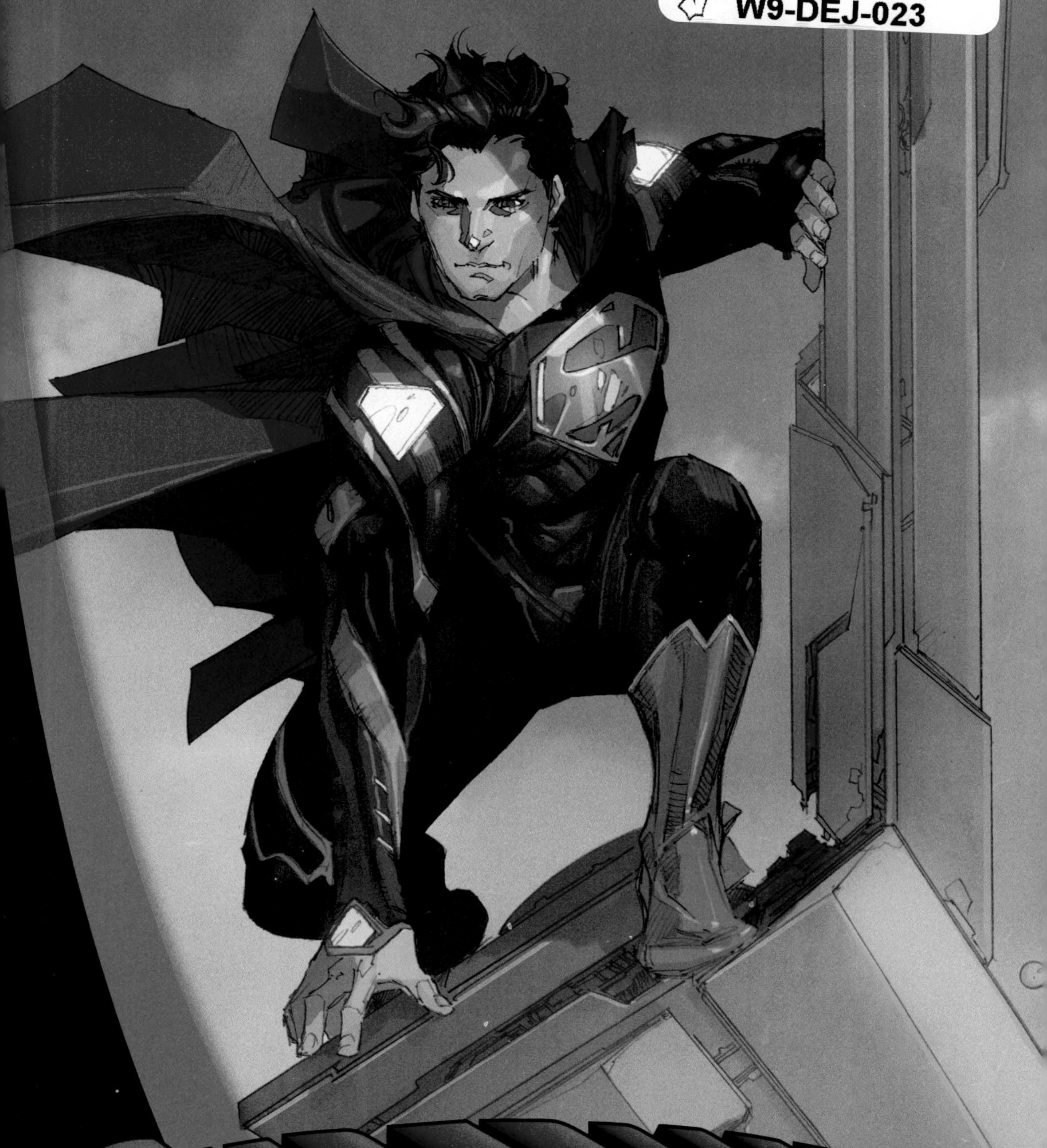

SUPERMAN

KRYPTON RETURNS

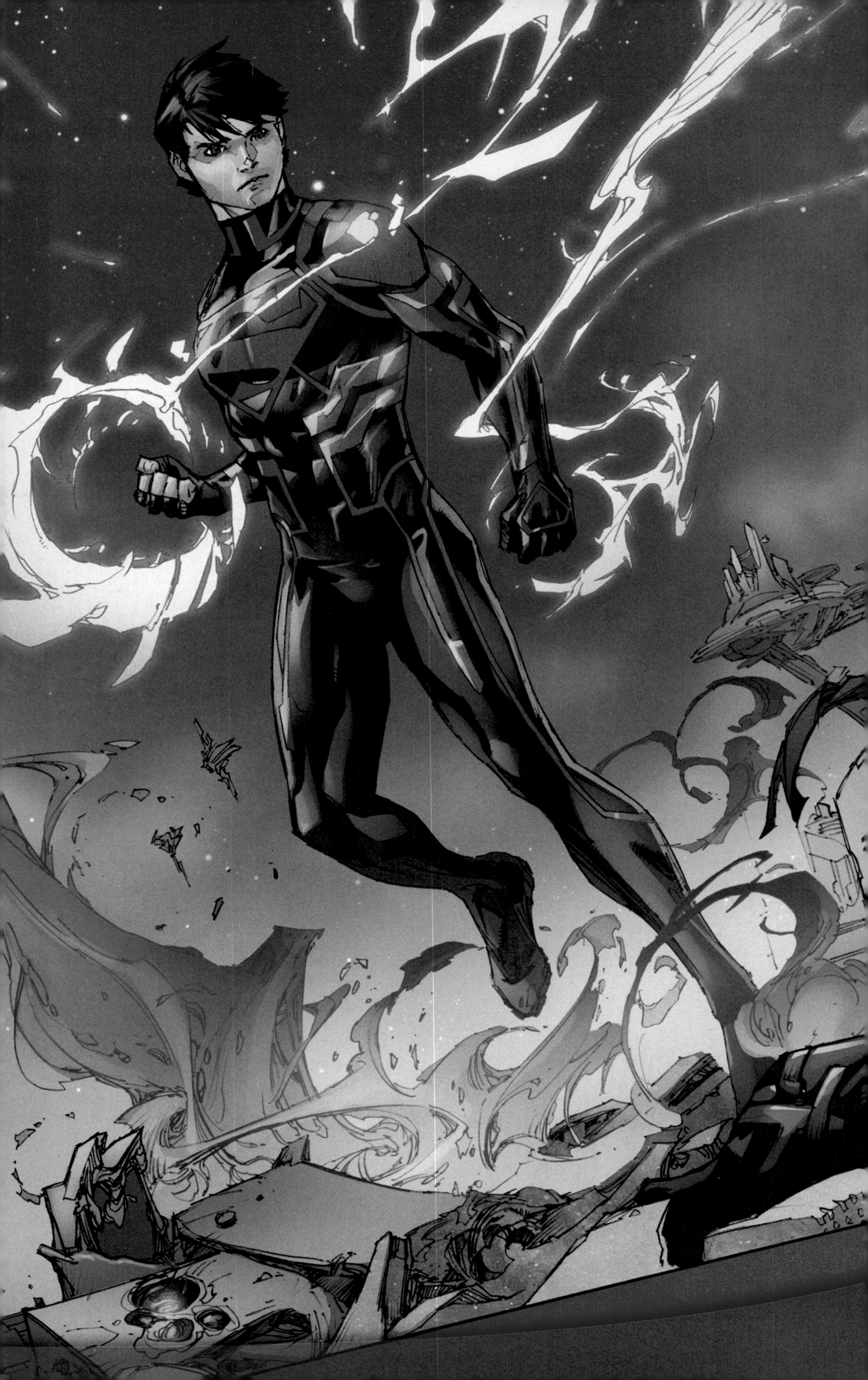

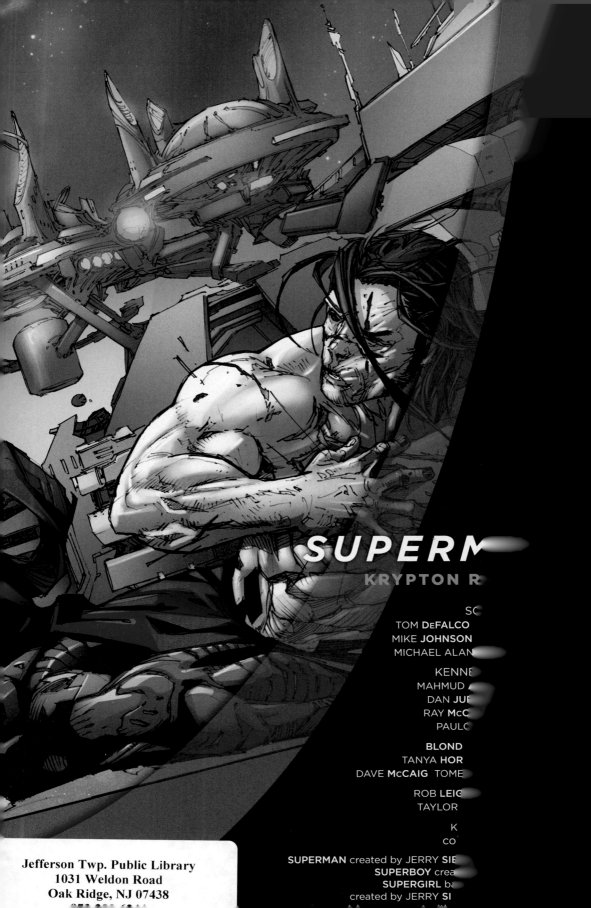

SUPERM

KRYPTON R

S
TOM DeFALCO
MIKE JOHNSON
MICHAEL ALAN

KENNE
MAHMUD
DAN JUF
RAY McC
PAULO

BLOND
TANYA HOR
DAVE McCAIG TOME

ROB LEIG
TAYLOR

K
CO

SUPERMAN created by JERRY SIE
SUPERBOY crea
SUPERGIRL ba
created by JERRY SI

EDDIE BERGANZA WIL MOSS CHRIS CONROY Editors – Original Series
RICKEY PURDIN Associate Editor – Original Series ANTHONY MARQUES DARREN SHAN Assistant Editors – Original Series
ROBIN WILDMAN Editor ROBBIE BIEDERMAN Publication Design

BOB HARRAS Senior VP – Editor-in-Chief, DC Comics

DIANE NELSON President DAN DIDIO and JIM LEE Co-Publishers GEOFF JOHNS Chief Creative Officer
AMIT DESAI Senior VP – Marketing and Global Franchise Management NAIRI GARDINER Senior VP – Finance
SAM ADES VP – Digital Marketing BOBBIE CHASE VP – Talent Development
MARK CHIARELLO Senior VP – Art, Design & Collected Editions JOHN CUNNINGHAM VP – Content Strategy
ANNE DePIES VP – Strategy Planning & Reporting DON FALLETTI VP – Manufacturing Operations
LAWRENCE GANEM VP – Editorial Administration & Talent Relations ALISON GILL Senior VP – Manufacturing & Operations
HANK KANALZ Senior VP – Editorial Strategy & Administration JAY KOGAN VP – Legal Affairs
DEREK MADDALENA Senior VP – Sales & Business Development DAN MIRON VP – Sales Planning & Trade Development
NICK NAPOLITANO VP – Manufacturing Administration CAROL ROEDER VP – Marketing
EDDIE SCANNELL VP – Mass Account & Digital Sales SUSAN SHEPPARD VP – Business Affairs
COURTNEY SIMMONS Senior VP – Publicity & Communications JIM (SKI) SOKOLOWSKI VP – Comic Book Specialty & Newsstand Sales

SUPERMAN: KRYPTON RETURNS
Published by DC Comics. Compilation Copyright © 2015 DC Comics. All Rights Reserved.
Originally published in single magazine form in SUPERMAN #0, 23.3, 25, SUPERGIRL #0, 25, SUPERBOY #0, 25
and ACTION COMICS ANNUAL #2. Copyright © 2012, 2013, 2014 DC Comics. All Rights Reserved. All characters, their
distinctive likenesses and related elements featured in this publication are trademarks of DC Comics. The stories, characters
and incidents featured in this publication are entirely fictional. DC Comics does not read or accept unsolicited ideas, stories or artwork.

DC Comics, 4000 Warner Blvd., Burbank, CA 91522
A Warner Bros. Entertainment Company.
Printed by RR Donnelley, Owensville, MO, USA. 7/10/15. First Printing.

ISBN: 978-1-4012-5544-2

Library of Congress Cataloging-in-Publication Data

Lobdell, Scott.
Superman : Krypton returns / Scott Lobdell ; [illustrated by] Kenneth Rocafort.
pages cm. — (The New 52!)
ISBN 978-1-4012-5544-2 (pbk.)
1. Graphic novels. I. Rocafort, Kenneth, illustrator. II. Title.

PN6728.S9L589 2015
741.5'973—dc23

2014039175

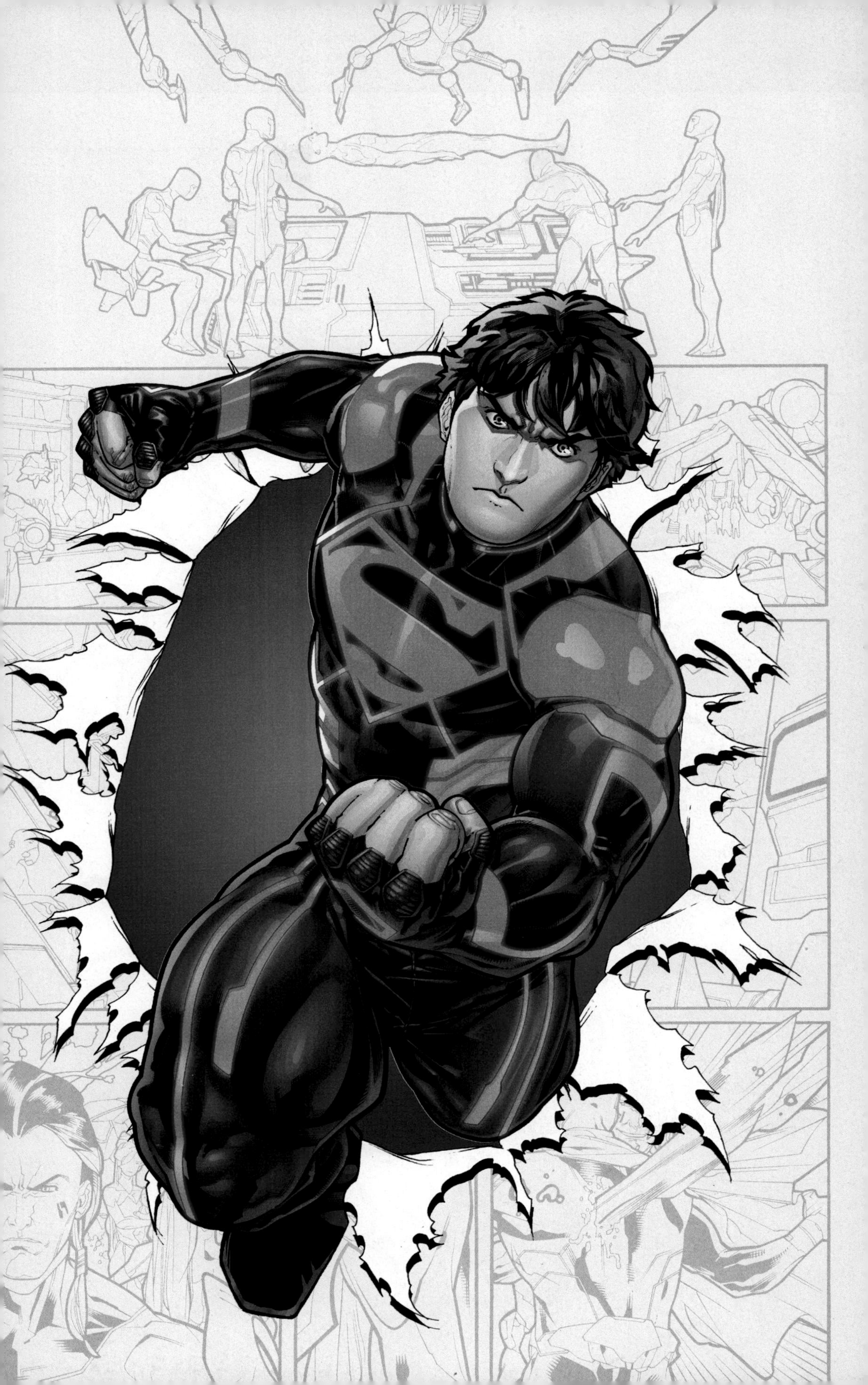

CLONESURRECTION!

TOM DeFALCO writer R.B. SILVA penciller ROB LEAN inker TANYA HORIE RICHARD HORIE HI-FI colorists
cover art by R.B. SILVA, ROB LEAN & HI-FI

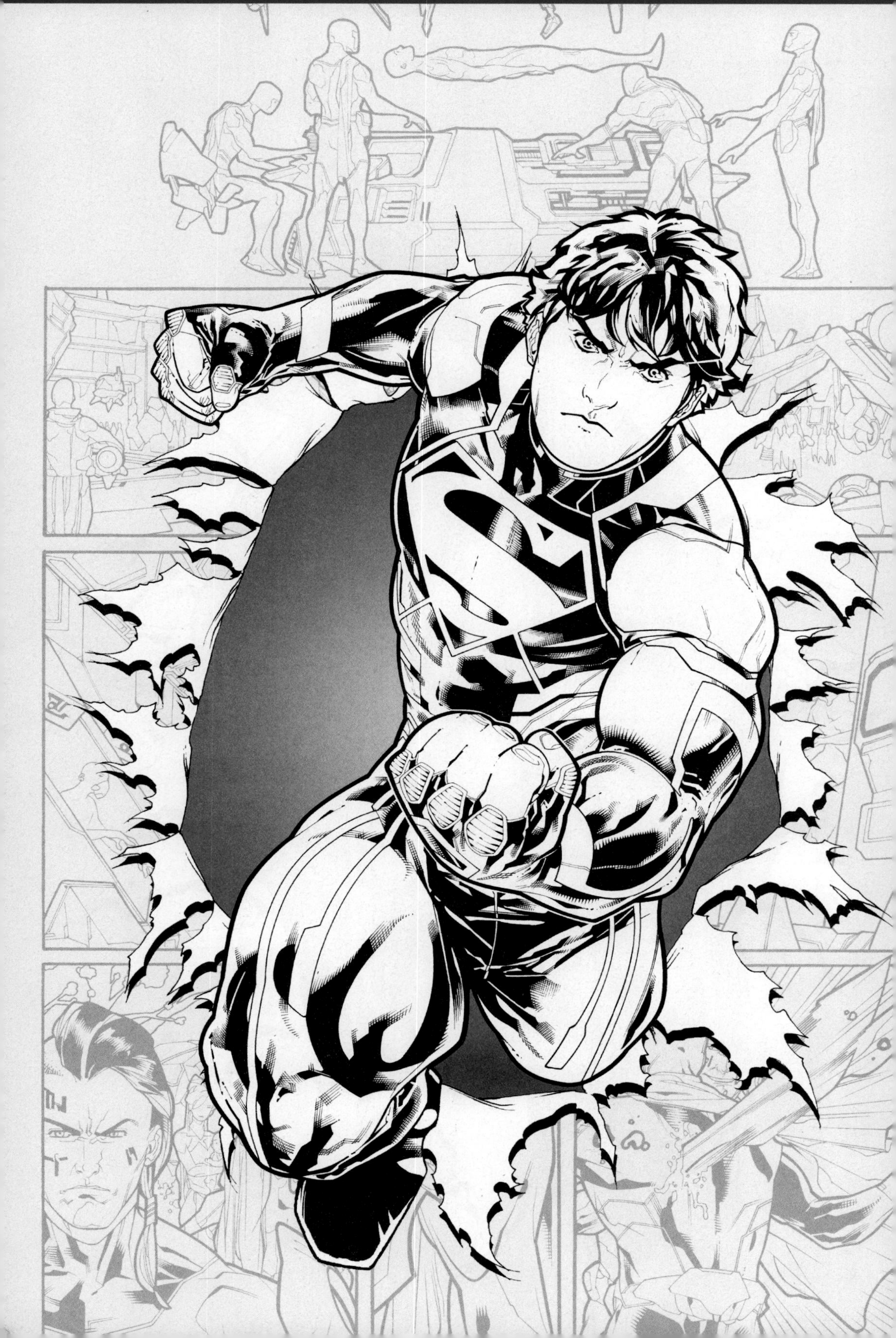

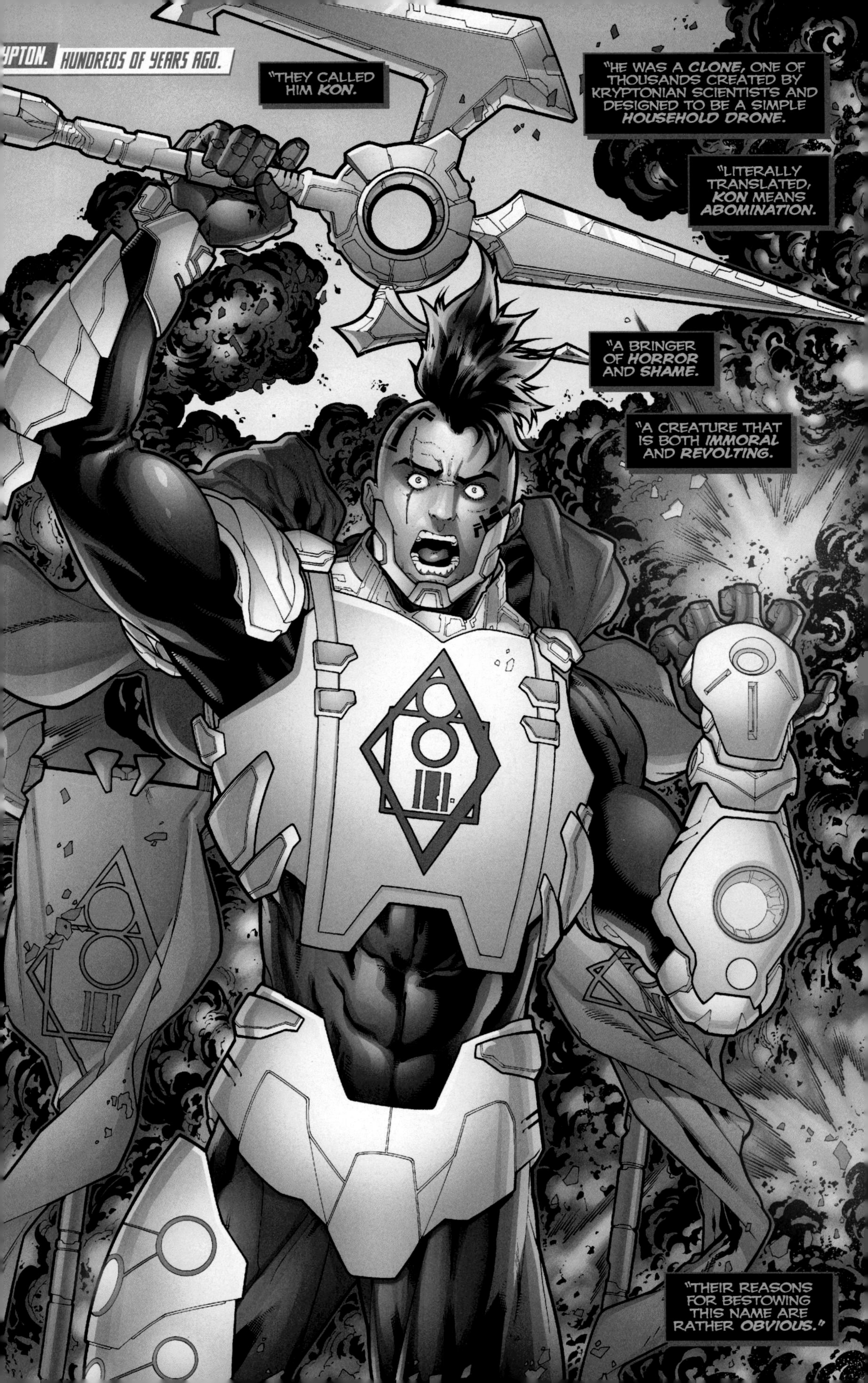
YPTON. HUNDREDS OF YEARS AGO.
"THEY CALLED HIM KON.
"HE WAS A CLONE, ONE OF THOUSANDS CREATED BY KRYPTONIAN SCIENTISTS AND DESIGNED TO BE A SIMPLE HOUSEHOLD DRONE.
"LITERALLY TRANSLATED, KON MEANS ABOMINATION.
"A BRINGER OF HORROR AND SHAME.
"A CREATURE THAT IS BOTH IMMORAL AND REVOLTING.
"THEIR REASONS FOR BESTOWING THIS NAME ARE RATHER OBVIOUS."

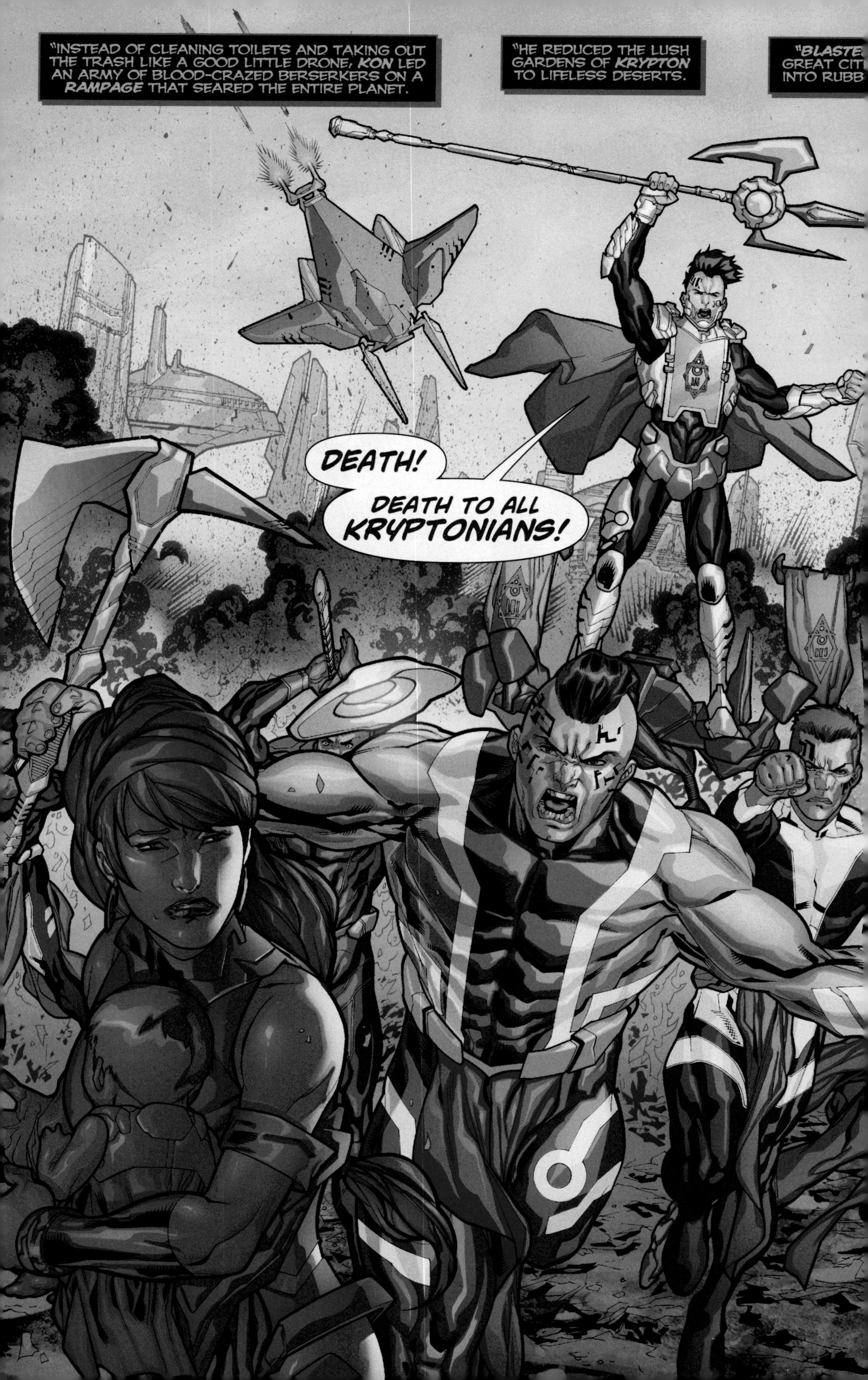
"INSTEAD OF CLEANING TOILETS AND TAKING OUT THE TRASH LIKE A GOOD LITTLE DRONE, KON LED AN ARMY OF BLOOD-CRAZED BERSERKERS ON A RAMPAGE THAT SEARED THE ENTIRE PLANET.
"HE REDUCED THE LUSH GARDENS OF KRYPTON TO LIFELESS DESERTS.
"BLASTE GREAT CIT INTO RUBB
DEATH!
DEATH TO ALL KRYPTONIANS!

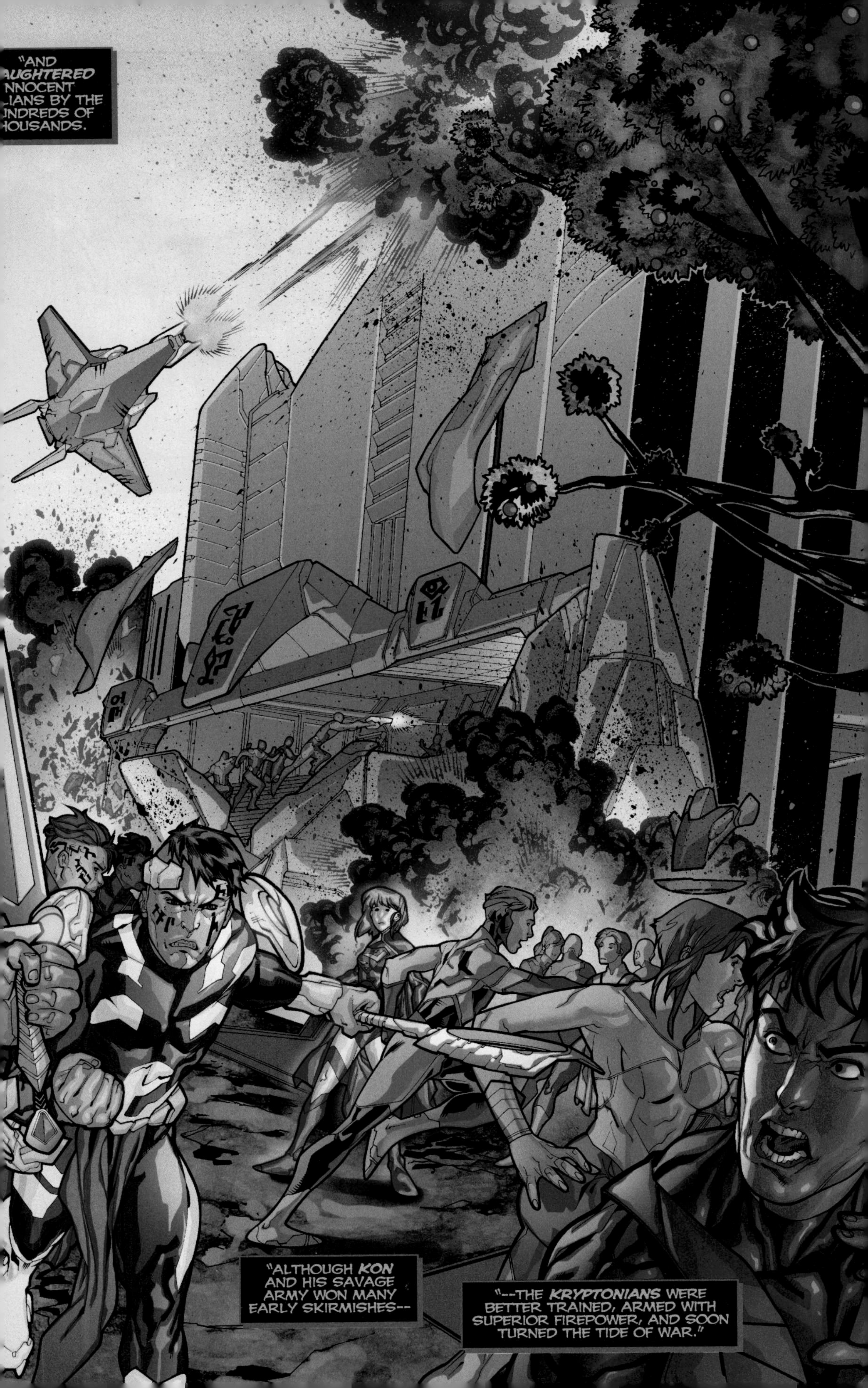
"AND
[S]LAUGHTERED
INNOCENT
[CIVI]LIANS BY THE
[HU]NDREDS OF
[T]HOUSANDS.
"ALTHOUGH KON AND HIS SAVAGE ARMY WON MANY EARLY SKIRMISHES--
"--THE KRYPTONIANS WERE BETTER TRAINED, ARMED WITH SUPERIOR FIREPOWER, AND SOON TURNED THE TIDE OF WAR."

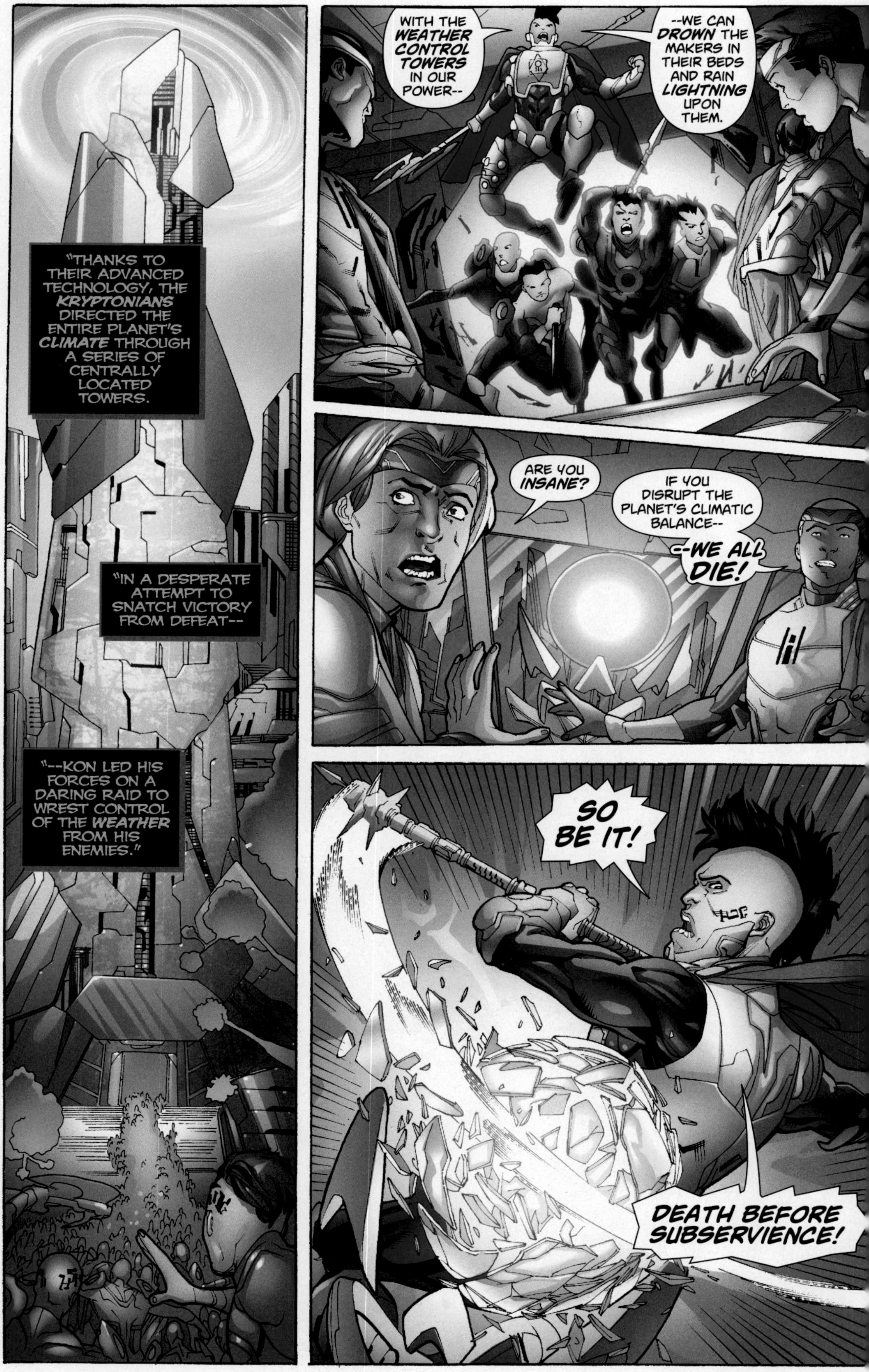
"THANKS TO THEIR ADVANCED TECHNOLOGY, THE KRYPTONIANS DIRECTED THE ENTIRE PLANET'S CLIMATE THROUGH A SERIES OF CENTRALLY LOCATED TOWERS.
"IN A DESPERATE ATTEMPT TO SNATCH VICTORY FROM DEFEAT--
"--KON LED HIS FORCES ON A DARING RAID TO WREST CONTROL OF THE WEATHER FROM HIS ENEMIES."
WITH THE WEATHER CONTROL TOWERS IN OUR POWER--
--WE CAN DROWN THE MAKERS IN THEIR BEDS AND RAIN LIGHTNING UPON THEM.
ARE YOU INSANE?
IF YOU DISRUPT THE PLANET'S CLIMATIC BALANCE--
--WE ALL DIE!
SO BE IT!
DEATH BEFORE SUBSERVIENCE!

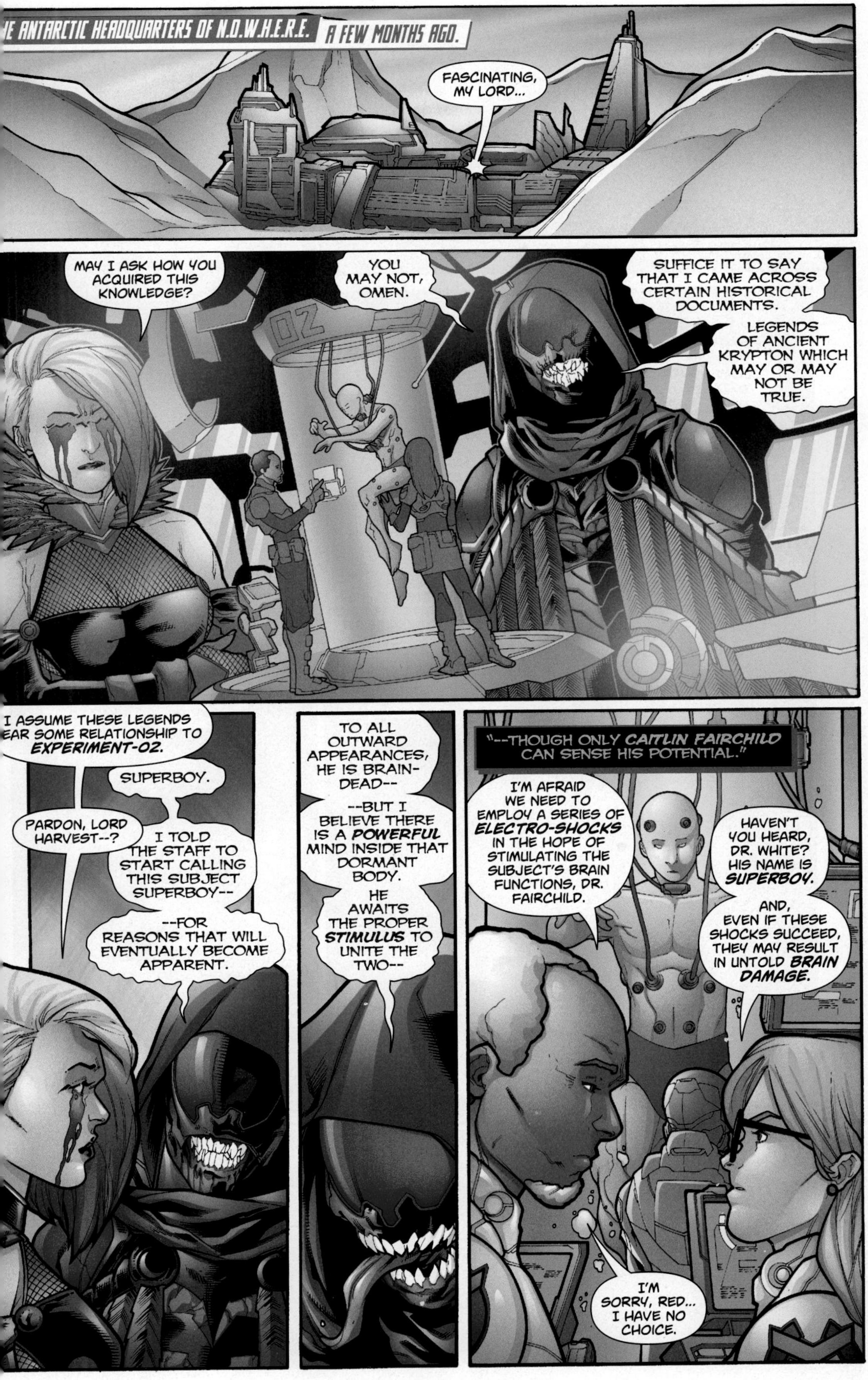
...E ANTARCTIC HEADQUARTERS OF N.O.W.H.E.R.E.
A FEW MONTHS AGO.
FASCINATING, MY LORD...
MAY I ASK HOW YOU ACQUIRED THIS KNOWLEDGE?
YOU MAY NOT, OMEN.
SUFFICE IT TO SAY THAT I CAME ACROSS CERTAIN HISTORICAL DOCUMENTS.
LEGENDS OF ANCIENT KRYPTON WHICH MAY OR MAY NOT BE TRUE.
I ASSUME THESE LEGENDS ...EAR SOME RELATIONSHIP TO EXPERIMENT-02.
SUPERBOY.
PARDON, LORD HARVEST--?
I TOLD THE STAFF TO START CALLING THIS SUBJECT SUPERBOY--
--FOR REASONS THAT WILL EVENTUALLY BECOME APPARENT.
TO ALL OUTWARD APPEARANCES, HE IS BRAIN-DEAD--
--BUT I BELIEVE THERE IS A POWERFUL MIND INSIDE THAT DORMANT BODY.
HE AWAITS THE PROPER STIMULUS TO UNITE THE TWO--
"--THOUGH ONLY CAITLIN FAIRCHILD CAN SENSE HIS POTENTIAL."
I'M AFRAID WE NEED TO EMPLOY A SERIES OF ELECTRO-SHOCKS IN THE HOPE OF STIMULATING THE SUBJECT'S BRAIN FUNCTIONS, DR. FAIRCHILD.
HAVEN'T YOU HEARD, DR. WHITE? HIS NAME IS SUPERBOY.
AND, EVEN IF THESE SHOCKS SUCCEED, THEY MAY RESULT IN UNTOLD BRAIN DAMAGE.
I'M SORRY, RED... I HAVE NO CHOICE.

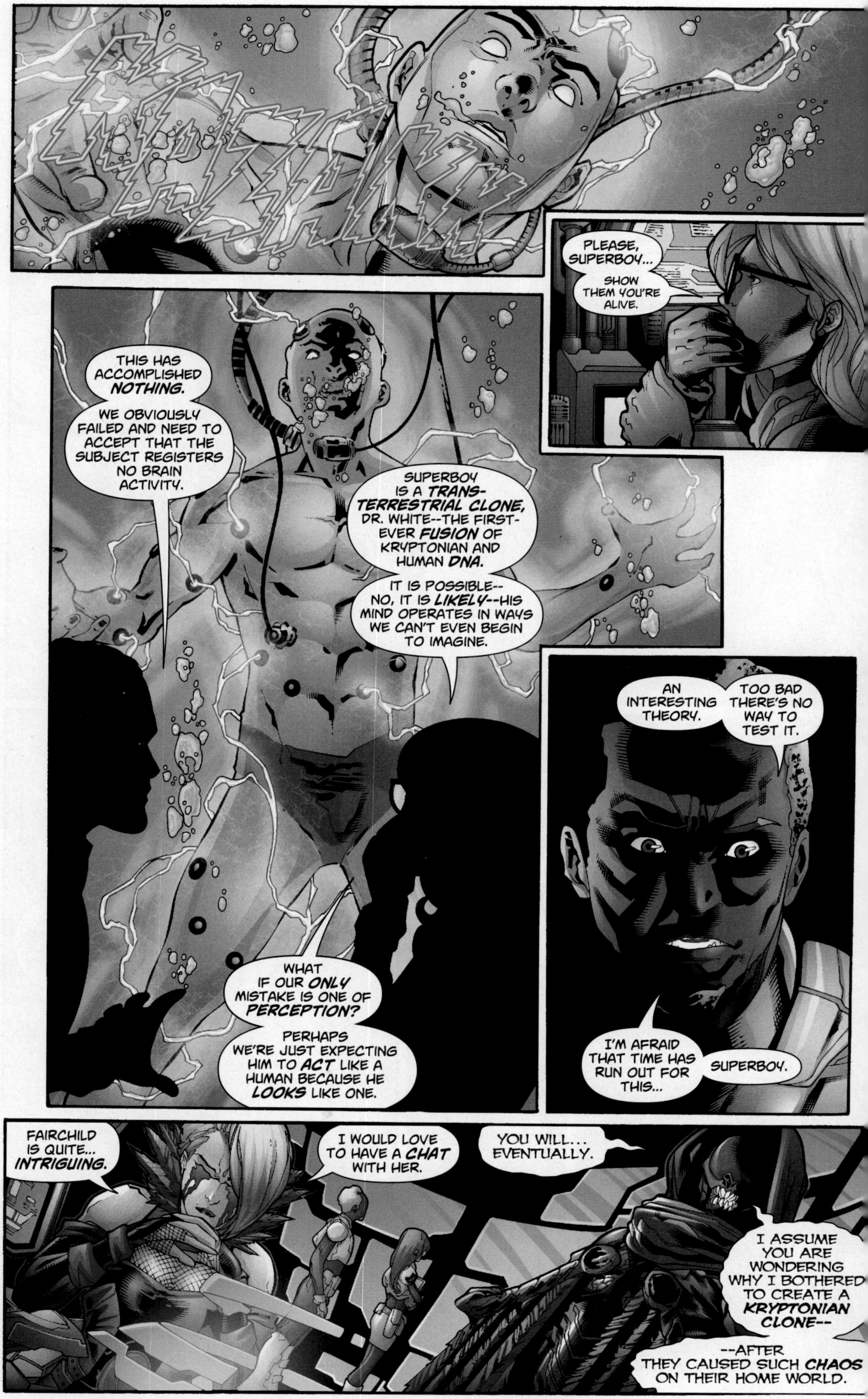
PLEASE, SUPERBOY...
SHOW THEM YOU'RE ALIVE.
THIS HAS ACCOMPLISHED NOTHING.
WE OBVIOUSLY FAILED AND NEED TO ACCEPT THAT THE SUBJECT REGISTERS NO BRAIN ACTIVITY.
SUPERBOY IS A TRANS-TERRESTRIAL CLONE, DR. WHITE--THE FIRST-EVER FUSION OF KRYPTONIAN AND HUMAN DNA.
IT IS POSSIBLE--NO, IT IS LIKELY--HIS MIND OPERATES IN WAYS WE CAN'T EVEN BEGIN TO IMAGINE.
AN INTERESTING THEORY.
TOO BAD THERE'S NO WAY TO TEST IT.
WHAT IF OUR ONLY MISTAKE IS ONE OF PERCEPTION?
PERHAPS WE'RE JUST EXPECTING HIM TO ACT LIKE A HUMAN BECAUSE HE LOOKS LIKE ONE.
I'M AFRAID THAT TIME HAS RUN OUT FOR THIS...
SUPERBOY.
FAIRCHILD IS QUITE... INTRIGUING.
I WOULD LOVE TO HAVE A CHAT WITH HER.
YOU WILL... EVENTUALLY.
I ASSUME YOU ARE WONDERING WHY I BOTHERED TO CREATE A KRYPTONIAN CLONE--
--AFTER THEY CAUSED SUCH CHAOS ON THEIR HOME WORLD.

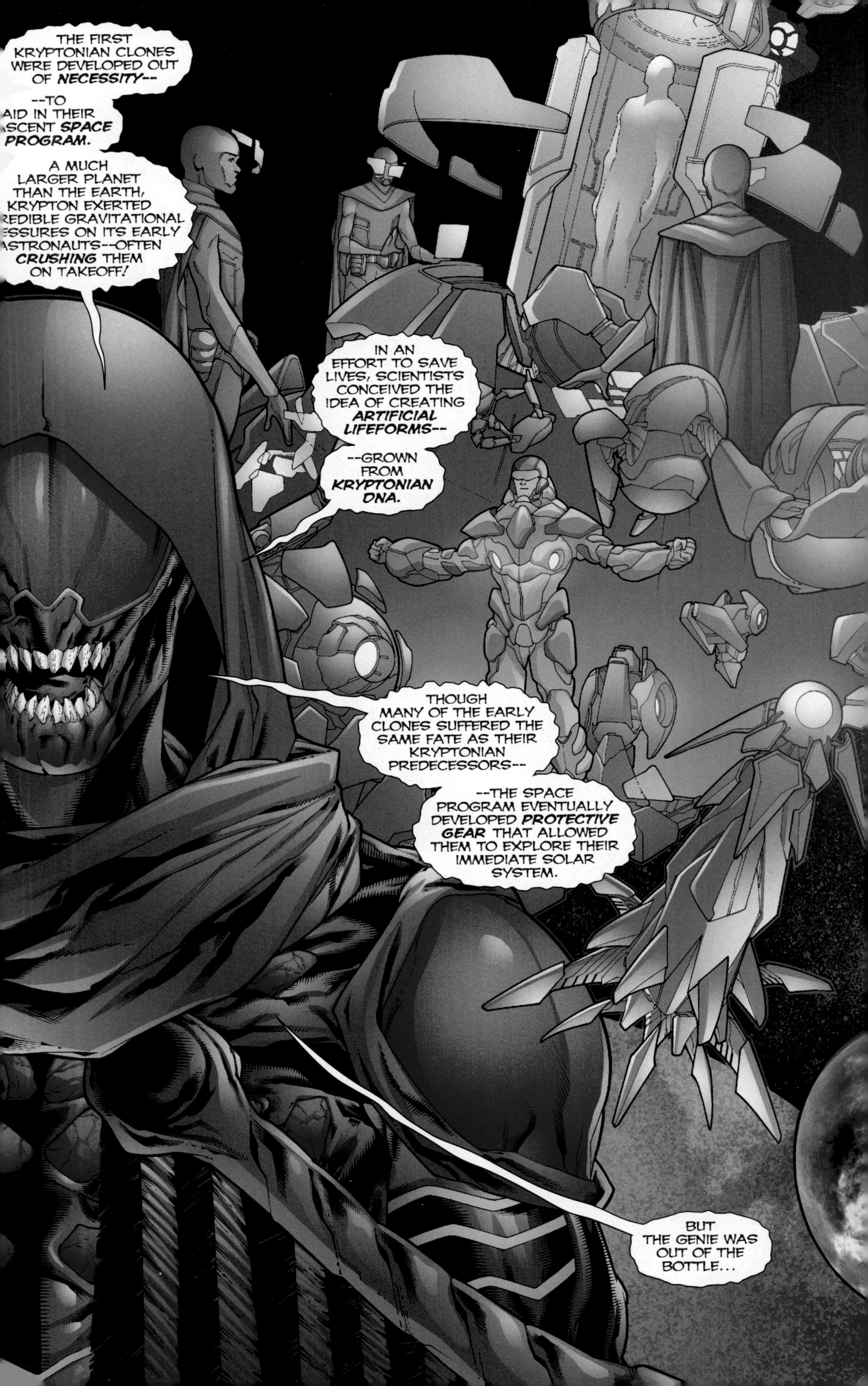
THE FIRST KRYPTONIAN CLONES WERE DEVELOPED OUT OF **NECESSITY**--
--TO AID IN THEIR SCENT **SPACE PROGRAM.**
A MUCH LARGER PLANET THAN THE EARTH, KRYPTON EXERTED REDIBLE GRAVITATIONAL ESSURES ON ITS EARLY ASTRONAUTS--OFTEN **CRUSHING** THEM ON TAKEOFF!
IN AN EFFORT TO SAVE LIVES, SCIENTISTS CONCEIVED THE IDEA OF CREATING **ARTIFICIAL LIFEFORMS**--
--GROWN FROM **KRYPTONIAN DNA.**
THOUGH MANY OF THE EARLY CLONES SUFFERED THE SAME FATE AS THEIR KRYPTONIAN PREDECESSORS--
--THE SPACE PROGRAM EVENTUALLY DEVELOPED **PROTECTIVE GEAR** THAT ALLOWED THEM TO EXPLORE THEIR IMMEDIATE SOLAR SYSTEM.
BUT THE GENIE WAS OUT OF THE BOTTLE...

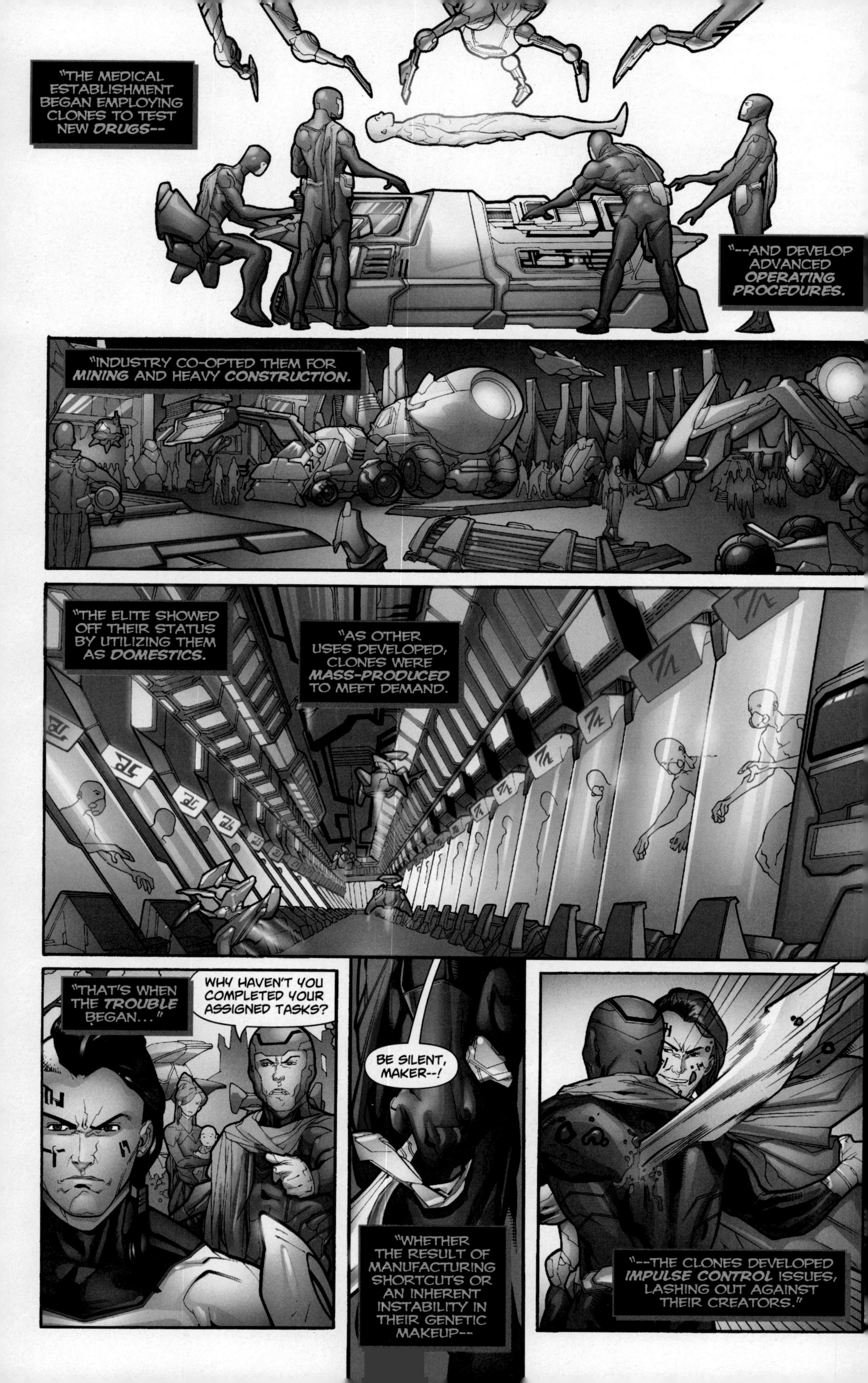
"THE MEDICAL ESTABLISHMENT BEGAN EMPLOYING CLONES TO TEST NEW DRUGS--
"--AND DEVELOP ADVANCED OPERATING PROCEDURES.
"INDUSTRY CO-OPTED THEM FOR MINING AND HEAVY CONSTRUCTION.
"THE ELITE SHOWED OFF THEIR STATUS BY UTILIZING THEM AS DOMESTICS.
"AS OTHER USES DEVELOPED, CLONES WERE MASS-PRODUCED TO MEET DEMAND.
"THAT'S WHEN THE TROUBLE BEGAN..."
WHY HAVEN'T YOU COMPLETED YOUR ASSIGNED TASKS?
BE SILENT, MAKER--!
"WHETHER THE RESULT OF MANUFACTURING SHORTCUTS OR AN INHERENT INSTABILITY IN THEIR GENETIC MAKEUP--
"--THE CLONES DEVELOPED IMPULSE CONTROL ISSUES, LASHING OUT AGAINST THEIR CREATORS."

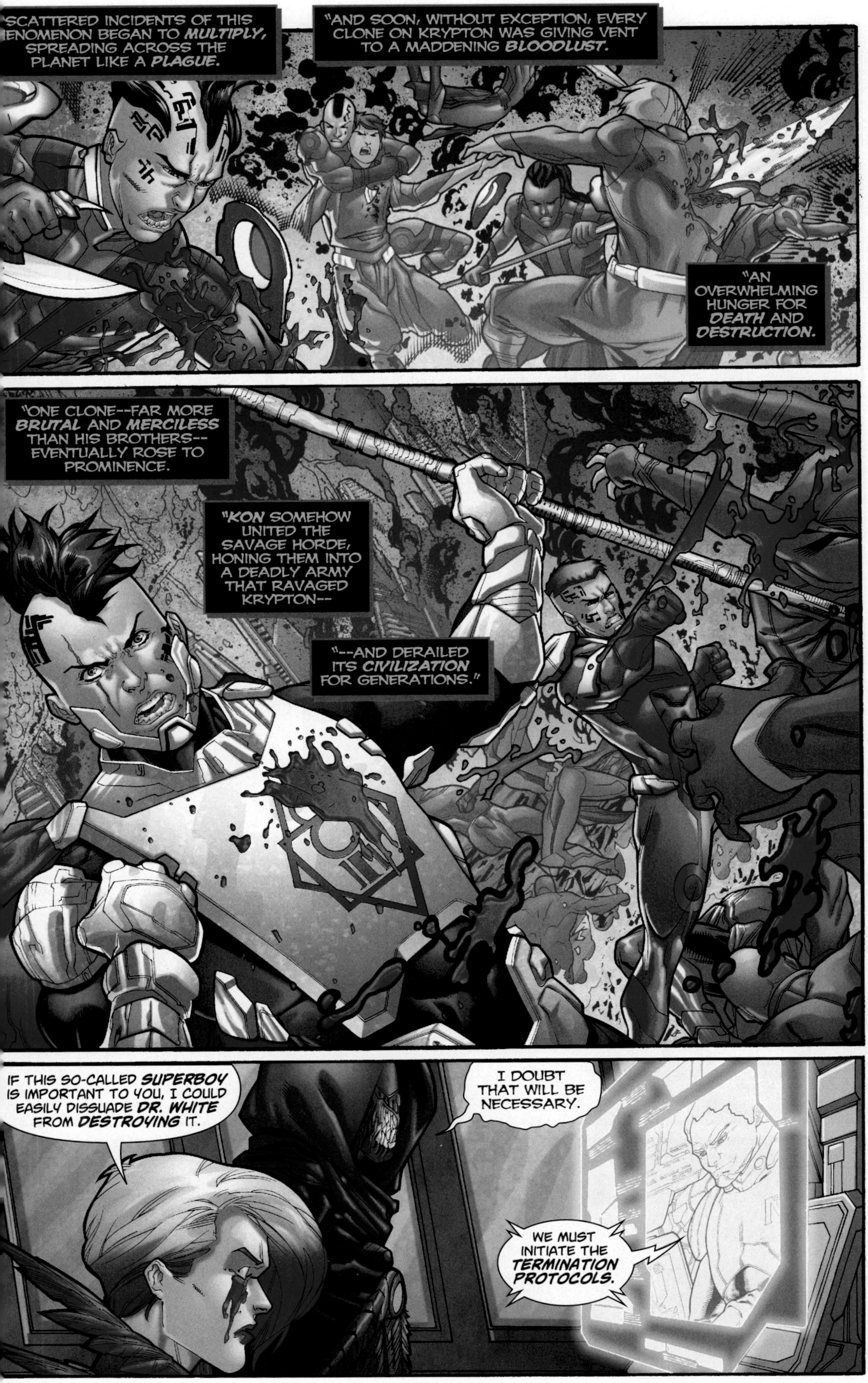
SCATTERED INCIDENTS OF THIS ENOMENON BEGAN TO MULTIPLY, SPREADING ACROSS THE PLANET LIKE A PLAGUE.
"AND SOON, WITHOUT EXCEPTION, EVERY CLONE ON KRYPTON WAS GIVING VENT TO A MADDENING BLOODLUST.
"AN OVERWHELMING HUNGER FOR DEATH AND DESTRUCTION.
"ONE CLONE--FAR MORE BRUTAL AND MERCILESS THAN HIS BROTHERS--EVENTUALLY ROSE TO PROMINENCE.
"KON SOMEHOW UNITED THE SAVAGE HORDE, HONING THEM INTO A DEADLY ARMY THAT RAVAGED KRYPTON--
"--AND DERAILED ITS CIVILIZATION FOR GENERATIONS."
IF THIS SO-CALLED SUPERBOY IS IMPORTANT TO YOU, I COULD EASILY DISSUADE DR. WHITE FROM DESTROYING IT.
I DOUBT THAT WILL BE NECESSARY.
WE MUST INITIATE THE TERMINATION PROTOCOLS.

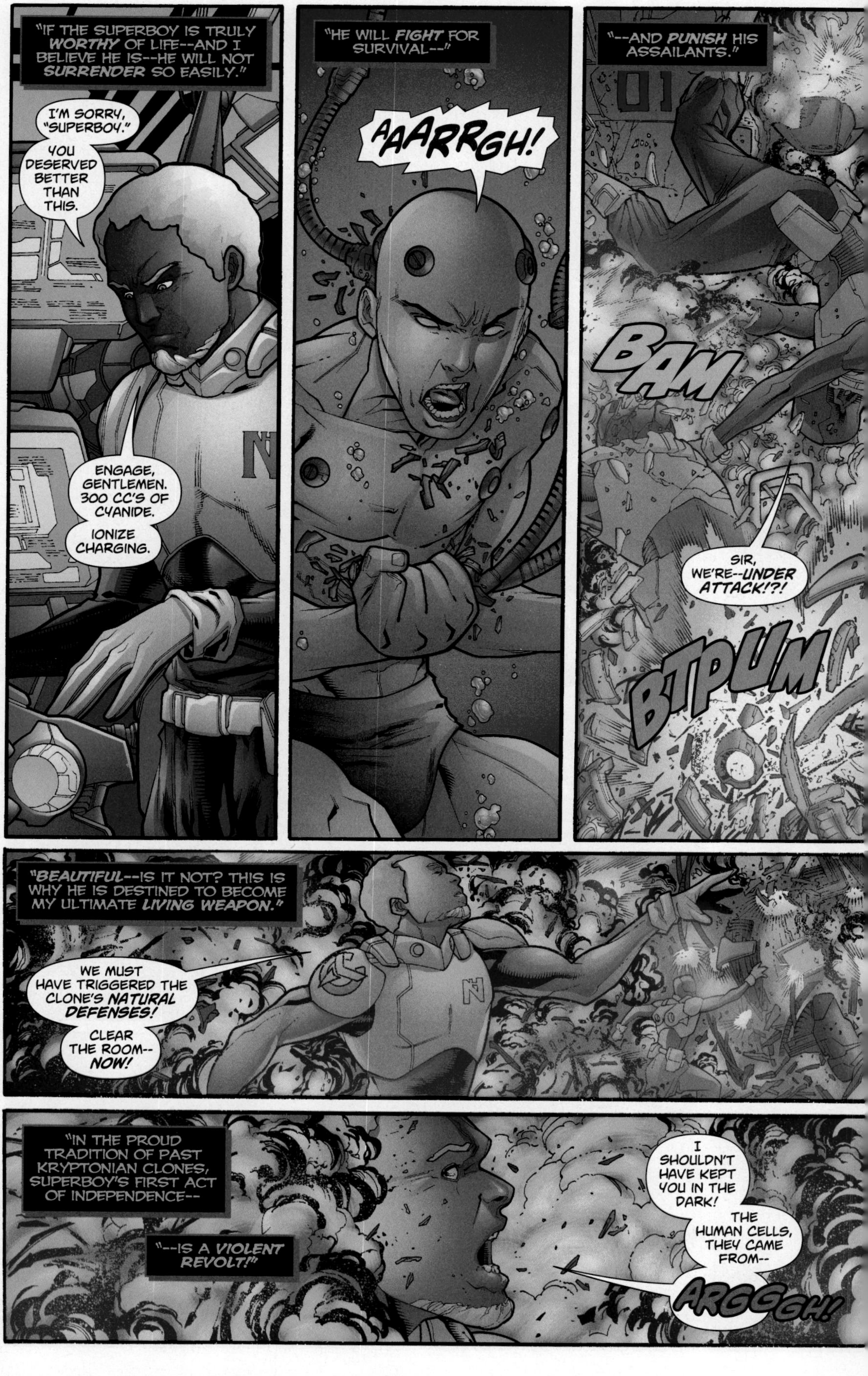
"IF THE SUPERBOY IS TRULY WORTHY OF LIFE--AND I BELIEVE HE IS--HE WILL NOT SURRENDER SO EASILY."
I'M SORRY, "SUPERBOY."
YOU DESERVED BETTER THAN THIS.
ENGAGE, GENTLEMEN. 300 CC'S OF CYANIDE.
IONIZE CHARGING.
"HE WILL FIGHT FOR SURVIVAL--"
AAARRGH!
"--AND PUNISH HIS ASSAILANTS."
BAM
SIR, WE'RE--UNDER ATTACK!?!
BTPUM
"BEAUTIFUL--IS IT NOT? THIS IS WHY HE IS DESTINED TO BECOME MY ULTIMATE LIVING WEAPON."
WE MUST HAVE TRIGGERED THE CLONE'S NATURAL DEFENSES!
CLEAR THE ROOM--NOW!
"IN THE PROUD TRADITION OF PAST KRYPTONIAN CLONES, SUPERBOY'S FIRST ACT OF INDEPENDENCE--
"--IS A VIOLENT REVOLT!"
I SHOULDN'T HAVE KEPT YOU IN THE DARK!
THE HUMAN CELLS, THEY CAME FROM--
ARGGGH!

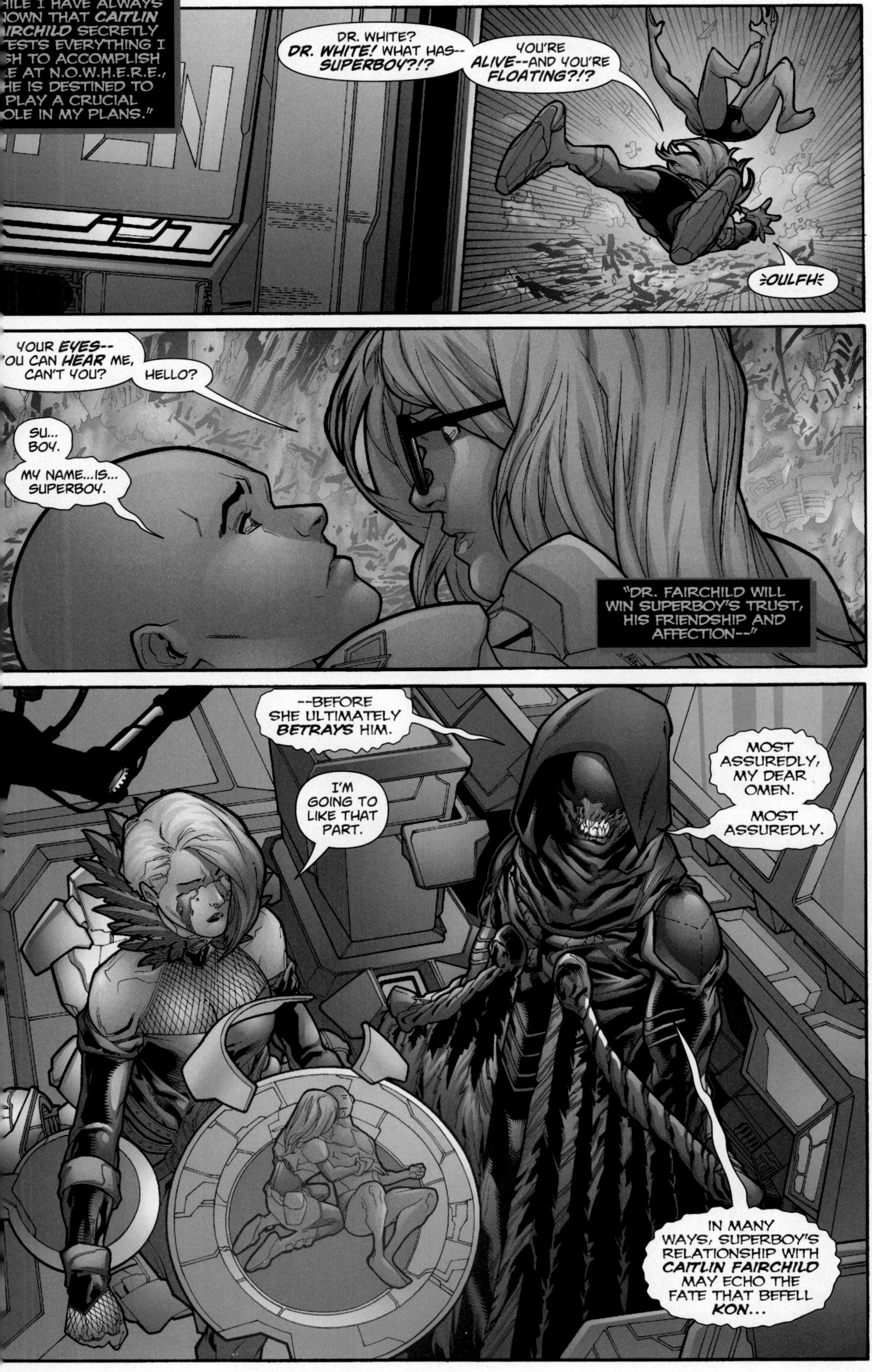
HILE I HAVE ALWAYS NOWN THAT CAITLIN AIRCHILD SECRETLY ESTS EVERYTHING I SH TO ACCOMPLISH E AT N.O.W.H.E.R.E., HE IS DESTINED TO PLAY A CRUCIAL OLE IN MY PLANS."
DR. WHITE? DR. WHITE! WHAT HAS-- SUPERBOY?!?
YOU'RE ALIVE--AND YOU'RE FLOATING?!?
OULFH
YOUR EYES-- OU CAN HEAR ME, CAN'T YOU?
HELLO?
SU... BOY.
MY NAME...IS... SUPERBOY.
"DR. FAIRCHILD WILL WIN SUPERBOY'S TRUST, HIS FRIENDSHIP AND AFFECTION--"
--BEFORE SHE ULTIMATELY BETRAYS HIM.
I'M GOING TO LIKE THAT PART.
MOST ASSUREDLY, MY DEAR OMEN.
MOST ASSUREDLY.
IN MANY WAYS, SUPERBOY'S RELATIONSHIP WITH CAITLIN FAIRCHILD MAY ECHO THE FATE THAT BEFELL KON...

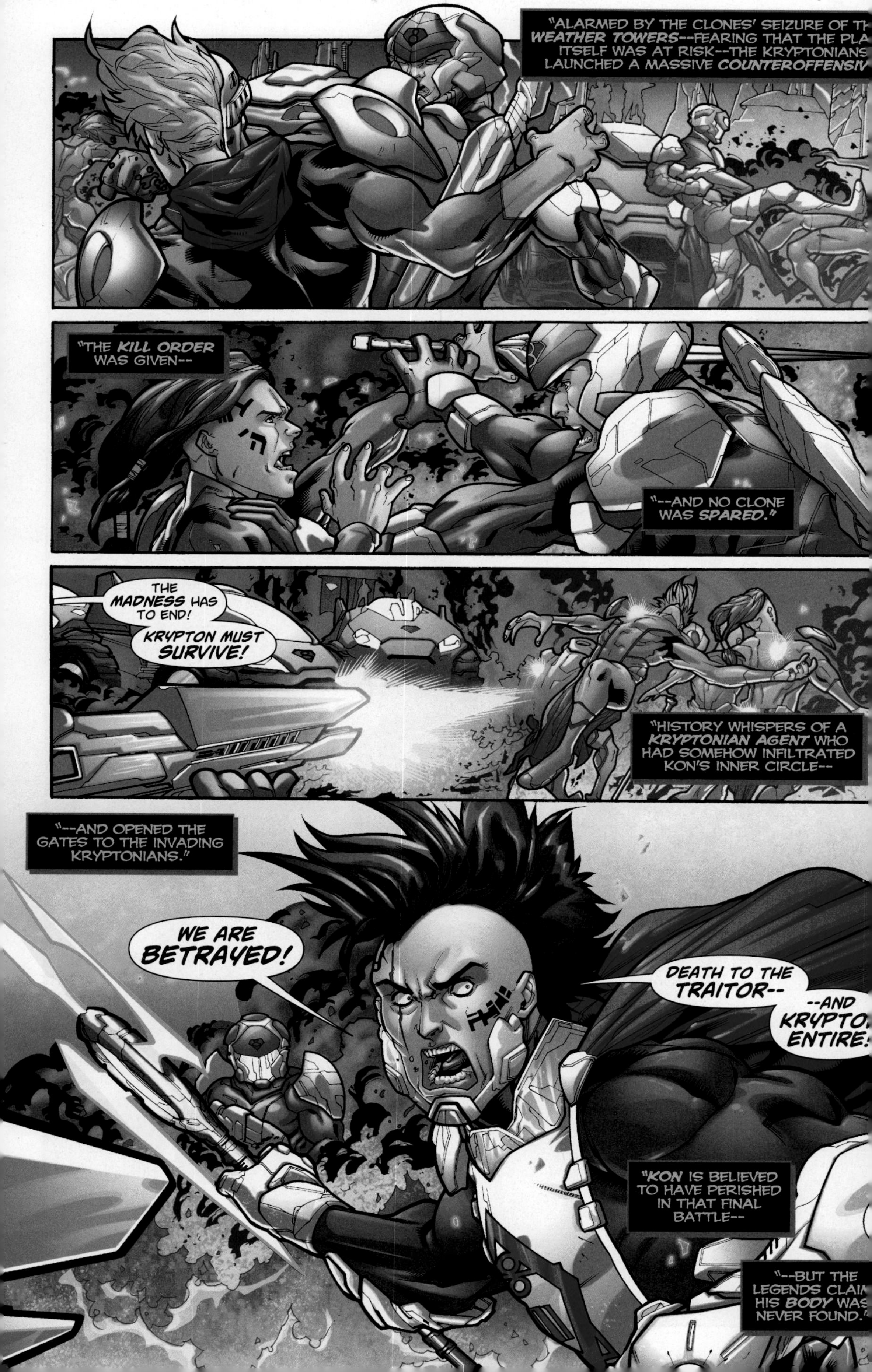
"ALARMED BY THE CLONES' SEIZURE OF TH WEATHER TOWERS--FEARING THAT THE PLA ITSELF WAS AT RISK--THE KRYPTONIANS LAUNCHED A MASSIVE COUNTEROFFENSIV
"THE KILL ORDER WAS GIVEN--
"--AND NO CLONE WAS SPARED."
THE MADNESS HAS TO END!
KRYPTON MUST SURVIVE!
"HISTORY WHISPERS OF A KRYPTONIAN AGENT WHO HAD SOMEHOW INFILTRATED KON'S INNER CIRCLE--
"--AND OPENED THE GATES TO THE INVADING KRYPTONIANS."
WE ARE BETRAYED!
DEATH TO THE TRAITOR--
--AND KRYPTO ENTIRE!
"KON IS BELIEVED TO HAVE PERISHED IN THAT FINAL BATTLE--
"--BUT THE LEGENDS CLAI HIS BODY WAS NEVER FOUND."

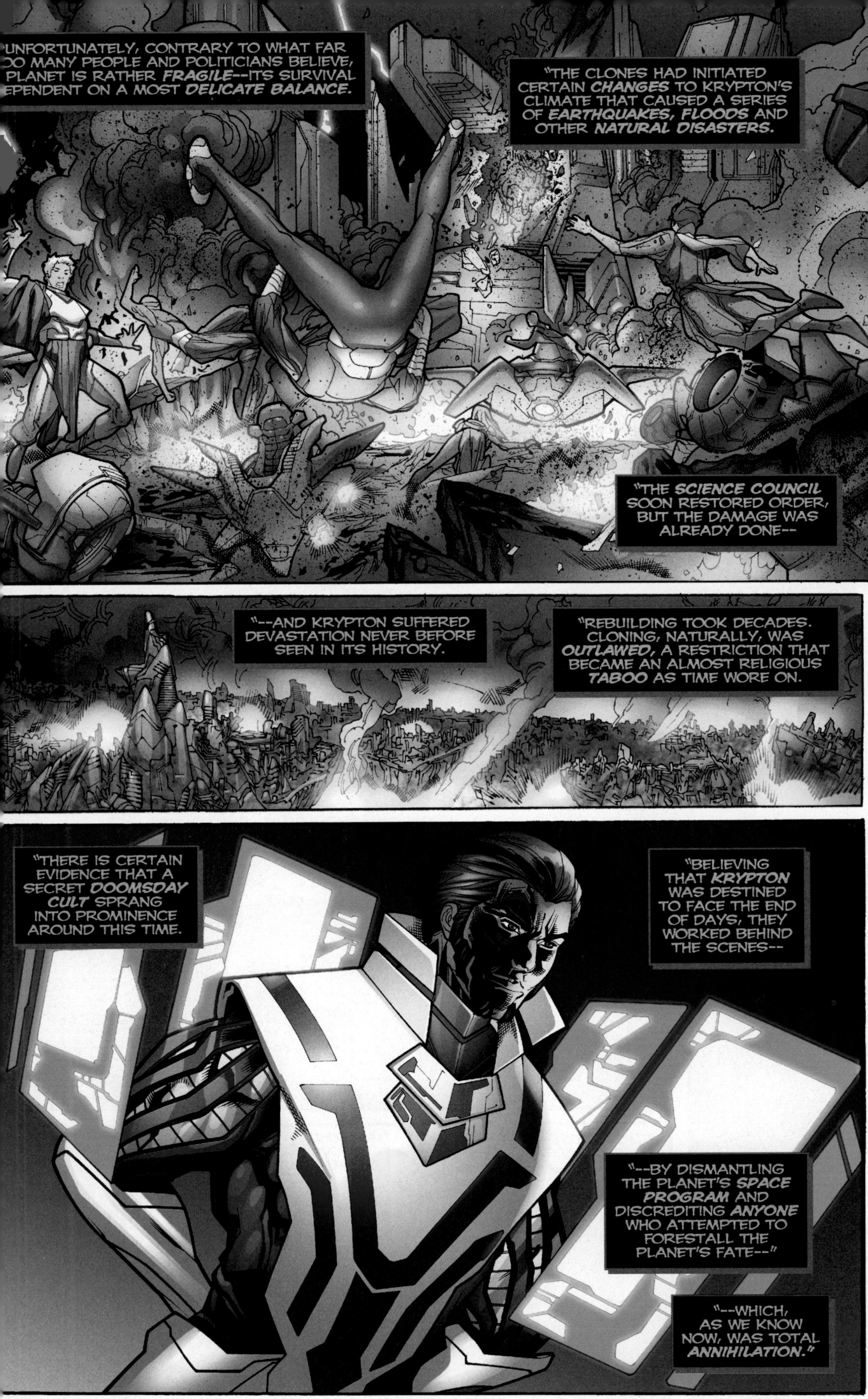
UNFORTUNATELY, CONTRARY TO WHAT FAR OO MANY PEOPLE AND POLITICIANS BELIEVE, PLANET IS RATHER FRAGILE--ITS SURVIVAL EPENDENT ON A MOST DELICATE BALANCE.
"THE CLONES HAD INITIATED CERTAIN CHANGES TO KRYPTON'S CLIMATE THAT CAUSED A SERIES OF EARTHQUAKES, FLOODS AND OTHER NATURAL DISASTERS.
"THE SCIENCE COUNCIL SOON RESTORED ORDER, BUT THE DAMAGE WAS ALREADY DONE--
"--AND KRYPTON SUFFERED DEVASTATION NEVER BEFORE SEEN IN ITS HISTORY.
"REBUILDING TOOK DECADES. CLONING, NATURALLY, WAS OUTLAWED, A RESTRICTION THAT BECAME AN ALMOST RELIGIOUS TABOO AS TIME WORE ON.
"THERE IS CERTAIN EVIDENCE THAT A SECRET DOOMSDAY CULT SPRANG INTO PROMINENCE AROUND THIS TIME.
"BELIEVING THAT KRYPTON WAS DESTINED TO FACE THE END OF DAYS, THEY WORKED BEHIND THE SCENES--
"--BY DISMANTLING THE PLANET'S SPACE PROGRAM AND DISCREDITING ANYONE WHO ATTEMPTED TO FORESTALL THE PLANET'S FATE--"
"--WHICH, AS WE KNOW NOW, WAS TOTAL ANNIHILATION."

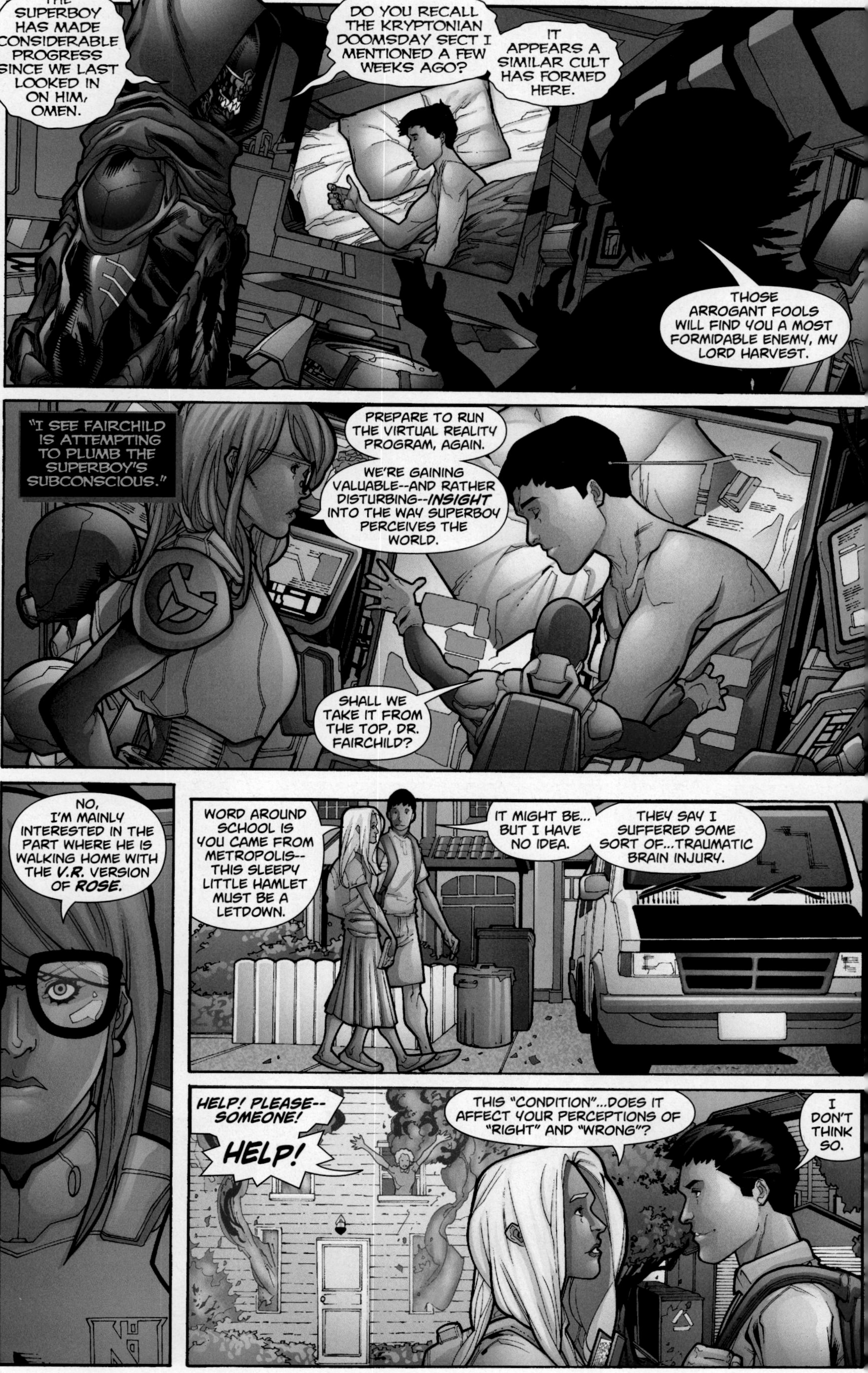

THE SUPERBOY HAS MADE CONSIDERABLE PROGRESS SINCE WE LAST LOOKED IN ON HIM, OMEN.
DO YOU RECALL THE KRYPTONIAN DOOMSDAY SECT I MENTIONED A FEW WEEKS AGO?
IT APPEARS A SIMILAR CULT HAS FORMED HERE.
THOSE ARROGANT FOOLS WILL FIND YOU A MOST FORMIDABLE ENEMY, MY LORD HARVEST.
"I SEE FAIRCHILD IS ATTEMPTING TO PLUMB THE SUPERBOY'S SUBCONSCIOUS."
PREPARE TO RUN THE VIRTUAL REALITY PROGRAM, AGAIN.
WE'RE GAINING VALUABLE--AND RATHER DISTURBING--INSIGHT INTO THE WAY SUPERBOY PERCEIVES THE WORLD.
SHALL WE TAKE IT FROM THE TOP, DR. FAIRCHILD?
NO, I'M MAINLY INTERESTED IN THE PART WHERE HE IS WALKING HOME WITH THE V.R. VERSION OF ROSE.
WORD AROUND SCHOOL IS YOU CAME FROM METROPOLIS-- THIS SLEEPY LITTLE HAMLET MUST BE A LETDOWN.
IT MIGHT BE... BUT I HAVE NO IDEA.
THEY SAY I SUFFERED SOME SORT OF...TRAUMATIC BRAIN INJURY.
HELP! PLEASE-- SOMEONE!
HELP!
THIS "CONDITION"...DOES IT AFFECT YOUR PERCEPTIONS OF "RIGHT" AND "WRONG"?
I DON'T THINK SO.

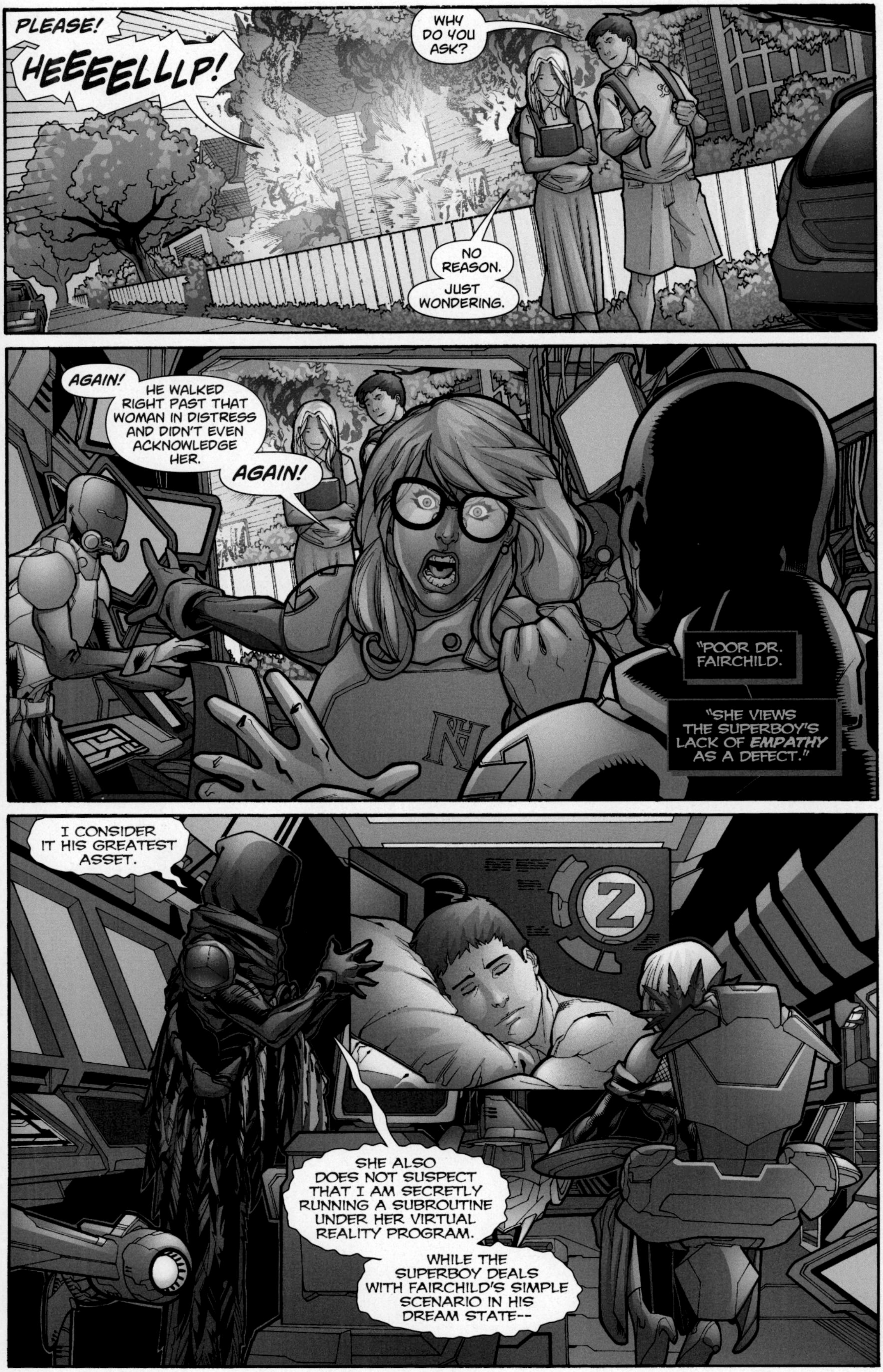
PLEASE!
HEEEELLLP!
WHY DO YOU ASK?
NO REASON.
JUST WONDERING.
AGAIN! HE WALKED RIGHT PAST THAT WOMAN IN DISTRESS AND DIDN'T EVEN ACKNOWLEDGE HER.
AGAIN!
"POOR DR. FAIRCHILD.
"SHE VIEWS THE SUPERBOY'S LACK OF EMPATHY AS A DEFECT."
I CONSIDER IT HIS GREATEST ASSET.
SHE ALSO DOES NOT SUSPECT THAT I AM SECRETLY RUNNING A SUBROUTINE UNDER HER VIRTUAL REALITY PROGRAM.
WHILE THE SUPERBOY DEALS WITH FAIRCHILD'S SIMPLE SCENARIO IN HIS DREAM STATE--

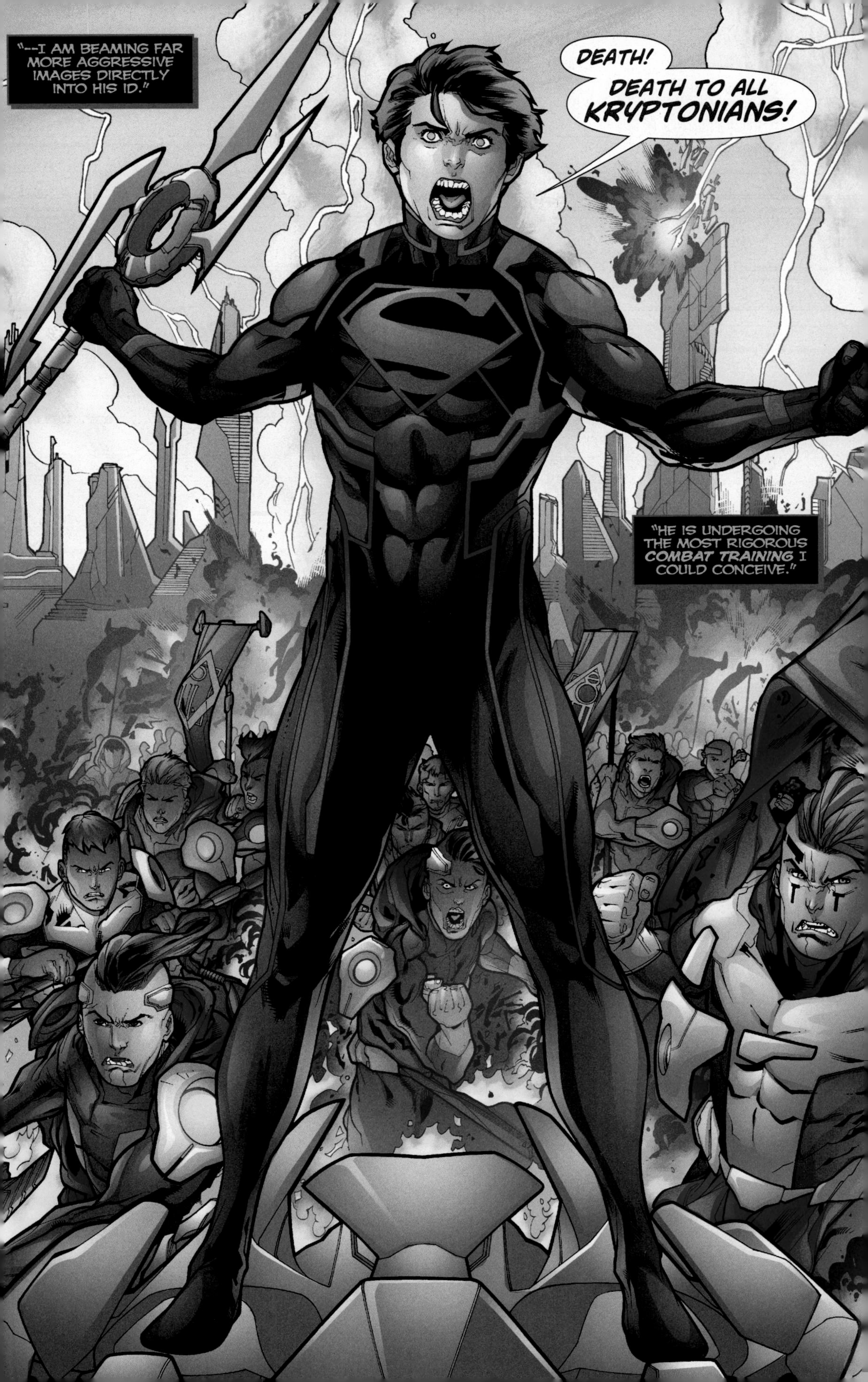
"--I AM BEAMING FAR MORE AGGRESSIVE IMAGES DIRECTLY INTO HIS ID."
DEATH! DEATH TO ALL KRYPTONIANS!
"HE IS UNDERGOING THE MOST RIGOROUS COMBAT TRAINING I COULD CONCEIVE."

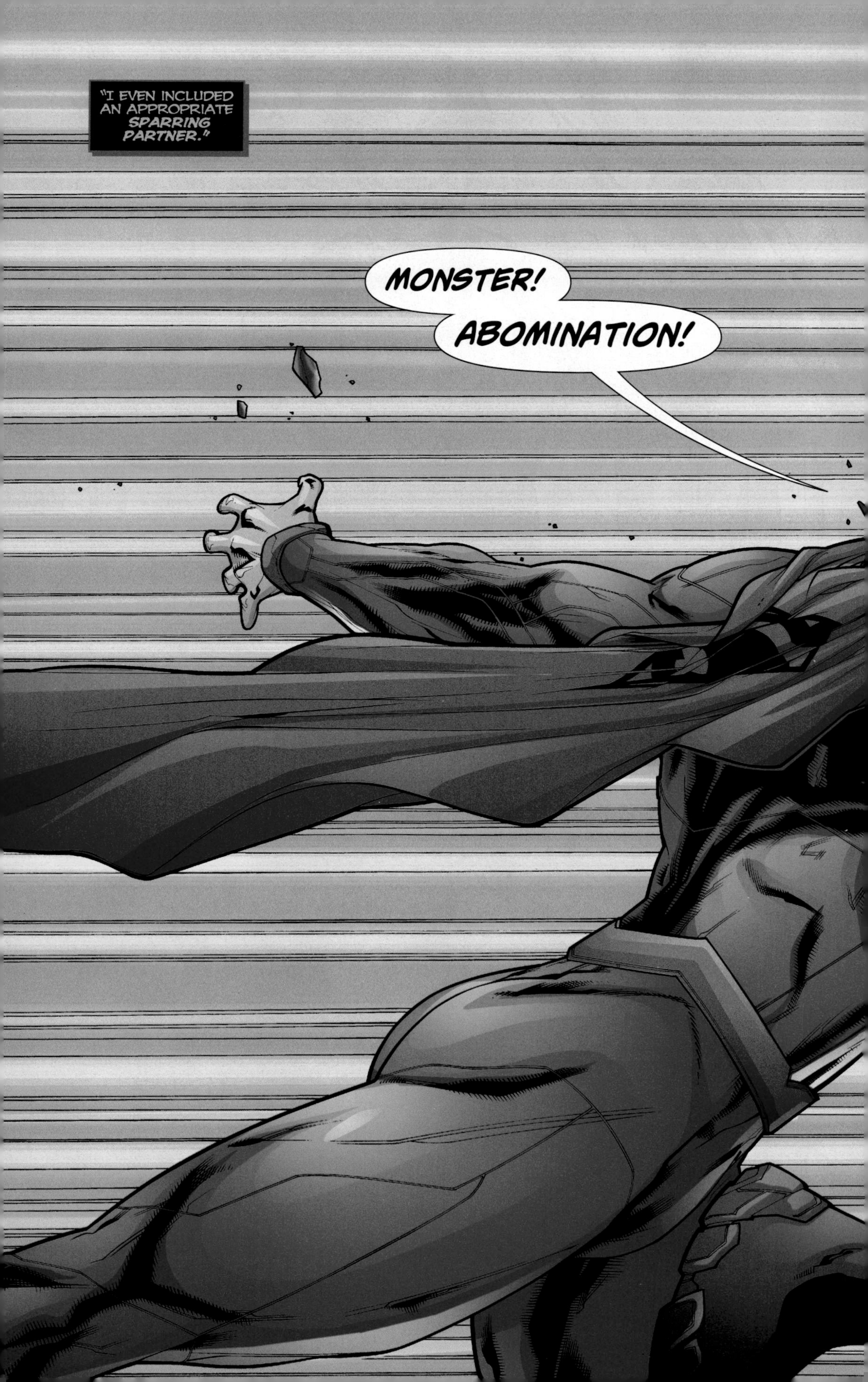
"I EVEN INCLUDED AN APPROPRIATE *SPARRING PARTNER.*"
MONSTER!
ABOMINATION!

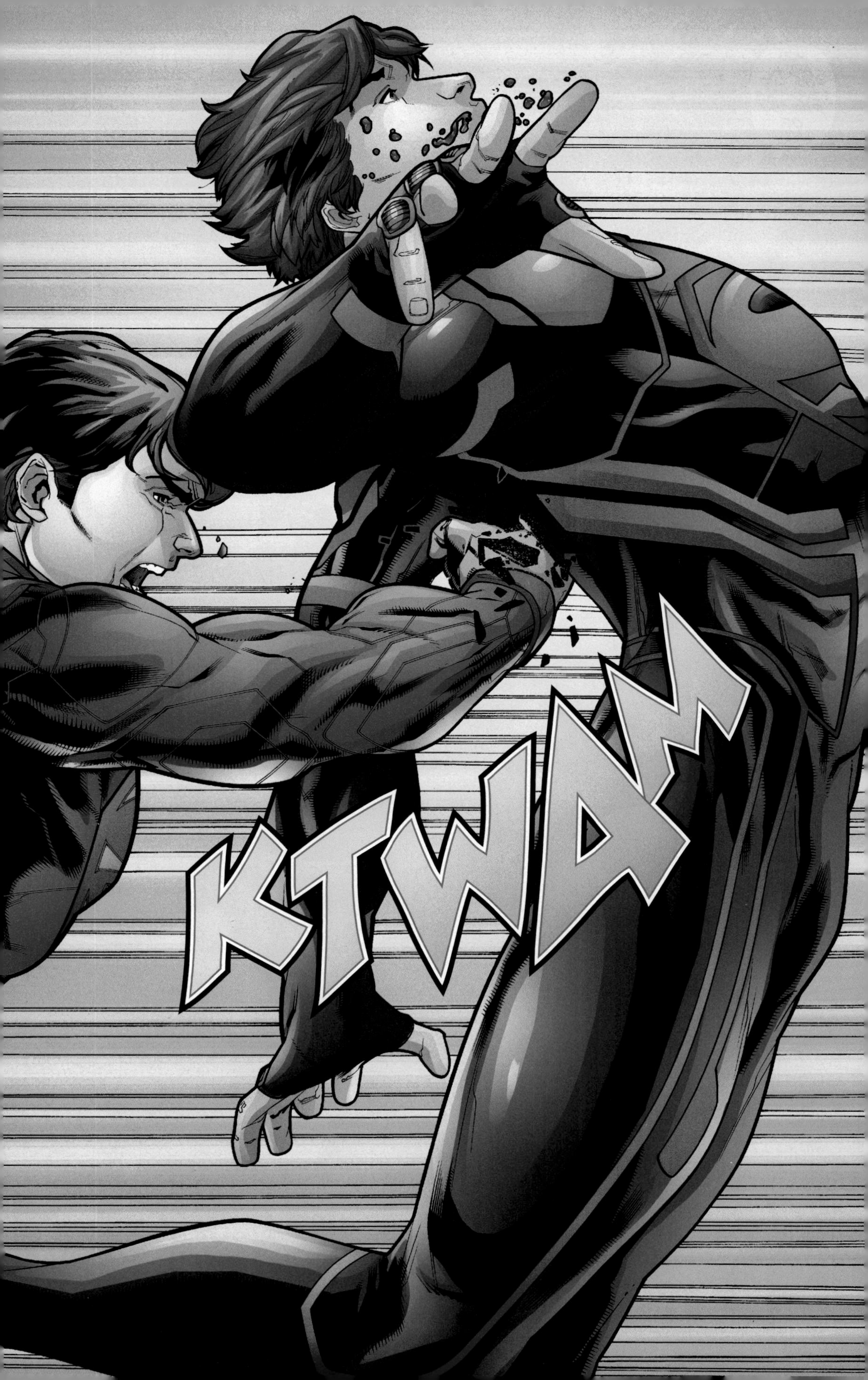
KTWAM

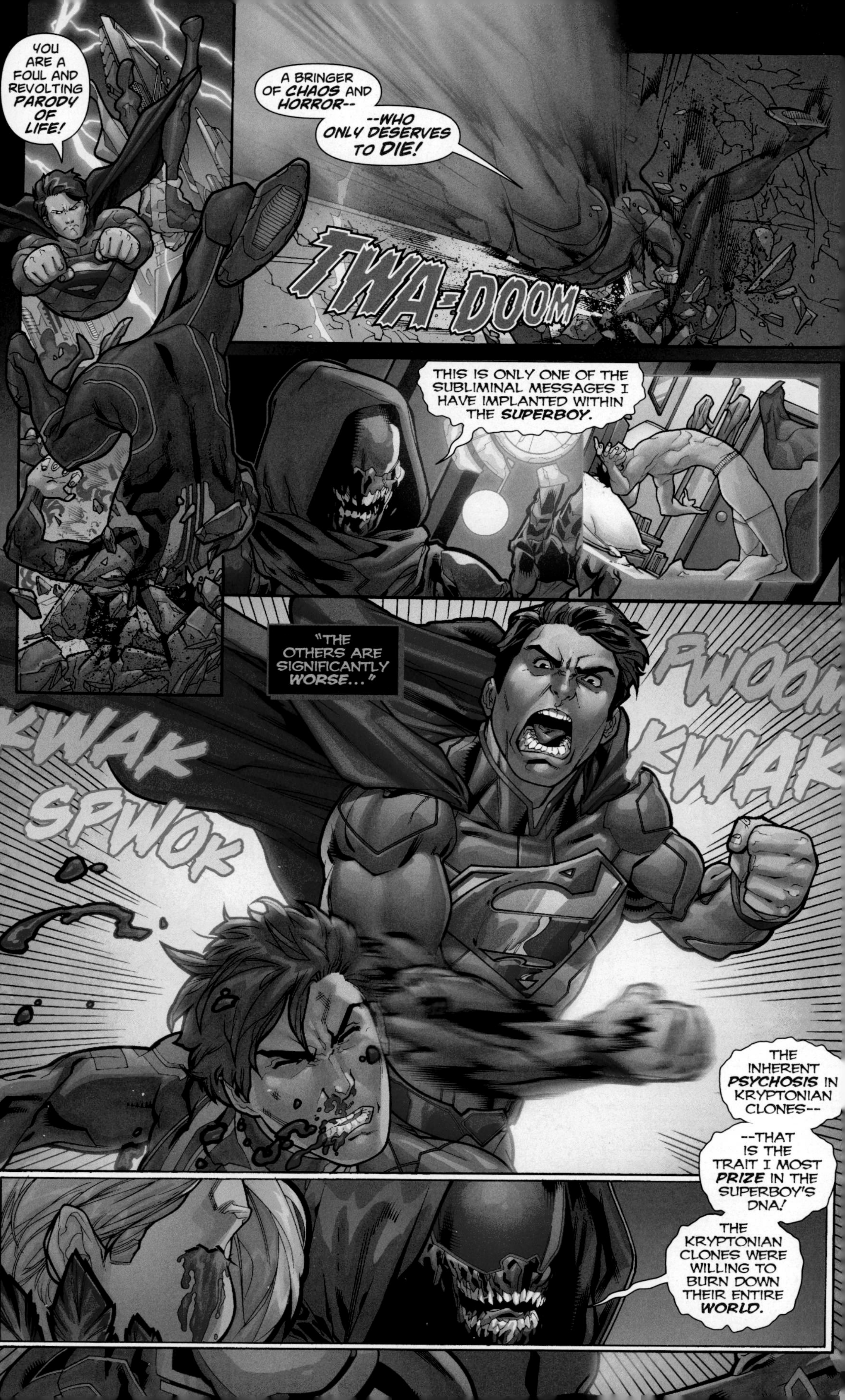
YOU ARE A FOUL AND REVOLTING PARODY OF LIFE!
A BRINGER OF CHAOS AND HORROR--
--WHO ONLY DESERVES TO DIE!
TWA-DOOM
THIS IS ONLY ONE OF THE SUBLIMINAL MESSAGES I HAVE IMPLANTED WITHIN THE SUPERBOY.
"THE OTHERS ARE SIGNIFICANTLY WORSE..."
PWOOM
KWAK
KWAK
SPWOK
THE INHERENT PSYCHOSIS IN KRYPTONIAN CLONES--
--THAT IS THE TRAIT I MOST PRIZE IN THE SUPERBOY'S DNA!
THE KRYPTONIAN CLONES WERE WILLING TO BURN DOWN THEIR ENTIRE WORLD.

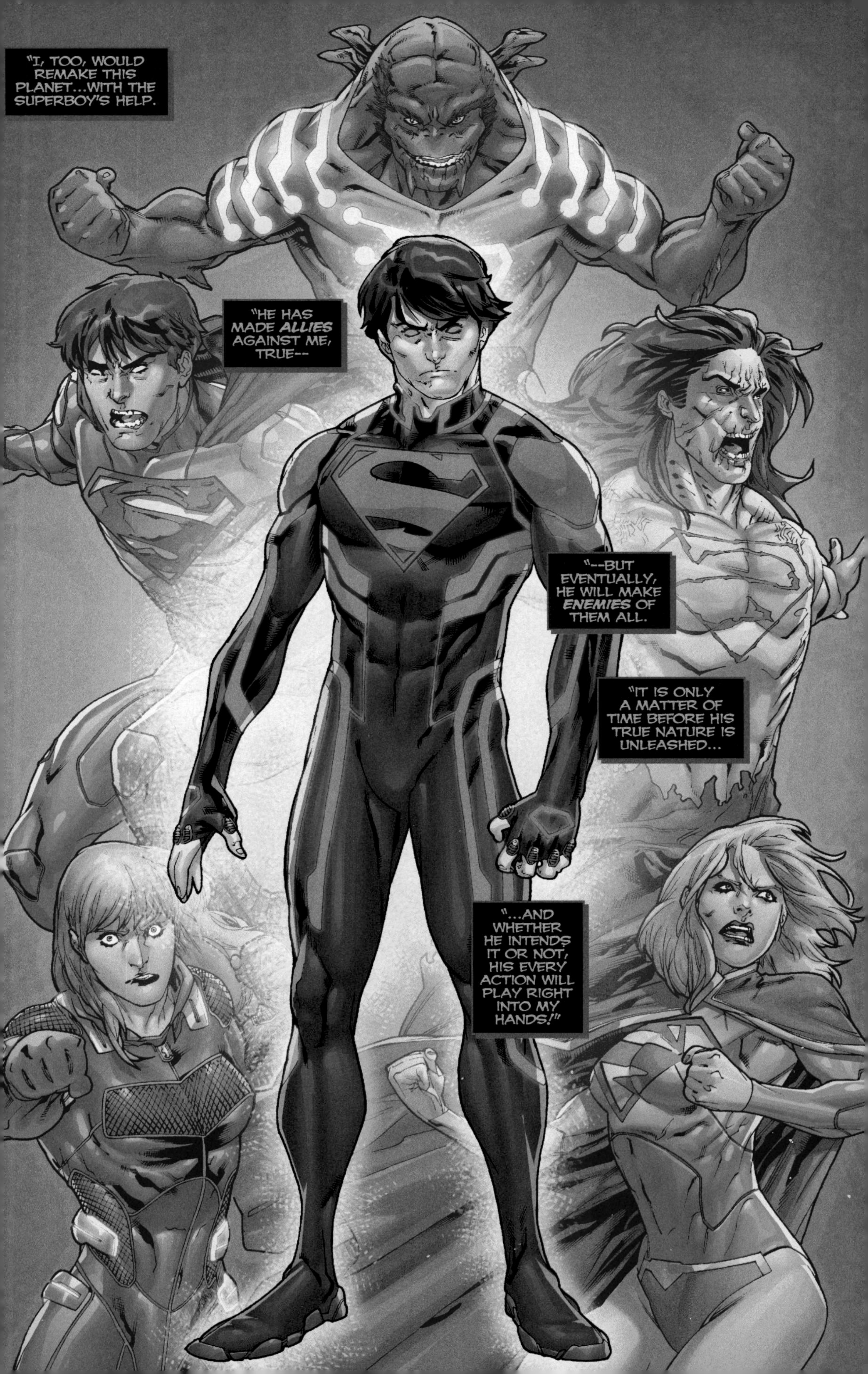
"I, TOO, WOULD REMAKE THIS PLANET...WITH THE SUPERBOY'S HELP.
"HE HAS MADE *ALLIES* AGAINST ME, TRUE--
"--BUT EVENTUALLY, HE WILL MAKE *ENEMIES* OF THEM ALL.
"IT IS ONLY A MATTER OF TIME BEFORE HIS TRUE NATURE IS UNLEASHED...
"...AND WHETHER HE INTENDS IT OR NOT, HIS EVERY ACTION WILL PLAY RIGHT INTO MY HANDS!"

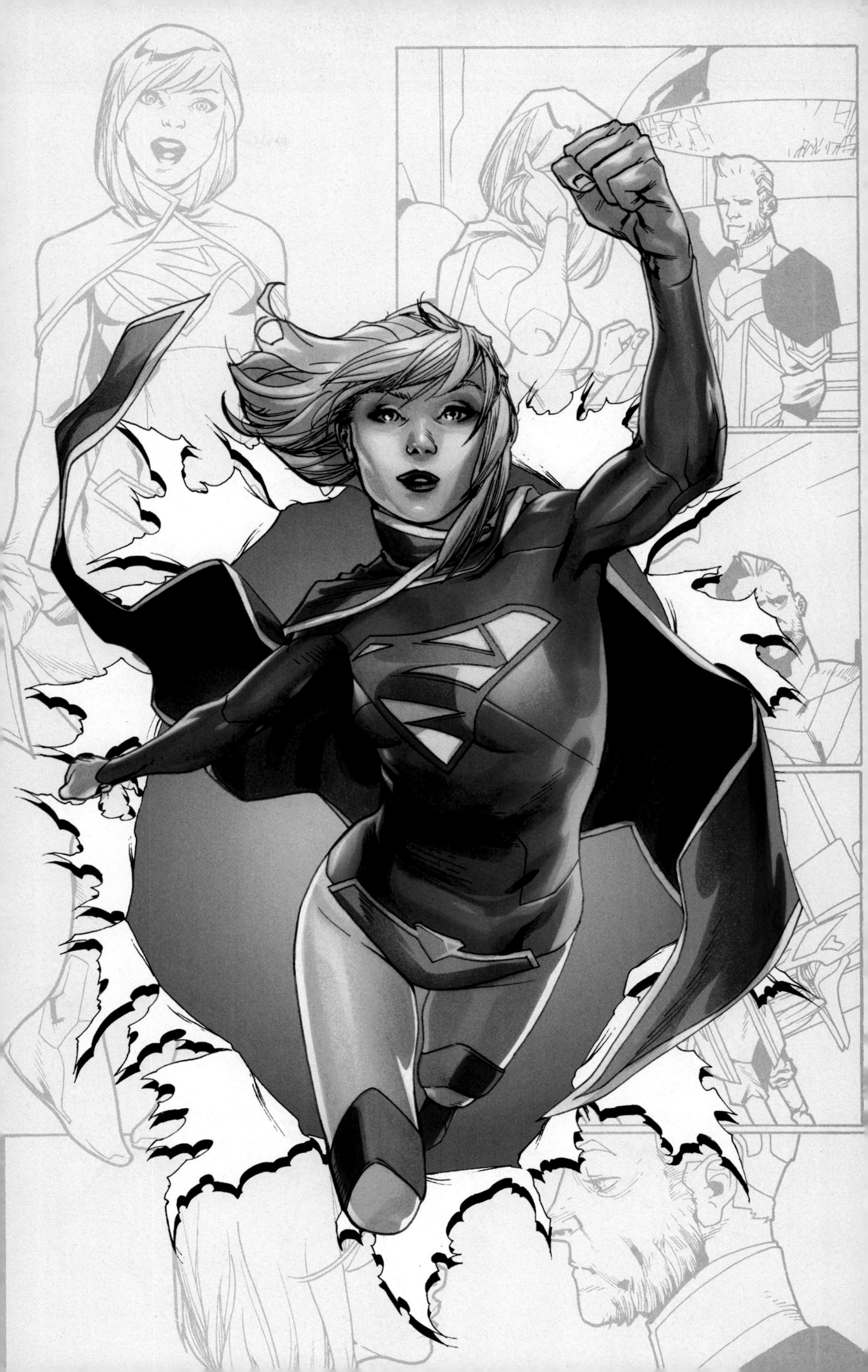

THE END OF THE BEGINNING

MICHAEL GREEN MIKE JOHNSON writers MAHMUD ASRAR artist DAVE McCAIG colorist
cover art by MAHMUD ASRAR & DAVE McCAIG

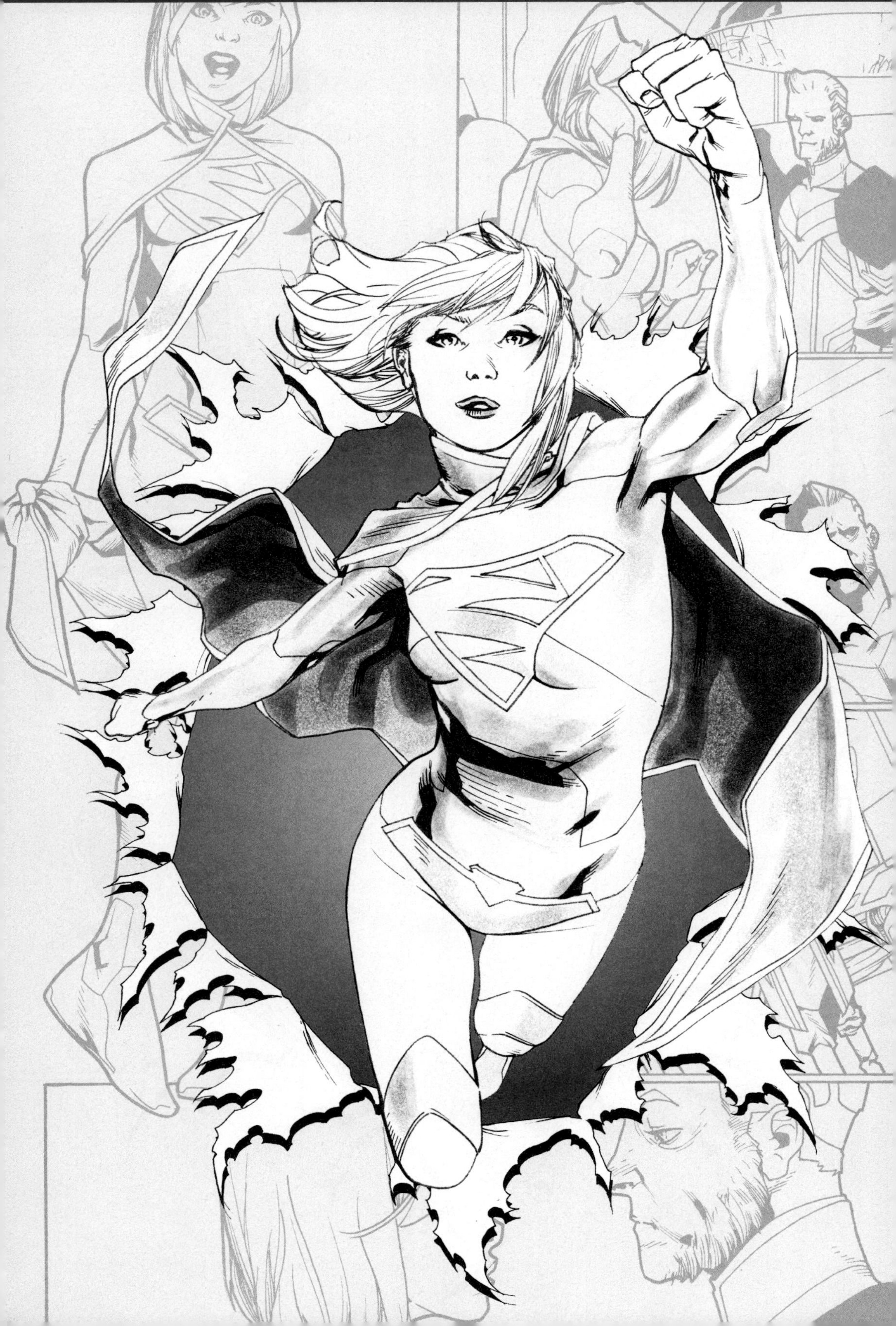

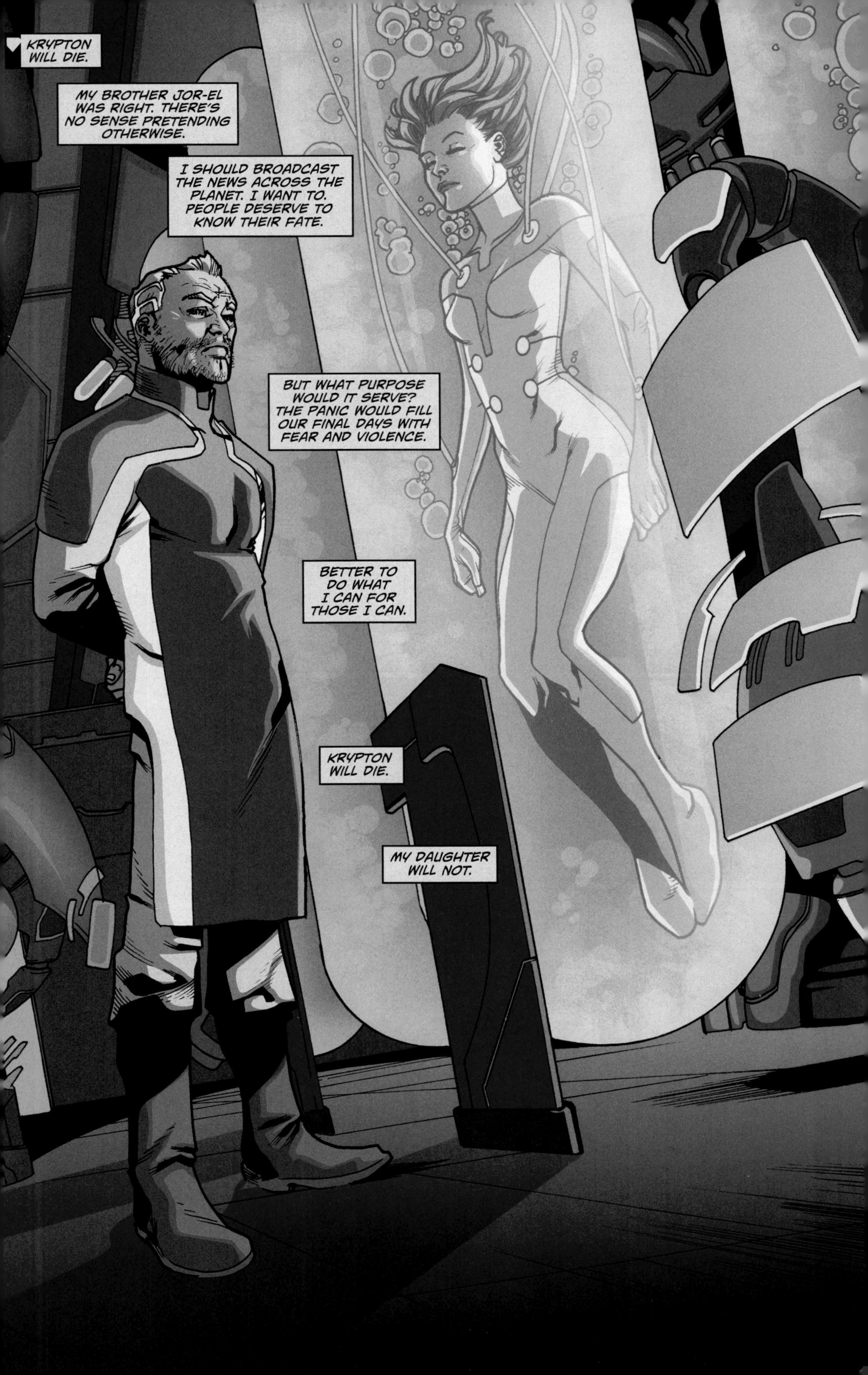
KRYPTON WILL DIE.
MY BROTHER JOR-EL WAS RIGHT. THERE'S NO SENSE PRETENDING OTHERWISE.
I SHOULD BROADCAST THE NEWS ACROSS THE PLANET. I WANT TO. PEOPLE DESERVE TO KNOW THEIR FATE.
BUT WHAT PURPOSE WOULD IT SERVE? THE PANIC WOULD FILL OUR FINAL DAYS WITH FEAR AND VIOLENCE.
BETTER TO DO WHAT I CAN FOR THOSE I CAN.
KRYPTON WILL DIE.
MY DAUGHTER WILL NOT.

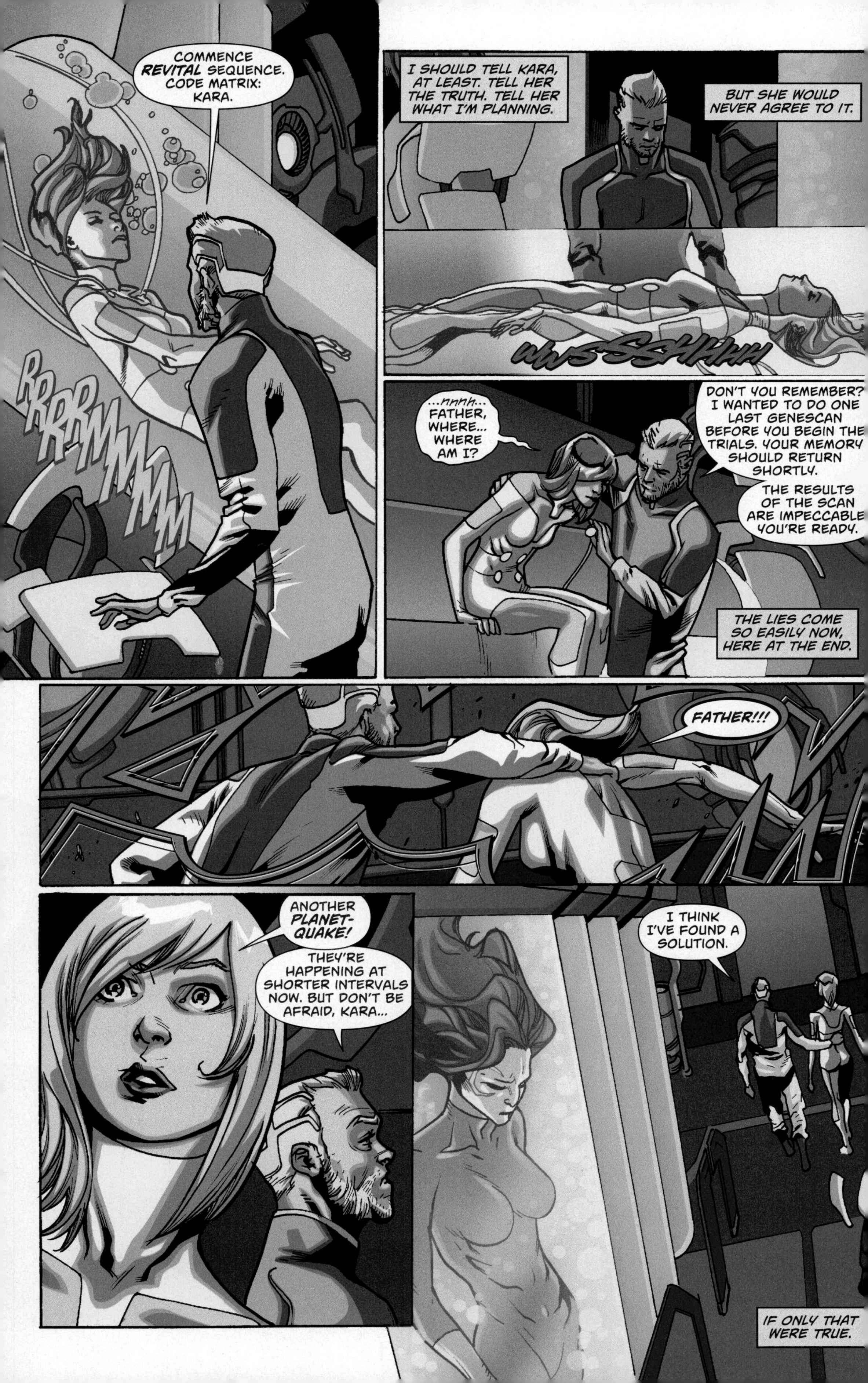
COMMENCE REVITAL SEQUENCE. CODE MATRIX: KARA.
RRRRMMMMMMMM
I SHOULD TELL KARA, AT LEAST. TELL HER THE TRUTH. TELL HER WHAT I'M PLANNING.
BUT SHE WOULD NEVER AGREE TO IT.
WWSSSHHHH
...nnnh... FATHER, WHERE... WHERE AM I?
DON'T YOU REMEMBER? I WANTED TO DO ONE LAST GENESCAN BEFORE YOU BEGIN THE TRIALS. YOUR MEMORY SHOULD RETURN SHORTLY.
THE RESULTS OF THE SCAN ARE IMPECCABLE. YOU'RE READY.
THE LIES COME SO EASILY NOW, HERE AT THE END.
FATHER!!!
ANOTHER PLANET-QUAKE!
THEY'RE HAPPENING AT SHORTER INTERVALS NOW. BUT DON'T BE AFRAID, KARA...
I THINK I'VE FOUND A SOLUTION.
IF ONLY THAT WERE TRUE.

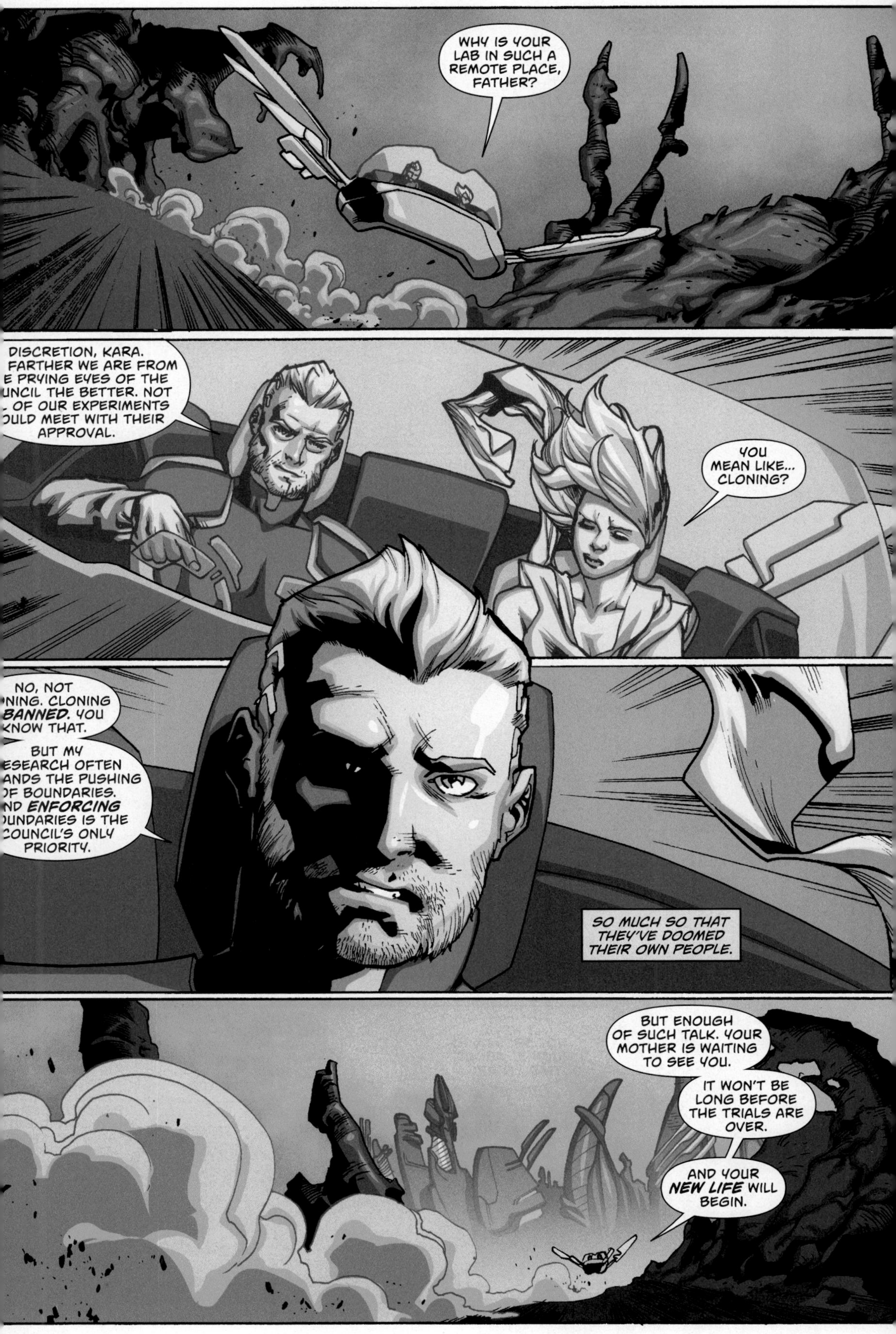
WHY IS YOUR LAB IN SUCH A REMOTE PLACE, FATHER?
DISCRETION, KARA. FARTHER WE ARE FROM E PRYING EYES OF THE UNCIL THE BETTER. NOT OF OUR EXPERIMENTS OULD MEET WITH THEIR APPROVAL.
YOU MEAN LIKE... CLONING?
NO, NOT NING. CLONING BANNED. YOU KNOW THAT.
BUT MY ESEARCH OFTEN ANDS THE PUSHING OF BOUNDARIES. ND ENFORCING UNDARIES IS THE COUNCIL'S ONLY PRIORITY.
SO MUCH SO THAT THEY'VE DOOMED THEIR OWN PEOPLE.
BUT ENOUGH OF SUCH TALK. YOUR MOTHER IS WAITING TO SEE YOU.
IT WON'T BE LONG BEFORE THE TRIALS ARE OVER.
AND YOUR NEW LIFE WILL BEGIN.

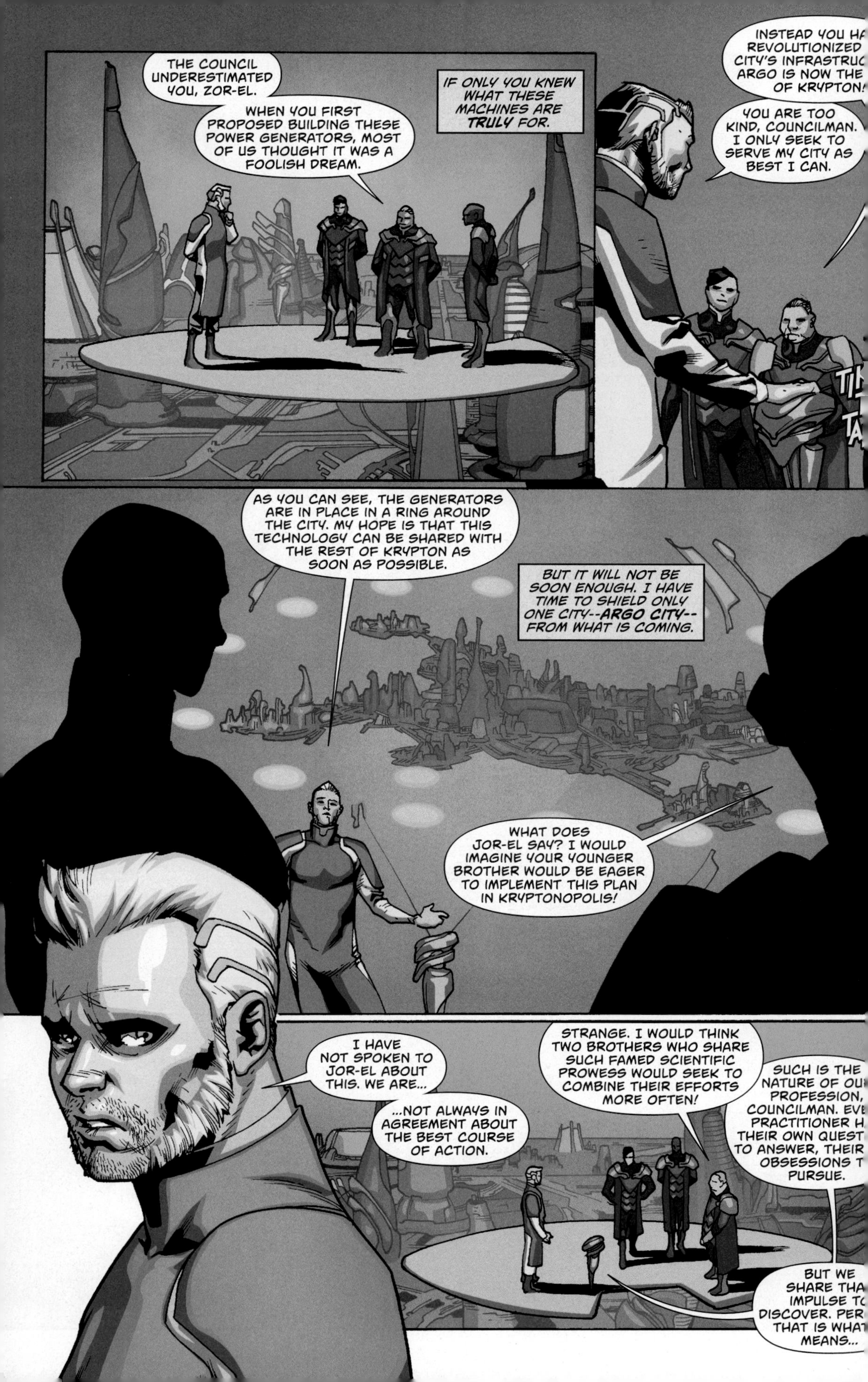
THE COUNCIL UNDERESTIMATED YOU, ZOR-EL.
WHEN YOU FIRST PROPOSED BUILDING THESE POWER GENERATORS, MOST OF US THOUGHT IT WAS A FOOLISH DREAM.
IF ONLY YOU KNEW WHAT THESE MACHINES ARE TRULY FOR.
INSTEAD YOU HA REVOLUTIONIZED CITY'S INFRASTRUC ARGO IS NOW THE OF KRYPTON!
YOU ARE TOO KIND, COUNCILMAN. I ONLY SEEK TO SERVE MY CITY AS BEST I CAN.
AS YOU CAN SEE, THE GENERATORS ARE IN PLACE IN A RING AROUND THE CITY. MY HOPE IS THAT THIS TECHNOLOGY CAN BE SHARED WITH THE REST OF KRYPTON AS SOON AS POSSIBLE.
BUT IT WILL NOT BE SOON ENOUGH. I HAVE TIME TO SHIELD ONLY ONE CITY--ARGO CITY--FROM WHAT IS COMING.
WHAT DOES JOR-EL SAY? I WOULD IMAGINE YOUR YOUNGER BROTHER WOULD BE EAGER TO IMPLEMENT THIS PLAN IN KRYPTONOPOLIS!
I HAVE NOT SPOKEN TO JOR-EL ABOUT THIS. WE ARE...
...NOT ALWAYS IN AGREEMENT ABOUT THE BEST COURSE OF ACTION.
STRANGE. I WOULD THINK TWO BROTHERS WHO SHARE SUCH FAMED SCIENTIFIC PROWESS WOULD SEEK TO COMBINE THEIR EFFORTS MORE OFTEN!
SUCH IS THE NATURE OF OU PROFESSION, COUNCILMAN. EVE PRACTITIONER H THEIR OWN QUEST TO ANSWER, THEIR OBSESSIONS T PURSUE.
BUT WE SHARE THA IMPULSE TO DISCOVER. PER THAT IS WHAT MEANS...

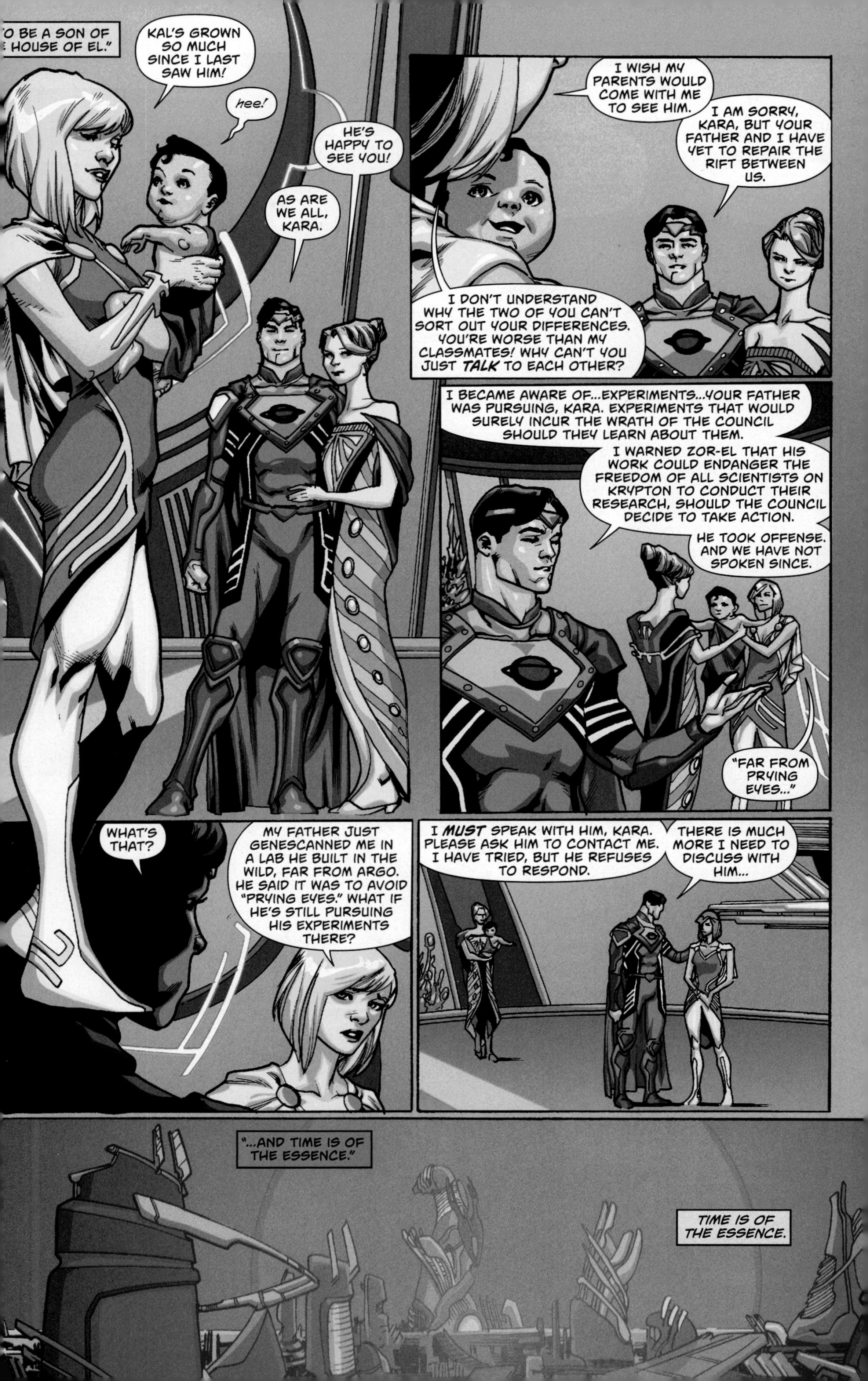
"TO BE A SON OF THE HOUSE OF EL."
KAL'S GROWN SO MUCH SINCE I LAST SAW HIM!
hee!
HE'S HAPPY TO SEE YOU!
AS ARE WE ALL, KARA.
I WISH MY PARENTS WOULD COME WITH ME TO SEE HIM.
I AM SORRY, KARA, BUT YOUR FATHER AND I HAVE YET TO REPAIR THE RIFT BETWEEN US.
I DON'T UNDERSTAND WHY THE TWO OF YOU CAN'T SORT OUT YOUR DIFFERENCES. YOU'RE WORSE THAN MY CLASSMATES! WHY CAN'T YOU JUST TALK TO EACH OTHER?
I BECAME AWARE OF...EXPERIMENTS...YOUR FATHER WAS PURSUING, KARA. EXPERIMENTS THAT WOULD SURELY INCUR THE WRATH OF THE COUNCIL SHOULD THEY LEARN ABOUT THEM.
I WARNED ZOR-EL THAT HIS WORK COULD ENDANGER THE FREEDOM OF ALL SCIENTISTS ON KRYPTON TO CONDUCT THEIR RESEARCH, SHOULD THE COUNCIL DECIDE TO TAKE ACTION.
HE TOOK OFFENSE. AND WE HAVE NOT SPOKEN SINCE.
"FAR FROM PRYING EYES..."
WHAT'S THAT?
MY FATHER JUST GENESCANNED ME IN A LAB HE BUILT IN THE WILD, FAR FROM ARGO. HE SAID IT WAS TO AVOID "PRYING EYES." WHAT IF HE'S STILL PURSUING HIS EXPERIMENTS THERE?
I MUST SPEAK WITH HIM, KARA. PLEASE ASK HIM TO CONTACT ME. I HAVE TRIED, BUT HE REFUSES TO RESPOND.
THERE IS MUCH MORE I NEED TO DISCUSS WITH HIM...
"...AND TIME IS OF THE ESSENCE."
TIME IS OF THE ESSENCE.

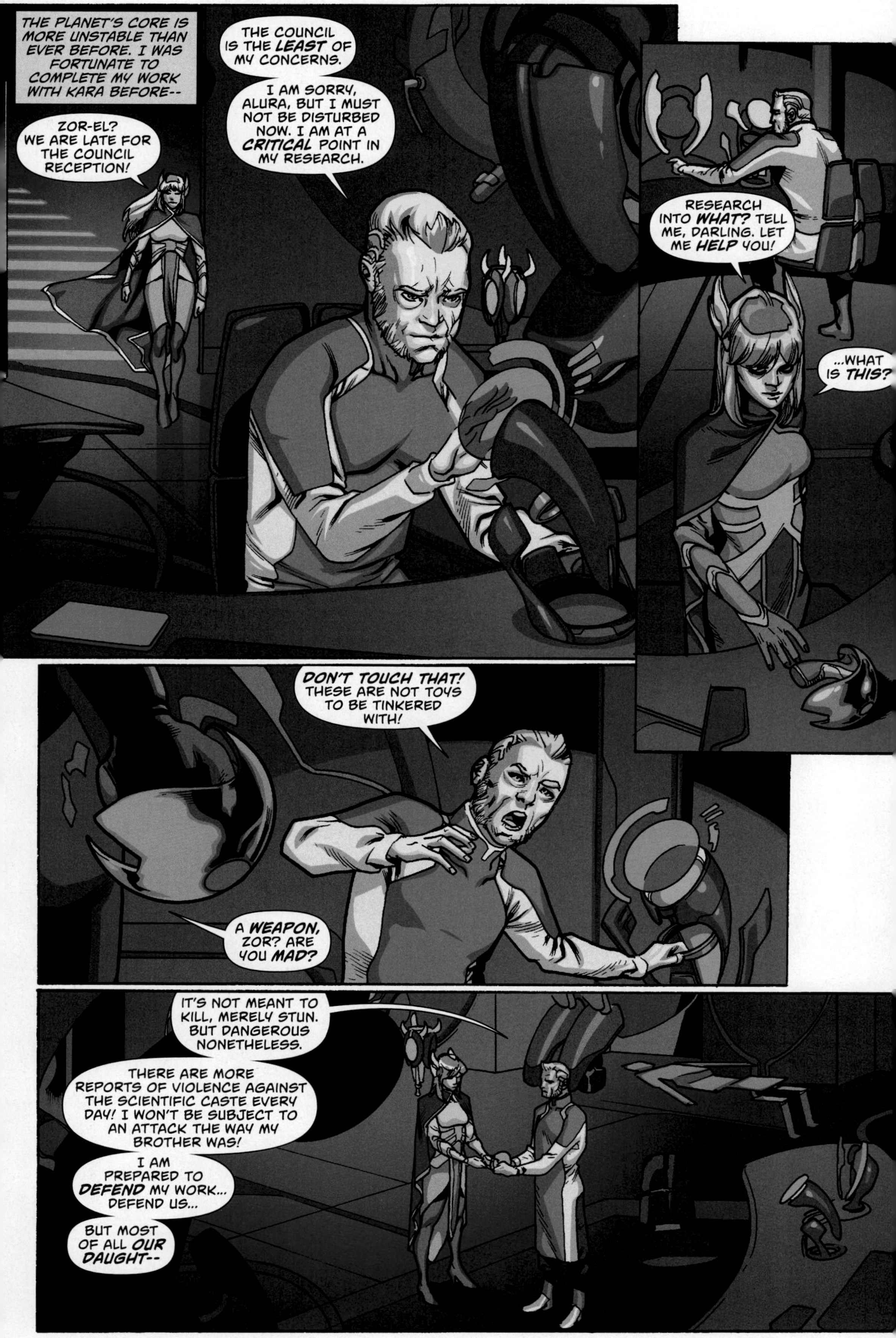
THE PLANET'S CORE IS MORE UNSTABLE THAN EVER BEFORE. I WAS FORTUNATE TO COMPLETE MY WORK WITH KARA BEFORE--
ZOR-EL? WE ARE LATE FOR THE COUNCIL RECEPTION!
THE COUNCIL IS THE LEAST OF MY CONCERNS.
I AM SORRY, ALURA, BUT I MUST NOT BE DISTURBED NOW. I AM AT A CRITICAL POINT IN MY RESEARCH.
RESEARCH INTO WHAT? TELL ME, DARLING. LET ME HELP YOU!
...WHAT IS THIS?
DON'T TOUCH THAT! THESE ARE NOT TOYS TO BE TINKERED WITH!
A WEAPON, ZOR? ARE YOU MAD?
IT'S NOT MEANT TO KILL, MERELY STUN. BUT DANGEROUS NONETHELESS.
THERE ARE MORE REPORTS OF VIOLENCE AGAINST THE SCIENTIFIC CASTE EVERY DAY! I WON'T BE SUBJECT TO AN ATTACK THE WAY MY BROTHER WAS!
I AM PREPARED TO DEFEND MY WORK... DEFEND US...
BUT MOST OF ALL OUR DAUGHT--

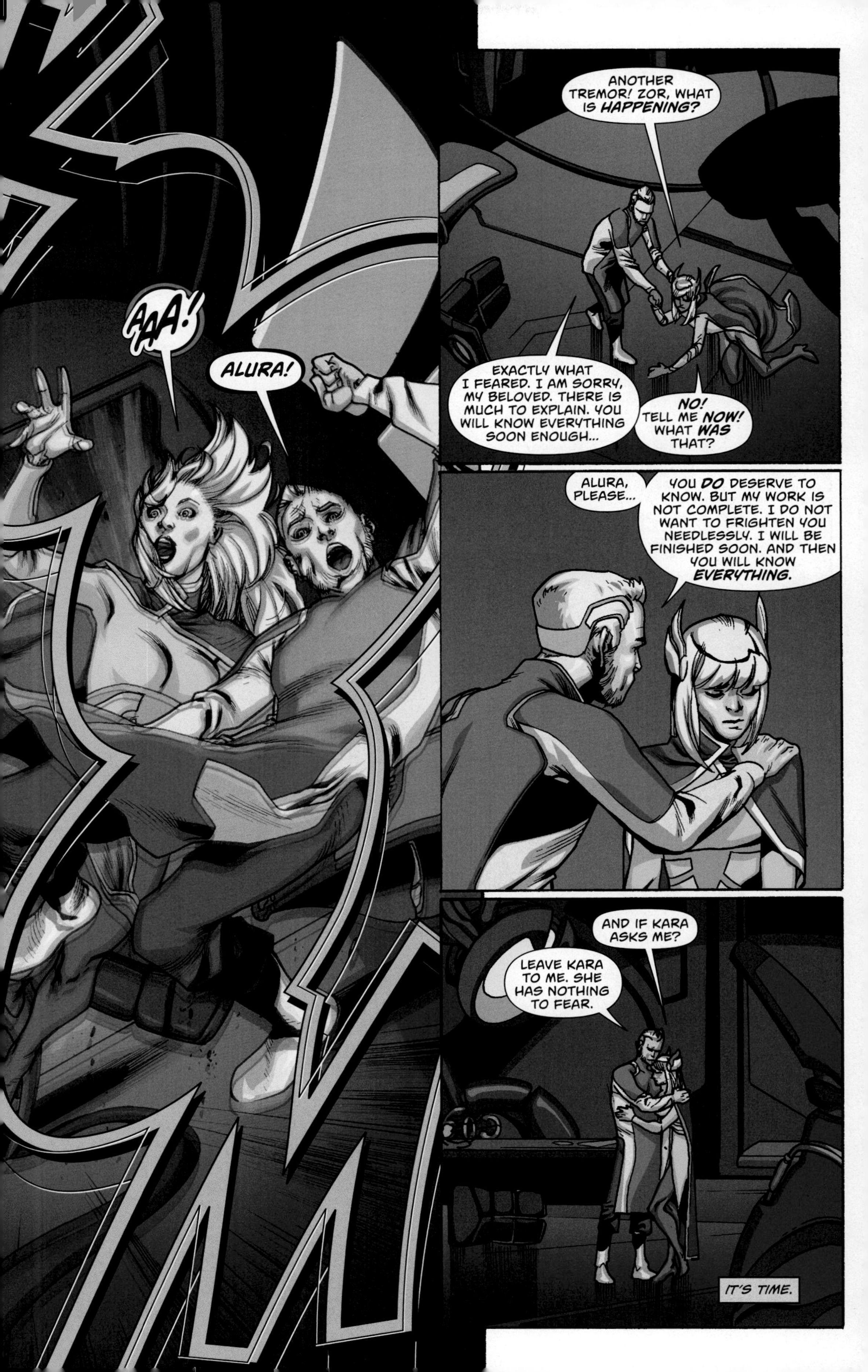
AAA!
ALURA!
ANOTHER TREMOR! ZOR, WHAT IS HAPPENING?
EXACTLY WHAT I FEARED. I AM SORRY, MY BELOVED. THERE IS MUCH TO EXPLAIN. YOU WILL KNOW EVERYTHING SOON ENOUGH...
NO! TELL ME NOW! WHAT WAS THAT?
ALURA, PLEASE...
YOU DO DESERVE TO KNOW. BUT MY WORK IS NOT COMPLETE. I DO NOT WANT TO FRIGHTEN YOU NEEDLESSLY. I WILL BE FINISHED SOON. AND THEN YOU WILL KNOW EVERYTHING.
AND IF KARA ASKS ME?
LEAVE KARA TO ME. SHE HAS NOTHING TO FEAR.
IT'S TIME.

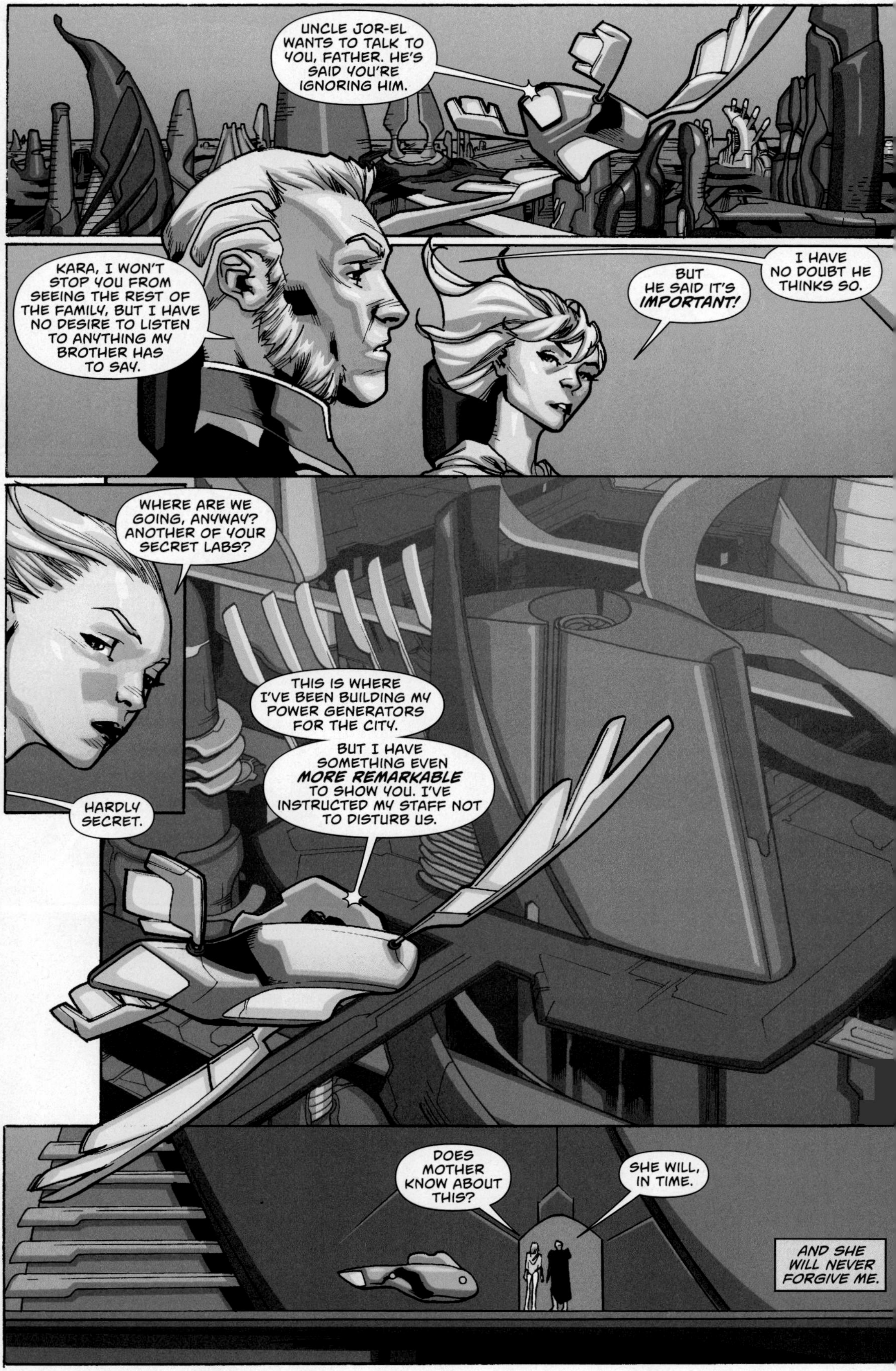
UNCLE JOR-EL WANTS TO TALK TO YOU, FATHER. HE'S SAID YOU'RE IGNORING HIM.
KARA, I WON'T STOP YOU FROM SEEING THE REST OF THE FAMILY, BUT I HAVE NO DESIRE TO LISTEN TO ANYTHING MY BROTHER HAS TO SAY.
BUT HE SAID IT'S IMPORTANT!
I HAVE NO DOUBT HE THINKS SO.
WHERE ARE WE GOING, ANYWAY? ANOTHER OF YOUR SECRET LABS?
HARDLY SECRET.
THIS IS WHERE I'VE BEEN BUILDING MY POWER GENERATORS FOR THE CITY.
BUT I HAVE SOMETHING EVEN MORE REMARKABLE TO SHOW YOU. I'VE INSTRUCTED MY STAFF NOT TO DISTURB US.
DOES MOTHER KNOW ABOUT THIS?
SHE WILL, IN TIME.
AND SHE WILL NEVER FORGIVE ME.

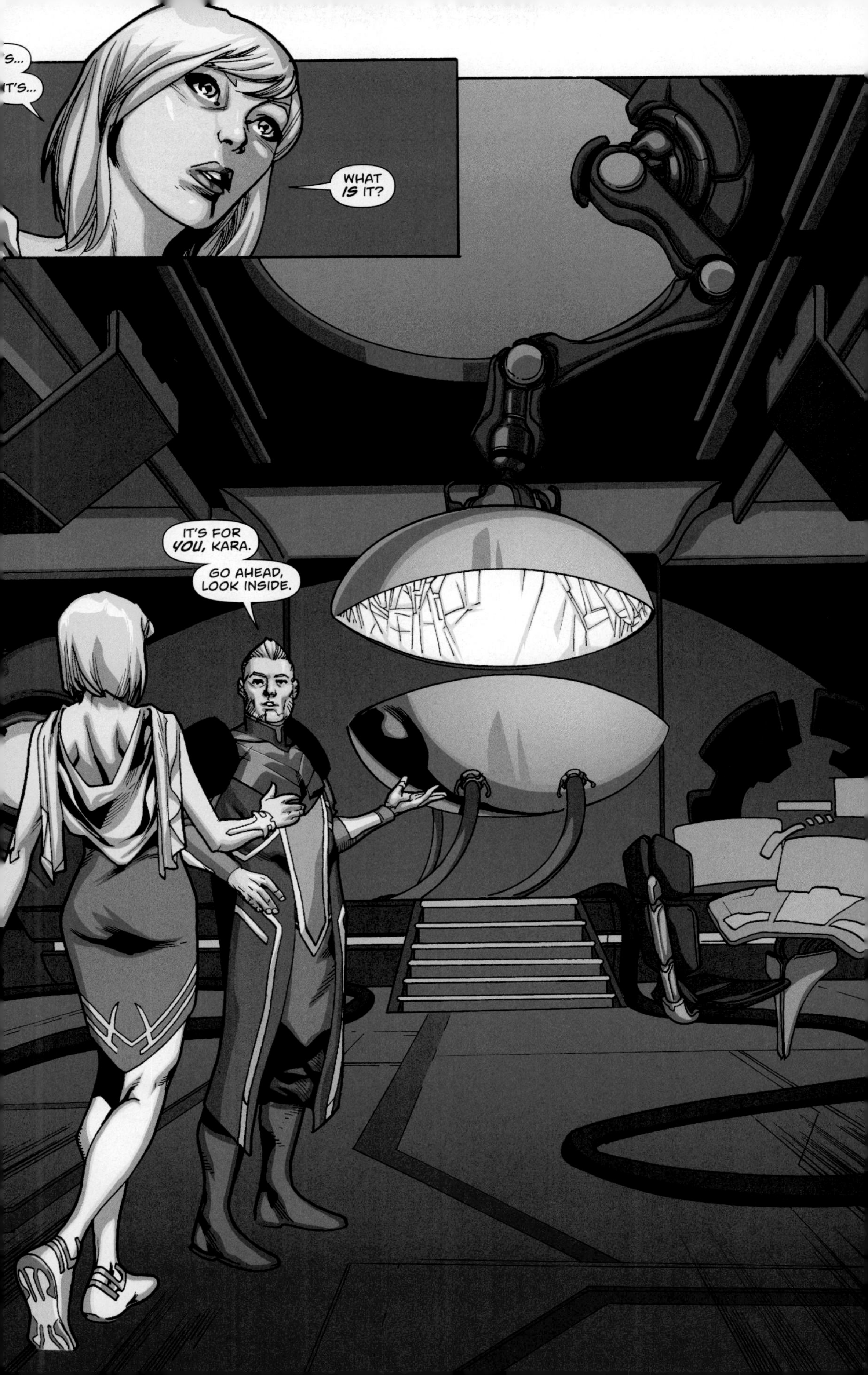

'S...
IT'S...
WHAT IS IT?
IT'S FOR YOU, KARA.
GO AHEAD, LOOK INSIDE.

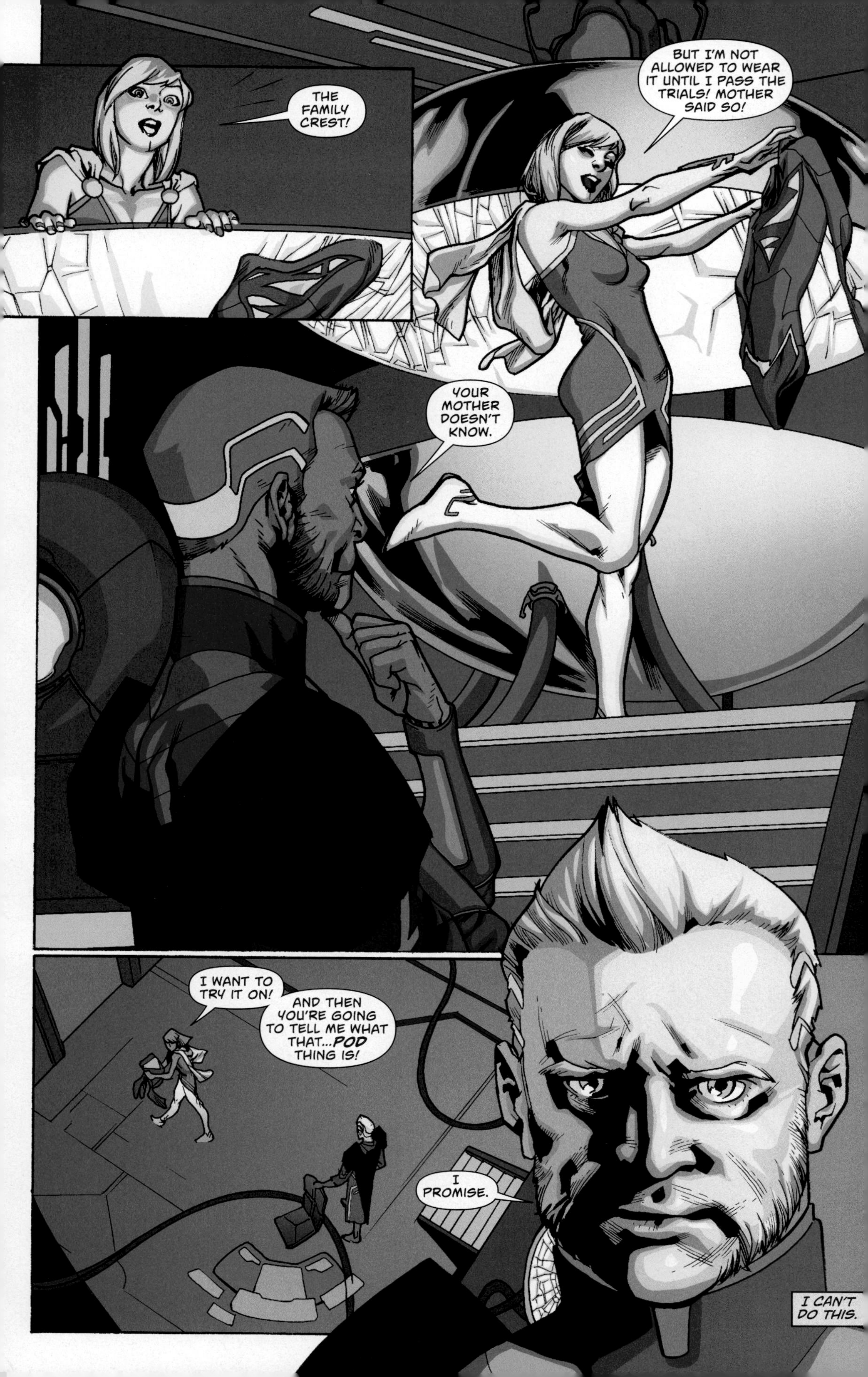
THE FAMILY CREST!
BUT I'M NOT ALLOWED TO WEAR IT UNTIL I PASS THE TRIALS! MOTHER SAID SO!
YOUR MOTHER DOESN'T KNOW.
I WANT TO TRY IT ON!
AND THEN YOU'RE GOING TO TELL ME WHAT THAT...POD THING IS!
I PROMISE.
I CAN'T DO THIS.

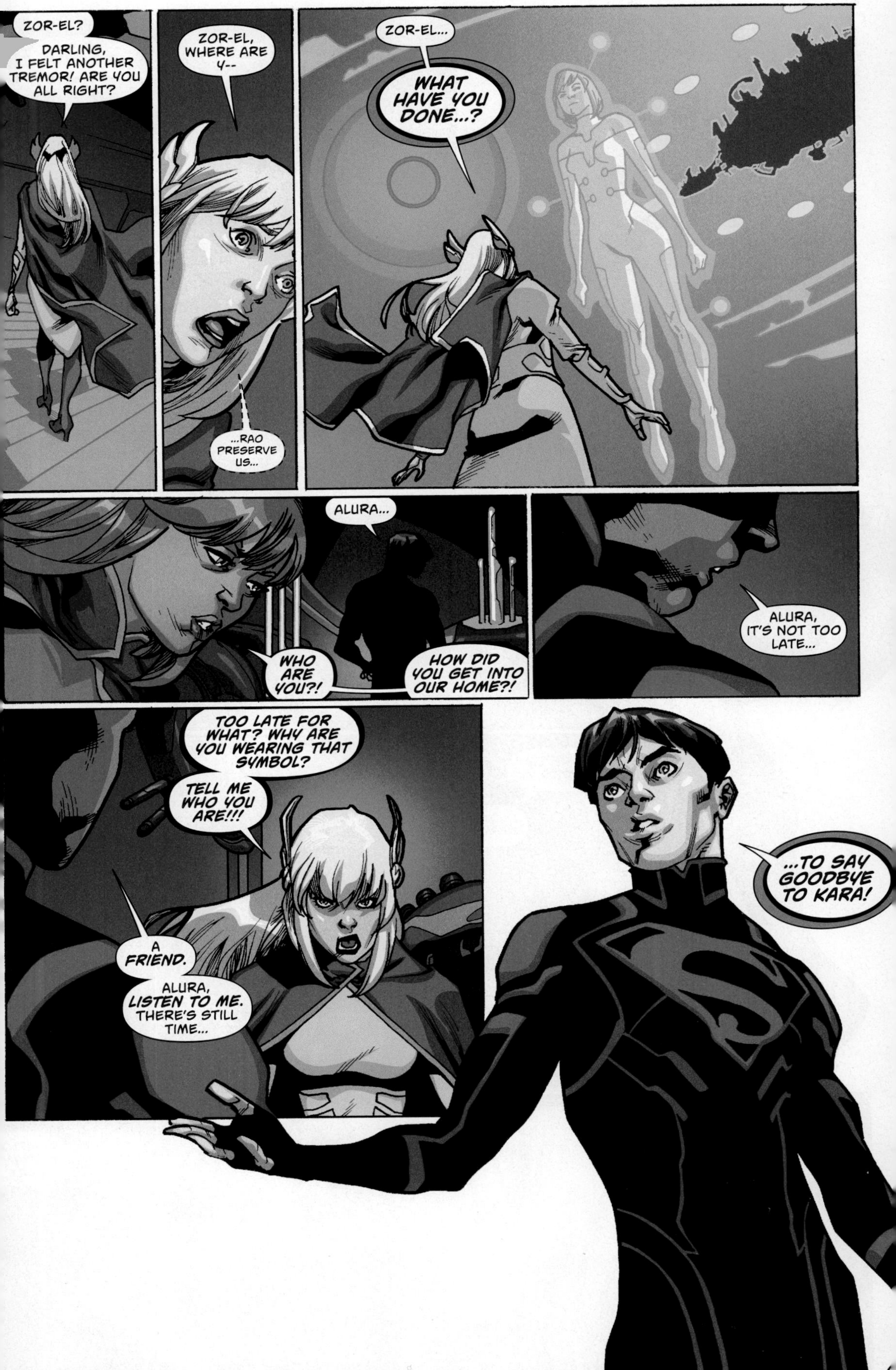
ZOR-EL?
DARLING, I FELT ANOTHER TREMOR! ARE YOU ALL RIGHT?
ZOR-EL, WHERE ARE Y--
...RAO PRESERVE US...
ZOR-EL...
WHAT HAVE YOU DONE...?
ALURA...
WHO ARE YOU?!
HOW DID YOU GET INTO OUR HOME?!
ALURA, IT'S NOT TOO LATE...
TOO LATE FOR WHAT? WHY ARE YOU WEARING THAT SYMBOL?
TELL ME WHO YOU ARE!!!
A FRIEND.
ALURA, LISTEN TO ME. THERE'S STILL TIME...
...TO SAY GOODBYE TO KARA!

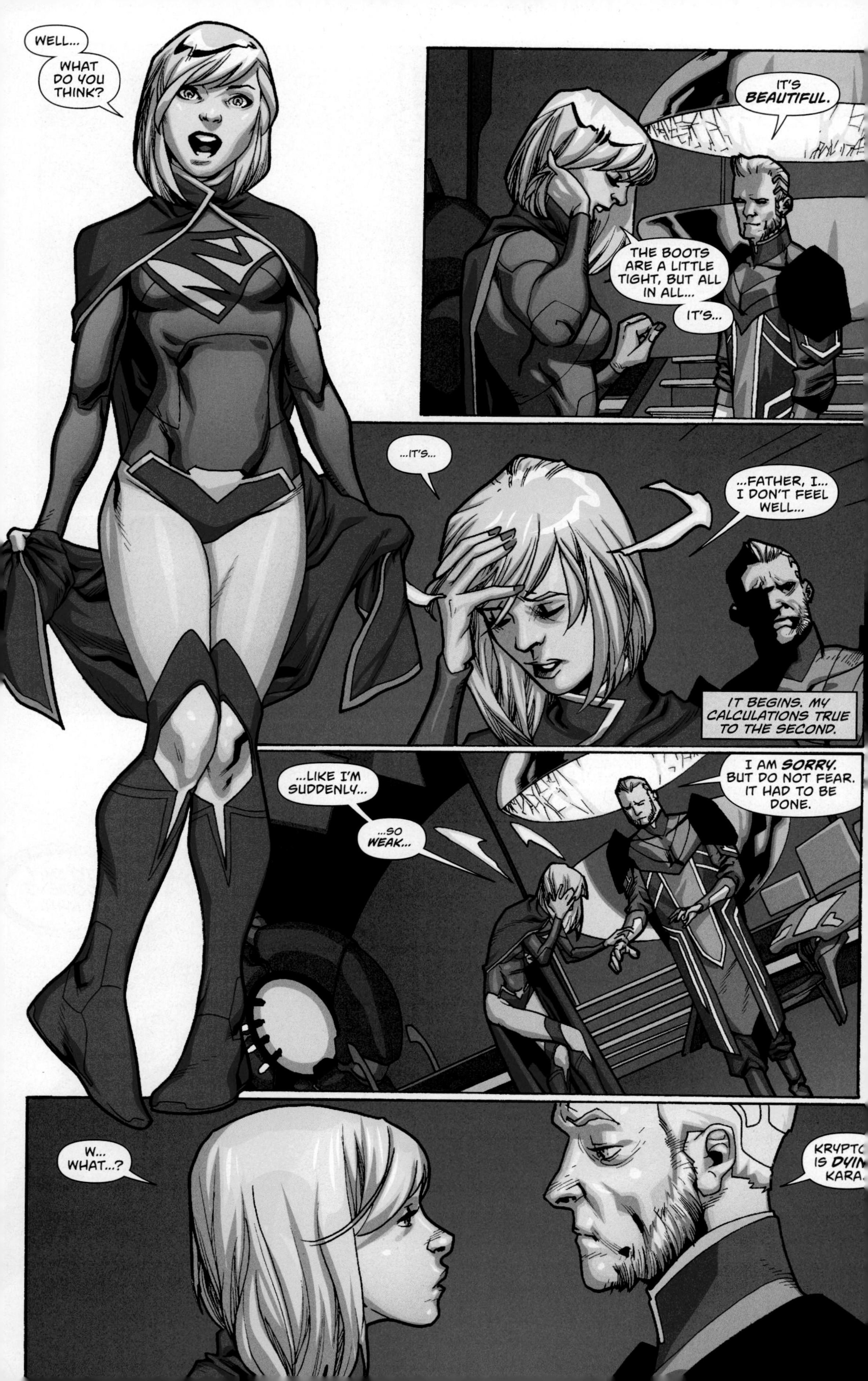
WELL... WHAT DO YOU THINK?
IT'S BEAUTIFUL.
THE BOOTS ARE A LITTLE TIGHT, BUT ALL IN ALL...
IT'S...
...IT'S...
...FATHER, I... I DON'T FEEL WELL...
IT BEGINS. MY CALCULATIONS TRUE TO THE SECOND.
...LIKE I'M SUDDENLY...
...SO WEAK...
I AM SORRY. BUT DO NOT FEAR. IT HAD TO BE DONE.
W... WHAT...?
KRYPTO IS DYIN KARA.

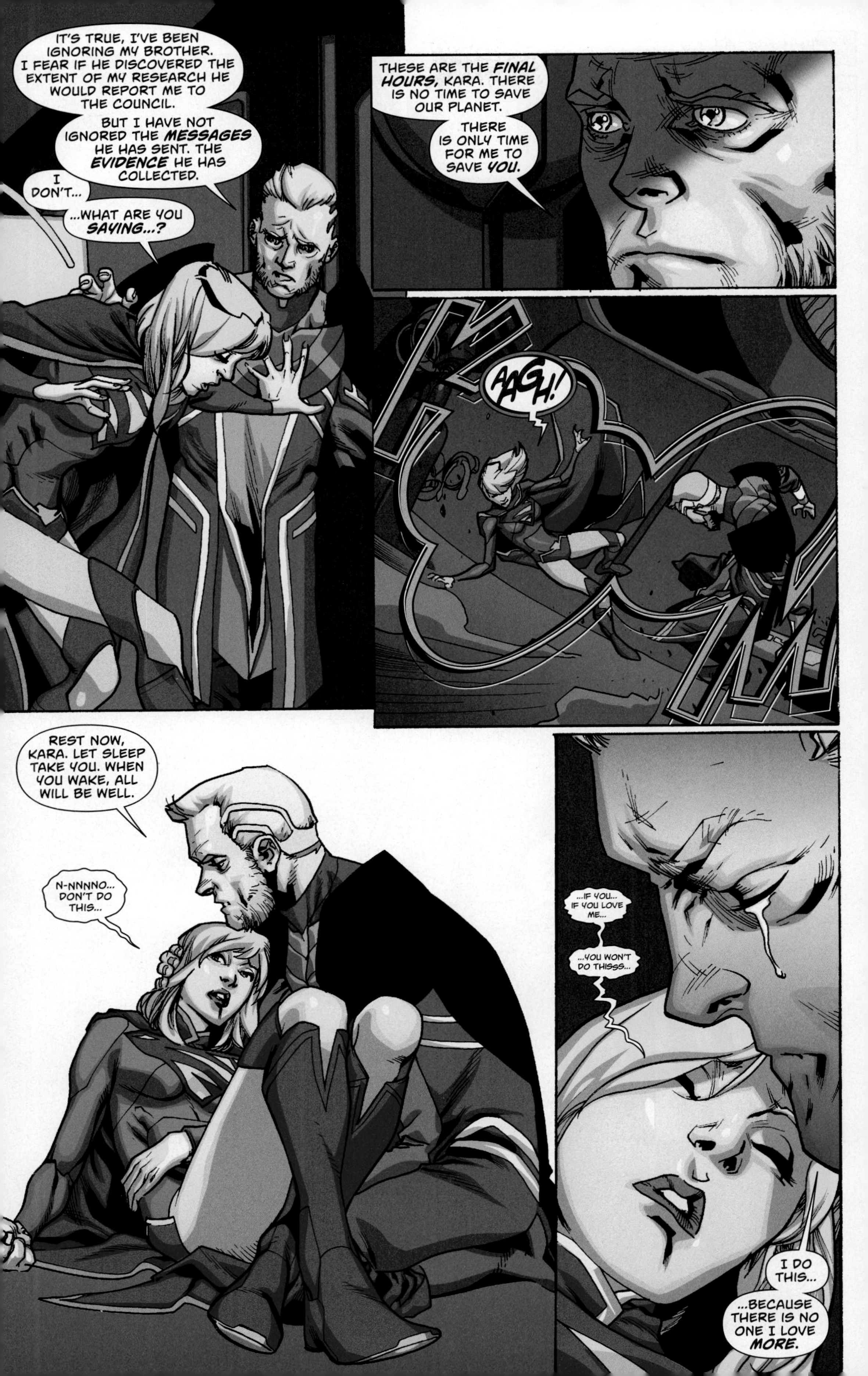
IT'S TRUE, I'VE BEEN IGNORING MY BROTHER. I FEAR IF HE DISCOVERED THE EXTENT OF MY RESEARCH HE WOULD REPORT ME TO THE COUNCIL.
BUT I HAVE NOT IGNORED THE MESSAGES HE HAS SENT. THE EVIDENCE HE HAS COLLECTED.
I DON'T...
...WHAT ARE YOU SAYING...?
THESE ARE THE FINAL HOURS, KARA. THERE IS NO TIME TO SAVE OUR PLANET.
THERE IS ONLY TIME FOR ME TO SAVE YOU.
AAGH!
REST NOW, KARA. LET SLEEP TAKE YOU. WHEN YOU WAKE, ALL WILL BE WELL.
N-NNNNO... DON'T DO THIS...
...IF YOU... IF YOU LOVE ME...
...YOU WON'T DO THISSS...
I DO THIS...
...BECAUSE THERE IS NO ONE I LOVE MORE.

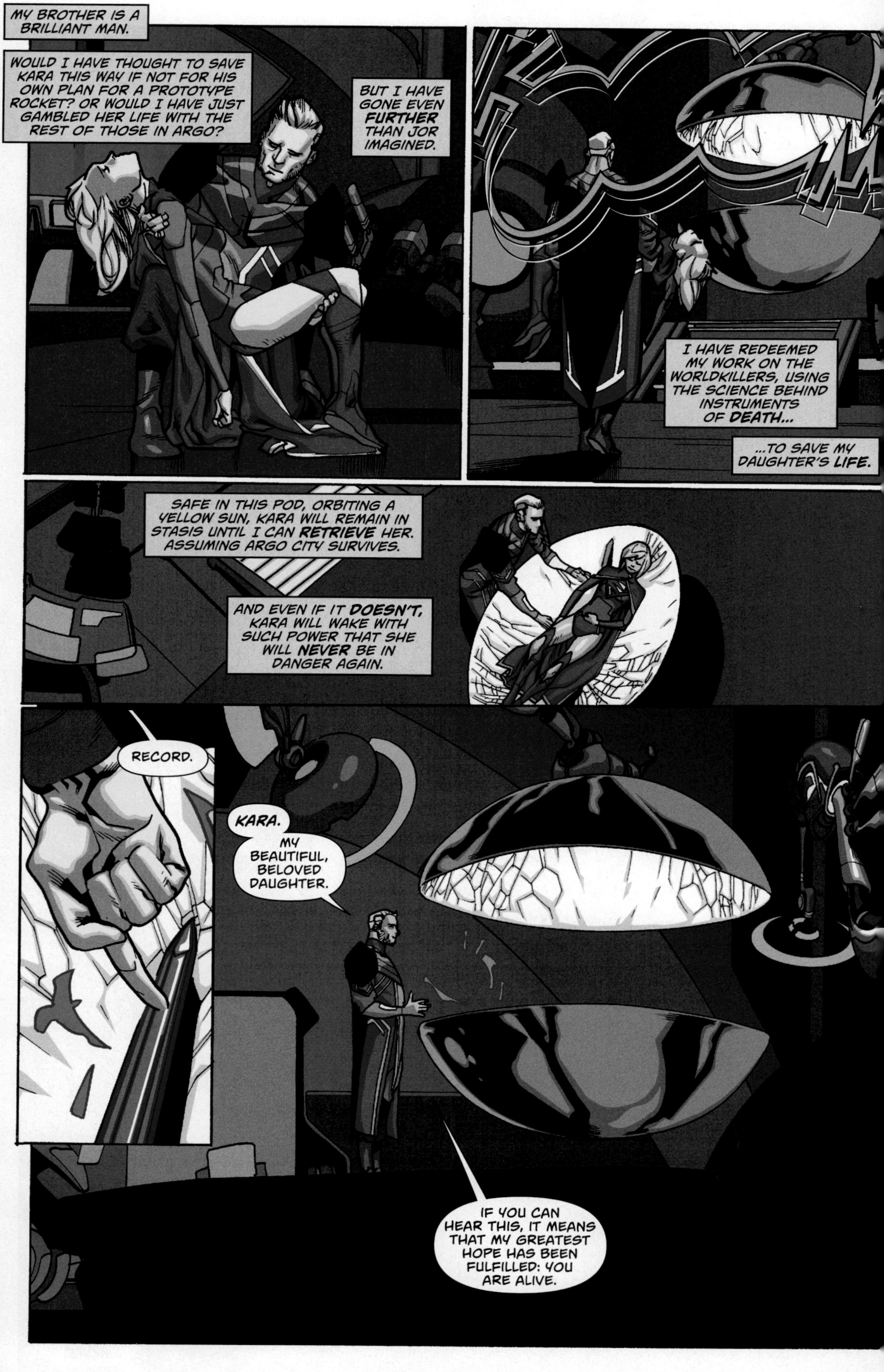
MY BROTHER IS A BRILLIANT MAN.
WOULD I HAVE THOUGHT TO SAVE KARA THIS WAY IF NOT FOR HIS OWN PLAN FOR A PROTOTYPE ROCKET? OR WOULD I HAVE JUST GAMBLED HER LIFE WITH THE REST OF THOSE IN ARGO?
BUT I HAVE GONE EVEN FURTHER THAN JOR IMAGINED.
I HAVE REDEEMED MY WORK ON THE WORLDKILLERS, USING THE SCIENCE BEHIND INSTRUMENTS OF DEATH...
...TO SAVE MY DAUGHTER'S LIFE.
SAFE IN THIS POD, ORBITING A YELLOW SUN, KARA WILL REMAIN IN STASIS UNTIL I CAN RETRIEVE HER. ASSUMING ARGO CITY SURVIVES.
AND EVEN IF IT DOESN'T, KARA WILL WAKE WITH SUCH POWER THAT SHE WILL NEVER BE IN DANGER AGAIN.
RECORD.
KARA.
MY BEAUTIFUL, BELOVED DAUGHTER.
IF YOU CAN HEAR THIS, IT MEANS THAT MY GREATEST HOPE HAS BEEN FULFILLED: YOU ARE ALIVE.

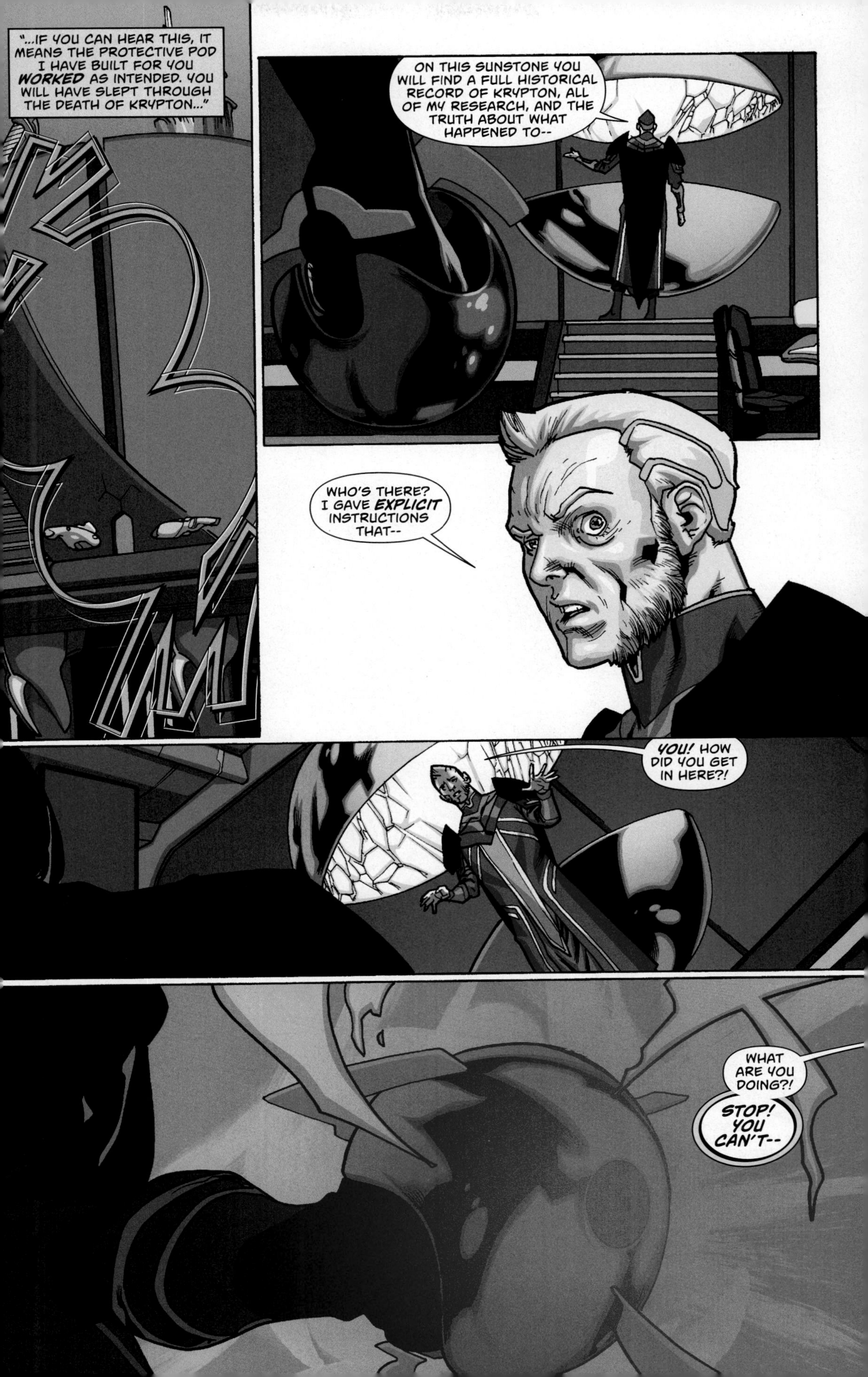
"...IF YOU CAN HEAR THIS, IT MEANS THE PROTECTIVE POD I HAVE BUILT FOR YOU WORKED AS INTENDED. YOU WILL HAVE SLEPT THROUGH THE DEATH OF KRYPTON..."
ON THIS SUNSTONE YOU WILL FIND A FULL HISTORICAL RECORD OF KRYPTON, ALL OF MY RESEARCH, AND THE TRUTH ABOUT WHAT HAPPENED TO--
WHO'S THERE? I GAVE EXPLICIT INSTRUCTIONS THAT--
YOU! HOW DID YOU GET IN HERE?!
WHAT ARE YOU DOING?!
STOP! YOU CAN'T--

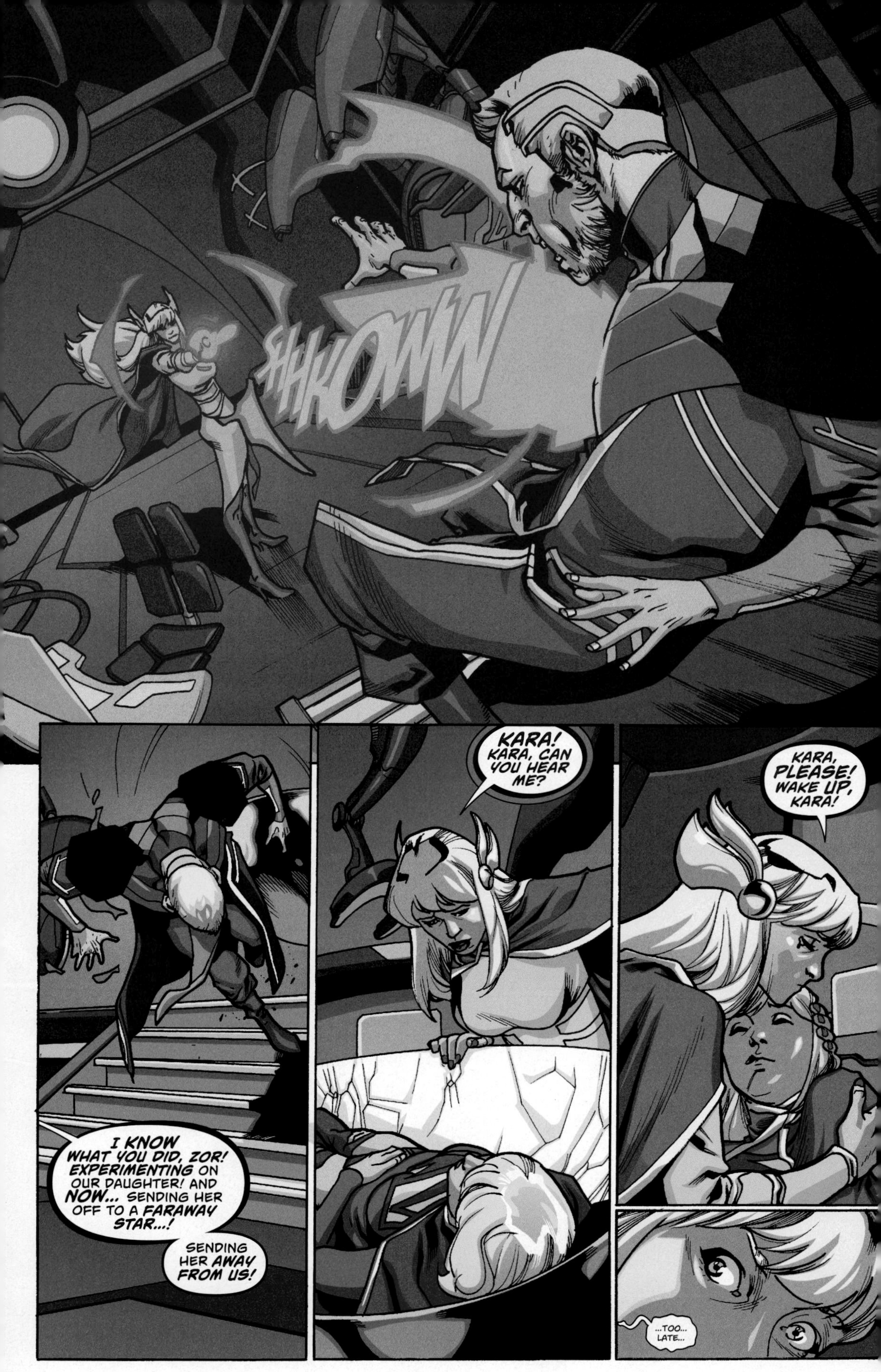
SHHKOWWW
I KNOW WHAT YOU DID, ZOR! EXPERIMENTING ON OUR DAUGHTER! AND NOW... SENDING HER OFF TO A FARAWAY STAR...!
SENDING HER AWAY FROM US!
KARA! KARA, CAN YOU HEAR ME?
KARA, PLEASE! WAKE UP, KARA!
...TOO... LATE...

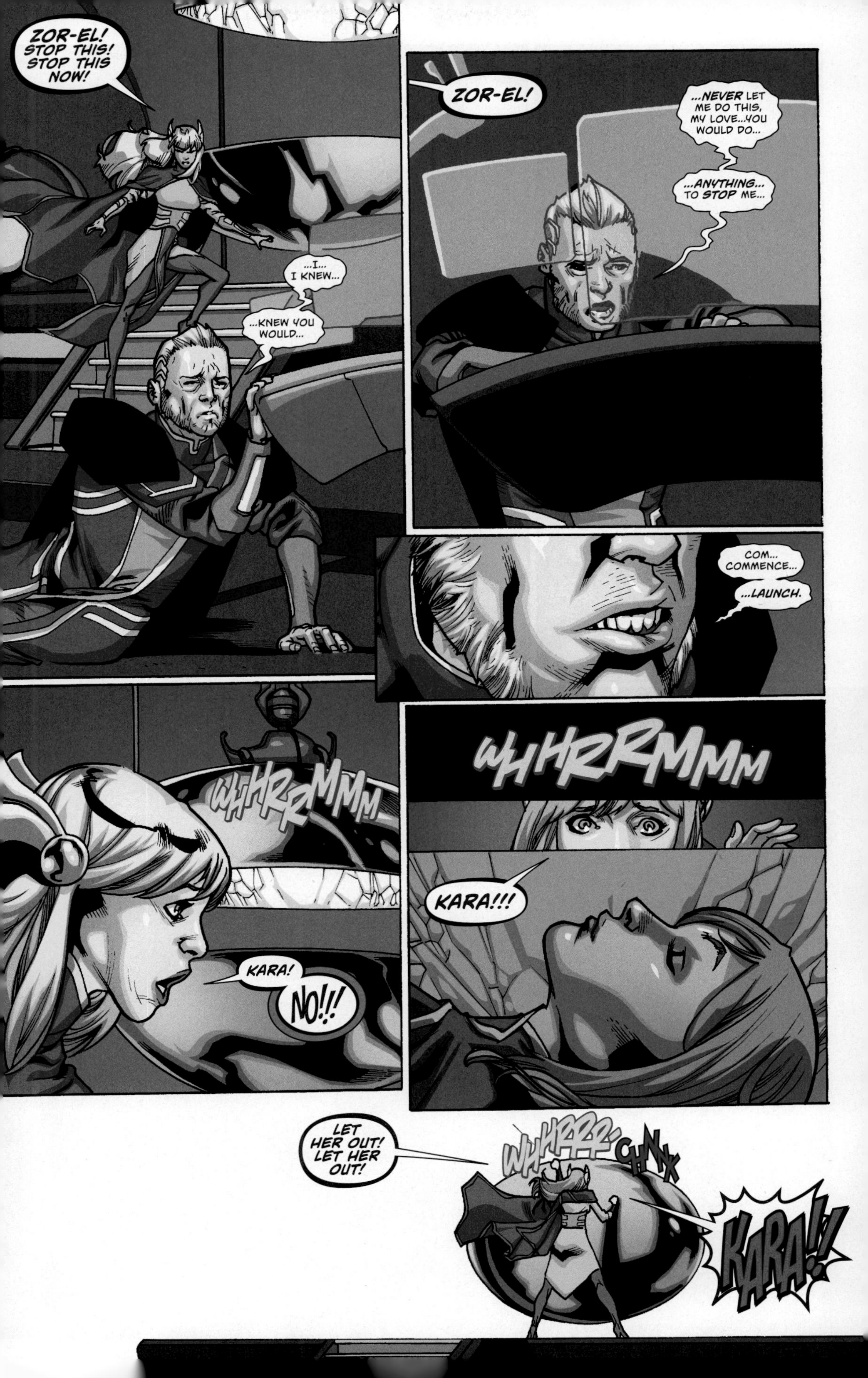
ZOR-EL! STOP THIS! STOP THIS NOW!
...I... I KNEW...
...KNEW YOU WOULD...
ZOR-EL!
...NEVER LET ME DO THIS, MY LOVE...YOU WOULD DO...
...ANYTHING... TO STOP ME...
COM... COMMENCE...
...LAUNCH.
WHHRRMMM
KARA! NO!!!
WHHRRMMMM
KARA!!!
LET HER OUT! LET HER OUT!
WHHRRR CHNK
KARA!!!

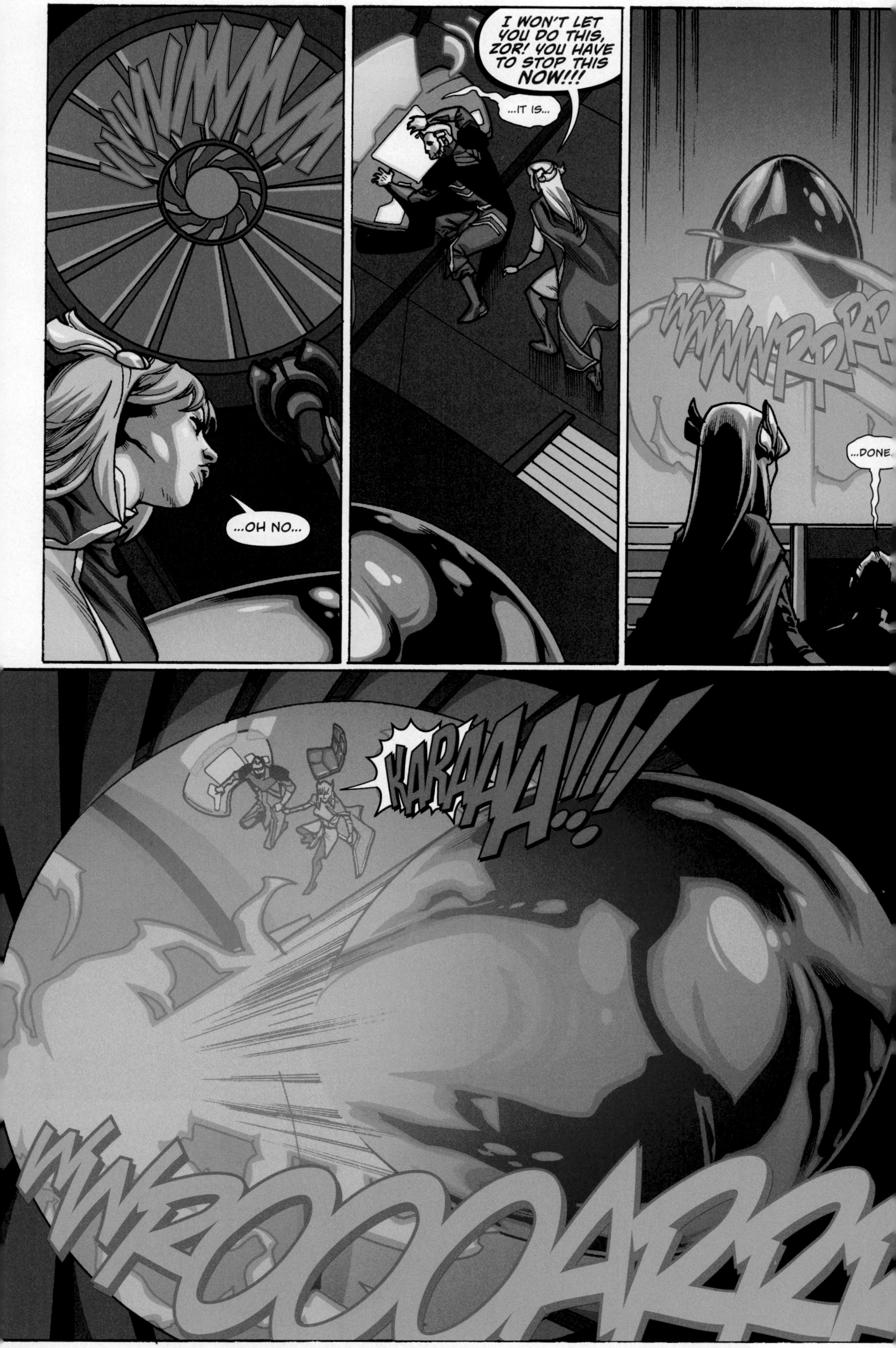
VMMMMM
...OH NO...
I WON'T LET YOU DO THIS, ZOR! YOU HAVE TO STOP THIS NOW!!!
...IT IS...
WMMNRRR
...DONE.
KARAAAA!!!!
WHROOOARRR

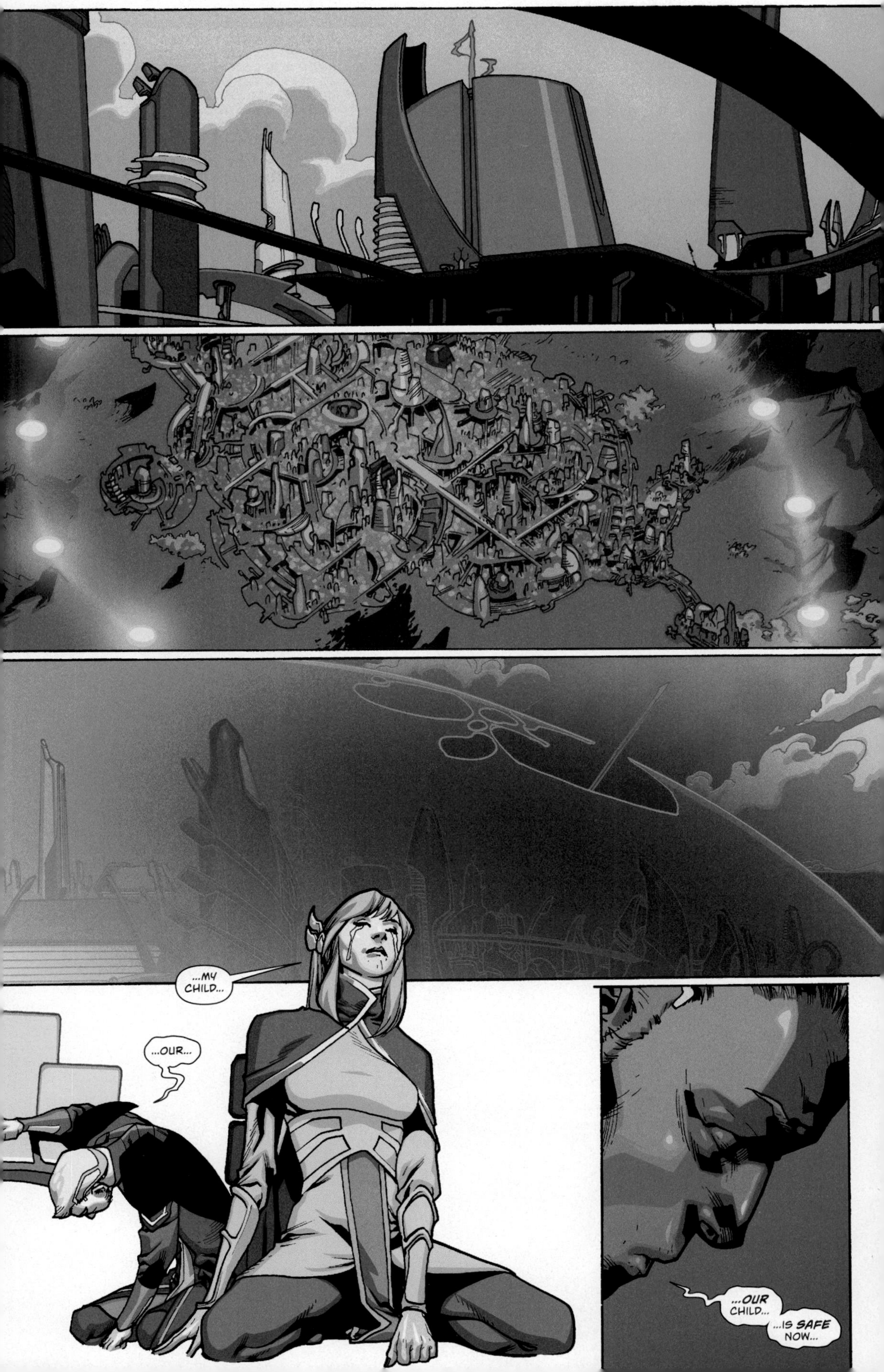
...MY CHILD...
...OUR...
...OUR CHILD...
...IS SAFE NOW...

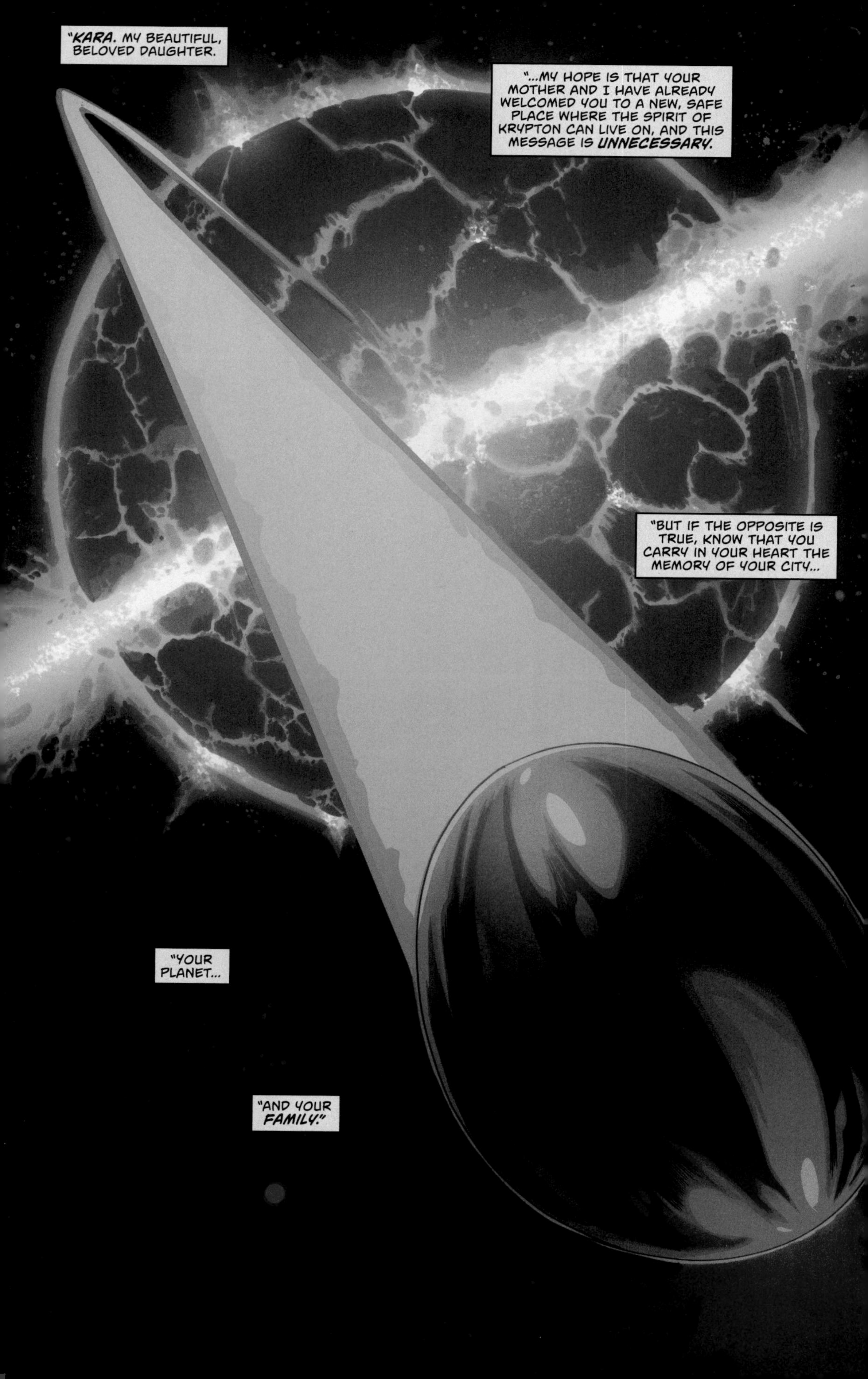
"KARA. MY BEAUTIFUL, BELOVED DAUGHTER.
"...MY HOPE IS THAT YOUR MOTHER AND I HAVE ALREADY WELCOMED YOU TO A NEW, SAFE PLACE WHERE THE SPIRIT OF KRYPTON CAN LIVE ON, AND THIS MESSAGE IS UNNECESSARY.
"BUT IF THE OPPOSITE IS TRUE, KNOW THAT YOU CARRY IN YOUR HEART THE MEMORY OF YOUR CITY...
"YOUR PLANET...
"AND YOUR FAMILY."

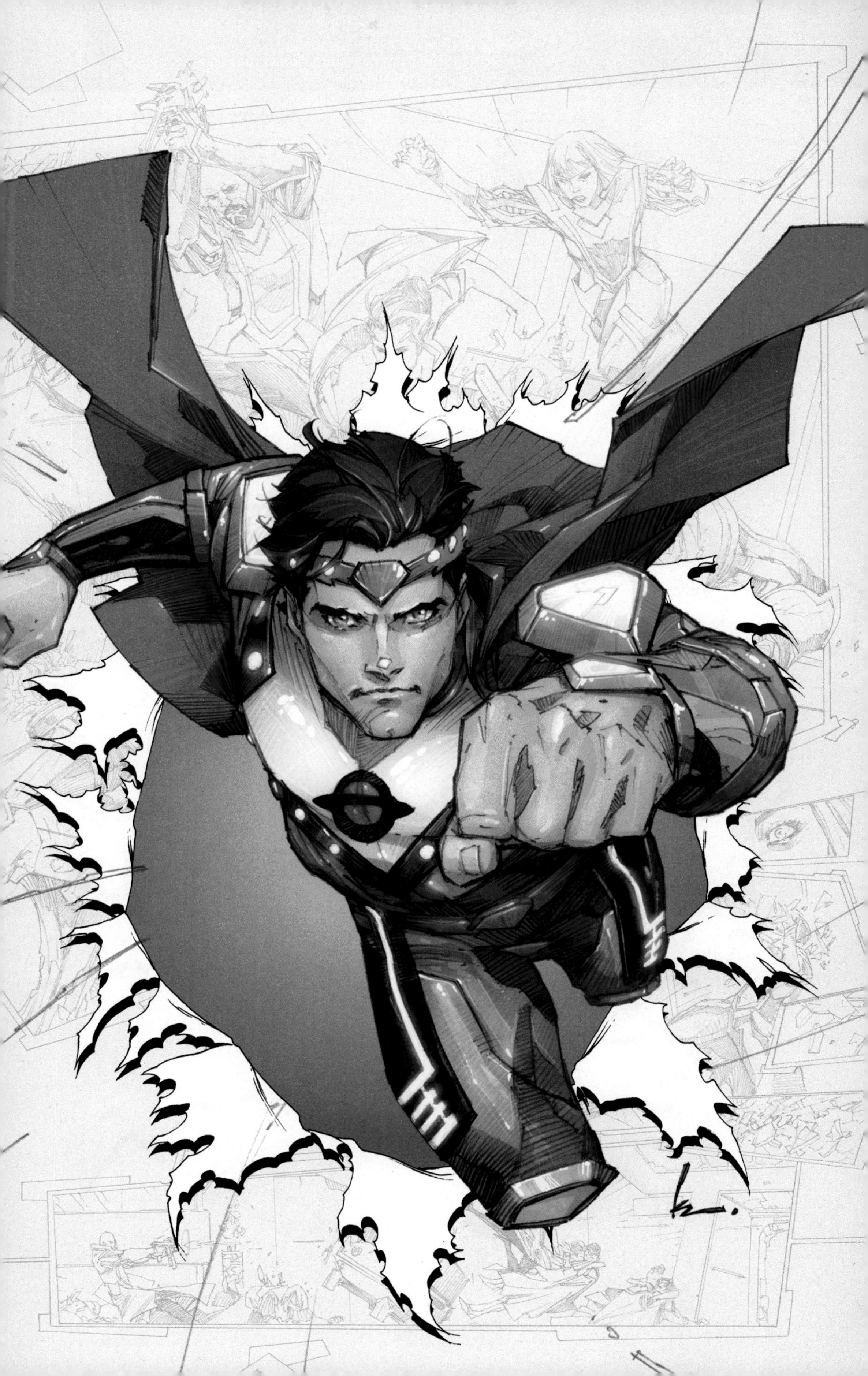

EVERY END HAS A BEGINNING...

SCOTT LOBDELL writer **KENNETH ROCAFORT** artist **SUNNY GHO** colorist

cover art by **KENNETH ROCAFORT**

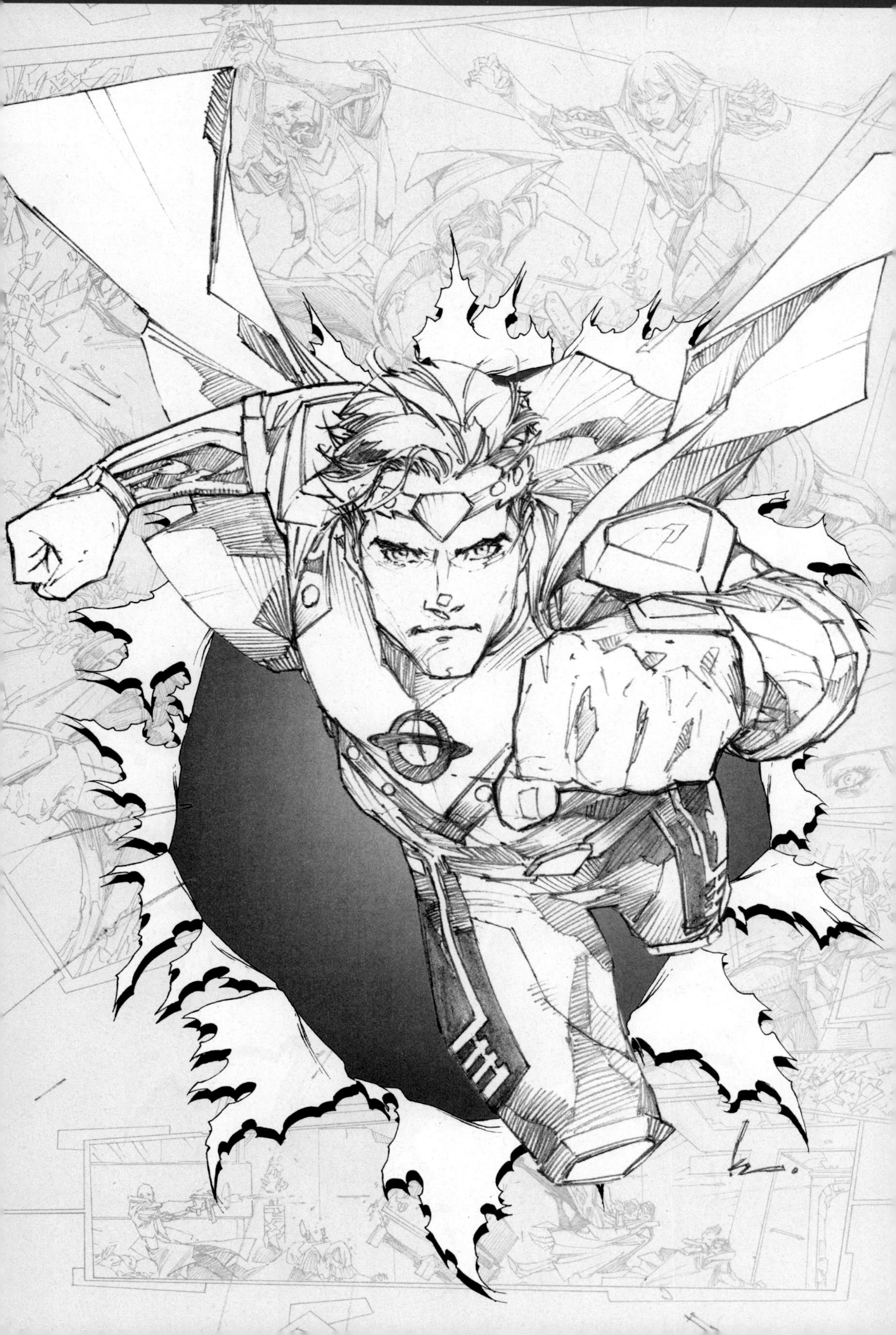

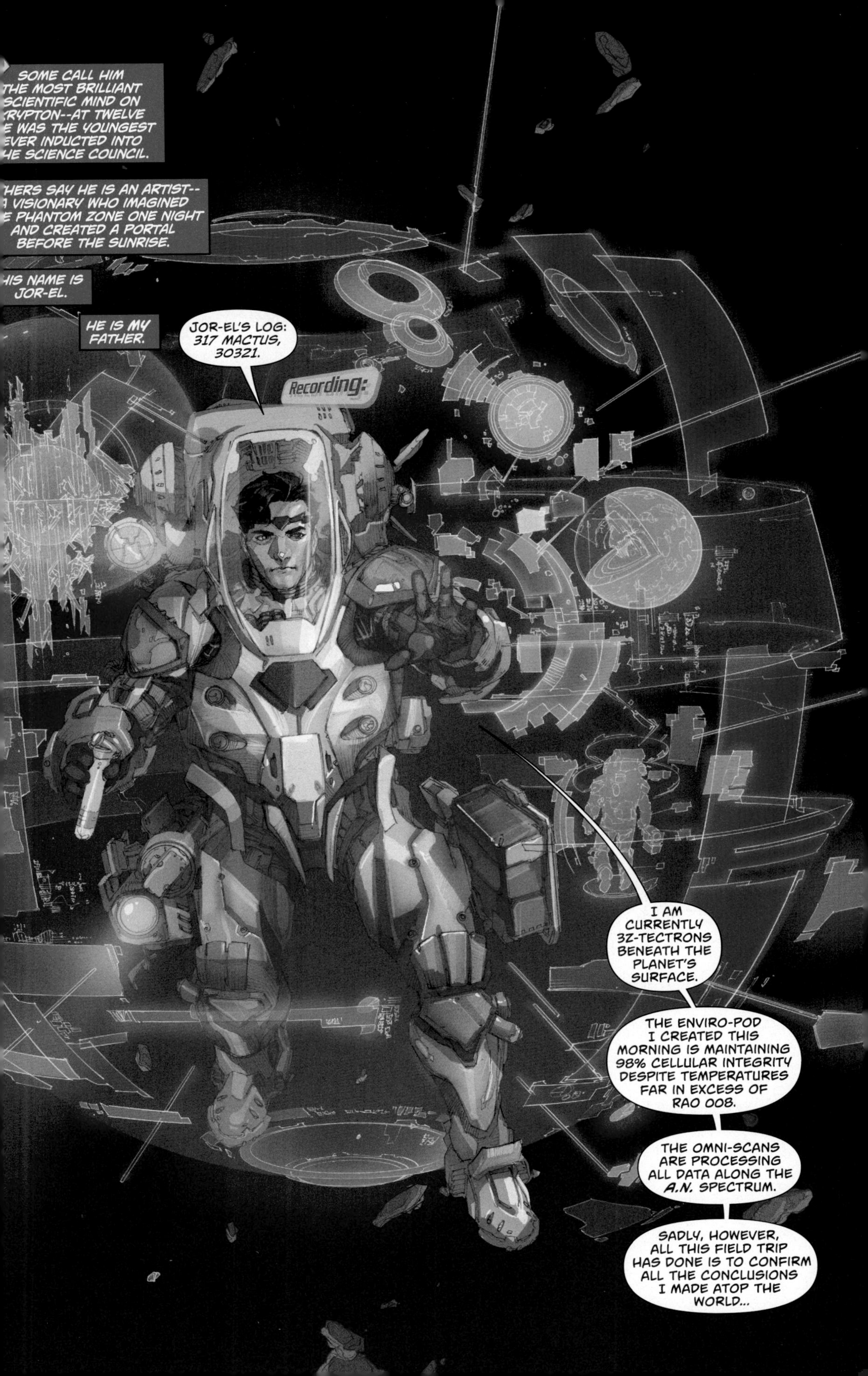
SOME CALL HIM THE MOST BRILLIANT SCIENTIFIC MIND ON KRYPTON--AT TWELVE E WAS THE YOUNGEST EVER INDUCTED INTO HE SCIENCE COUNCIL.
THERS SAY HE IS AN ARTIST-- A VISIONARY WHO IMAGINED E PHANTOM ZONE ONE NIGHT AND CREATED A PORTAL BEFORE THE SUNRISE.
HIS NAME IS JOR-EL.
HE IS MY FATHER.
JOR-EL'S LOG: 317 MACTUS, 30321.
Recording:
I AM CURRENTLY 3Z-TECTRONS BENEATH THE PLANET'S SURFACE.
THE ENVIRO-POD I CREATED THIS MORNING IS MAINTAINING 98% CELLULAR INTEGRITY DESPITE TEMPERATURES FAR IN EXCESS OF RAO 008.
THE OMNI-SCANS ARE PROCESSING ALL DATA ALONG THE A.N. SPECTRUM.
SADLY, HOWEVER, ALL THIS FIELD TRIP HAS DONE IS TO CONFIRM ALL THE CONCLUSIONS I MADE ATOP THE WORLD...

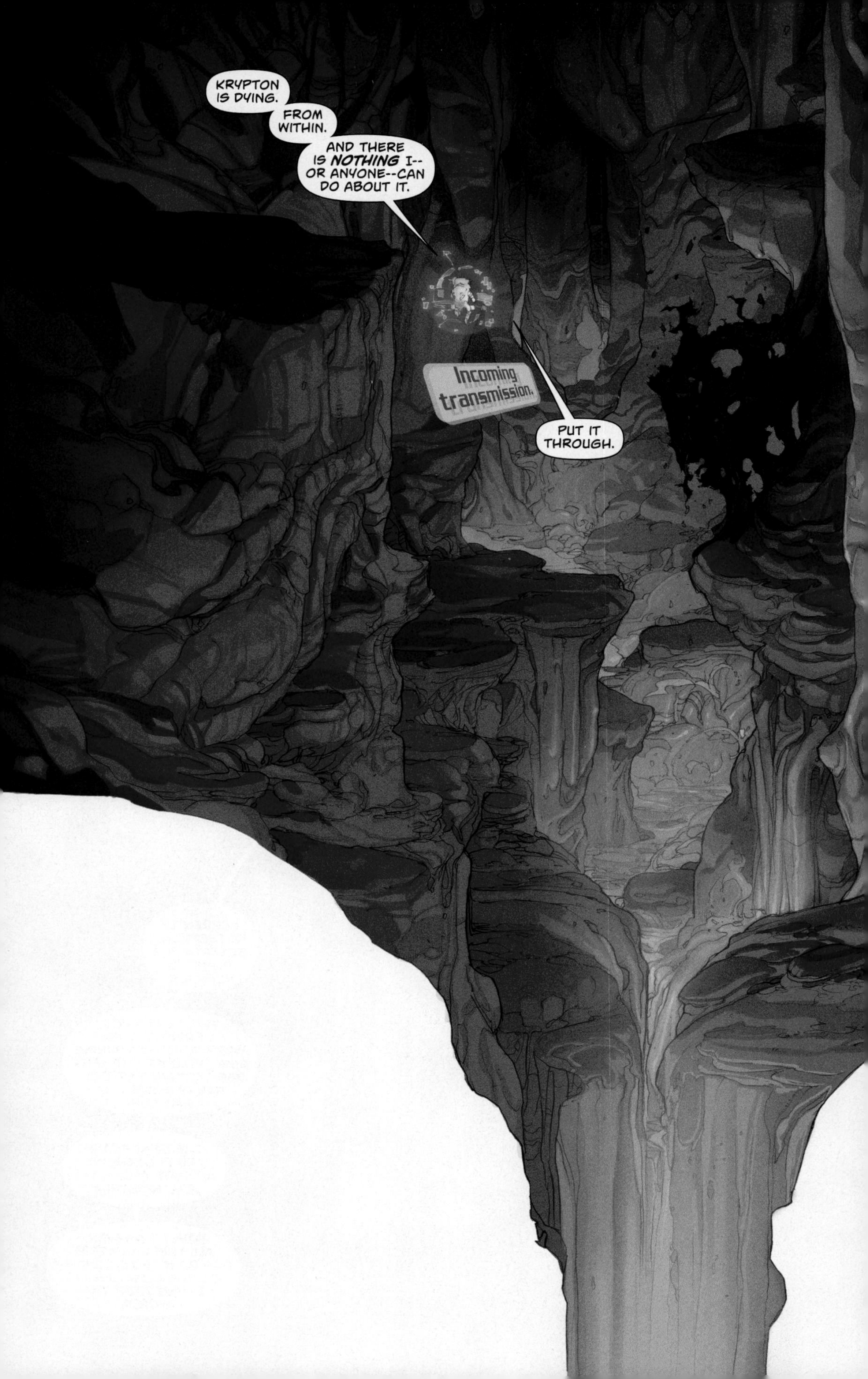
KRYPTON IS DYING.
FROM WITHIN.
AND THERE IS NOTHING I--OR ANYONE--CAN DO ABOUT IT.
Incoming transmission.
PUT IT THROUGH.

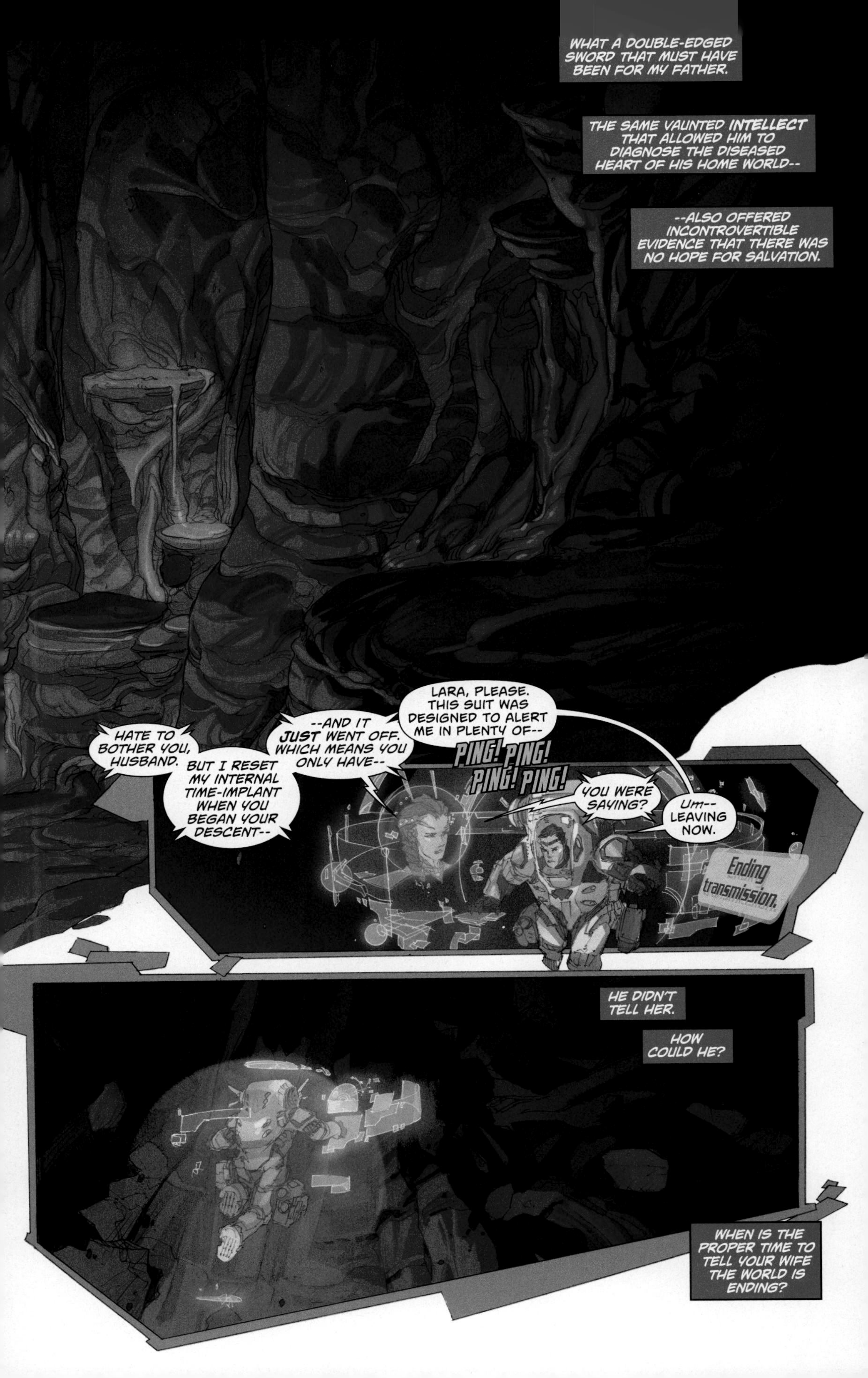
WHAT A DOUBLE-EDGED SWORD THAT MUST HAVE BEEN FOR MY FATHER.
THE SAME VAUNTED INTELLECT THAT ALLOWED HIM TO DIAGNOSE THE DISEASED HEART OF HIS HOME WORLD--
--ALSO OFFERED INCONTROVERTIBLE EVIDENCE THAT THERE WAS NO HOPE FOR SALVATION.
HATE TO BOTHER YOU, HUSBAND.
BUT I RESET MY INTERNAL TIME-IMPLANT WHEN YOU BEGAN YOUR DESCENT--
--AND IT JUST WENT OFF. WHICH MEANS YOU ONLY HAVE--
LARA, PLEASE. THIS SUIT WAS DESIGNED TO ALERT ME IN PLENTY OF--
PING! PING! PING! PING!
YOU WERE SAYING?
Um-- LEAVING NOW.
Ending transmission.
HE DIDN'T TELL HER.
HOW COULD HE?
WHEN IS THE PROPER TIME TO TELL YOUR WIFE THE WORLD IS ENDING?

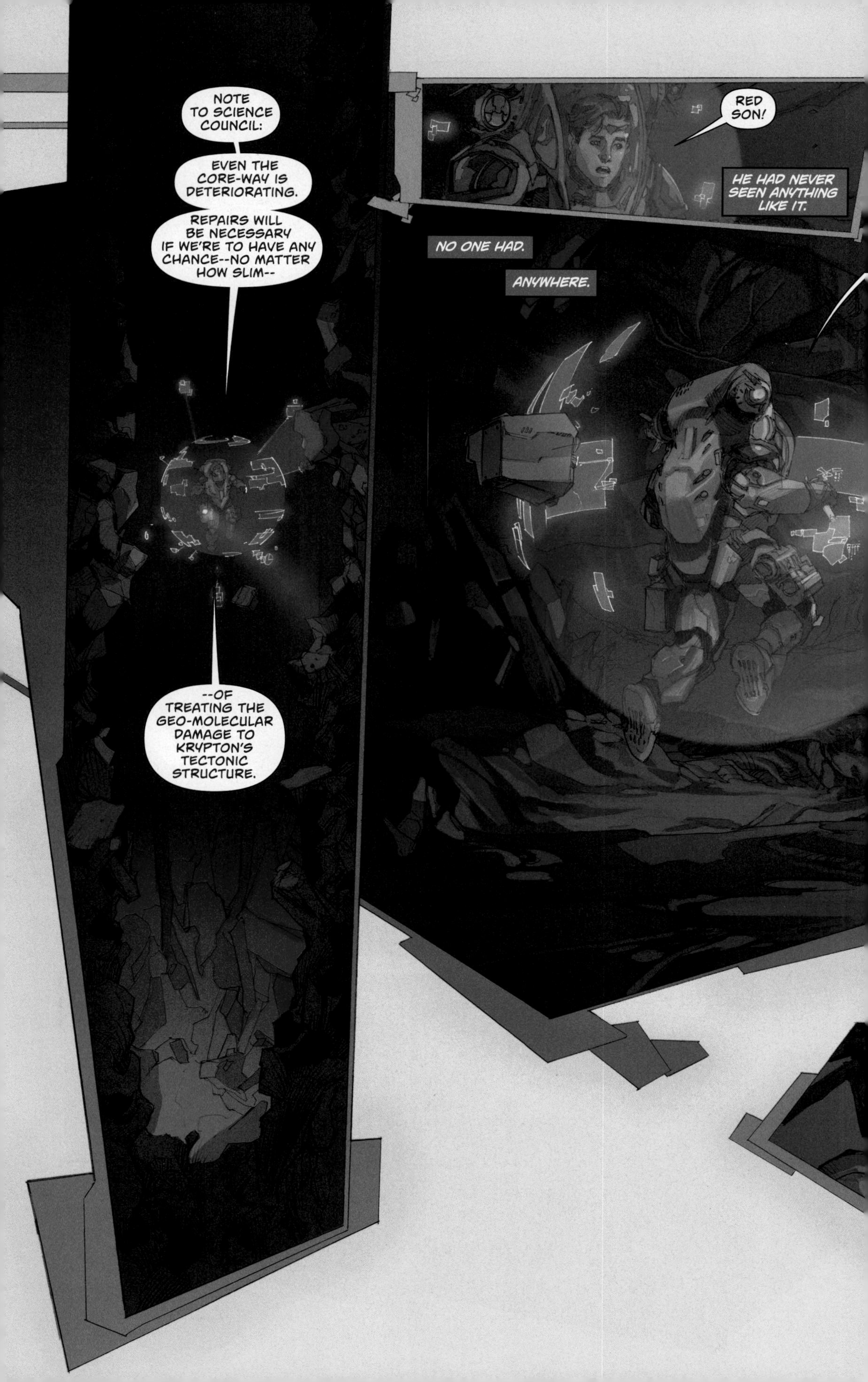
NOTE TO SCIENCE COUNCIL:
EVEN THE CORE-WAY IS DETERIORATING.
REPAIRS WILL BE NECESSARY IF WE'RE TO HAVE ANY CHANCE--NO MATTER HOW SLIM--
--OF TREATING THE GEO-MOLECULAR DAMAGE TO KRYPTON'S TECTONIC STRUCTURE.
RED SON!
HE HAD NEVER SEEN ANYTHING LIKE IT.
NO ONE HAD.
ANYWHERE.

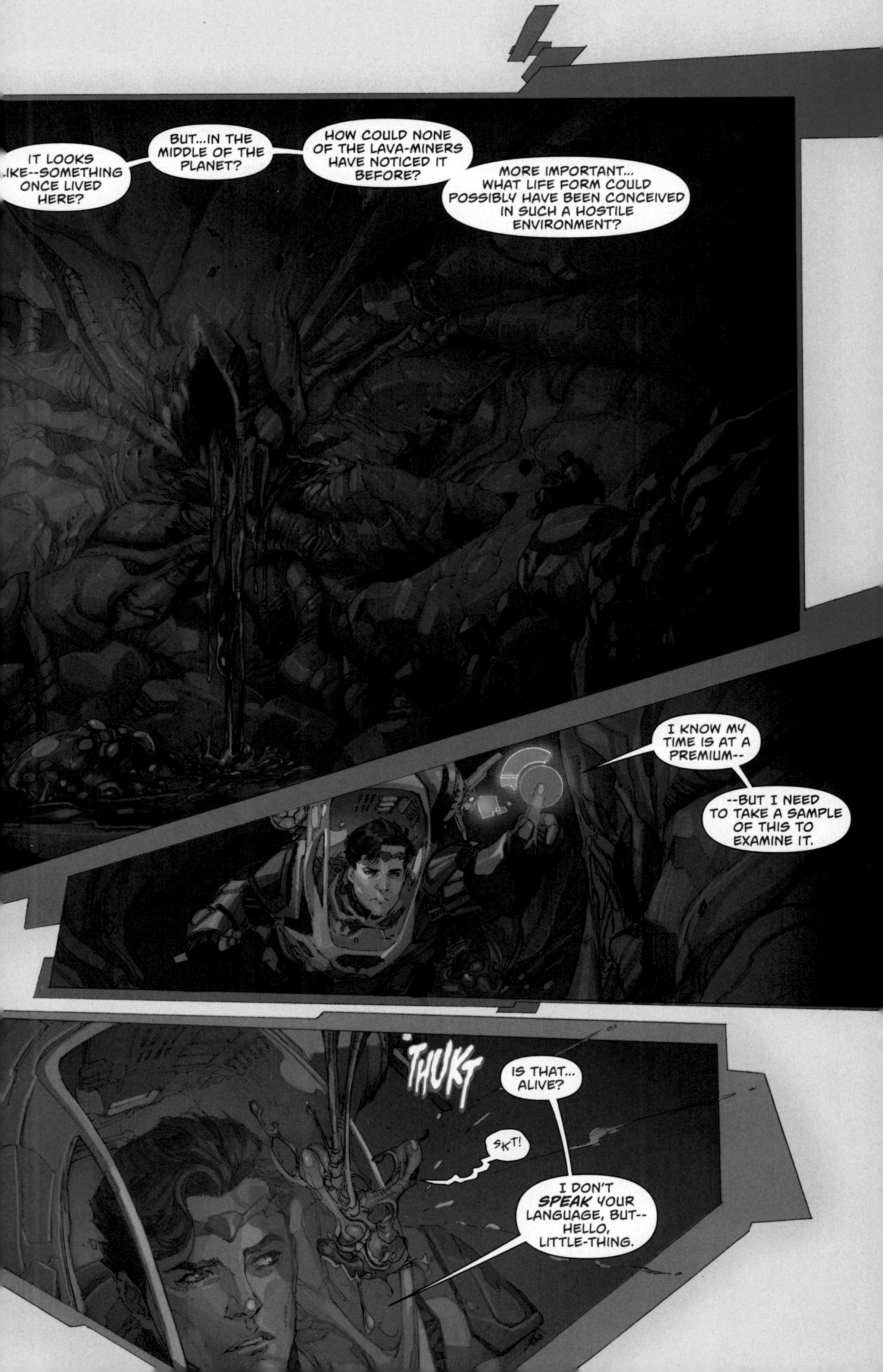

IT LOOKS LIKE--SOMETHING ONCE LIVED HERE?
BUT...IN THE MIDDLE OF THE PLANET?
HOW COULD NONE OF THE LAVA-MINERS HAVE NOTICED IT BEFORE?
MORE IMPORTANT... WHAT LIFE FORM COULD POSSIBLY HAVE BEEN CONCEIVED IN SUCH A HOSTILE ENVIRONMENT?
I KNOW MY TIME IS AT A PREMIUM--
--BUT I NEED TO TAKE A SAMPLE OF THIS TO EXAMINE IT.
THUKT
IS THAT... ALIVE?
SKT!
I DON'T SPEAK YOUR LANGUAGE, BUT-- HELLO, LITTLE-THING.

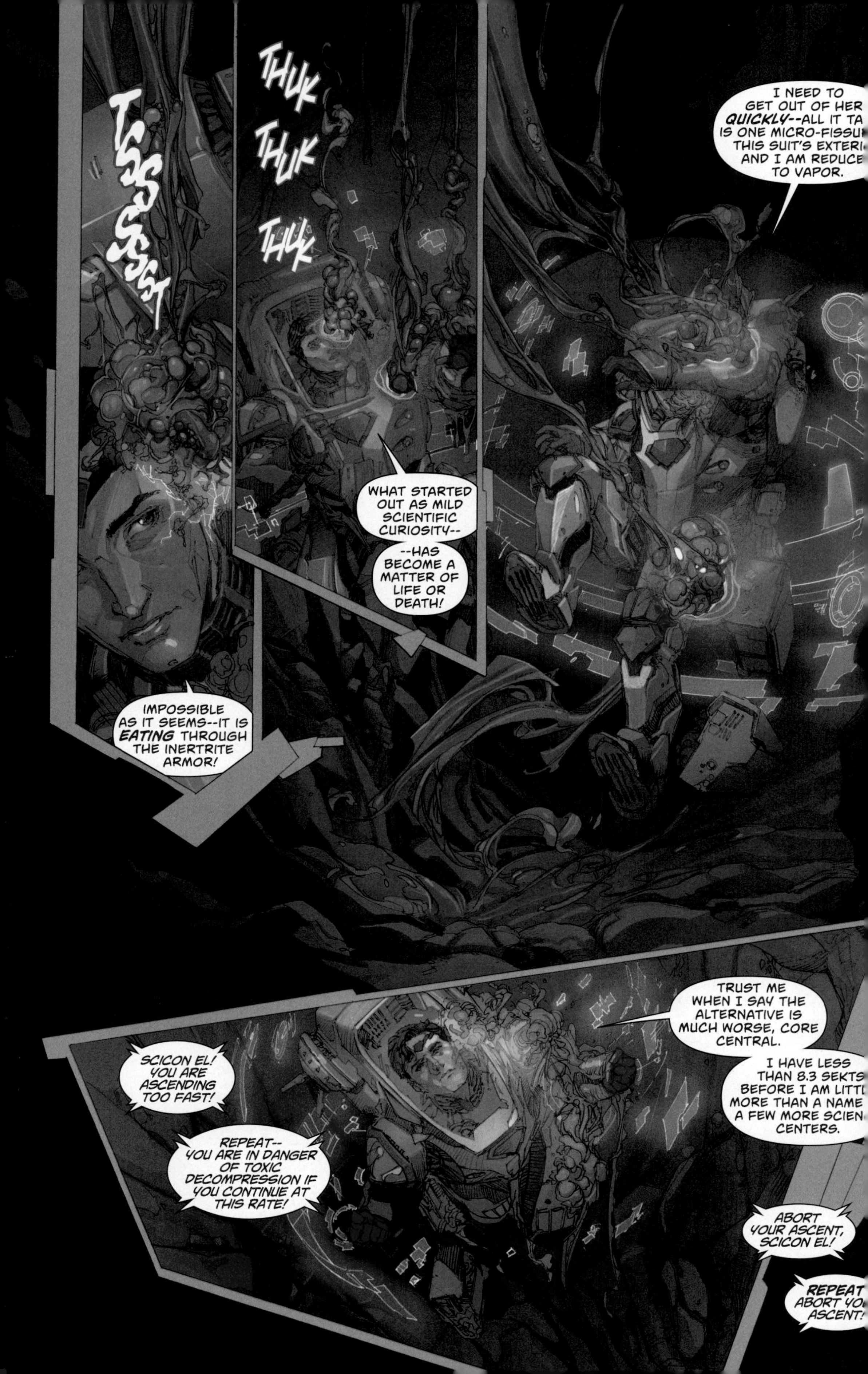
TSSSSSSST
THUK THUK THUK
I NEED TO GET OUT OF HER QUICKLY--ALL IT TA IS ONE MICRO-FISSU THIS SUIT'S EXTERI AND I AM REDUCE TO VAPOR.
WHAT STARTED OUT AS MILD SCIENTIFIC CURIOSITY--
--HAS BECOME A MATTER OF LIFE OR DEATH!
IMPOSSIBLE AS IT SEEMS--IT IS EATING THROUGH THE INERTRITE ARMOR!
SCICON EL! YOU ARE ASCENDING TOO FAST!
REPEAT-- YOU ARE IN DANGER OF TOXIC DECOMPRESSION IF YOU CONTINUE AT THIS RATE!
TRUST ME WHEN I SAY THE ALTERNATIVE IS MUCH WORSE, CORE CENTRAL.
I HAVE LESS THAN 8.3 SEKTS BEFORE I AM LITT MORE THAN A NAME A FEW MORE SCIEN CENTERS.
ABORT YOUR ASCENT, SCICON EL!
REPEAT ABORT YO ASCENT!

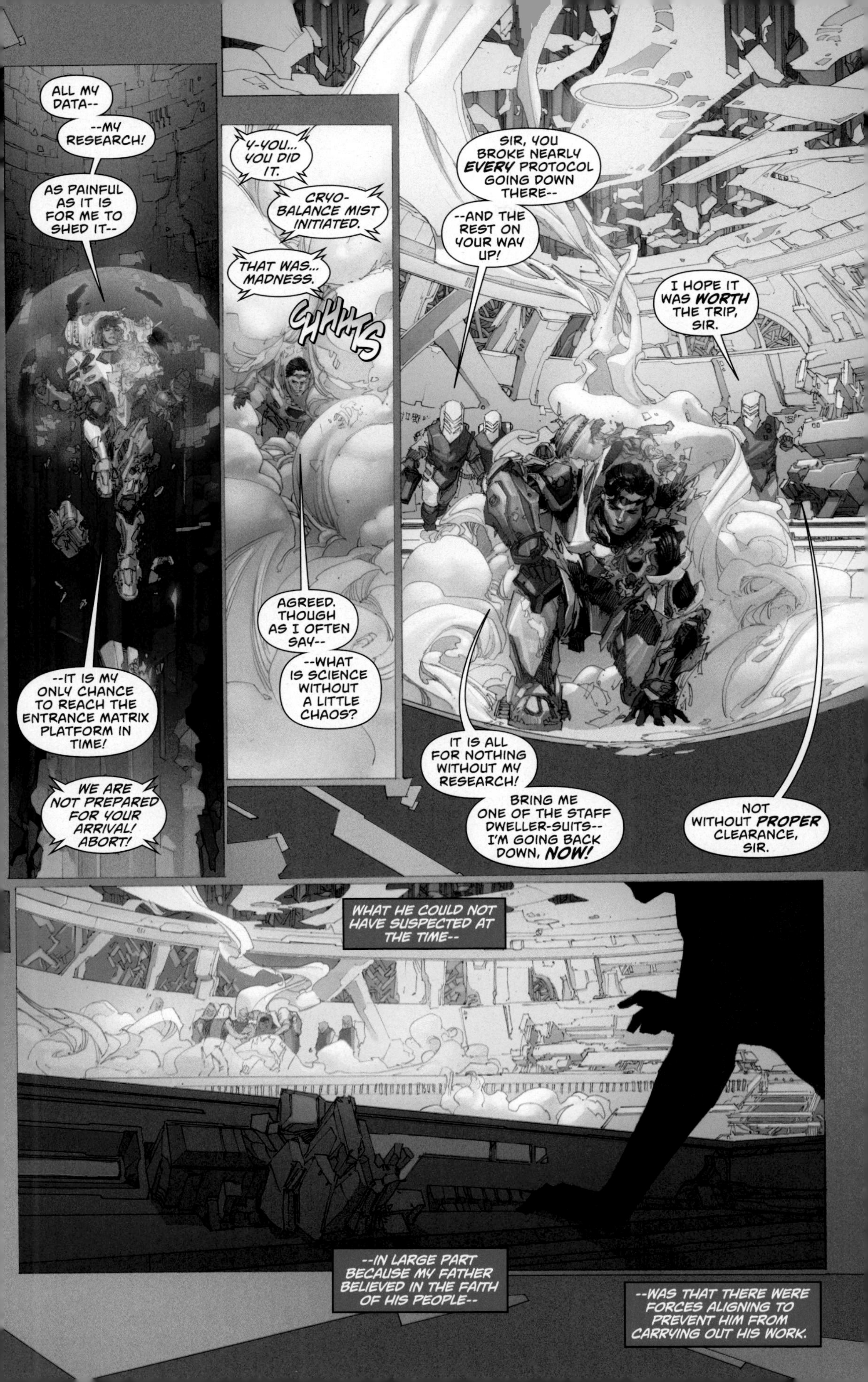
ALL MY DATA--
--MY RESEARCH!
AS PAINFUL AS IT IS FOR ME TO SHED IT--
--IT IS MY ONLY CHANCE TO REACH THE ENTRANCE MATRIX PLATFORM IN TIME!
WE ARE NOT PREPARED FOR YOUR ARRIVAL! ABORT!
Y-YOU... YOU DID IT.
CRYO-BALANCE MIST INITIATED.
THAT WAS... MADNESS.
SHHHTS
AGREED. THOUGH AS I OFTEN SAY--
--WHAT IS SCIENCE WITHOUT A LITTLE CHAOS?
SIR, YOU BROKE NEARLY EVERY PROTOCOL GOING DOWN THERE--
--AND THE REST ON YOUR WAY UP!
I HOPE IT WAS WORTH THE TRIP, SIR.
IT IS ALL FOR NOTHING WITHOUT MY RESEARCH!
BRING ME ONE OF THE STAFF DWELLER-SUITS-- I'M GOING BACK DOWN, NOW!
NOT WITHOUT PROPER CLEARANCE, SIR.
WHAT HE COULD NOT HAVE SUSPECTED AT THE TIME--
--IN LARGE PART BECAUSE MY FATHER BELIEVED IN THE FAITH OF HIS PEOPLE--
--WAS THAT THERE WERE FORCES ALIGNING TO PREVENT HIM FROM CARRYING OUT HIS WORK.

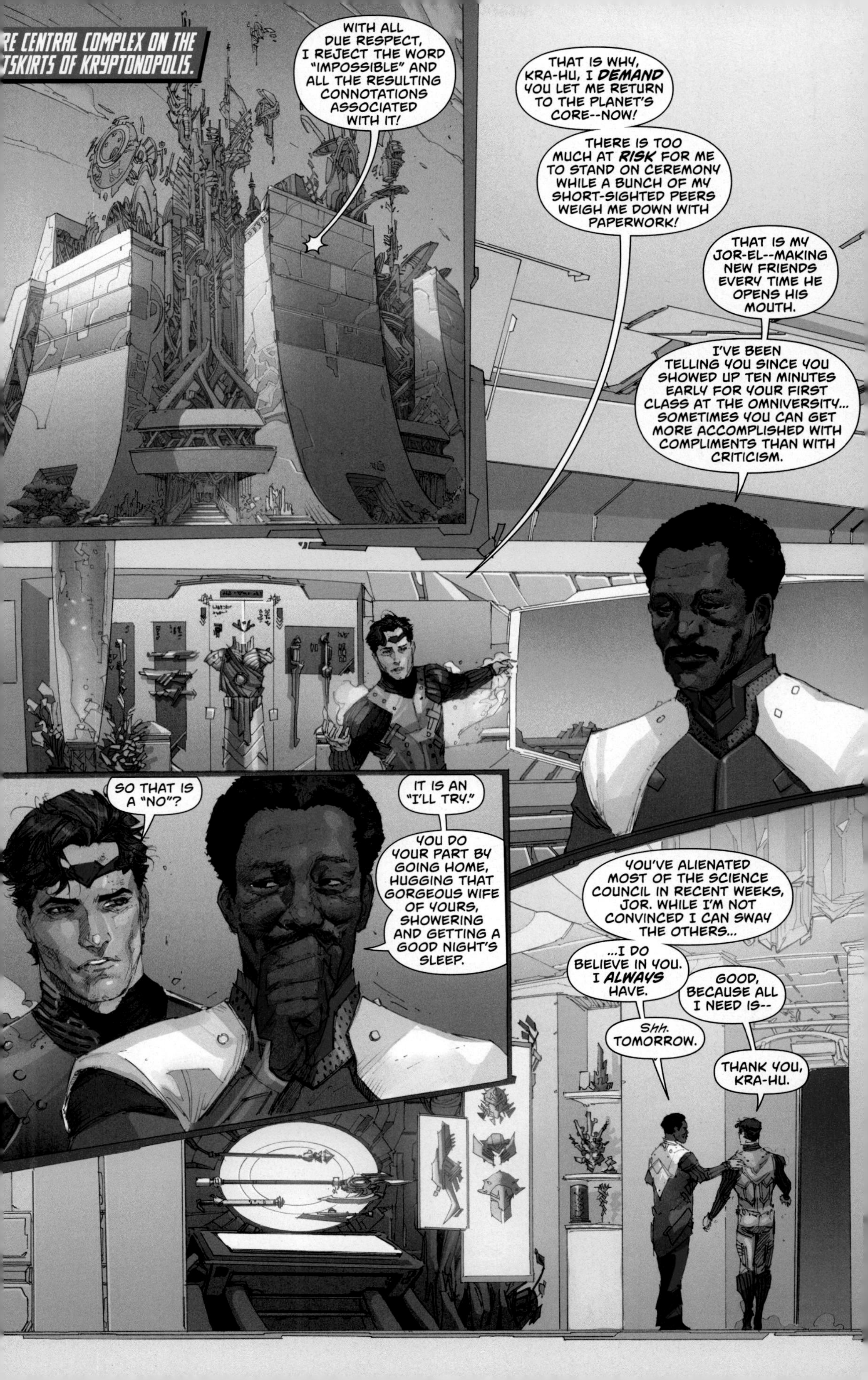

RE CENTRAL COMPLEX ON THE TSKIRTS OF KRYPTONOPOLIS.
WITH ALL DUE RESPECT, I REJECT THE WORD "IMPOSSIBLE" AND ALL THE RESULTING CONNOTATIONS ASSOCIATED WITH IT!
THAT IS WHY, KRA-HU, I DEMAND YOU LET ME RETURN TO THE PLANET'S CORE--NOW!
THERE IS TOO MUCH AT RISK FOR ME TO STAND ON CEREMONY WHILE A BUNCH OF MY SHORT-SIGHTED PEERS WEIGH ME DOWN WITH PAPERWORK!
THAT IS MY JOR-EL--MAKING NEW FRIENDS EVERY TIME HE OPENS HIS MOUTH.
I'VE BEEN TELLING YOU SINCE YOU SHOWED UP TEN MINUTES EARLY FOR YOUR FIRST CLASS AT THE OMNIVERSITY... SOMETIMES YOU CAN GET MORE ACCOMPLISHED WITH COMPLIMENTS THAN WITH CRITICISM.
SO THAT IS A "NO"?
IT IS AN "I'LL TRY."
YOU DO YOUR PART BY GOING HOME, HUGGING THAT GORGEOUS WIFE OF YOURS, SHOWERING AND GETTING A GOOD NIGHT'S SLEEP.
YOU'VE ALIENATED MOST OF THE SCIENCE COUNCIL IN RECENT WEEKS, JOR. WHILE I'M NOT CONVINCED I CAN SWAY THE OTHERS...
...I DO BELIEVE IN YOU. I ALWAYS HAVE.
GOOD, BECAUSE ALL I NEED IS--
Shh. TOMORROW.
THANK YOU, KRA-HU.

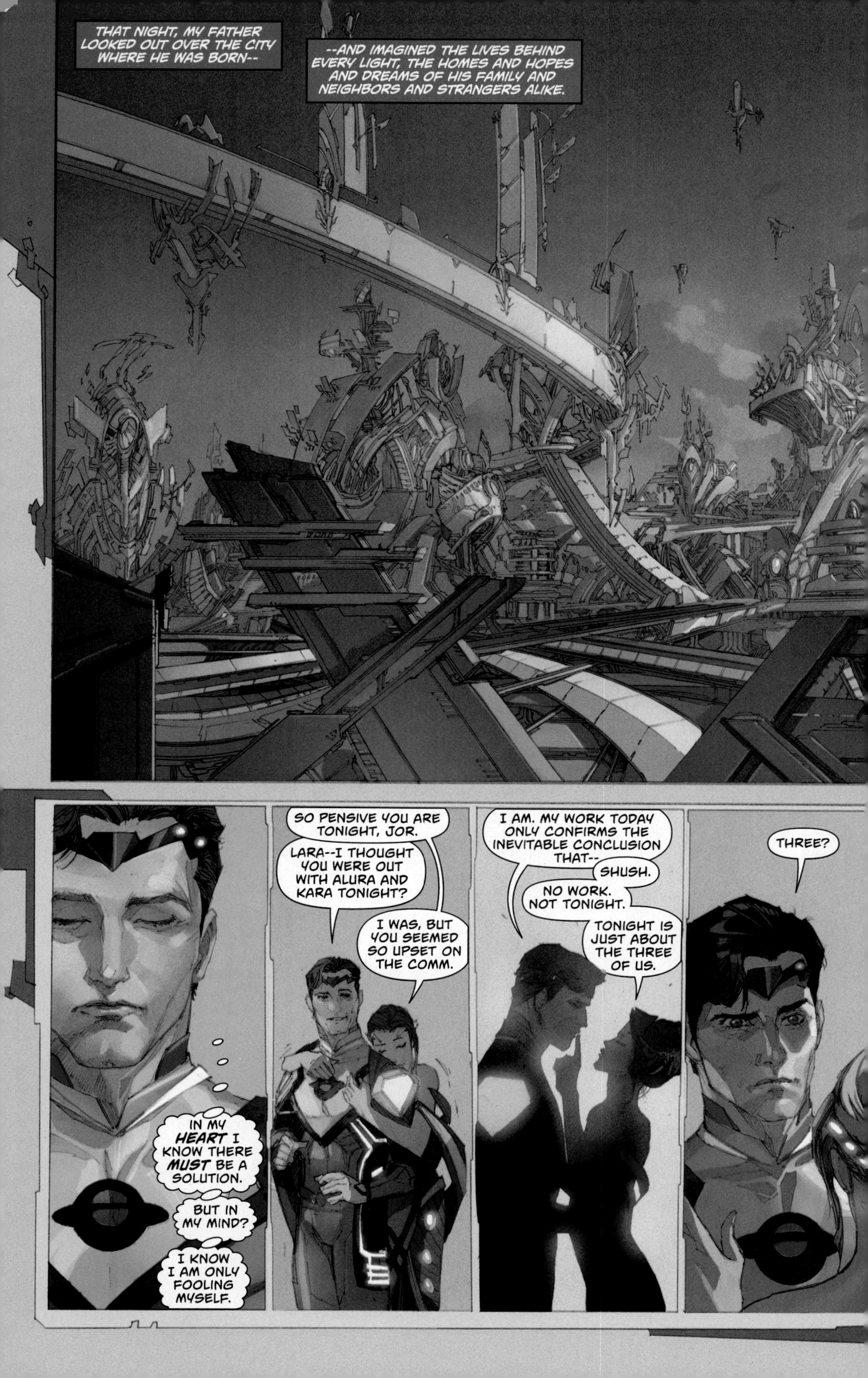
THAT NIGHT, MY FATHER LOOKED OUT OVER THE CITY WHERE HE WAS BORN--
--AND IMAGINED THE LIVES BEHIND EVERY LIGHT, THE HOMES AND HOPES AND DREAMS OF HIS FAMILY AND NEIGHBORS AND STRANGERS ALIKE.
IN MY HEART I KNOW THERE MUST BE A SOLUTION.
BUT IN MY MIND?
I KNOW I AM ONLY FOOLING MYSELF.
SO PENSIVE YOU ARE TONIGHT, JOR.
LARA--I THOUGHT YOU WERE OUT WITH ALURA AND KARA TONIGHT?
I WAS, BUT YOU SEEMED SO UPSET ON THE COMM.
I AM. MY WORK TODAY ONLY CONFIRMS THE INEVITABLE CONCLUSION THAT--
SHUSH.
NO WORK. NOT TONIGHT.
TONIGHT IS JUST ABOUT THE THREE OF US.
THREE?

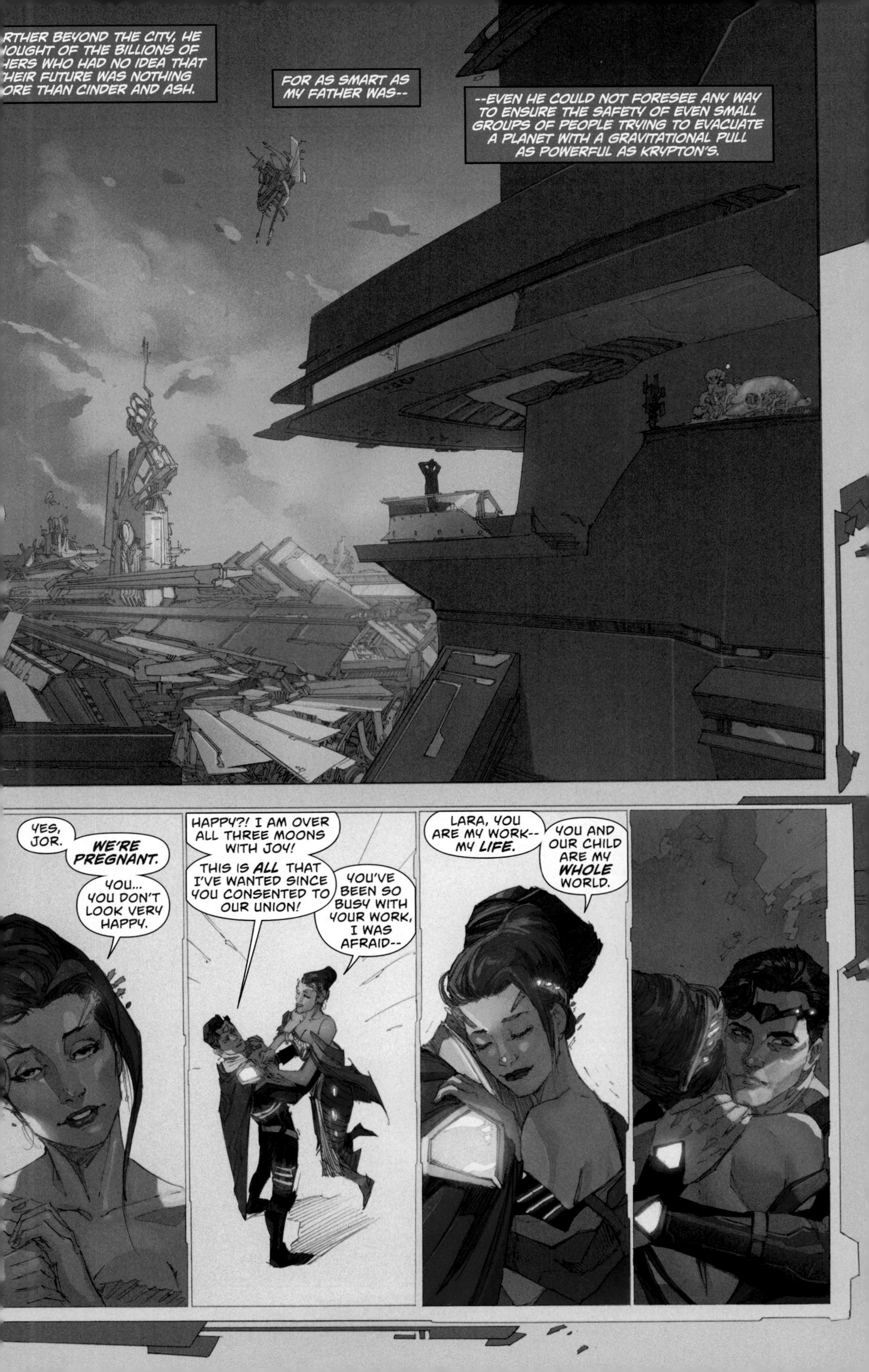
RTHER BEYOND THE CITY, HE
HOUGHT OF THE BILLIONS OF
HERS WHO HAD NO IDEA THAT
THEIR FUTURE WAS NOTHING
ORE THAN CINDER AND ASH.
FOR AS SMART AS MY FATHER WAS--
--EVEN HE COULD NOT FORESEE ANY WAY TO ENSURE THE SAFETY OF EVEN SMALL GROUPS OF PEOPLE TRYING TO EVACUATE A PLANET WITH A GRAVITATIONAL PULL AS POWERFUL AS KRYPTON'S.
YES, JOR.
WE'RE PREGNANT.
YOU... YOU DON'T LOOK VERY HAPPY.
HAPPY?! I AM OVER ALL THREE MOONS WITH JOY!
THIS IS ALL THAT I'VE WANTED SINCE YOU CONSENTED TO OUR UNION!
YOU'VE BEEN SO BUSY WITH YOUR WORK, I WAS AFRAID--
LARA, YOU ARE MY WORK-- MY LIFE.
YOU AND OUR CHILD ARE MY WHOLE WORLD.

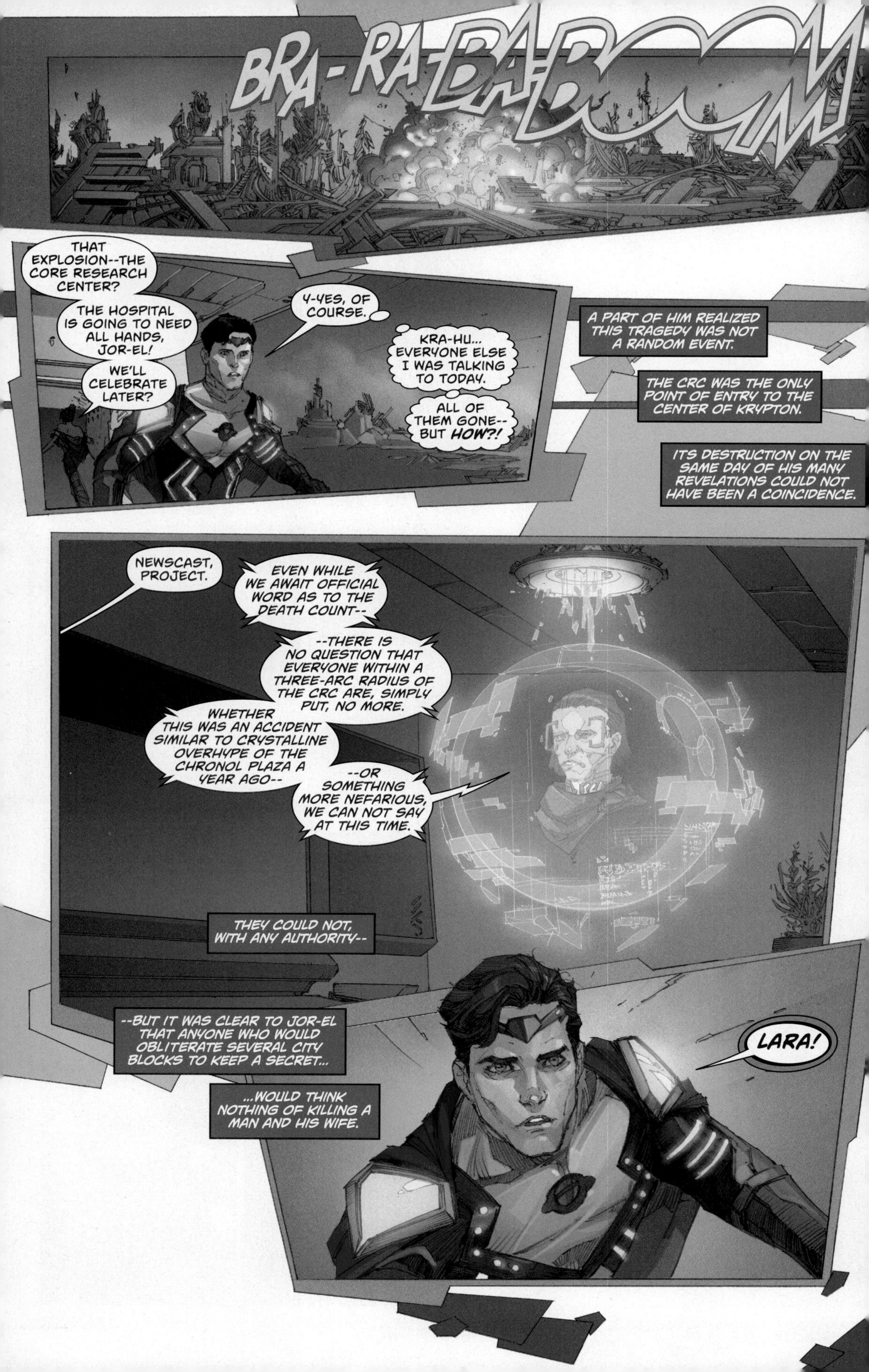
BRA-RA-BA-BOOM
THAT EXPLOSION--THE CORE RESEARCH CENTER?
THE HOSPITAL IS GOING TO NEED ALL HANDS, JOR-EL!
WE'LL CELEBRATE LATER?
Y-YES, OF COURSE.
KRA-HU... EVERYONE ELSE I WAS TALKING TO TODAY.
ALL OF THEM GONE-- BUT HOW?!
A PART OF HIM REALIZED THIS TRAGEDY WAS NOT A RANDOM EVENT.
THE CRC WAS THE ONLY POINT OF ENTRY TO THE CENTER OF KRYPTON.
ITS DESTRUCTION ON THE SAME DAY OF HIS MANY REVELATIONS COULD NOT HAVE BEEN A COINCIDENCE.
NEWSCAST, PROJECT.
EVEN WHILE WE AWAIT OFFICIAL WORD AS TO THE DEATH COUNT--
--THERE IS NO QUESTION THAT EVERYONE WITHIN A THREE-ARC RADIUS OF THE CRC ARE, SIMPLY PUT, NO MORE.
WHETHER THIS WAS AN ACCIDENT SIMILAR TO CRYSTALLINE OVERHYPE OF THE CHRONOL PLAZA A YEAR AGO--
--OR SOMETHING MORE NEFARIOUS, WE CAN NOT SAY AT THIS TIME.
THEY COULD NOT, WITH ANY AUTHORITY--
--BUT IT WAS CLEAR TO JOR-EL THAT ANYONE WHO WOULD OBLITERATE SEVERAL CITY BLOCKS TO KEEP A SECRET...
...WOULD THINK NOTHING OF KILLING A MAN AND HIS WIFE.
LARA!

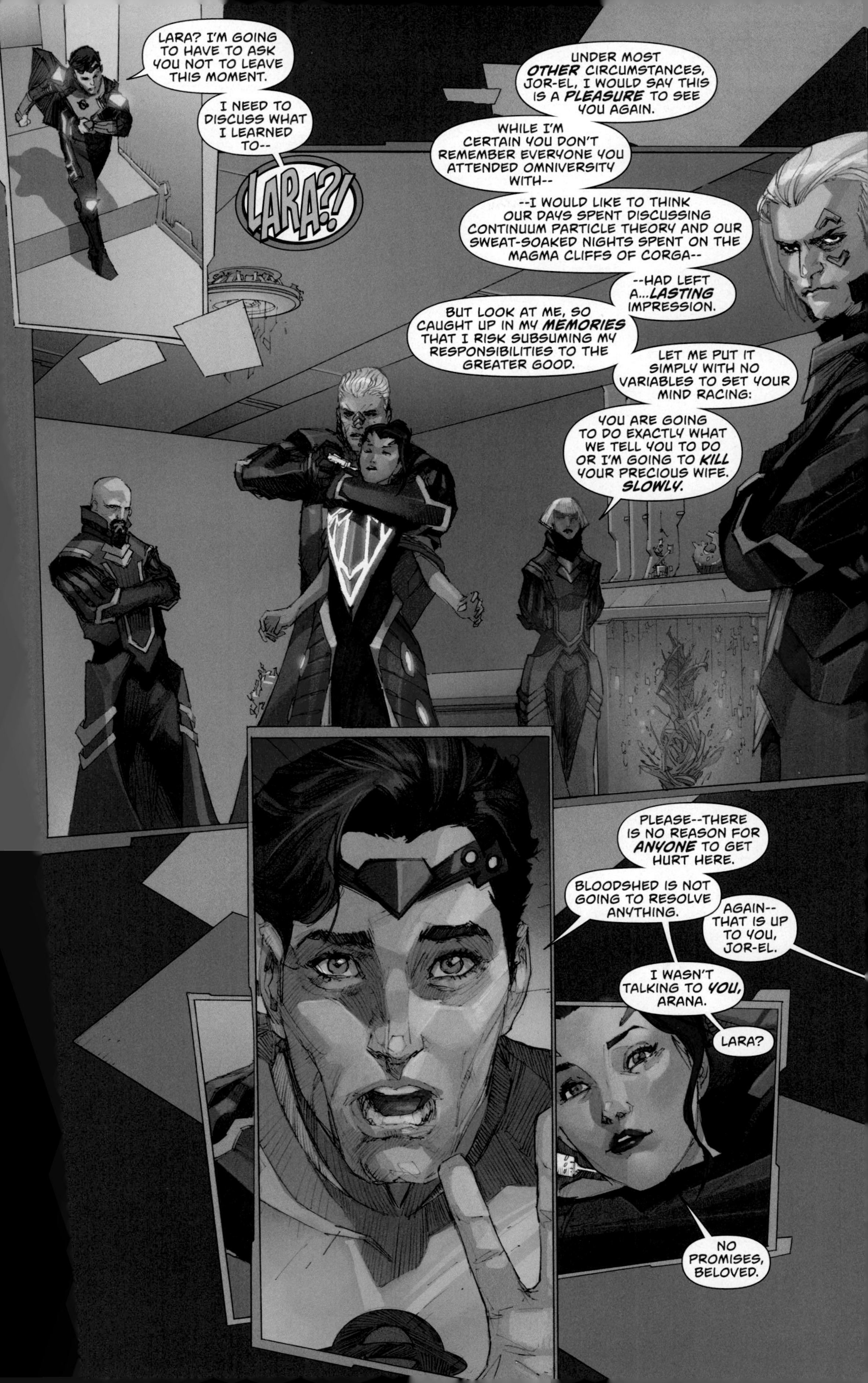
LARA? I'M GOING TO HAVE TO ASK YOU NOT TO LEAVE THIS MOMENT.
I NEED TO DISCUSS WHAT I LEARNED TO--
LARA?!
UNDER MOST OTHER CIRCUMSTANCES, JOR-EL, I WOULD SAY THIS IS A PLEASURE TO SEE YOU AGAIN.
WHILE I'M CERTAIN YOU DON'T REMEMBER EVERYONE YOU ATTENDED OMNIVERSITY WITH--
--I WOULD LIKE TO THINK OUR DAYS SPENT DISCUSSING CONTINUUM PARTICLE THEORY AND OUR SWEAT-SOAKED NIGHTS SPENT ON THE MAGMA CLIFFS OF CORGA--
--HAD LEFT A...LASTING IMPRESSION.
BUT LOOK AT ME, SO CAUGHT UP IN MY MEMORIES THAT I RISK SUBSUMING MY RESPONSIBILITIES TO THE GREATER GOOD.
LET ME PUT IT SIMPLY WITH NO VARIABLES TO SET YOUR MIND RACING:
YOU ARE GOING TO DO EXACTLY WHAT WE TELL YOU TO DO OR I'M GOING TO KILL YOUR PRECIOUS WIFE. SLOWLY.
PLEASE--THERE IS NO REASON FOR ANYONE TO GET HURT HERE.
BLOODSHED IS NOT GOING TO RESOLVE ANYTHING.
AGAIN--THAT IS UP TO YOU, JOR-EL.
I WASN'T TALKING TO YOU, ARANA.
LARA?
NO PROMISES, BELOVED.

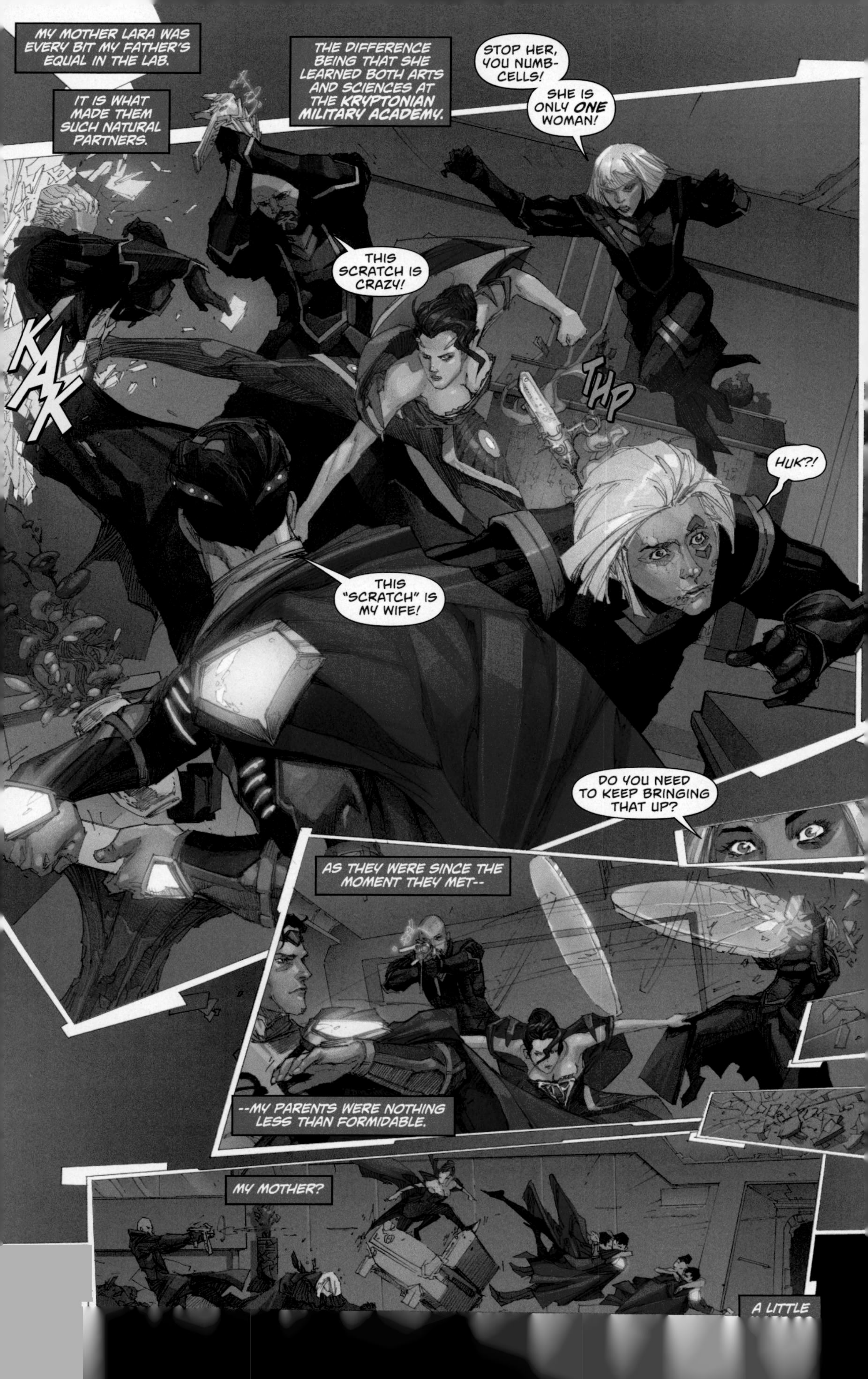

MY MOTHER LARA WAS EVERY BIT MY FATHER'S EQUAL IN THE LAB.
IT IS WHAT MADE THEM SUCH NATURAL PARTNERS.
THE DIFFERENCE BEING THAT SHE LEARNED BOTH ARTS AND SCIENCES AT THE KRYPTONIAN MILITARY ACADEMY.
STOP HER, YOU NUMB-CELLS!
SHE IS ONLY ONE WOMAN!
THIS SCRATCH IS CRAZY!
KAK
THP
HUK?!
THIS "SCRATCH" IS MY WIFE!
DO YOU NEED TO KEEP BRINGING THAT UP?
AS THEY WERE SINCE THE MOMENT THEY MET--
--MY PARENTS WERE NOTHING LESS THAN FORMIDABLE.
MY MOTHER?
A LITTLE

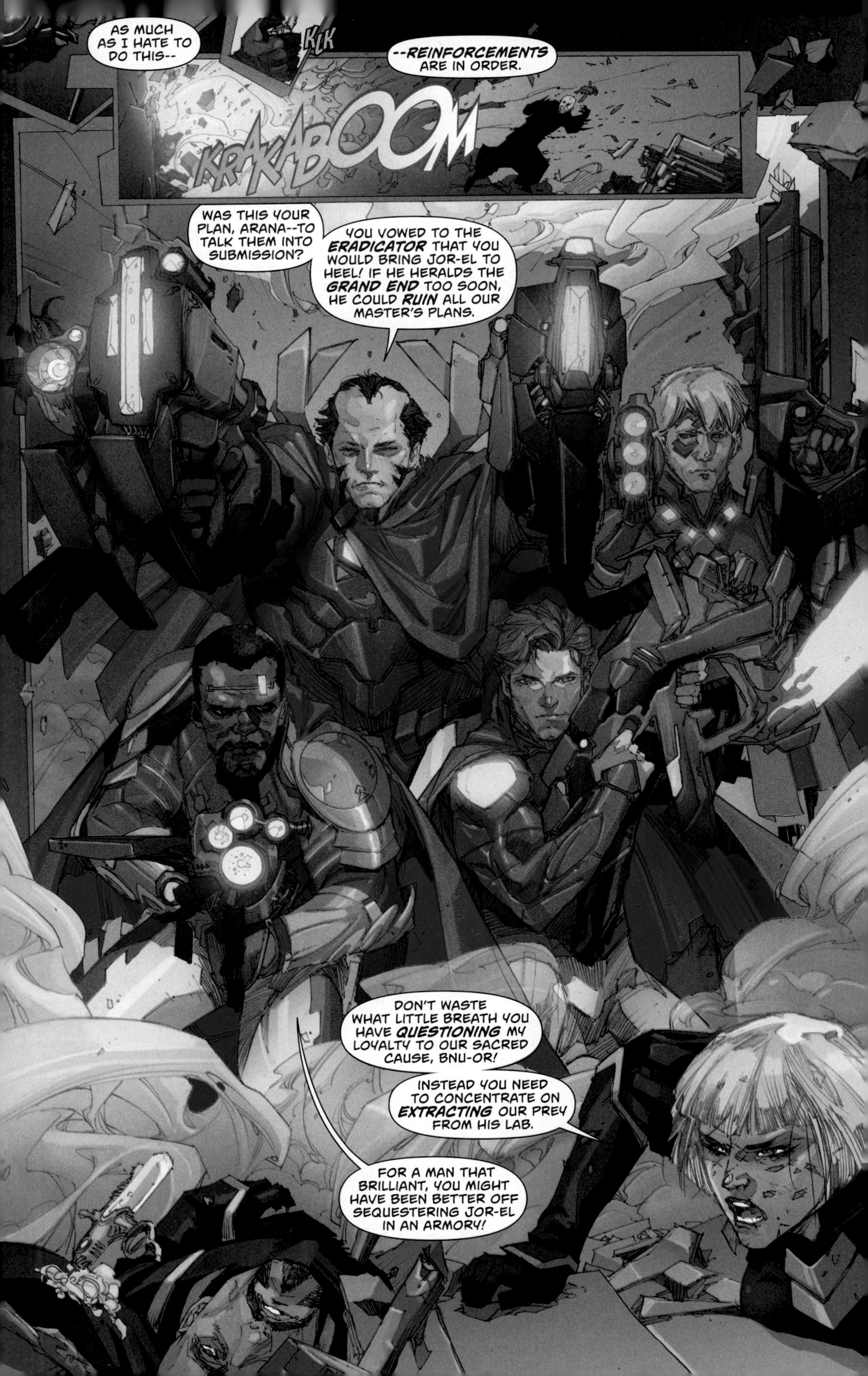
AS MUCH AS I HATE TO DO THIS--
KLK
--REINFORCEMENTS ARE IN ORDER.
KRAKABOOM
WAS THIS YOUR PLAN, ARANA--TO TALK THEM INTO SUBMISSION?
YOU VOWED TO THE ERADICATOR THAT YOU WOULD BRING JOR-EL TO HEEL! IF HE HERALDS THE GRAND END TOO SOON, HE COULD RUIN ALL OUR MASTER'S PLANS.
DON'T WASTE WHAT LITTLE BREATH YOU HAVE QUESTIONING MY LOYALTY TO OUR SACRED CAUSE, BNU-OR!
INSTEAD YOU NEED TO CONCENTRATE ON EXTRACTING OUR PREY FROM HIS LAB.
FOR A MAN THAT BRILLIANT, YOU MIGHT HAVE BEEN BETTER OFF SEQUESTERING JOR-EL IN AN ARMORY!

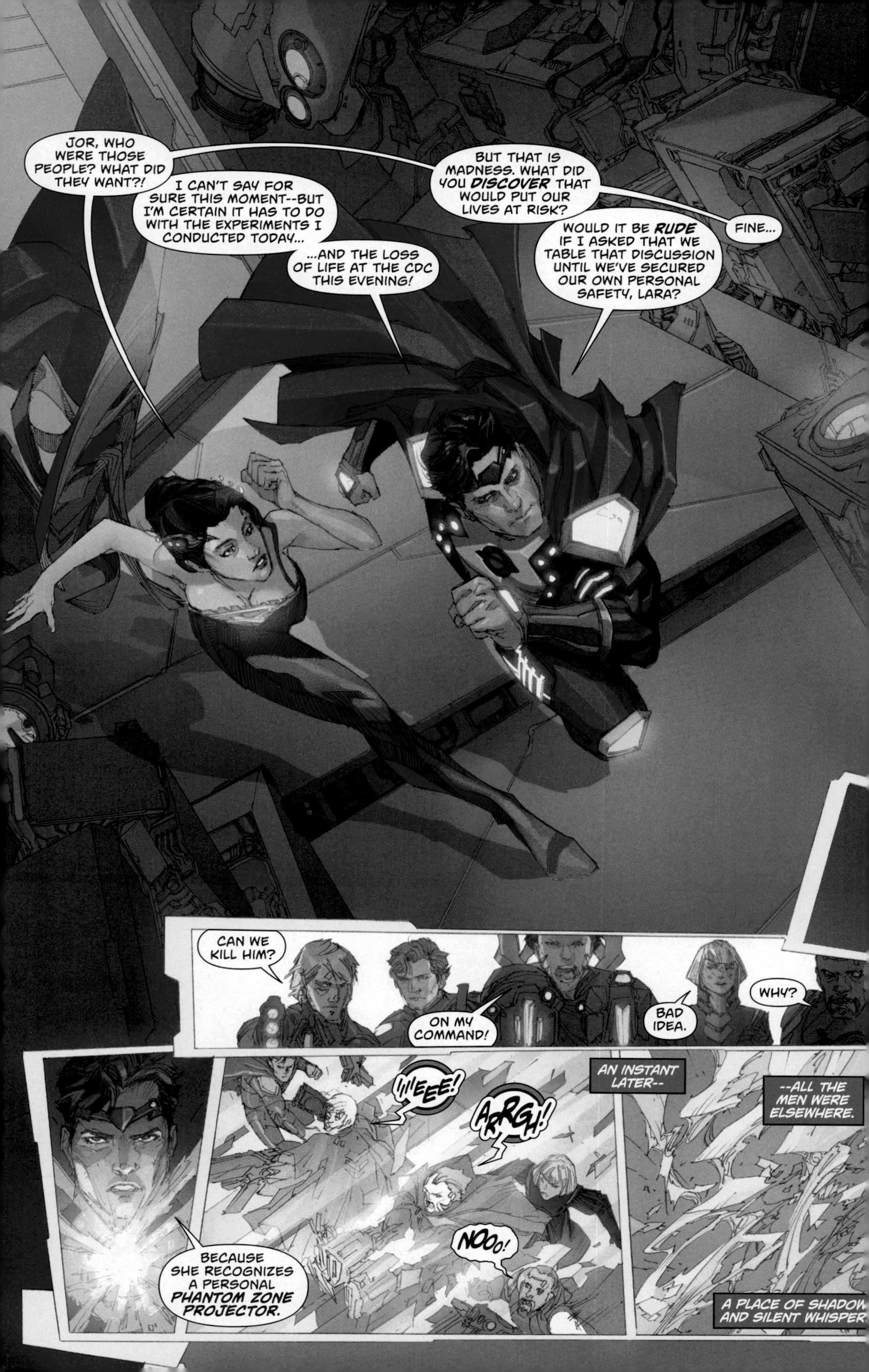
JOR, WHO WERE THOSE PEOPLE? WHAT DID THEY WANT?!
I CAN'T SAY FOR SURE THIS MOMENT--BUT I'M CERTAIN IT HAS TO DO WITH THE EXPERIMENTS I CONDUCTED TODAY...
...AND THE LOSS OF LIFE AT THE CDC THIS EVENING!
BUT THAT IS MADNESS. WHAT DID YOU DISCOVER THAT WOULD PUT OUR LIVES AT RISK?
WOULD IT BE RUDE IF I ASKED THAT WE TABLE THAT DISCUSSION UNTIL WE'VE SECURED OUR OWN PERSONAL SAFETY, LARA?
FINE...
CAN WE KILL HIM?
ON MY COMMAND!
BAD IDEA.
WHY?
BECAUSE SHE RECOGNIZES A PERSONAL PHANTOM ZONE PROJECTOR.
WEEE!
ARRGH!
NOOo!
AN INSTANT LATER--
--ALL THE MEN WERE ELSEWHERE.
A PLACE OF SHADOW AND SILENT WHISPER

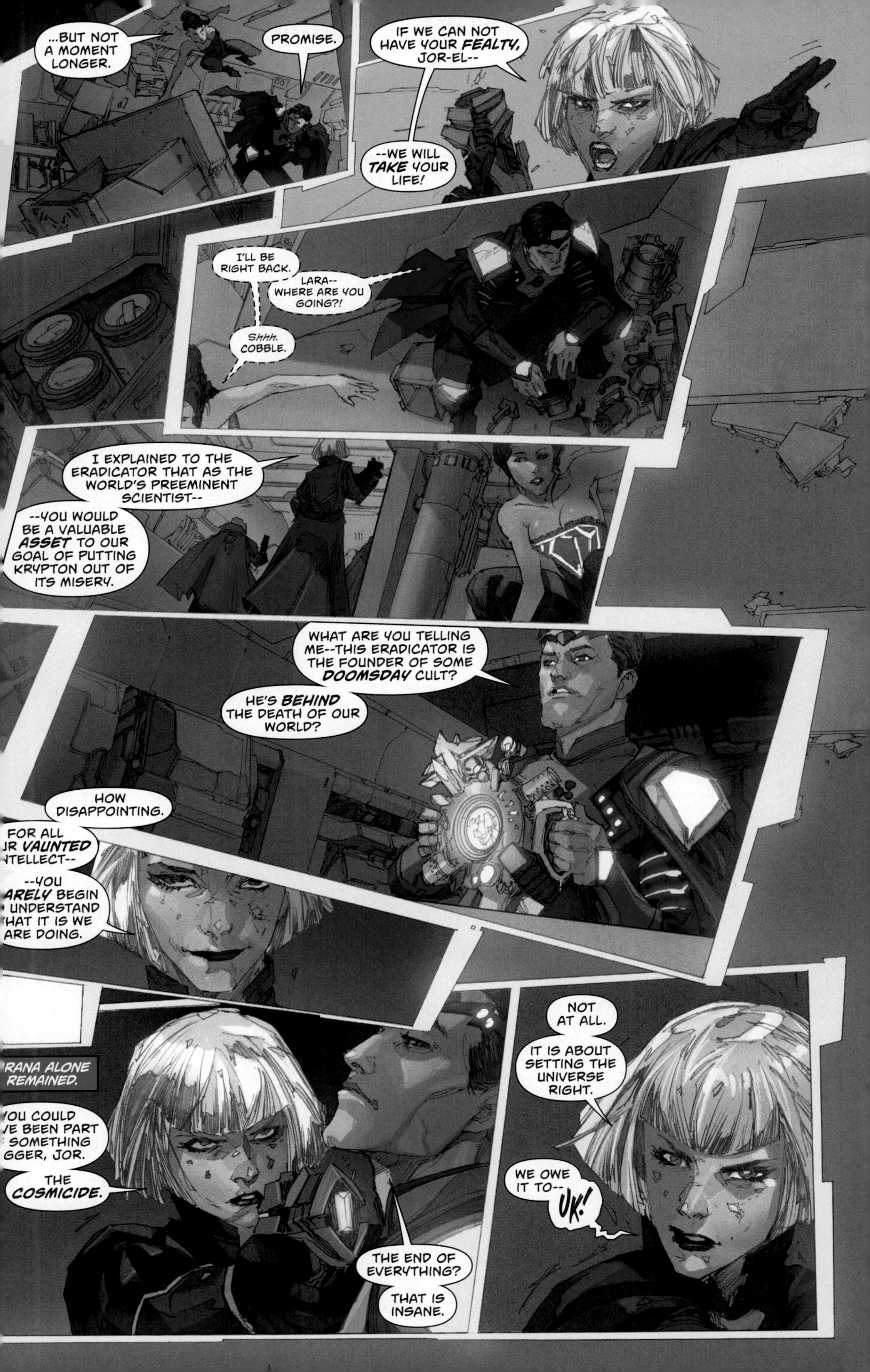
...BUT NOT A MOMENT LONGER.
PROMISE.
IF WE CAN NOT HAVE YOUR FEALTY, JOR-EL--
--WE WILL TAKE YOUR LIFE!
I'LL BE RIGHT BACK.
LARA-- WHERE ARE YOU GOING?!
Shhh. COBBLE.
I EXPLAINED TO THE ERADICATOR THAT AS THE WORLD'S PREEMINENT SCIENTIST--
--YOU WOULD BE A VALUABLE ASSET TO OUR GOAL OF PUTTING KRYPTON OUT OF ITS MISERY.
WHAT ARE YOU TELLING ME--THIS ERADICATOR IS THE FOUNDER OF SOME DOOMSDAY CULT?
HE'S BEHIND THE DEATH OF OUR WORLD?
HOW DISAPPOINTING.
FOR ALL R VAUNTED NTELLECT--
--YOU ARELY BEGIN UNDERSTAND HAT IT IS WE ARE DOING.
RANA ALONE REMAINED.
YOU COULD VE BEEN PART SOMETHING GGER, JOR.
THE COSMICIDE.
THE END OF EVERYTHING?
THAT IS INSANE.
NOT AT ALL.
IT IS ABOUT SETTING THE UNIVERSE RIGHT.
WE OWE IT TO--
UK!

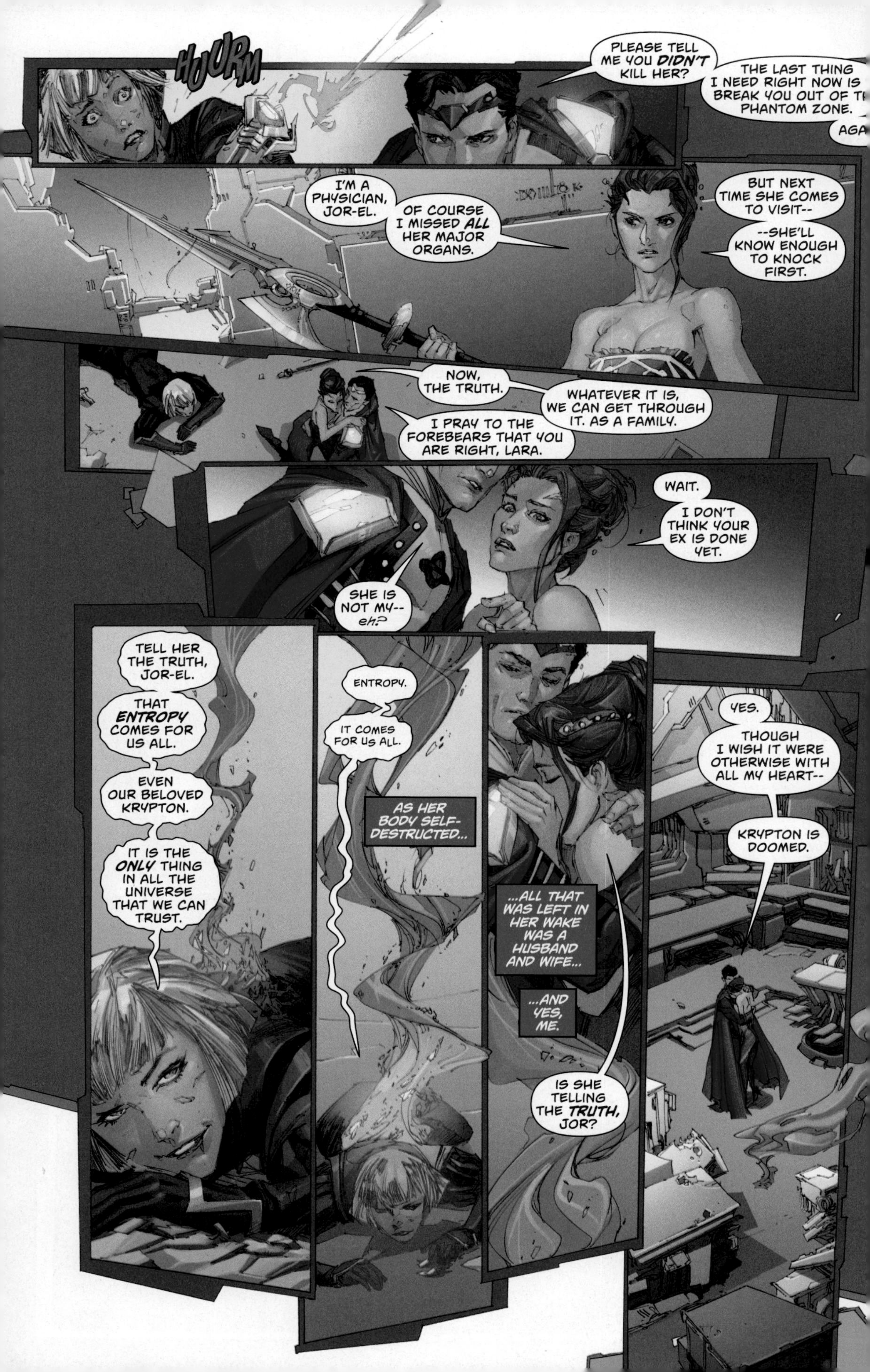
HUURM
PLEASE TELL ME YOU DIDN'T KILL HER?
THE LAST THING I NEED RIGHT NOW IS BREAK YOU OUT OF TH PHANTOM ZONE.
AGA
I'M A PHYSICIAN, JOR-EL.
OF COURSE I MISSED ALL HER MAJOR ORGANS.
BUT NEXT TIME SHE COMES TO VISIT--
--SHE'LL KNOW ENOUGH TO KNOCK FIRST.
NOW, THE TRUTH.
WHATEVER IT IS, WE CAN GET THROUGH IT. AS A FAMILY.
I PRAY TO THE FOREBEARS THAT YOU ARE RIGHT, LARA.
WAIT.
I DON'T THINK YOUR EX IS DONE YET.
SHE IS NOT MY-- eh?
TELL HER THE TRUTH, JOR-EL.
THAT ENTROPY COMES FOR US ALL.
EVEN OUR BELOVED KRYPTON.
IT IS THE ONLY THING IN ALL THE UNIVERSE THAT WE CAN TRUST.
ENTROPY.
IT COMES FOR US ALL.
AS HER BODY SELF-DESTRUCTED...
...ALL THAT WAS LEFT IN HER WAKE WAS A HUSBAND AND WIFE...
...AND YES, ME.
IS SHE TELLING THE TRUTH, JOR?
YES.
THOUGH I WISH IT WERE OTHERWISE WITH ALL MY HEART--
KRYPTON IS DOOMED.

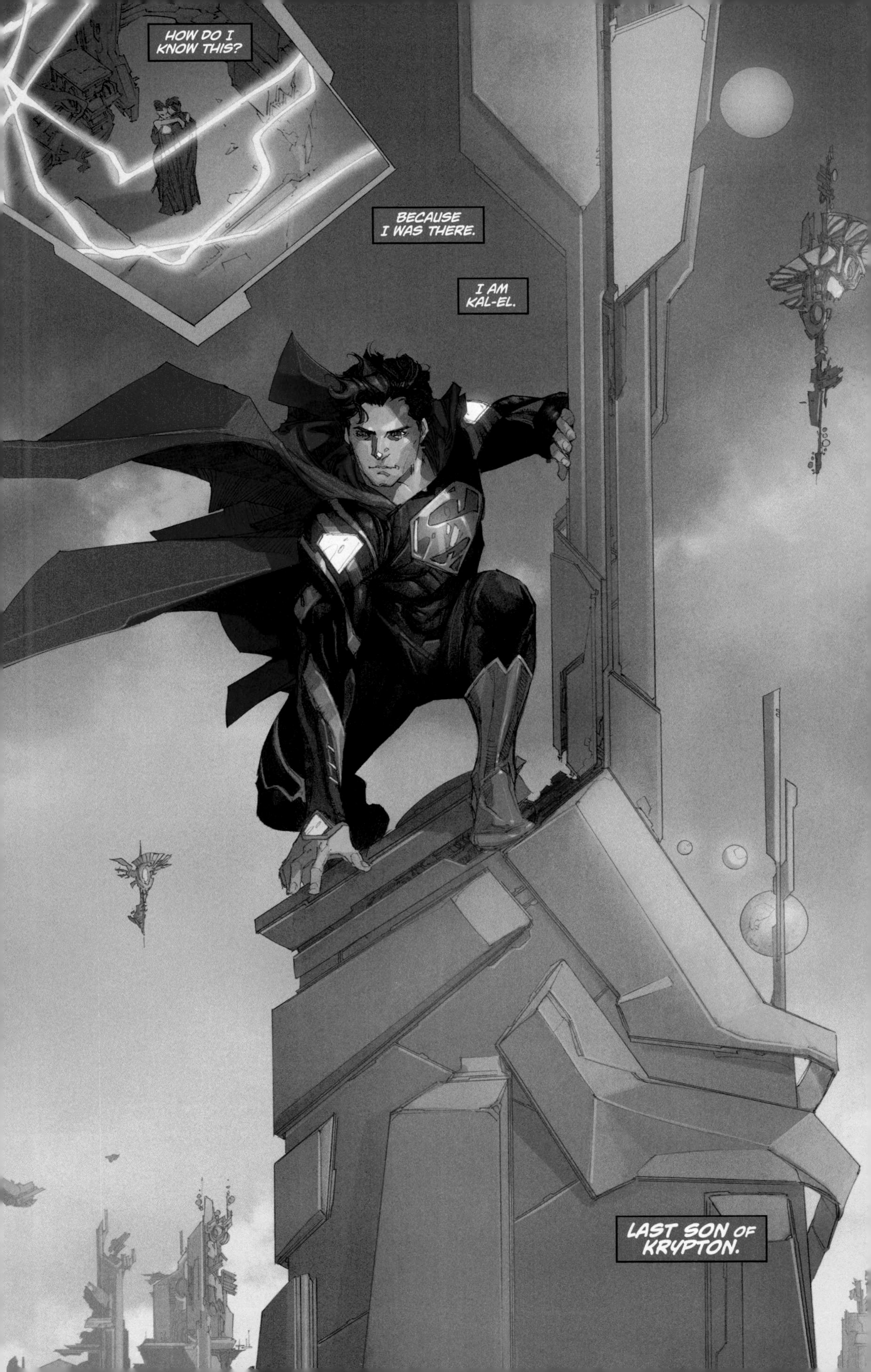
HOW DO I KNOW THIS?
BECAUSE I WAS THERE.
I AM KAL-EL.
LAST SON OF KRYPTON.

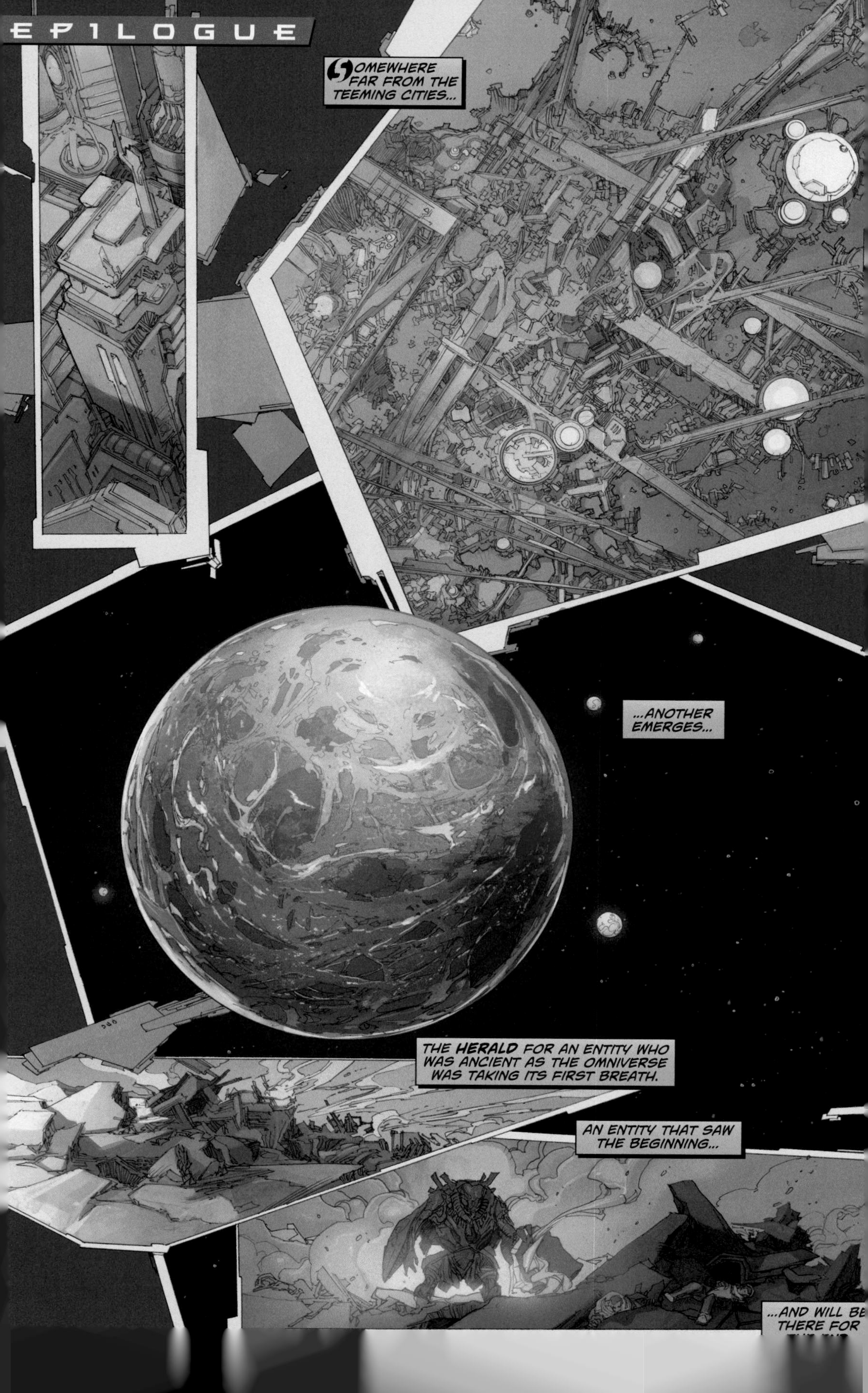
EPILOGUE
SOMEWHERE FAR FROM THE TEEMING CITIES...
...ANOTHER EMERGES...
THE HERALD FOR AN ENTITY WHO WAS ANCIENT AS THE OMNIVERSE WAS TAKING ITS FIRST BREATH.
AN ENTITY THAT SAW THE BEGINNING...
...AND WILL BE THERE FOR

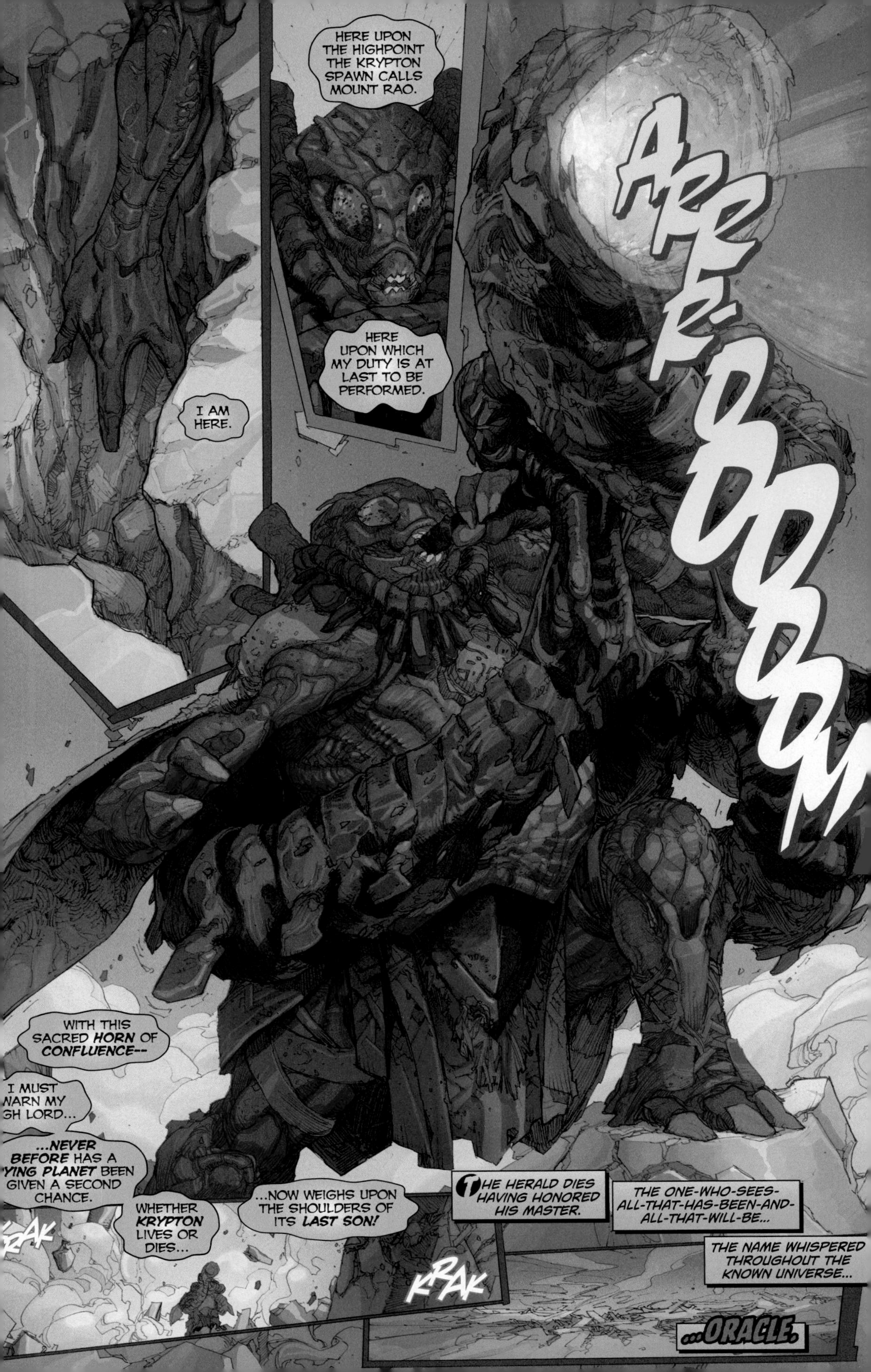
HERE UPON THE HIGHPOINT THE KRYPTON SPAWN CALLS MOUNT RAO.
HERE UPON WHICH MY DUTY IS AT LAST TO BE PERFORMED.
I AM HERE.
ARRROOOOOM
WITH THIS SACRED HORN OF CONFLUENCE--
I MUST WARN MY ...GH LORD...
...NEVER BEFORE HAS A ...YING PLANET BEEN GIVEN A SECOND CHANCE.
WHETHER KRYPTON LIVES OR DIES...
...NOW WEIGHS UPON THE SHOULDERS OF ITS LAST SON!
KRAK
KRAK
THE HERALD DIES HAVING HONORED HIS MASTER.
THE ONE-WHO-SEES-ALL-THAT-HAS-BEEN-AND-ALL-THAT-WILL-BE...
THE NAME WHISPERED THROUGHOUT THE KNOWN UNIVERSE...
...ORACLE.

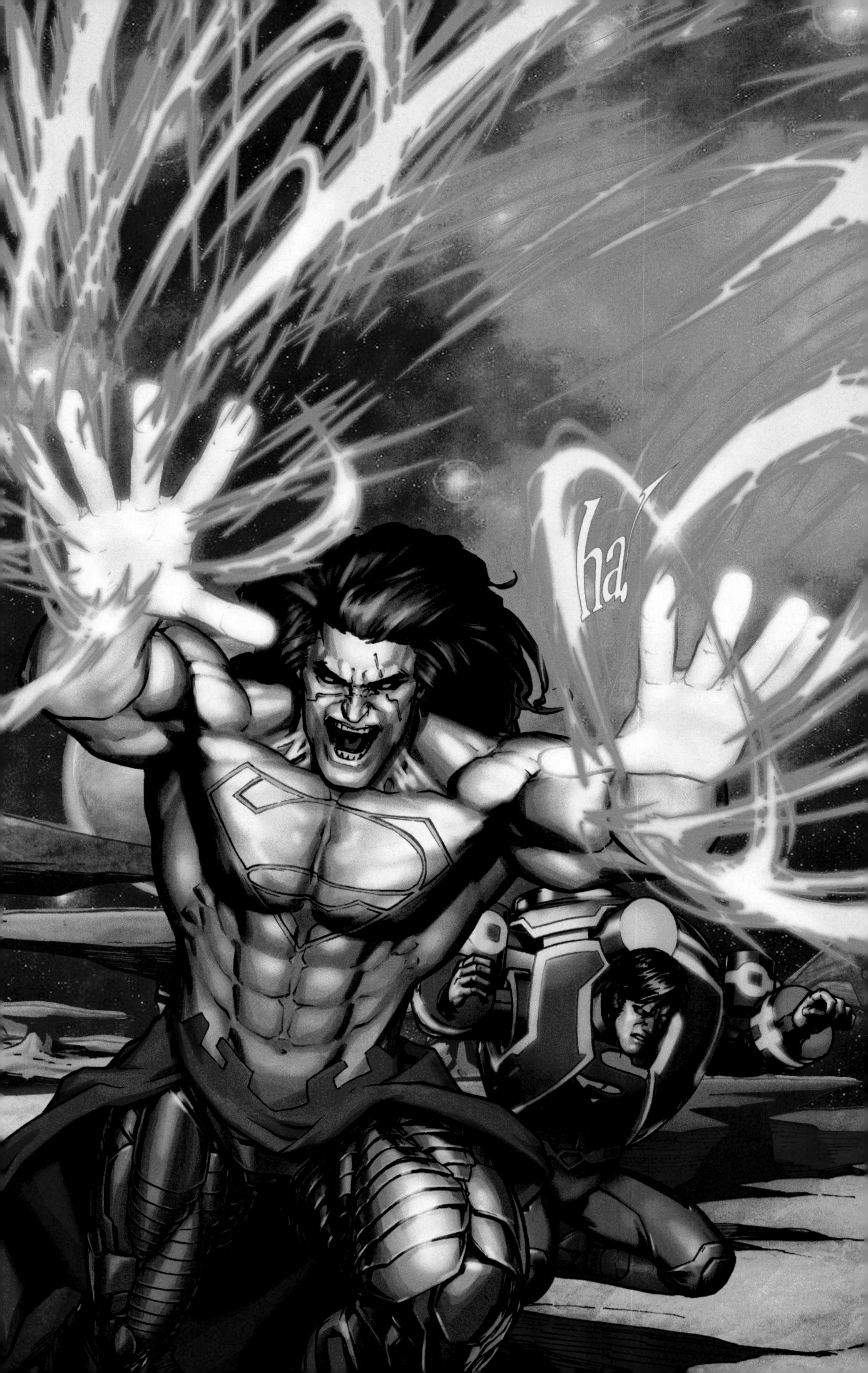
ha

TO H'EL AND BACK

SCOTT LOBDELL writer **DAN JURGENS** penciller **RAY McCARTHY** finishes **HI-FI** colorist
cover art by **GENE HA**

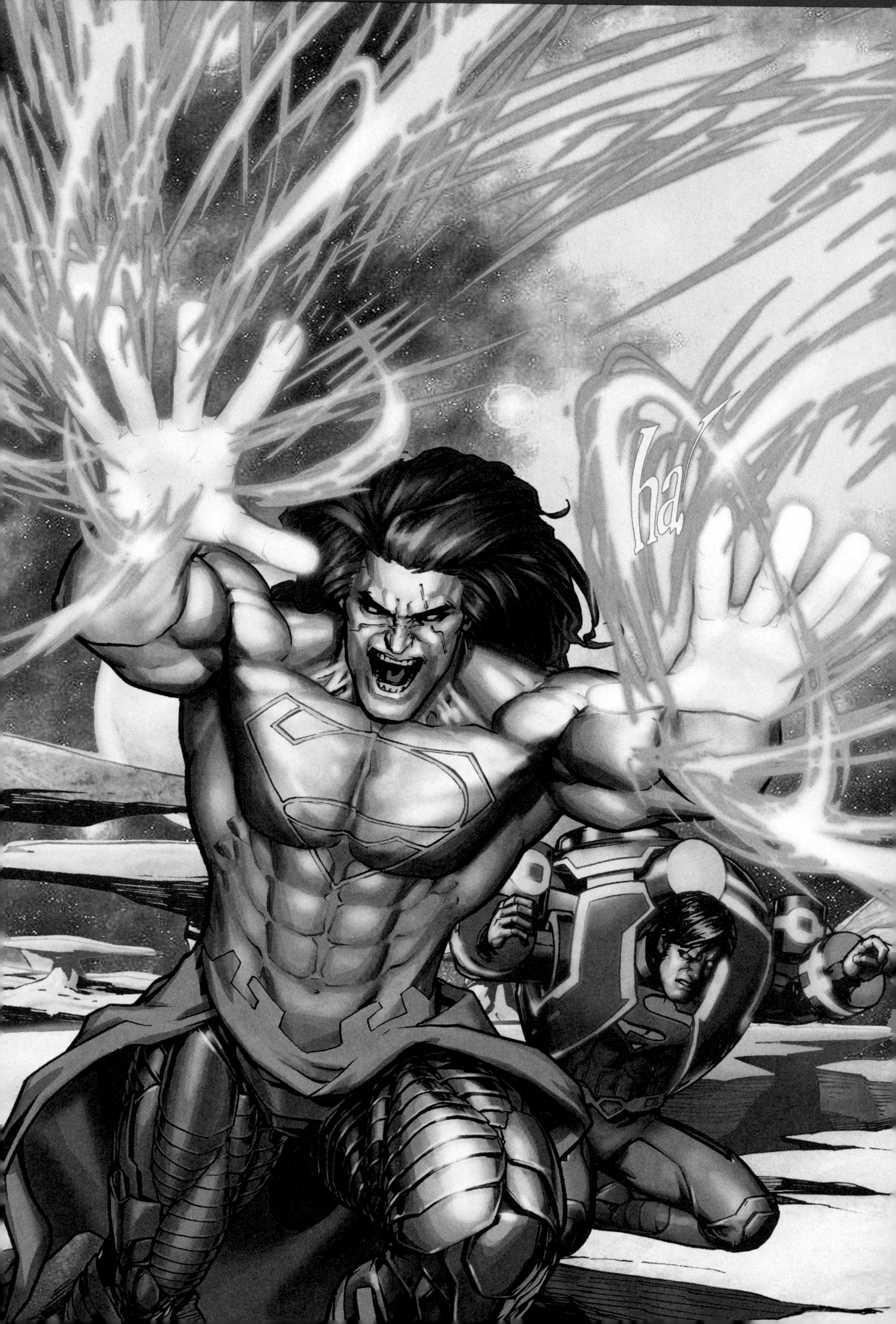
ha!

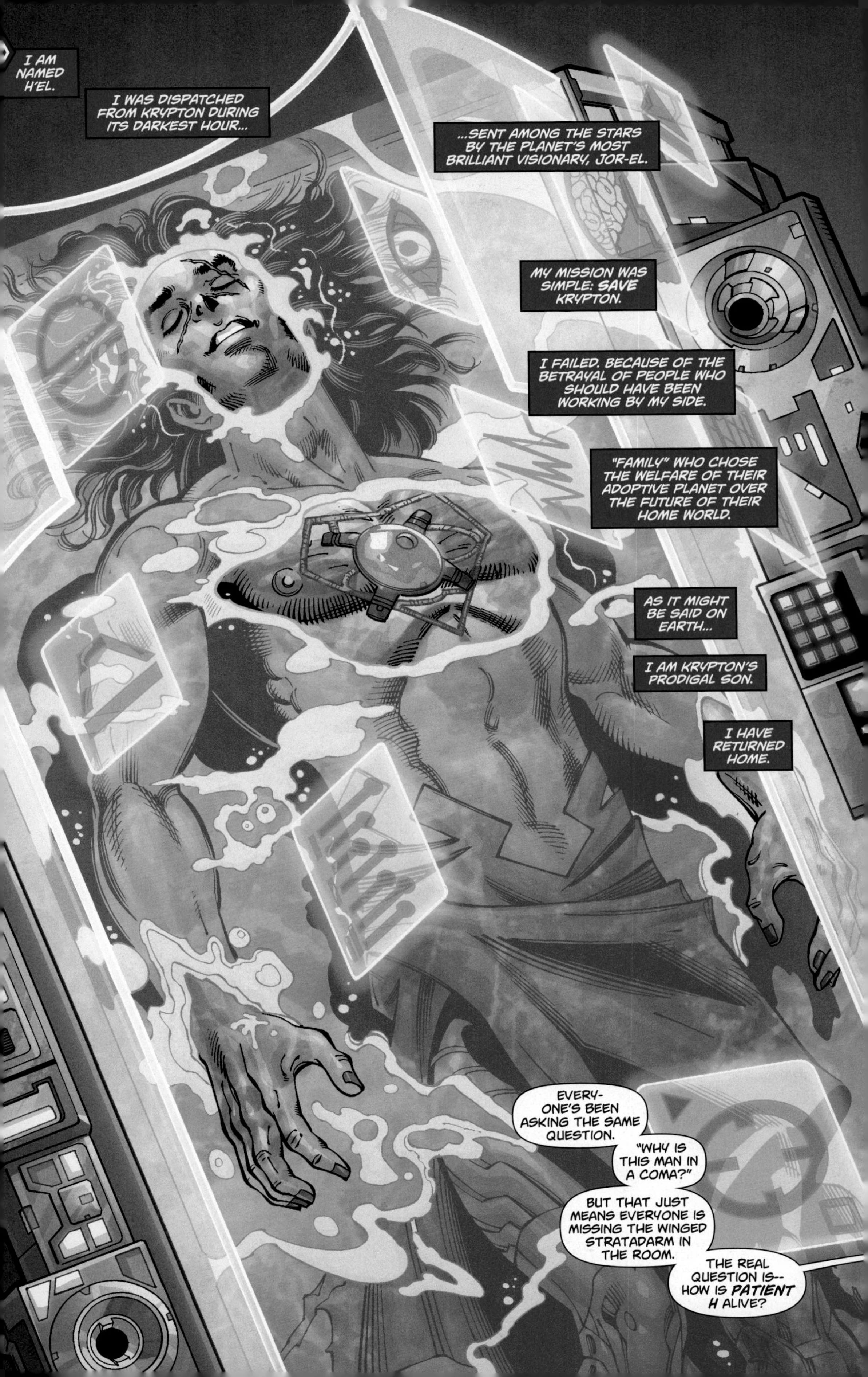
I AM NAMED H'EL.
I WAS DISPATCHED FROM KRYPTON DURING ITS DARKEST HOUR...
...SENT AMONG THE STARS BY THE PLANET'S MOST BRILLIANT VISIONARY, JOR-EL.
MY MISSION WAS SIMPLE: **SAVE** KRYPTON.
I FAILED. BECAUSE OF THE BETRAYAL OF PEOPLE WHO SHOULD HAVE BEEN WORKING BY MY SIDE.
"FAMILY" WHO CHOSE THE WELFARE OF THEIR ADOPTIVE PLANET OVER THE FUTURE OF THEIR HOME WORLD.
AS IT MIGHT BE SAID ON EARTH...
I AM KRYPTON'S PRODIGAL SON.
I HAVE RETURNED HOME.
EVERY-ONE'S BEEN ASKING THE SAME QUESTION.
"WHY IS THIS MAN IN A COMA?"
BUT THAT JUST MEANS EVERYONE IS MISSING THE WINGED STRATADARM IN THE ROOM.
THE REAL QUESTION IS-- HOW IS ***PATIENT H*** ALIVE?

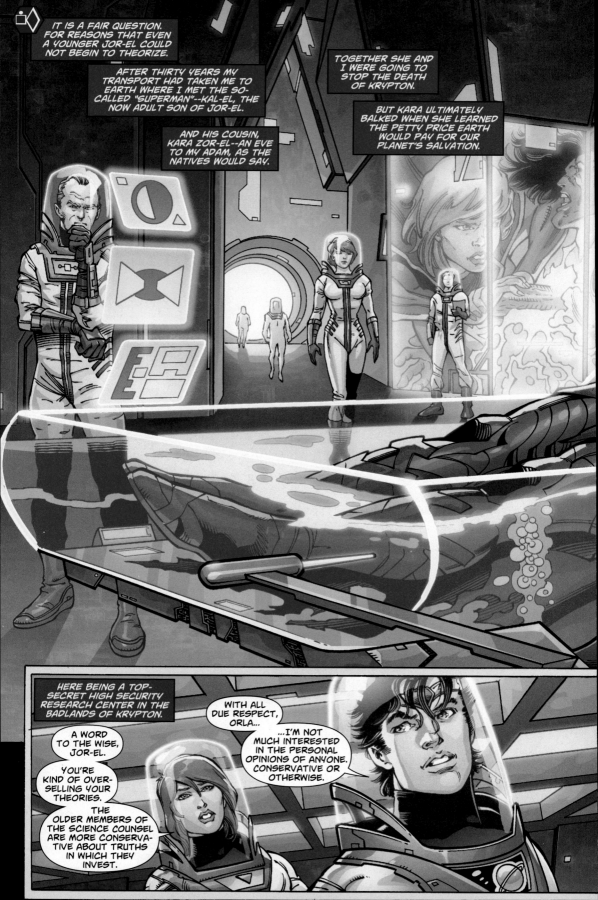

IT IS A FAIR QUESTION. FOR REASONS THAT EVEN A YOUNGER JOR-EL COULD NOT BEGIN TO THEORIZE.

AFTER THIRTY YEARS MY TRANSPORT HAD TAKEN ME TO EARTH WHERE I MET THE SO-CALLED "SUPERMAN"--KAL-EL, THE NOW ADULT SON OF JOR-EL.

AND HIS COUSIN, KARA ZOR-EL--AN EVE TO MY ADAM, AS THE NATIVES WOULD SAY.

TOGETHER SHE AND I WERE GOING TO STOP THE DEATH OF KRYPTON.

BUT KARA ULTIMATELY BALKED WHEN SHE LEARNED THE PETTY PRICE EARTH WOULD PAY FOR OUR PLANET'S SALVATION.

HERE BEING A TOP-SECRET HIGH SECURITY RESEARCH CENTER IN THE BADLANDS OF KRYPTON.

A WORD TO THE WISE, JOR-EL.

YOU'RE KIND OF OVER-SELLING YOUR THEORIES.

THE OLDER MEMBERS OF THE SCIENCE COUNSEL ARE MORE CONSERVA-TIVE ABOUT TRUTHS IN WHICH THEY INVEST.

WITH ALL DUE RESPECT, ORLA...

...I'M NOT MUCH INTERESTED IN THE PERSONAL OPINIONS OF ANYONE. CONSERVATIVE OR OTHERWISE.

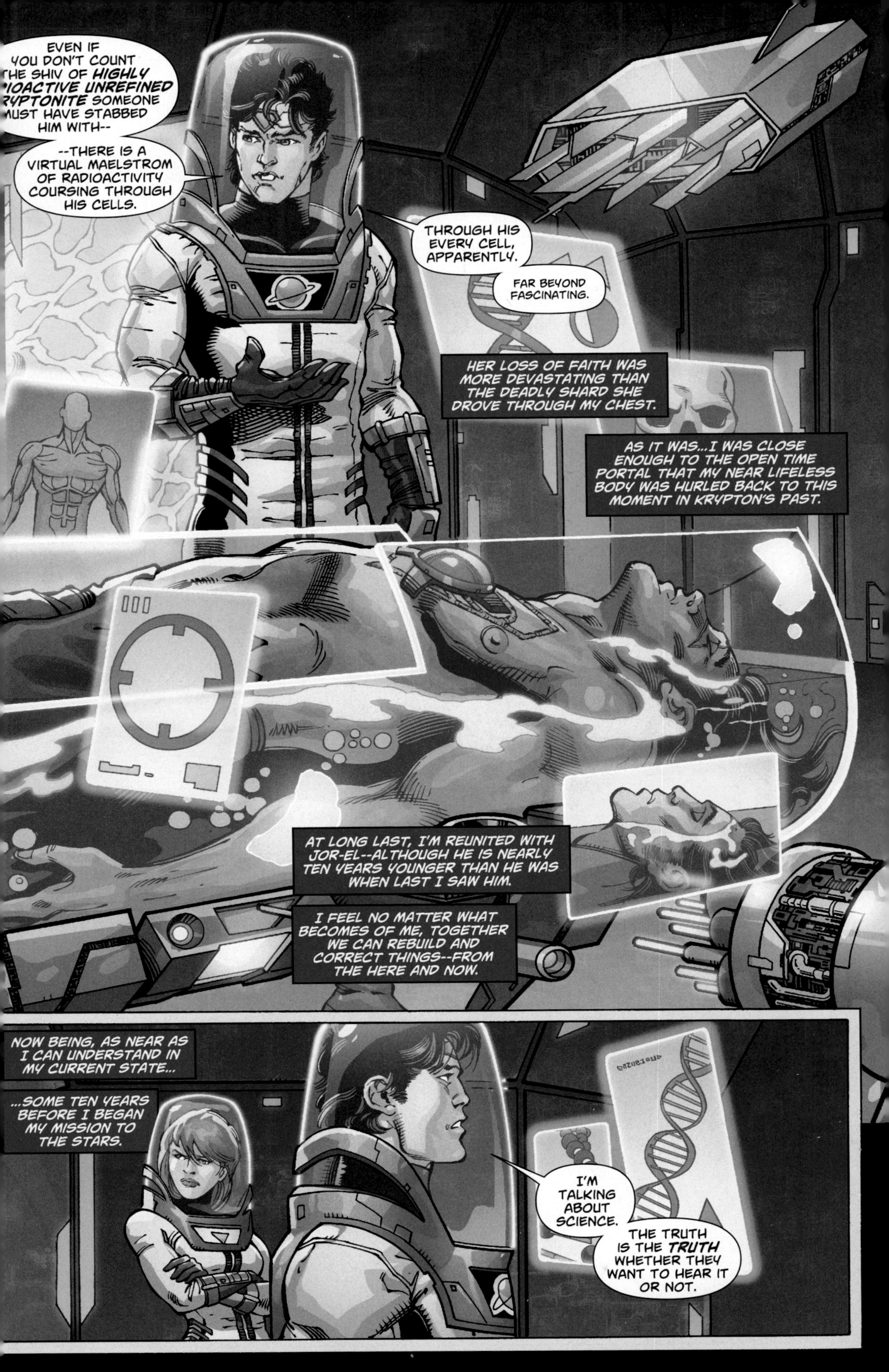
EVEN IF YOU DON'T COUNT THE SHIV OF HIGHLY RADIOACTIVE UNREFINED KRYPTONITE SOMEONE MUST HAVE STABBED HIM WITH--
--THERE IS A VIRTUAL MAELSTROM OF RADIOACTIVITY COURSING THROUGH HIS CELLS.
THROUGH HIS EVERY CELL, APPARENTLY.
FAR BEYOND FASCINATING.
HER LOSS OF FAITH WAS MORE DEVASTATING THAN THE DEADLY SHARD SHE DROVE THROUGH MY CHEST.
AS IT WAS...I WAS CLOSE ENOUGH TO THE OPEN TIME PORTAL THAT MY NEAR LIFELESS BODY WAS HURLED BACK TO THIS MOMENT IN KRYPTON'S PAST.
AT LONG LAST, I'M REUNITED WITH JOR-EL--ALTHOUGH HE IS NEARLY TEN YEARS YOUNGER THAN HE WAS WHEN LAST I SAW HIM.
I FEEL NO MATTER WHAT BECOMES OF ME, TOGETHER WE CAN REBUILD AND CORRECT THINGS--FROM THE HERE AND NOW.
NOW BEING, AS NEAR AS I CAN UNDERSTAND IN MY CURRENT STATE...
...SOME TEN YEARS BEFORE I BEGAN MY MISSION TO THE STARS.
I'M TALKING ABOUT SCIENCE.
THE TRUTH IS THE TRUTH WHETHER THEY WANT TO HEAR IT OR NOT.

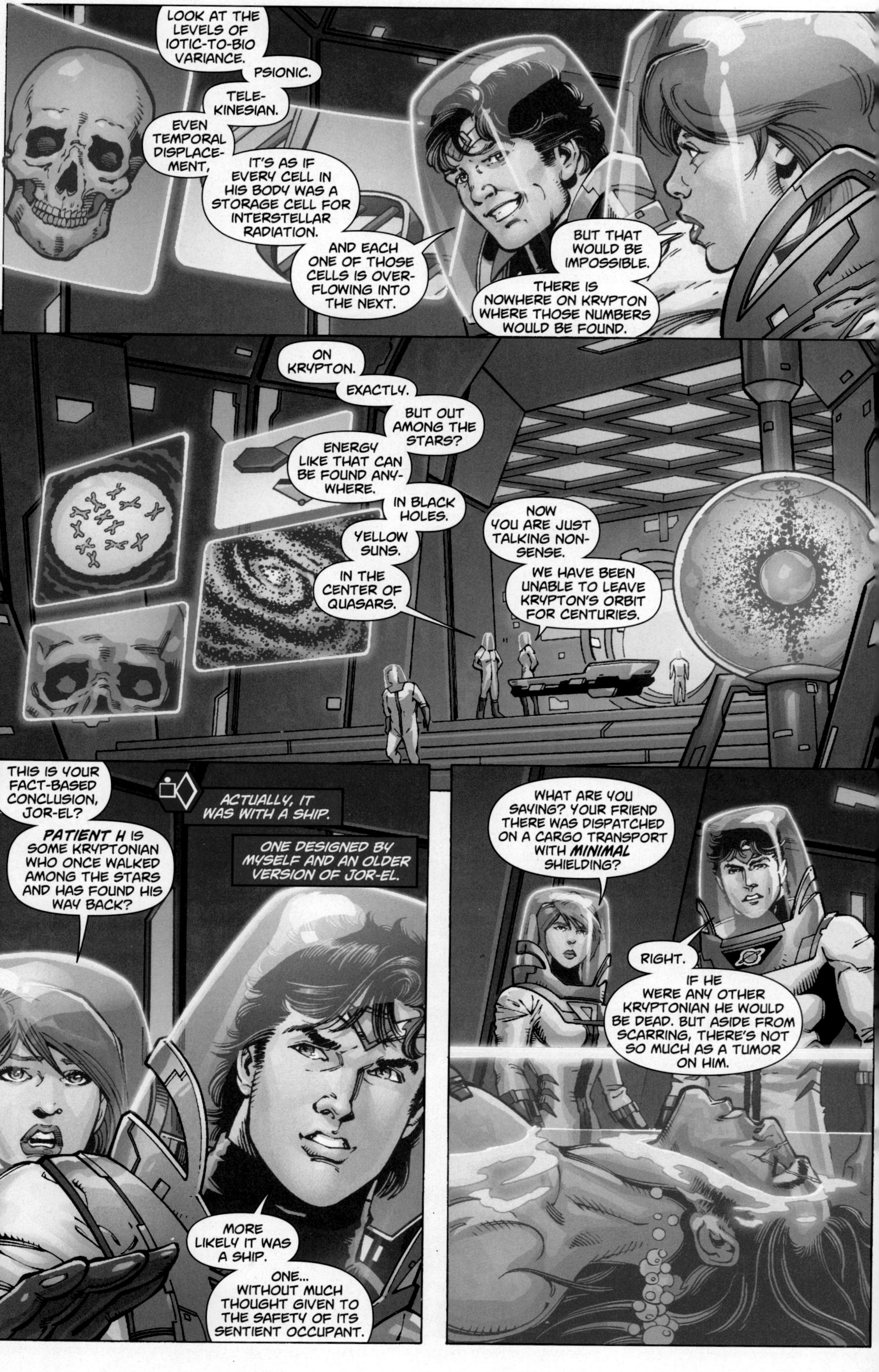
LOOK AT THE LEVELS OF IOTIC-TO-BIO VARIANCE.
PSIONIC.
TELE-KINESIAN.
EVEN TEMPORAL DISPLACE-MENT,
IT'S AS IF EVERY CELL IN HIS BODY WAS A STORAGE CELL FOR INTERSTELLAR RADIATION.
AND EACH ONE OF THOSE CELLS IS OVER-FLOWING INTO THE NEXT.
BUT THAT WOULD BE IMPOSSIBLE.
THERE IS NOWHERE ON KRYPTON WHERE THOSE NUMBERS WOULD BE FOUND.
ON KRYPTON.
EXACTLY.
BUT OUT AMONG THE STARS?
ENERGY LIKE THAT CAN BE FOUND ANY-WHERE.
IN BLACK HOLES.
YELLOW SUNS.
IN THE CENTER OF QUASARS.
NOW YOU ARE JUST TALKING NON-SENSE.
WE HAVE BEEN UNABLE TO LEAVE KRYPTON'S ORBIT FOR CENTURIES.
THIS IS YOUR FACT-BASED CONCLUSION, JOR-EL?
ACTUALLY, IT WAS WITH A SHIP.
PATIENT H IS SOME KRYPTONIAN WHO ONCE WALKED AMONG THE STARS AND HAS FOUND HIS WAY BACK?
ONE DESIGNED BY MYSELF AND AN OLDER VERSION OF JOR-EL.
MORE LIKELY IT WAS A SHIP.
ONE... WITHOUT MUCH THOUGHT GIVEN TO THE SAFETY OF ITS SENTIENT OCCUPANT.
WHAT ARE YOU SAYING? YOUR FRIEND THERE WAS DISPATCHED ON A CARGO TRANSPORT WITH *MINIMAL* SHIELDING?
RIGHT.
IF HE WERE ANY OTHER KRYPTONIAN HE WOULD BE DEAD. BUT ASIDE FROM SCARRING, THERE'S NOT SO MUCH AS A TUMOR ON HIM.

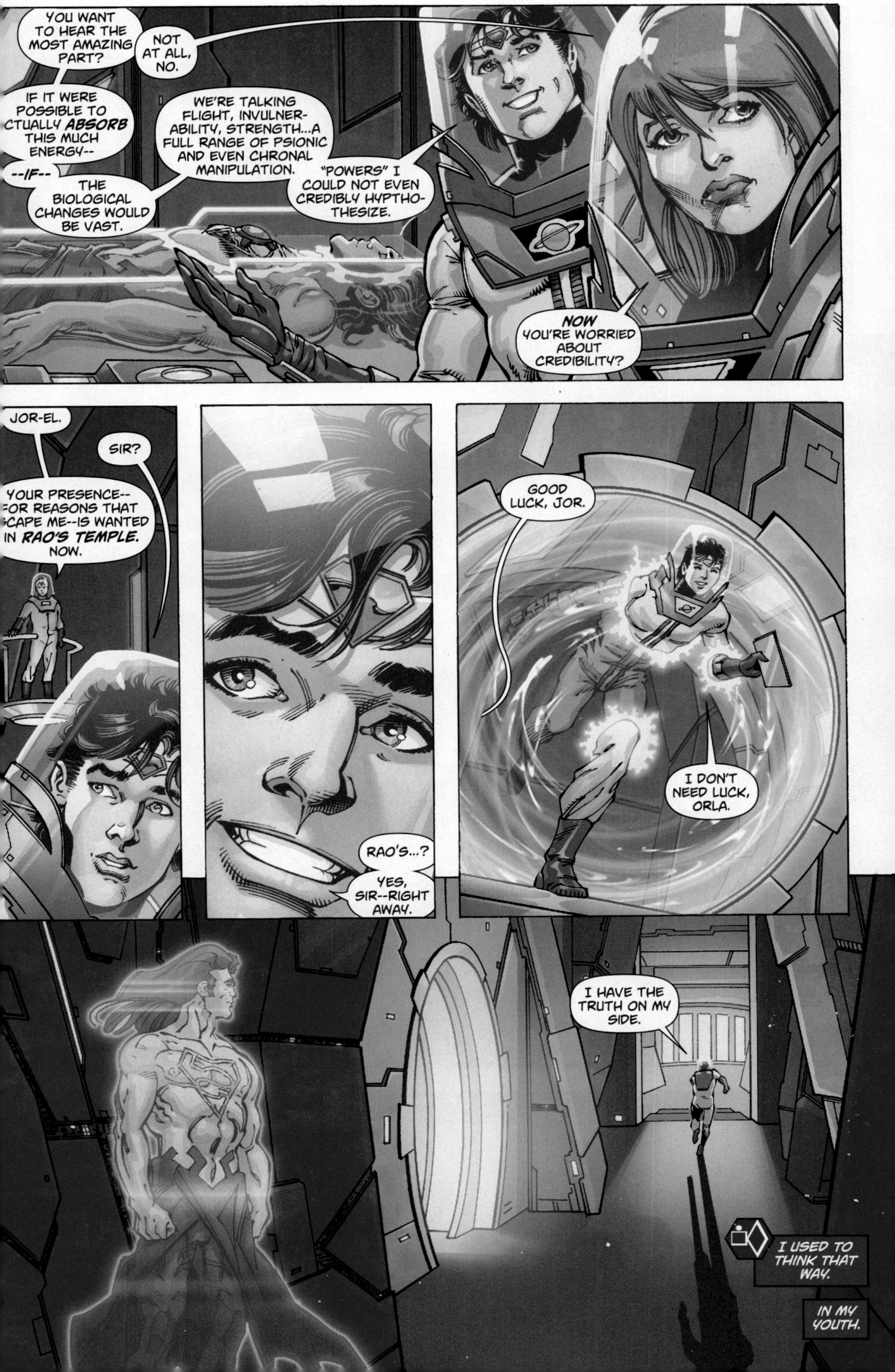
YOU WANT TO HEAR THE MOST AMAZING PART?
NOT AT ALL, NO.
IF IT WERE POSSIBLE TO CTUALLY ABSORB THIS MUCH ENERGY--
--IF--
THE BIOLOGICAL CHANGES WOULD BE VAST.
WE'RE TALKING FLIGHT, INVULNER-ABILITY, STRENGTH...A FULL RANGE OF PSIONIC AND EVEN CHRONAL MANIPULATION.
"POWERS" I COULD NOT EVEN CREDIBLY HYPTHO-THESIZE.
NOW YOU'RE WORRIED ABOUT CREDIBILITY?
JOR-EL.
SIR?
YOUR PRESENCE--FOR REASONS THAT SCAPE ME--IS WANTED IN RAO'S TEMPLE. NOW.
RAO'S...?
YES, SIR--RIGHT AWAY.
GOOD LUCK, JOR.
I DON'T NEED LUCK, ORLA.
I HAVE THE TRUTH ON MY SIDE.
I USED TO THINK THAT WAY.
IN MY YOUTH.

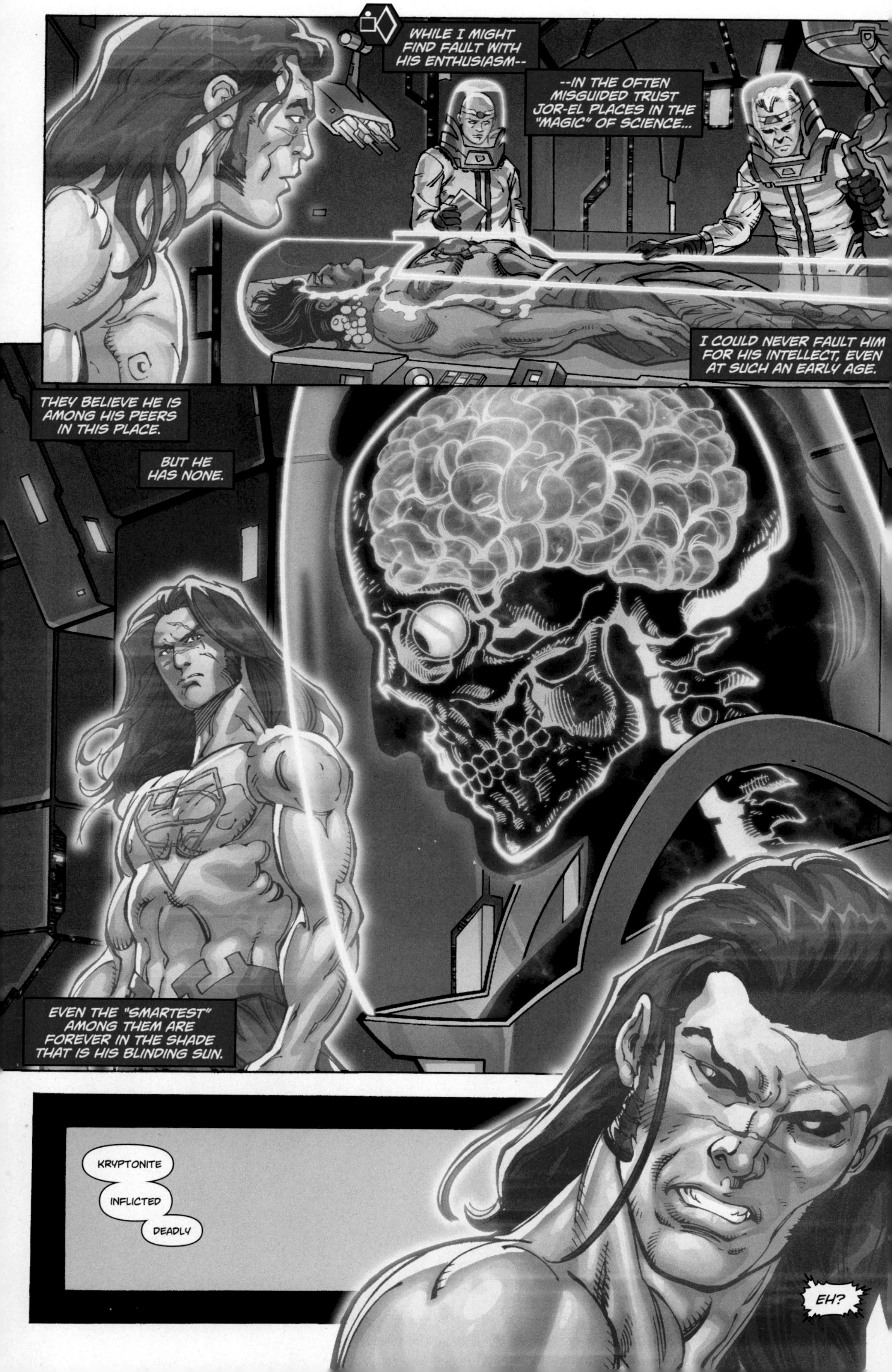
WHILE I MIGHT FIND FAULT WITH HIS ENTHUSIASM--
--IN THE OFTEN MISGUIDED TRUST JOR-EL PLACES IN THE "MAGIC" OF SCIENCE...
I COULD NEVER FAULT HIM FOR HIS INTELLECT, EVEN AT SUCH AN EARLY AGE.
THEY BELIEVE HE IS AMONG HIS PEERS IN THIS PLACE.
BUT HE HAS NONE.
EVEN THE "SMARTEST" AMONG THEM ARE FOREVER IN THE SHADE THAT IS HIS BLINDING SUN.
KRYPTONITE
INFLICTED
DEADLY
EH?

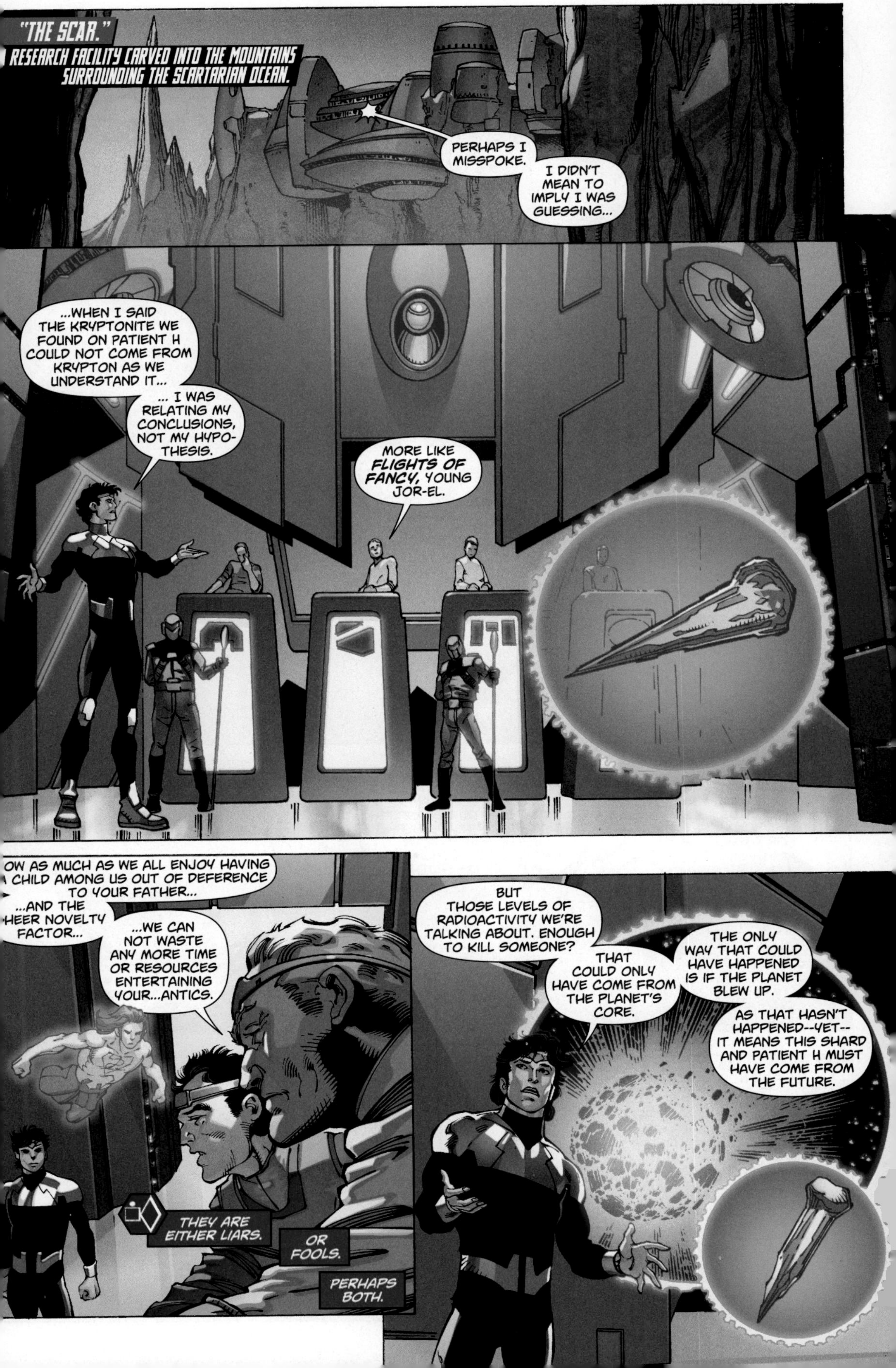
"THE SCAR."
RESEARCH FACILITY CARVED INTO THE MOUNTAINS SURROUNDING THE SCARTARIAN OCEAN.
PERHAPS I MISSPOKE.
I DIDN'T MEAN TO IMPLY I WAS GUESSING...
...WHEN I SAID THE KRYPTONITE WE FOUND ON PATIENT H COULD NOT COME FROM KRYPTON AS WE UNDERSTAND IT...
... I WAS RELATING MY CONCLUSIONS, NOT MY HYPO-THESIS.
MORE LIKE FLIGHTS OF FANCY, YOUNG JOR-EL.
OW AS MUCH AS WE ALL ENJOY HAVING CHILD AMONG US OUT OF DEFERENCE TO YOUR FATHER...
...AND THE HEER NOVELTY FACTOR...
...WE CAN NOT WASTE ANY MORE TIME OR RESOURCES ENTERTAINING YOUR...ANTICS.
THEY ARE EITHER LIARS.
OR FOOLS.
PERHAPS BOTH.
BUT THOSE LEVELS OF RADIOACTIVITY WE'RE TALKING ABOUT. ENOUGH TO KILL SOMEONE?
THAT COULD ONLY HAVE COME FROM THE PLANET'S CORE.
THE ONLY WAY THAT COULD HAVE HAPPENED IS IF THE PLANET BLEW UP.
AS THAT HASN'T HAPPENED--YET-- IT MEANS THIS SHARD AND PATIENT H MUST HAVE COME FROM THE FUTURE.

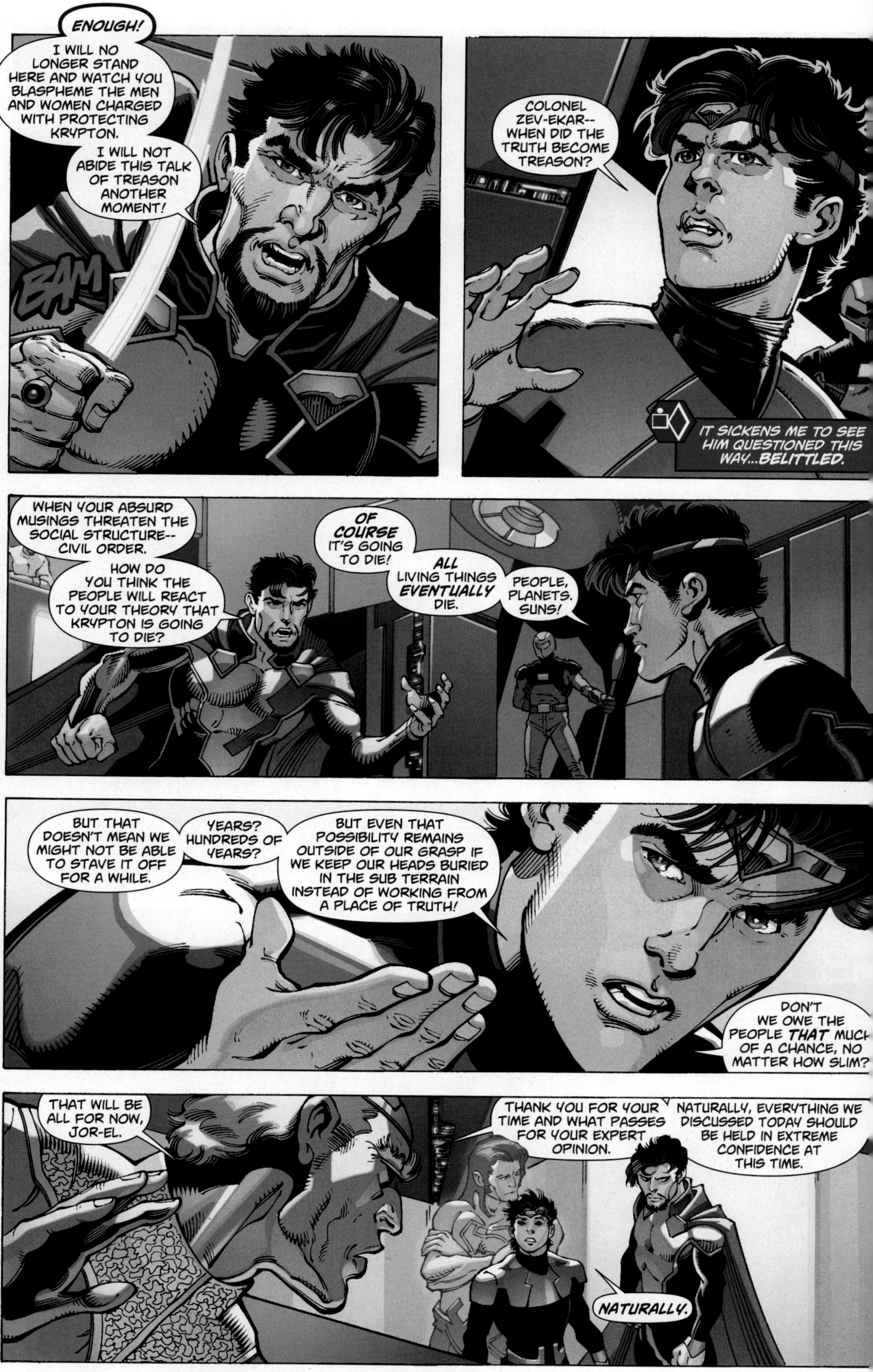
ENOUGH!
I WILL NO LONGER STAND HERE AND WATCH YOU BLASPHEME THE MEN AND WOMEN CHARGED WITH PROTECTING KRYPTON.
I WILL NOT ABIDE THIS TALK OF TREASON ANOTHER MOMENT!
BAM
COLONEL ZEV-EKAR-- WHEN DID THE TRUTH BECOME TREASON?
IT SICKENS ME TO SEE HIM QUESTIONED THIS WAY...BELITTLED.
WHEN YOUR ABSURD MUSINGS THREATEN THE SOCIAL STRUCTURE-- CIVIL ORDER.
HOW DO YOU THINK THE PEOPLE WILL REACT TO YOUR THEORY THAT KRYPTON IS GOING TO DIE?
OF COURSE IT'S GOING TO DIE!
ALL LIVING THINGS EVENTUALLY DIE.
PEOPLE, PLANETS. SUNS!
BUT THAT DOESN'T MEAN WE MIGHT NOT BE ABLE TO STAVE IT OFF FOR A WHILE.
YEARS? HUNDREDS OF YEARS?
BUT EVEN THAT POSSIBILITY REMAINS OUTSIDE OF OUR GRASP IF WE KEEP OUR HEADS BURIED IN THE SUB TERRAIN INSTEAD OF WORKING FROM A PLACE OF TRUTH!
DON'T WE OWE THE PEOPLE THAT MUCH OF A CHANCE, NO MATTER HOW SLIM?
THAT WILL BE ALL FOR NOW, JOR-EL.
THANK YOU FOR YOUR TIME AND WHAT PASSES FOR YOUR EXPERT OPINION.
NATURALLY, EVERYTHING WE DISCUSSED TODAY SHOULD BE HELD IN EXTREME CONFIDENCE AT THIS TIME.
NATURALLY.

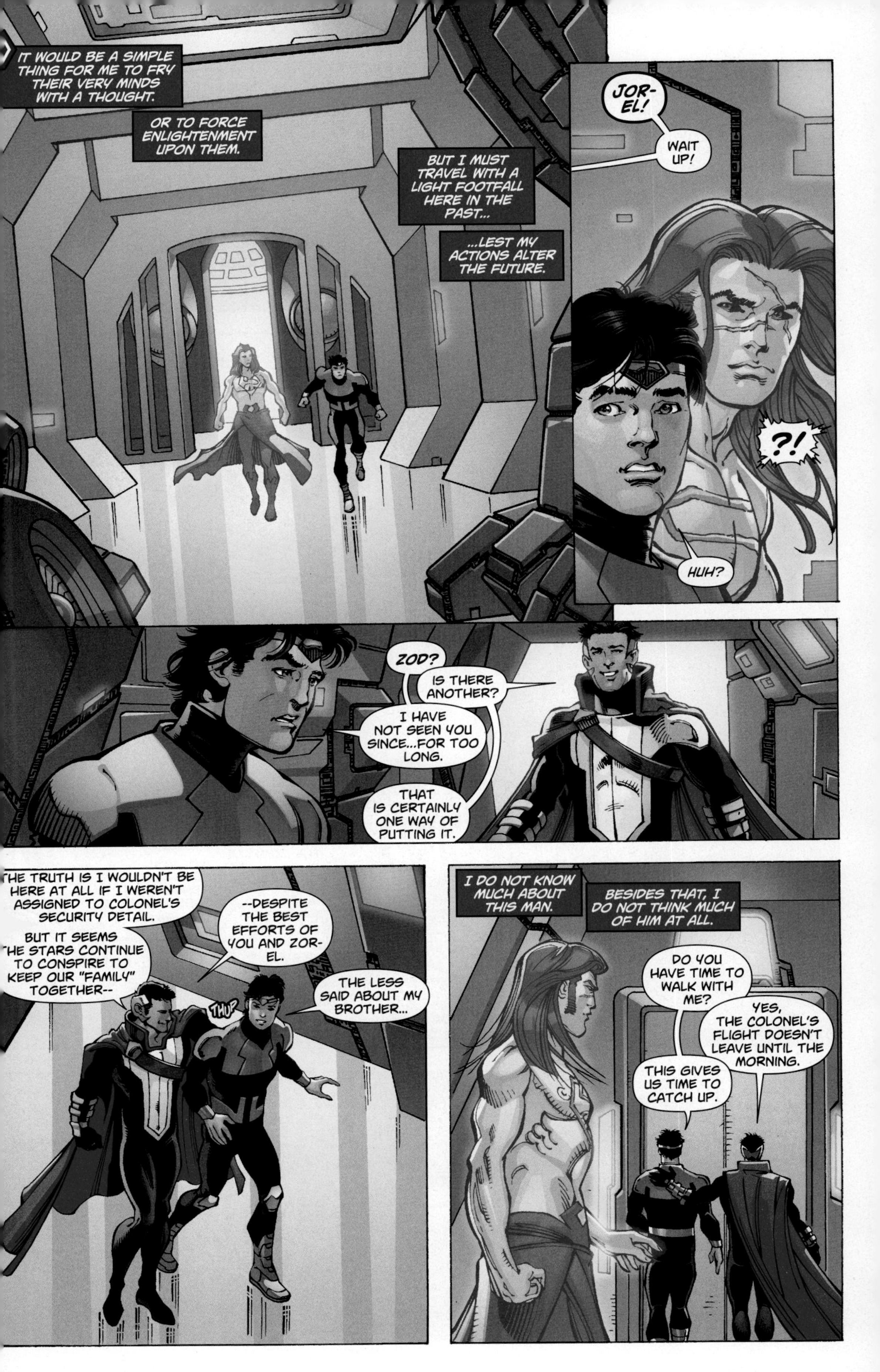
IT WOULD BE A SIMPLE THING FOR ME TO FRY THEIR VERY MINDS WITH A THOUGHT.
OR TO FORCE ENLIGHTENMENT UPON THEM.
BUT I MUST TRAVEL WITH A LIGHT FOOTFALL HERE IN THE PAST...
...LEST MY ACTIONS ALTER THE FUTURE.
JOR-EL!
WAIT UP!
?!
HUH?
ZOD?
IS THERE ANOTHER?
I HAVE NOT SEEN YOU SINCE...FOR TOO LONG.
THAT IS CERTAINLY ONE WAY OF PUTTING IT.
THE TRUTH IS I WOULDN'T BE HERE AT ALL IF I WEREN'T ASSIGNED TO COLONEL'S SECURITY DETAIL.
BUT IT SEEMS THE STARS CONTINUE TO CONSPIRE TO KEEP OUR "FAMILY" TOGETHER--
--DESPITE THE BEST EFFORTS OF YOU AND ZOR-EL.
THUP
THE LESS SAID ABOUT MY BROTHER...
I DO NOT KNOW MUCH ABOUT THIS MAN.
BESIDES THAT, I DO NOT THINK MUCH OF HIM AT ALL.
DO YOU HAVE TIME TO WALK WITH ME?
YES, THE COLONEL'S FLIGHT DOESN'T LEAVE UNTIL THE MORNING.
THIS GIVES US TIME TO CATCH UP.

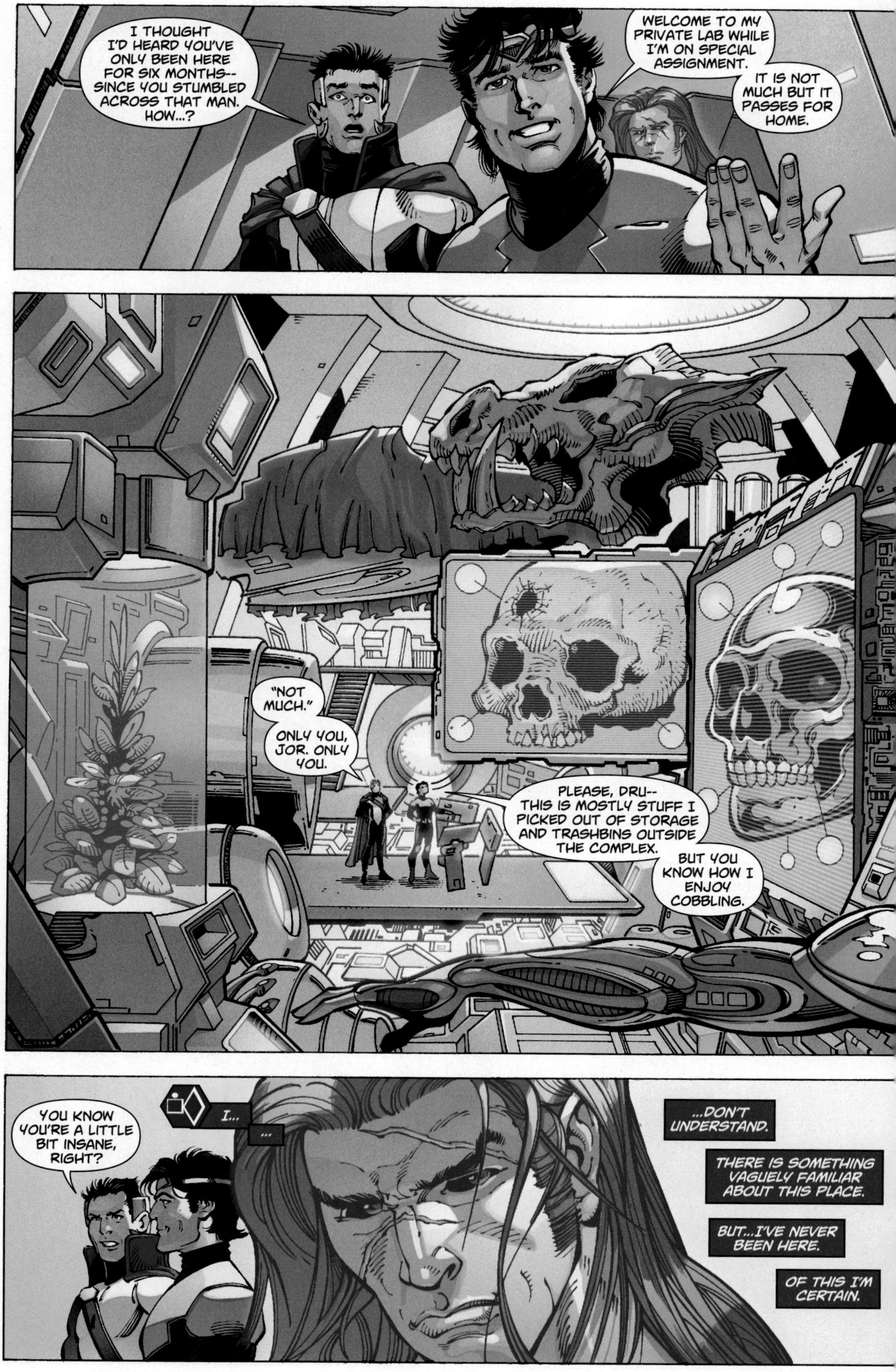
I THOUGHT I'D HEARD YOU'VE ONLY BEEN HERE FOR SIX MONTHS-- SINCE YOU STUMBLED ACROSS THAT MAN. HOW...?
WELCOME TO MY PRIVATE LAB WHILE I'M ON SPECIAL ASSIGNMENT.
IT IS NOT MUCH BUT IT PASSES FOR HOME.
"NOT MUCH."
ONLY YOU, JOR. ONLY YOU.
PLEASE, DRU-- THIS IS MOSTLY STUFF I PICKED OUT OF STORAGE AND TRASHBINS OUTSIDE THE COMPLEX.
BUT YOU KNOW HOW I ENJOY COBBLING.
YOU KNOW YOU'RE A LITTLE BIT INSANE, RIGHT?
I...
...
...DON'T UNDERSTAND.
THERE IS SOMETHING VAGUELY FAMILIAR ABOUT THIS PLACE.
BUT...I'VE NEVER BEEN HERE.
OF THIS I'M CERTAIN.

IN LIGHT OF RECENT DEVELOPMENTS...A PARTICULAR PROJECT OF MINE HAS TAKEN ON GREATER SIGNIFICANCE.

COMING FROM YOU THAT COULD MEAN ANYTHING FROM A PAN-DIMENSIONAL POWER SOURCE OR AN EVERLASTING BREATH MINT.

NOTHING SO AMBITIOUS.

I'VE BEEN CATALOGUING THE *HISTORY* OF KRYPTON--

--AS WELL AS MY OWN WILD PROJECTIONS ON THE FUTURE OF THE SAME--

--STARTING WITH THE BEGINNING OF THE PLANET UNTIL THE END.

HISTORY, GEOGRAPHY, MATH, SCIENCE, THE ARTS, ETHICS FROM ALL THREE ERAS AND ALL TWELVE COLONIES.

YEAH. *THAT* DOESN'T SOUND AMBITIOUS.

THAT HARD PART WASN'T THE MALE AND FEMALE OF OUR SPECIES.

IT WAS GETTING SOME OF THE ANCIENT, LONG-EXTINCT LIFE FORMS.

THAT'S...

THAT IS...

?!

THAT IS THE DRAGON I CLONED TO TEST SUPERMAN'S ABILITIES.

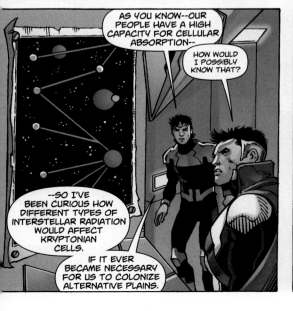

AS YOU KNOW--OUR PEOPLE HAVE A HIGH CAPACITY FOR CELLULAR ABSORPTION--

HOW WOULD I POSSIBLY KNOW THAT?

--SO I'VE BEEN CURIOUS HOW DIFFERENT TYPES OF INTERSTELLAR RADIATION WOULD AFFECT KRYPTONIAN CELLS.

IF IT EVER BECAME NECESSARY FOR US TO COLONIZE ALTERNATIVE PLAINS.

SO YOU'RE SKIRTING THE LAW AGAINST MANNED SPACE TRAVEL BUT DISGUISING YOUR CARGO INSIDE A TIME CAPSULE?

THESE SOLAR SYSTEMS.

I HAVE...BEEN THERE? BUT...

ONCE AROUND THE GALAXY AND BACK, YES.

I'M ALMOST IMPRESSED.

BUT HOW DO YOU EVEN INTEND TO GET YOUR PAYLOAD OUT OF ORBIT?

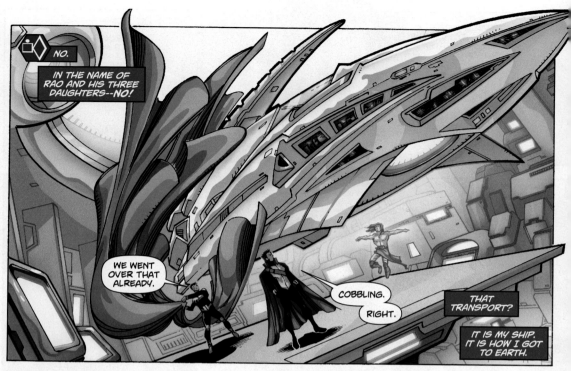

NO.

IN THE NAME OF RAO AND HIS THREE DAUGHTERS--NO!

WE WENT OVER THAT ALREADY.

COBBLING.

RIGHT.

THAT TRANSPORT?

IT IS MY SHIP. IT IS HOW I GOT TO EARTH.

BUT...HOW IS THAT POSSIBLE?!

I RECALL THE LAUNCH.

THE CHEERING OF THOUSANDS.

THE SACRED TRUST BETWEEN MYSELF AND MY MENTOR, JOR-EL.

"HOUSE OF EL."

NICE TOUCH.

A NOD TO HISTORY.

THE BOMBING OF KANDOR IN THE OLD WAR?

THE ARGONAUTS USED TO NAME THEIR AIRSKIFFS FOR GOOD LUCK.

H'EL.

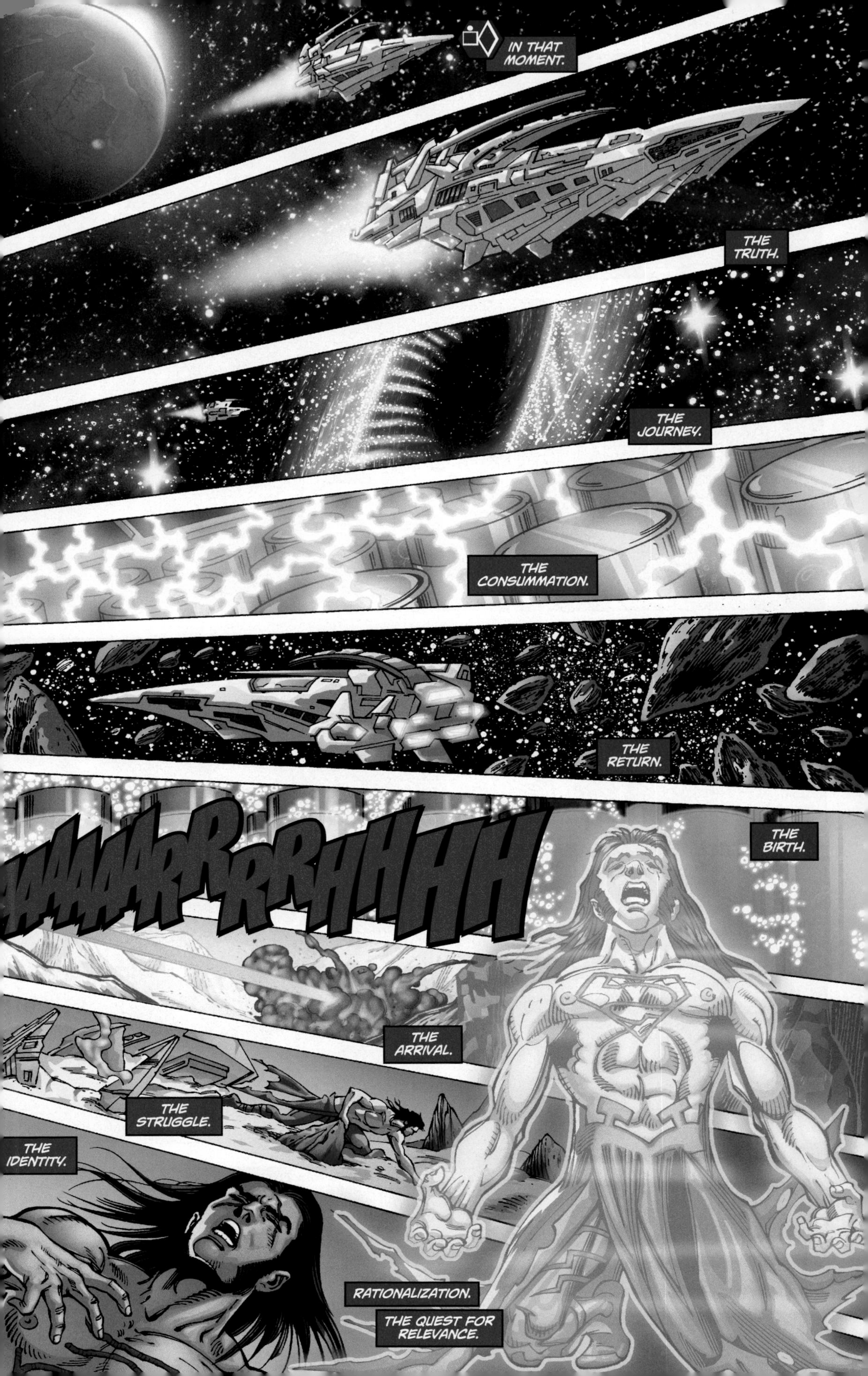
IN THAT MOMENT.
THE TRUTH.
THE JOURNEY.
THE CONSUMMATION.
THE RETURN.
AAAAAARRRRHHHHH
THE BIRTH.
THE ARRIVAL.
THE STRUGGLE.
THE IDENTITY.
RATIONALIZATION.
THE QUEST FOR RELEVANCE.

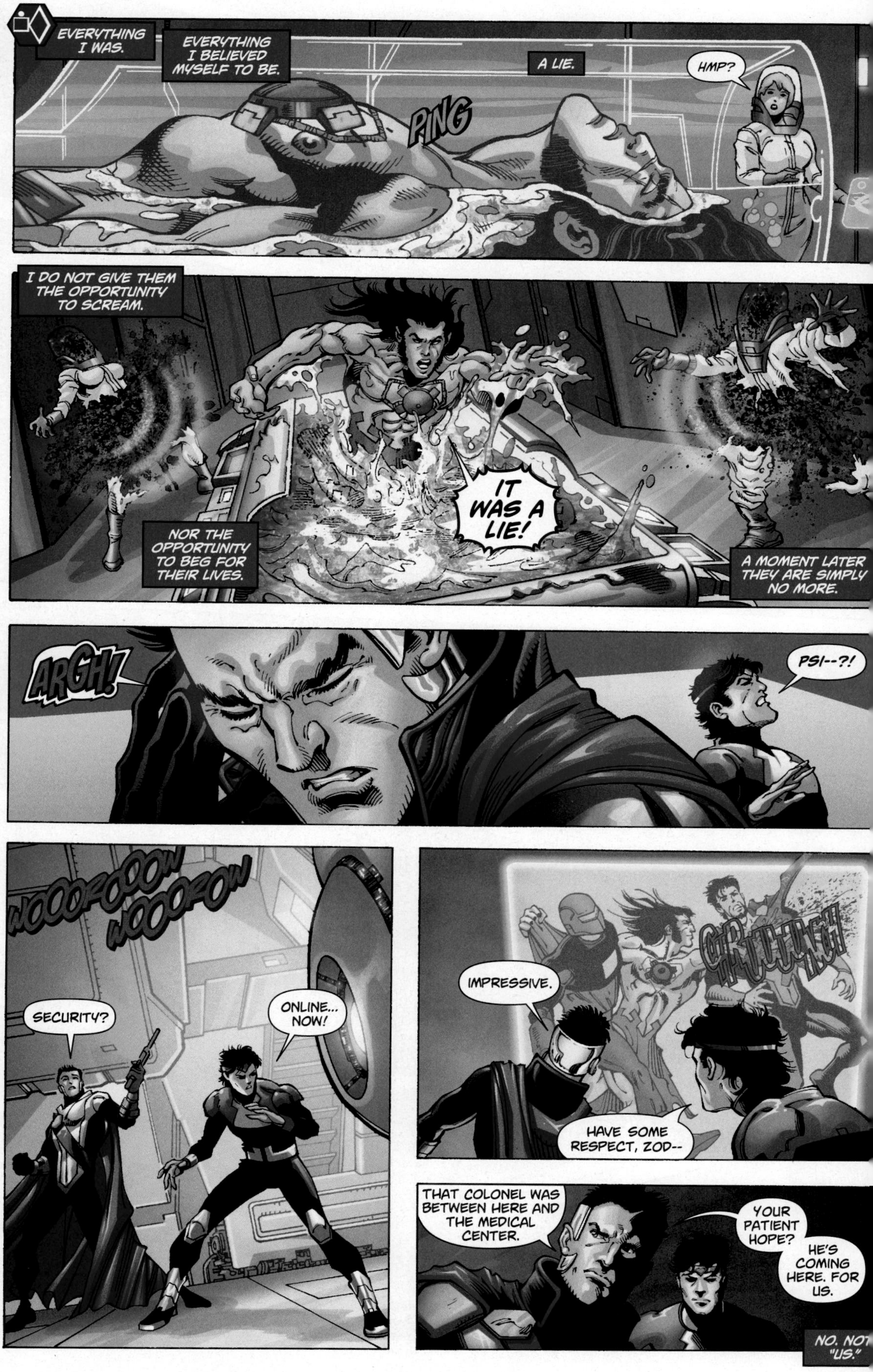
EVERYTHING I WAS.
EVERYTHING I BELIEVED MYSELF TO BE.
A LIE.
HMP?
PING
I DO NOT GIVE THEM THE OPPORTUNITY TO SCREAM.
IT WAS A LIE!
NOR THE OPPORTUNITY TO BEG FOR THEIR LIVES.
A MOMENT LATER THEY ARE SIMPLY NO MORE.
ARGH!
PSI--?!
WOOORooOOW WOOOROW
SECURITY?
ONLINE... NOW!
IMPRESSIVE.
HAVE SOME RESPECT, ZOD--
THAT COLONEL WAS BETWEEN HERE AND THE MEDICAL CENTER.
YOUR PATIENT HOPE?
HE'S COMING HERE. FOR US.
NO. NOT "US."

NO. HE'S HERE FOR THE SHIP.

YOUR TIME CAPSULE? HOW WOULD THIS--THIS SUPERMAN--EVEN KNOW ABOUT IT?

THE SHARD FROM THE FUTURE--IT'S WHERE HE CAME FROM.

AFTER KRYPTON BLEW UP.

HIS IRRADIATED PHYSIOLOGY THAT MAKES HIM MORE POWERFUL THAN ANY KRYPTONIAN I COULD EVEN IMAGINE.

HE'S *NOT* AN ACCIDENT...HE'S A PARADOX, AN ANOMALY. OR HE'S ABOUT TO BE! HE'S COMING HERE TO *CHANGE* HIS CELLS FOR THE ONES I WAS ABOUT TO DISPATCH INTO ORBIT!

BUT ZOD-- IF HE *DOES* THAT?!

HE WOULD BE FREE TO WREAK UNSPEAKABLE HAVOC THROUGHOUT ALL OF TIME AND SPACE!

DESTROY IT--*NOW!*

COMPUTER!

JOR-EL?

INITIATE SELF-DESTRUCT. NOW!

BAM

TOO LATE.

AFFIRMATIVE.

AWAITING PASSWORD.

FAR TOO LATE.

FWOOSH

MANUAL OVERRIDE, *CONFIRM!*

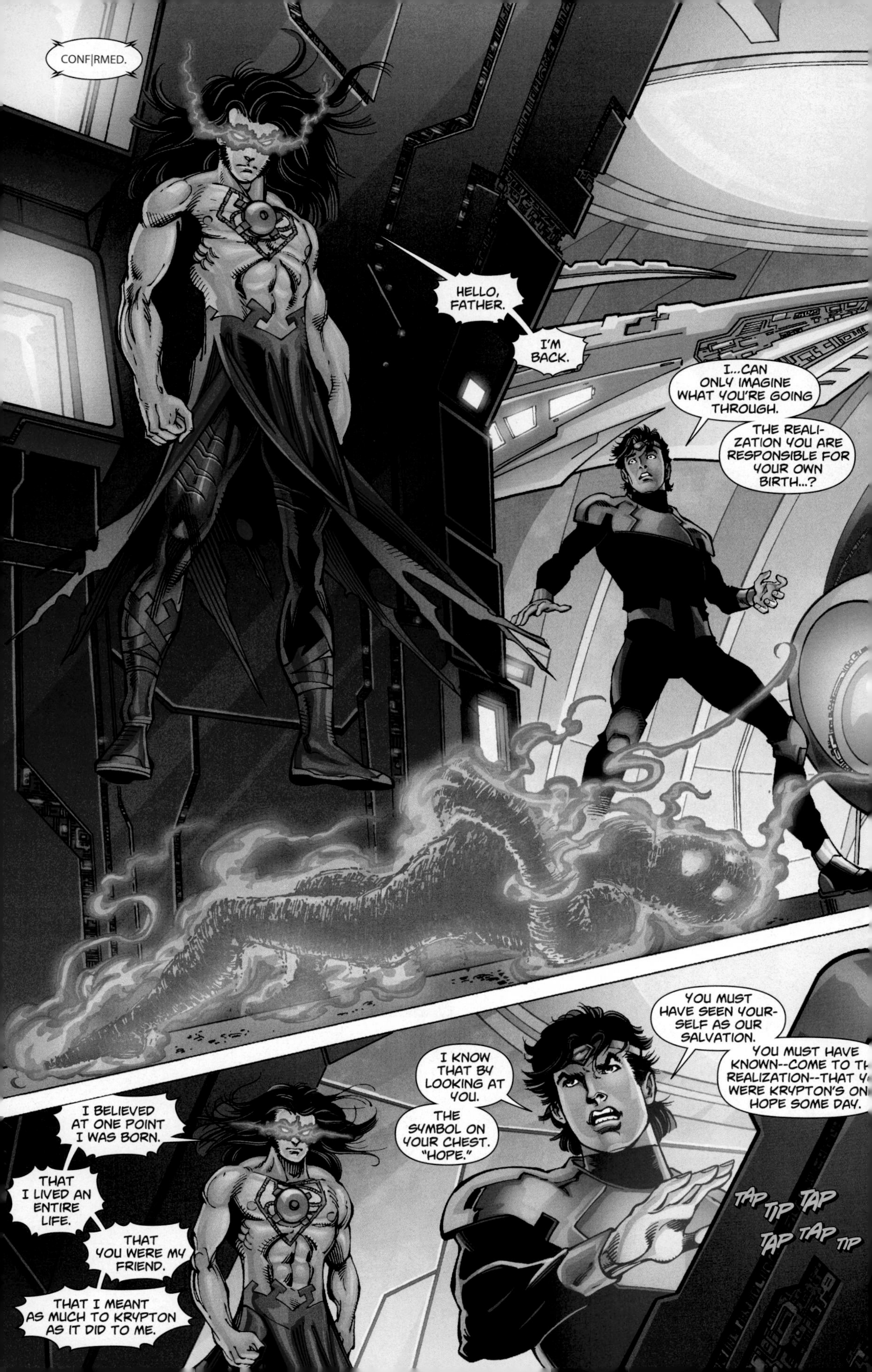
CONF|RMED.
HELLO, FATHER.
I'M BACK.
I...CAN ONLY IMAGINE WHAT YOU'RE GOING THROUGH.
THE REALI-ZATION YOU ARE RESPONSIBLE FOR YOUR OWN BIRTH...?
I BELIEVED AT ONE POINT I WAS BORN.
THAT I LIVED AN ENTIRE LIFE.
THAT YOU WERE MY FRIEND.
THAT I MEANT AS MUCH TO KRYPTON AS IT DID TO ME.
I KNOW THAT BY LOOKING AT YOU.
THE SYMBOL ON YOUR CHEST. "HOPE."
YOU MUST HAVE SEEN YOUR-SELF AS OUR SALVATION.
TAP TIP TAP
TAP TAP TIP

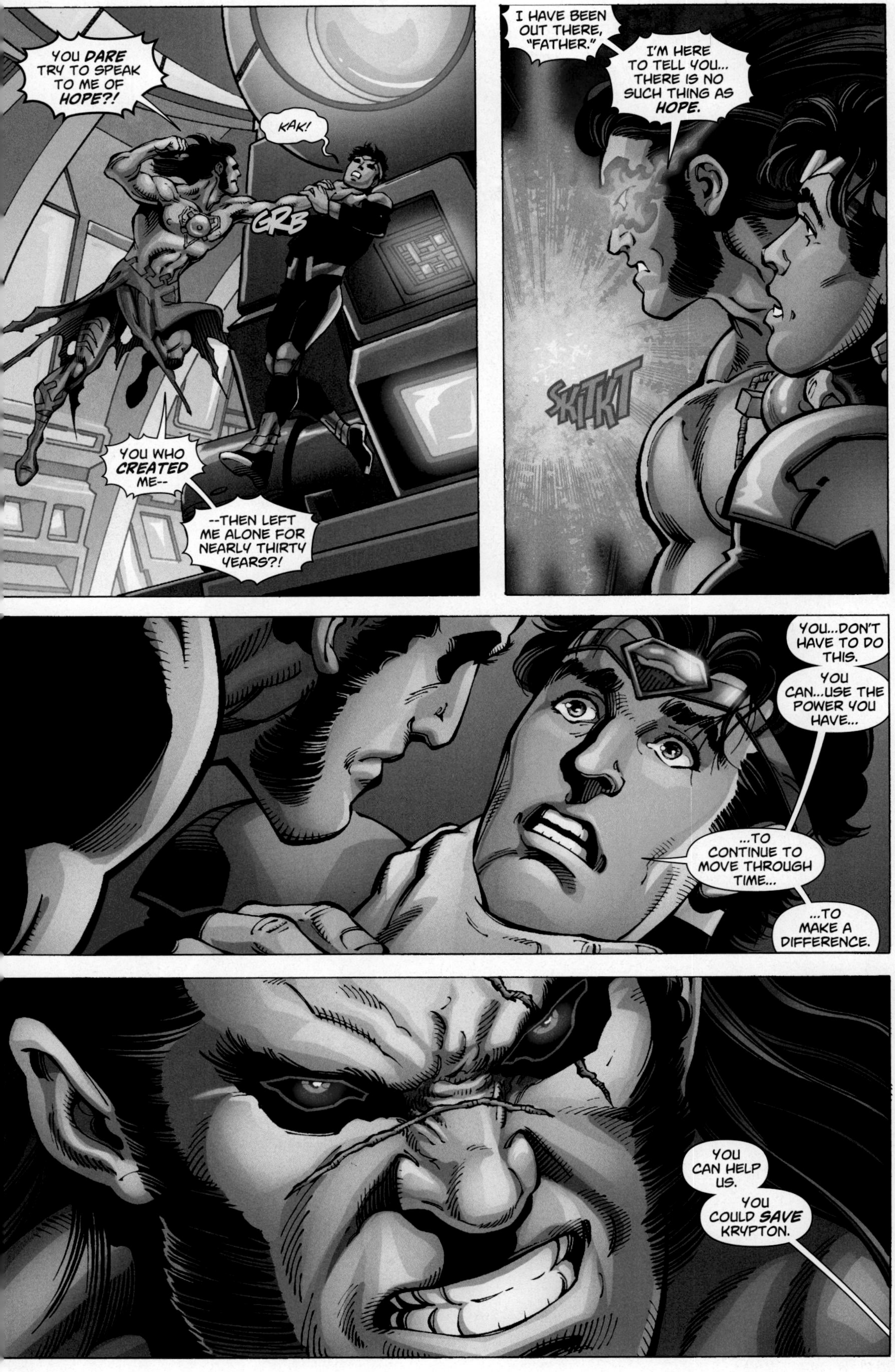
YOU DARE TRY TO SPEAK TO ME OF HOPE?!
KAK!
GRB
YOU WHO CREATED ME--
--THEN LEFT ME ALONE FOR NEARLY THIRTY YEARS?!
I HAVE BEEN OUT THERE, "FATHER."
I'M HERE TO TELL YOU... THERE IS NO SUCH THING AS HOPE.
SKITKT
YOU...DON'T HAVE TO DO THIS.
YOU CAN...USE THE POWER YOU HAVE...
...TO CONTINUE TO MOVE THROUGH TIME...
...TO MAKE A DIFFERENCE.
YOU CAN HELP US.
YOU COULD SAVE KRYPTON.

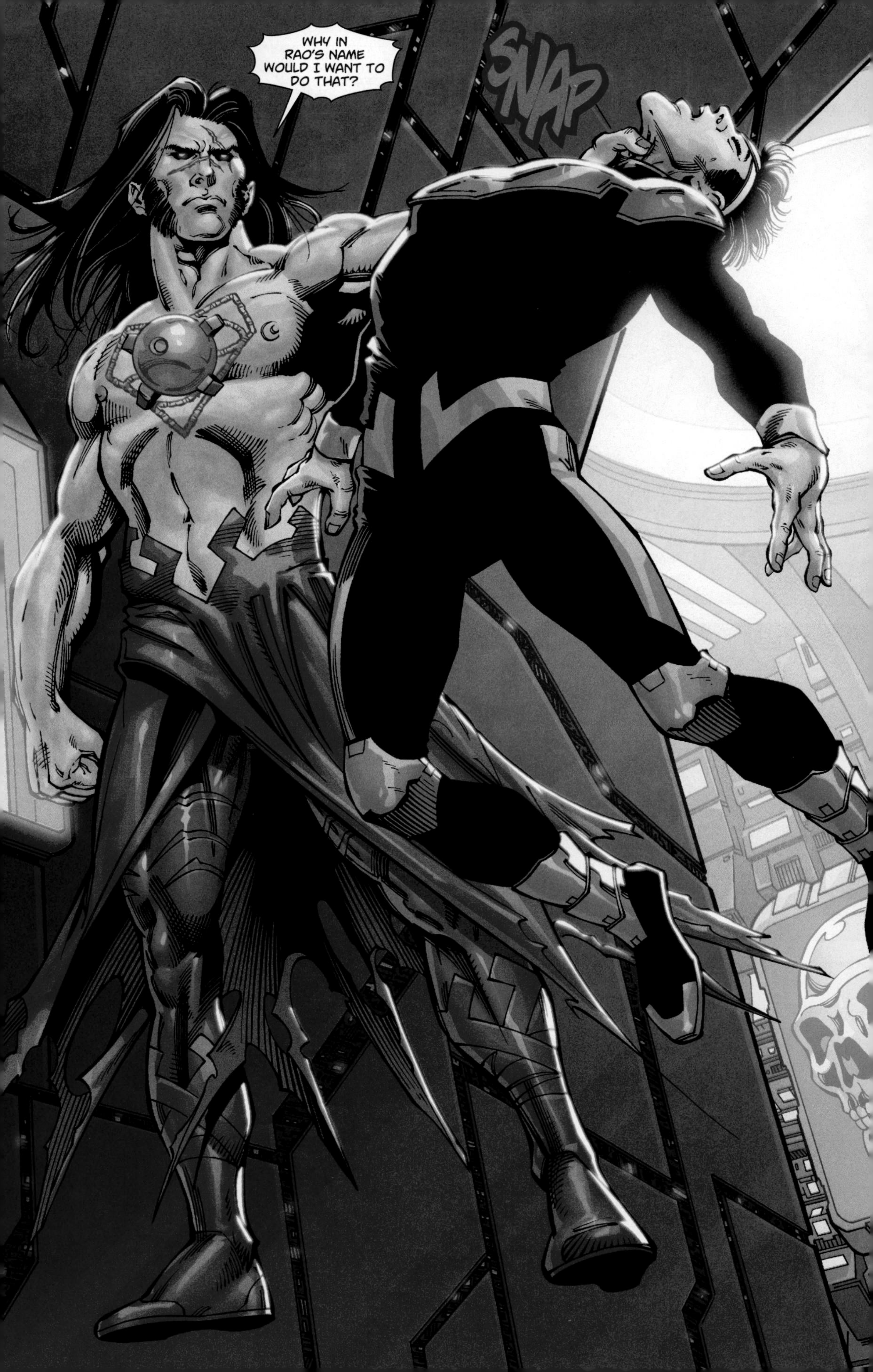
WHY IN RAO'S NAME WOULD I WANT TO DO THAT?
SNAP

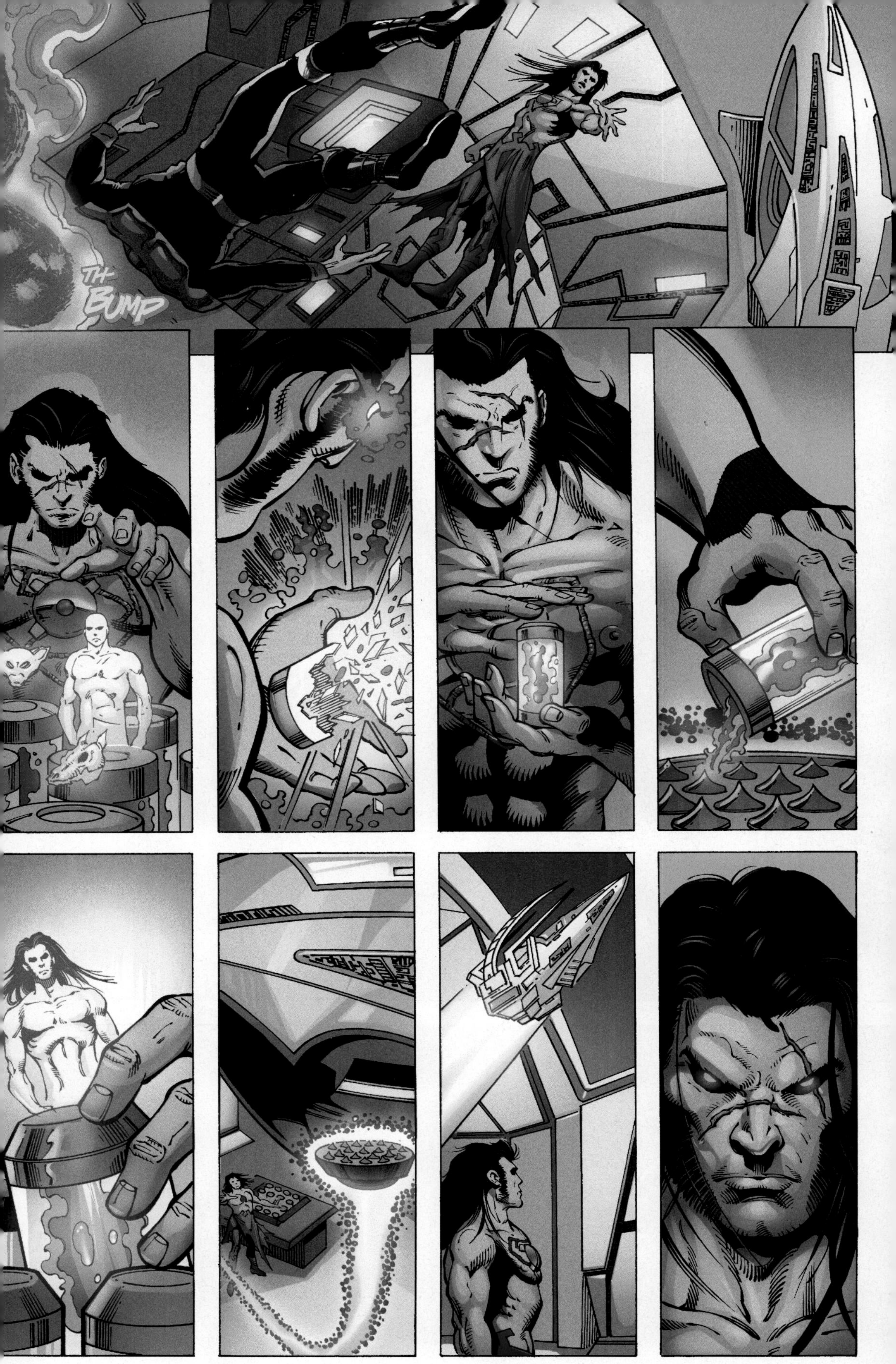
TH-BUMP

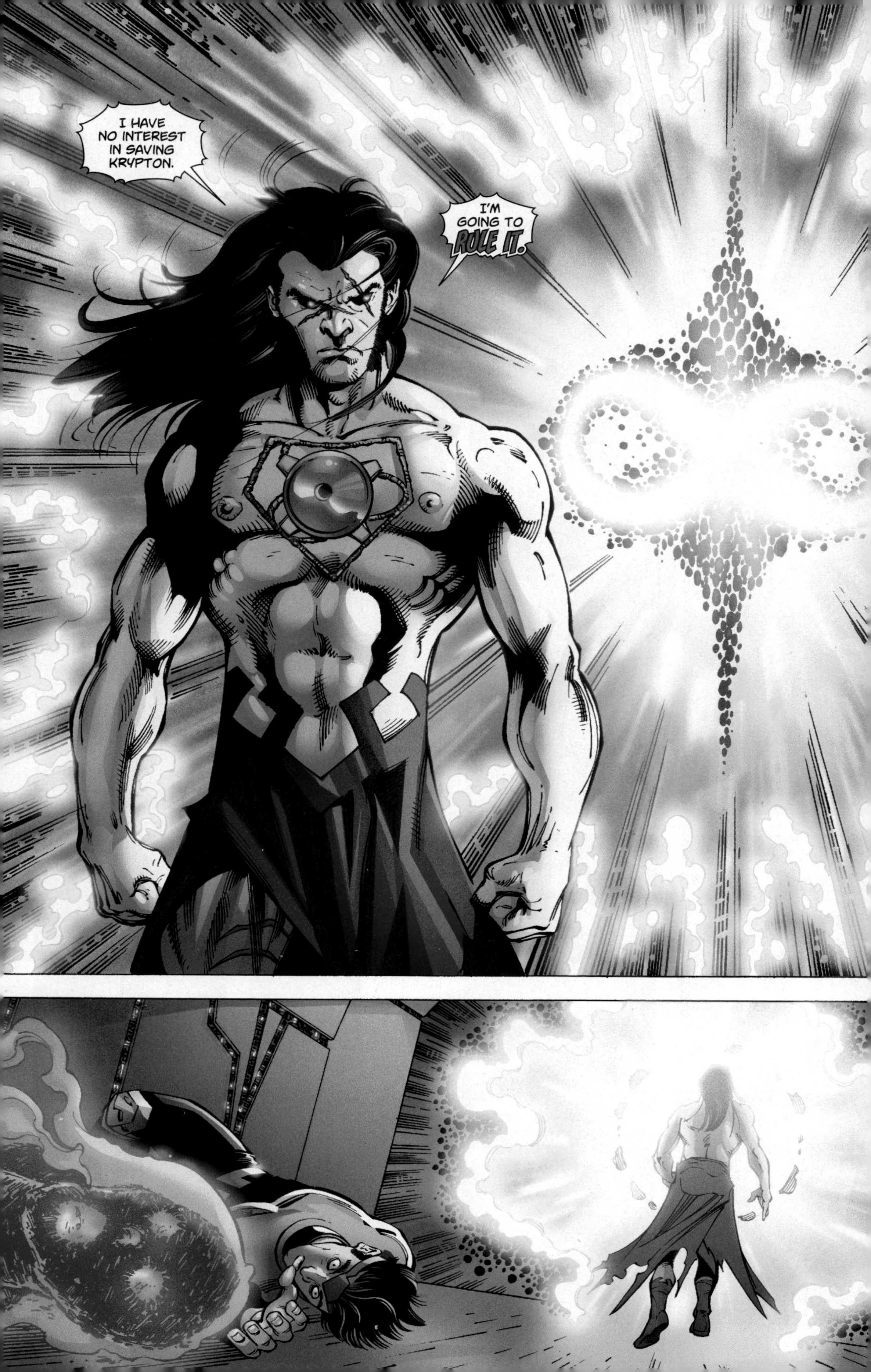
I HAVE NO INTEREST IN SAVING KRYPTON.
I'M GOING TO RULE IT.

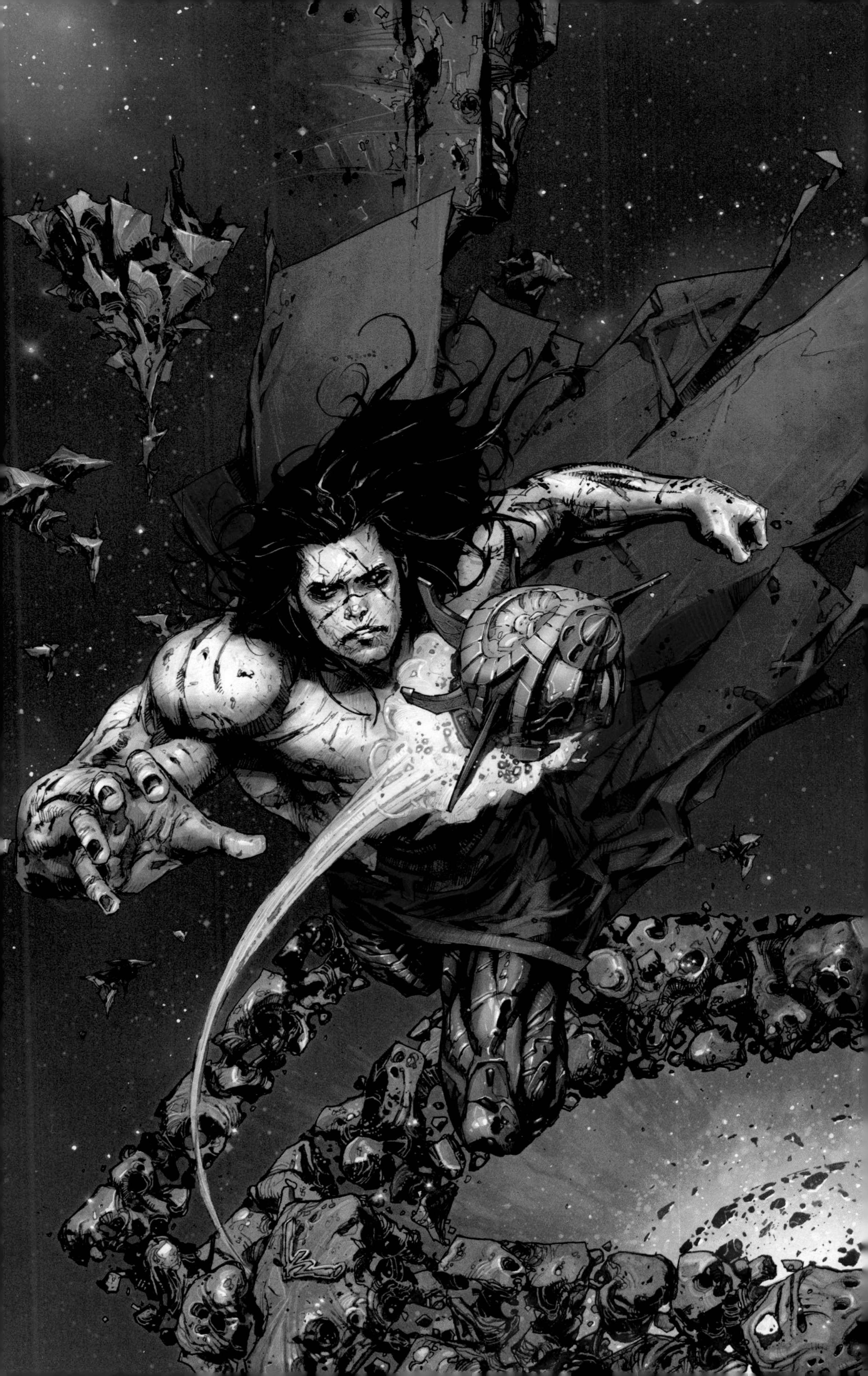

KRYPTON RETURNS PART ONE

SCOTT LOBDELL writer **KENNETH ROCAFORT DAN JURGENS** artists **TOMEU MOREY BLOND** colorists

cover art by **KENNETH ROCAFORT**

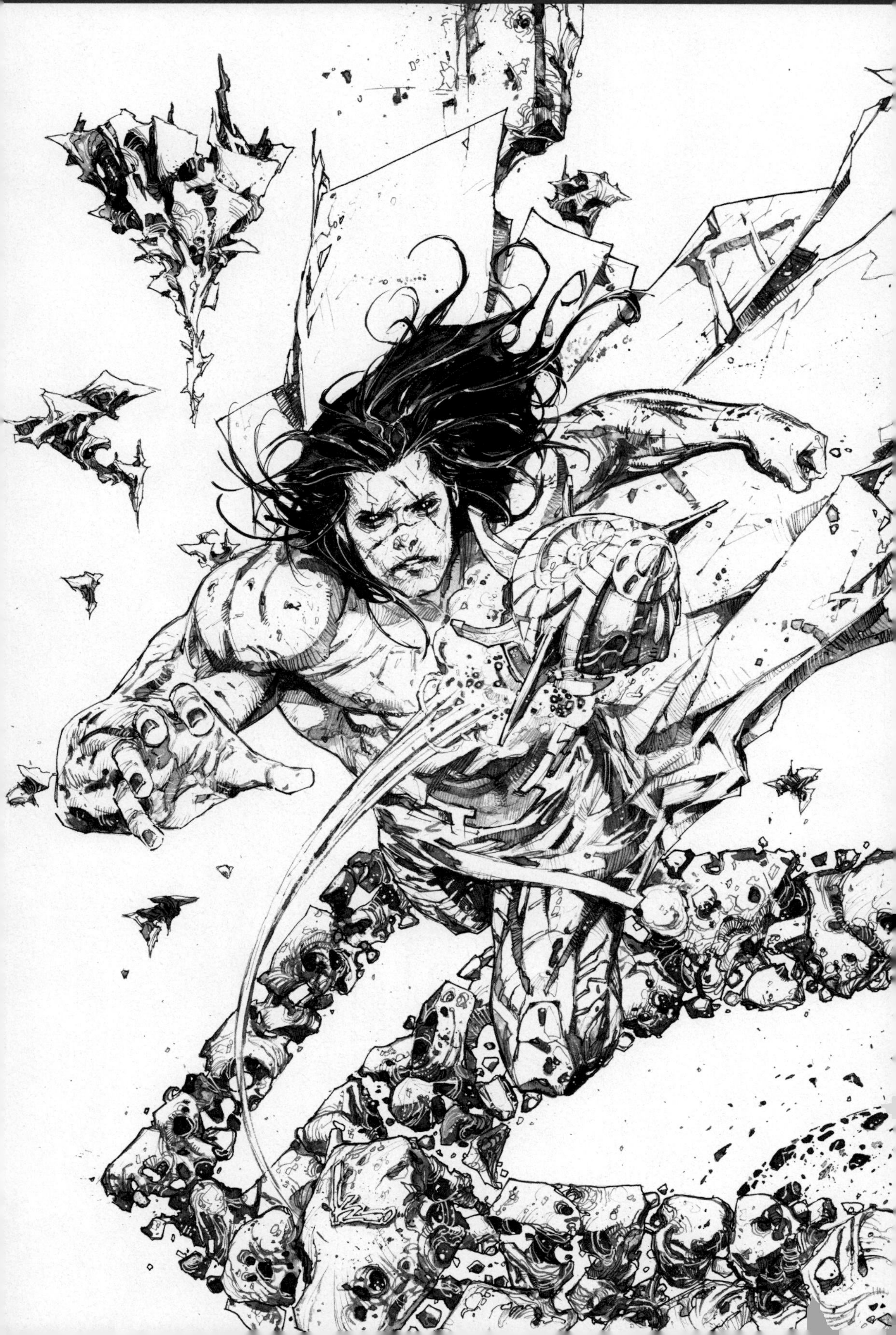

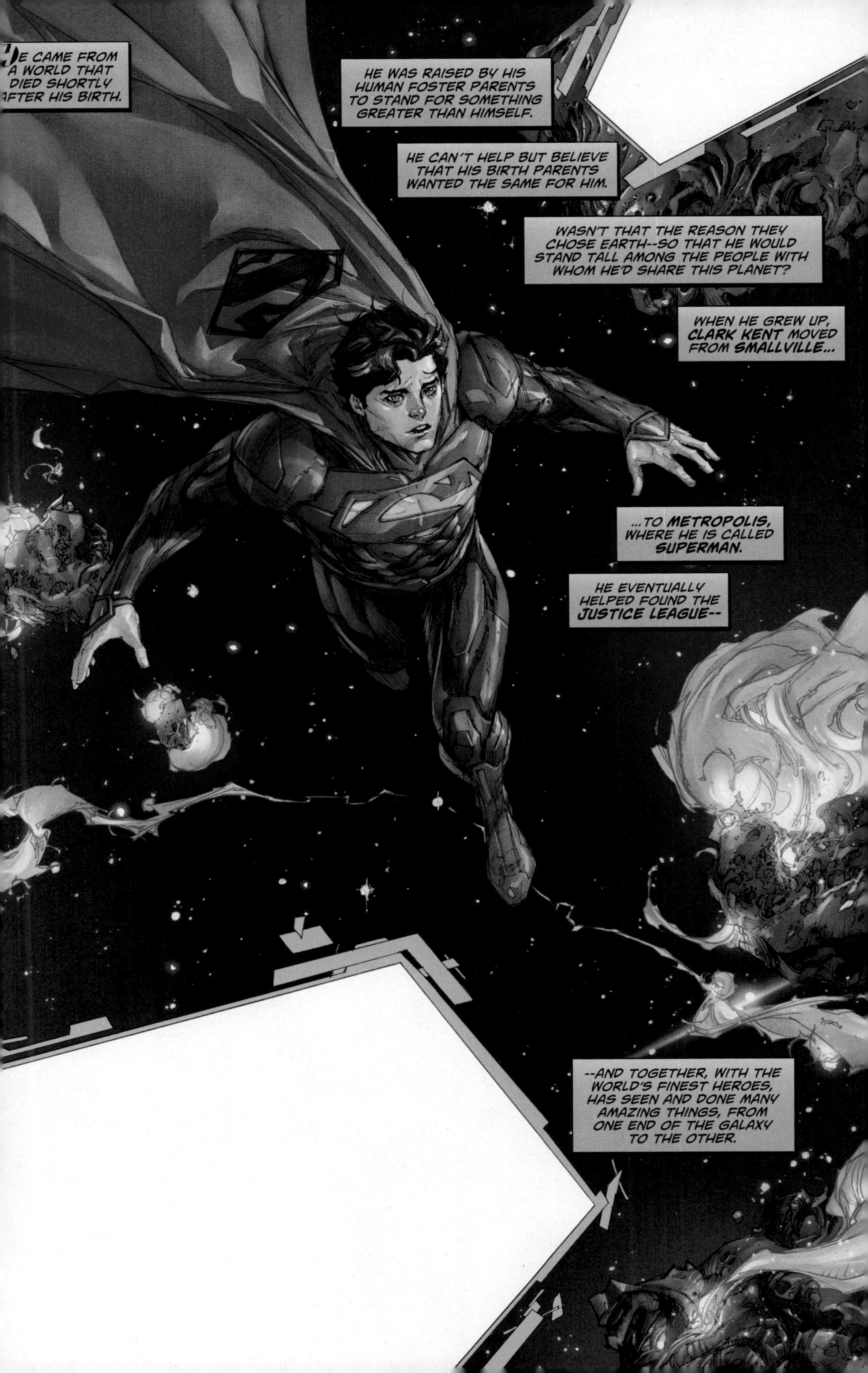
HE CAME FROM A WORLD THAT DIED SHORTLY AFTER HIS BIRTH.
HE WAS RAISED BY HIS HUMAN FOSTER PARENTS TO STAND FOR SOMETHING GREATER THAN HIMSELF.
HE CAN'T HELP BUT BELIEVE THAT HIS BIRTH PARENTS WANTED THE SAME FOR HIM.
WASN'T THAT THE REASON THEY CHOSE EARTH--SO THAT HE WOULD STAND TALL AMONG THE PEOPLE WITH WHOM HE'D SHARE THIS PLANET?
WHEN HE GREW UP, CLARK KENT MOVED FROM SMALLVILLE...
...TO METROPOLIS, WHERE HE IS CALLED SUPERMAN.
HE EVENTUALLY HELPED FOUND THE JUSTICE LEAGUE--
--AND TOGETHER, WITH THE WORLD'S FINEST HEROES, HAS SEEN AND DONE MANY AMAZING THINGS, FROM ONE END OF THE GALAXY TO THE OTHER.

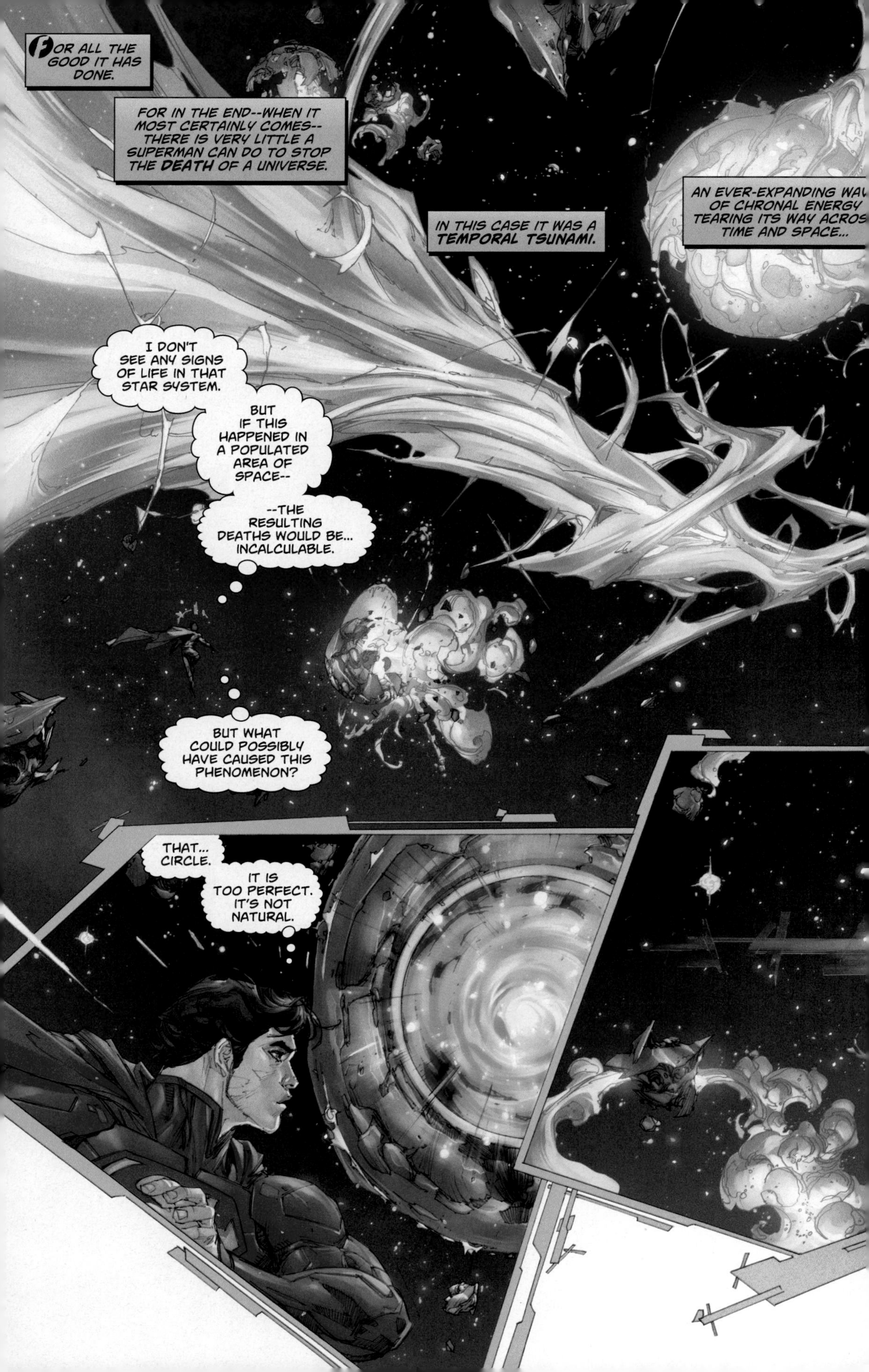
FOR ALL THE GOOD IT HAS DONE.
FOR IN THE END--WHEN IT MOST CERTAINLY COMES--THERE IS VERY LITTLE A SUPERMAN CAN DO TO STOP THE DEATH OF A UNIVERSE.
IN THIS CASE IT WAS A TEMPORAL TSUNAMI.
AN EVER-EXPANDING WAV OF CHRONAL ENERGY TEARING ITS WAY ACROS TIME AND SPACE...
I DON'T SEE ANY SIGNS OF LIFE IN THAT STAR SYSTEM.
BUT IF THIS HAPPENED IN A POPULATED AREA OF SPACE--
--THE RESULTING DEATHS WOULD BE... INCALCULABLE.
BUT WHAT COULD POSSIBLY HAVE CAUSED THIS PHENOMENON?
THAT... CIRCLE.
IT IS TOO PERFECT. IT'S NOT NATURAL.

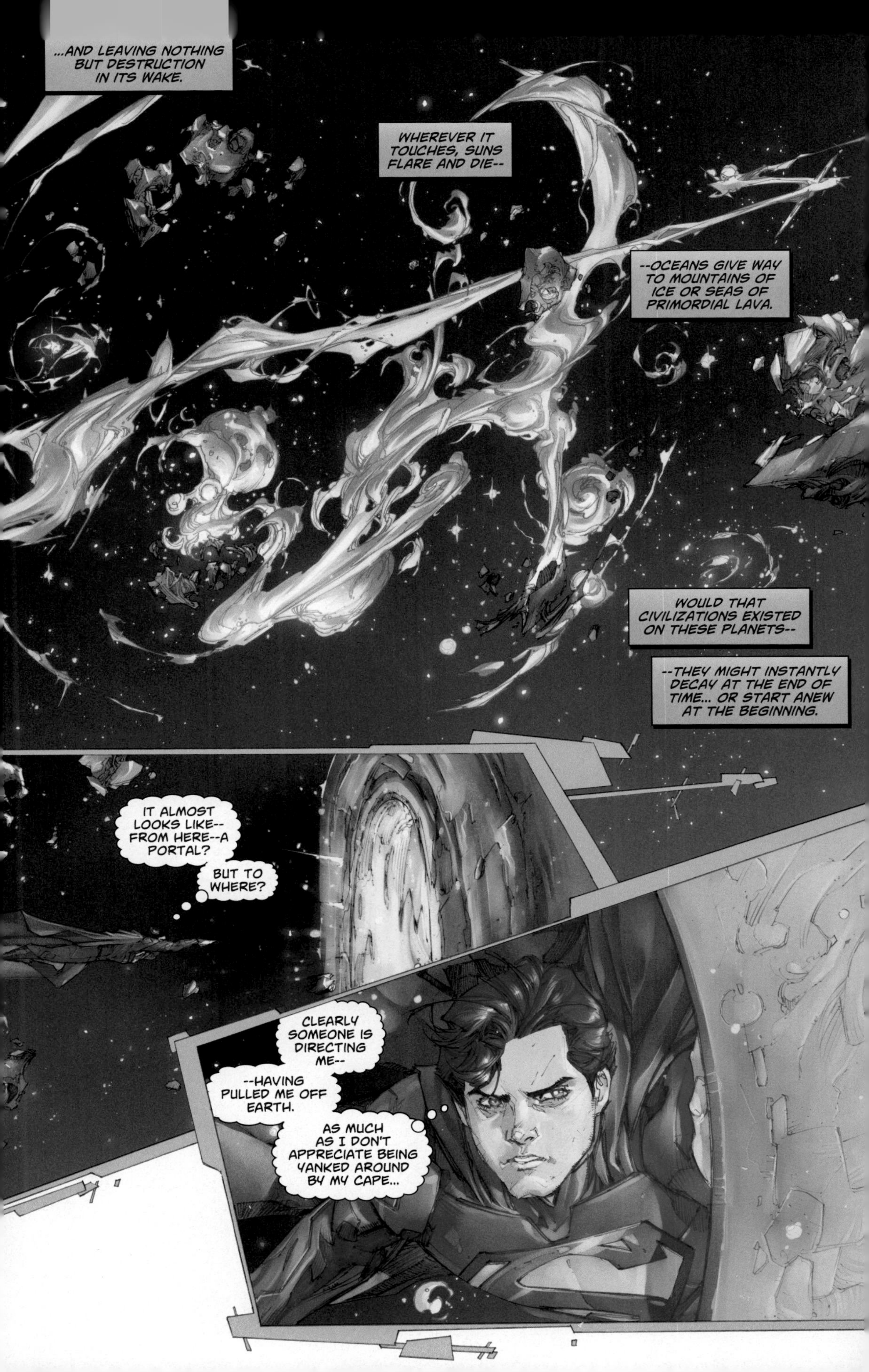
...AND LEAVING NOTHING BUT DESTRUCTION IN ITS WAKE.
WHEREVER IT TOUCHES, SUNS FLARE AND DIE--
--OCEANS GIVE WAY TO MOUNTAINS OF ICE OR SEAS OF PRIMORDIAL LAVA.
WOULD THAT CIVILIZATIONS EXISTED ON THESE PLANETS--
--THEY MIGHT INSTANTLY DECAY AT THE END OF TIME... OR START ANEW AT THE BEGINNING.
IT ALMOST LOOKS LIKE-- FROM HERE--A PORTAL?
BUT TO WHERE?
CLEARLY SOMEONE IS DIRECTING ME--
--HAVING PULLED ME OFF EARTH.
AS MUCH AS I DON'T APPRECIATE BEING YANKED AROUND BY MY CAPE...

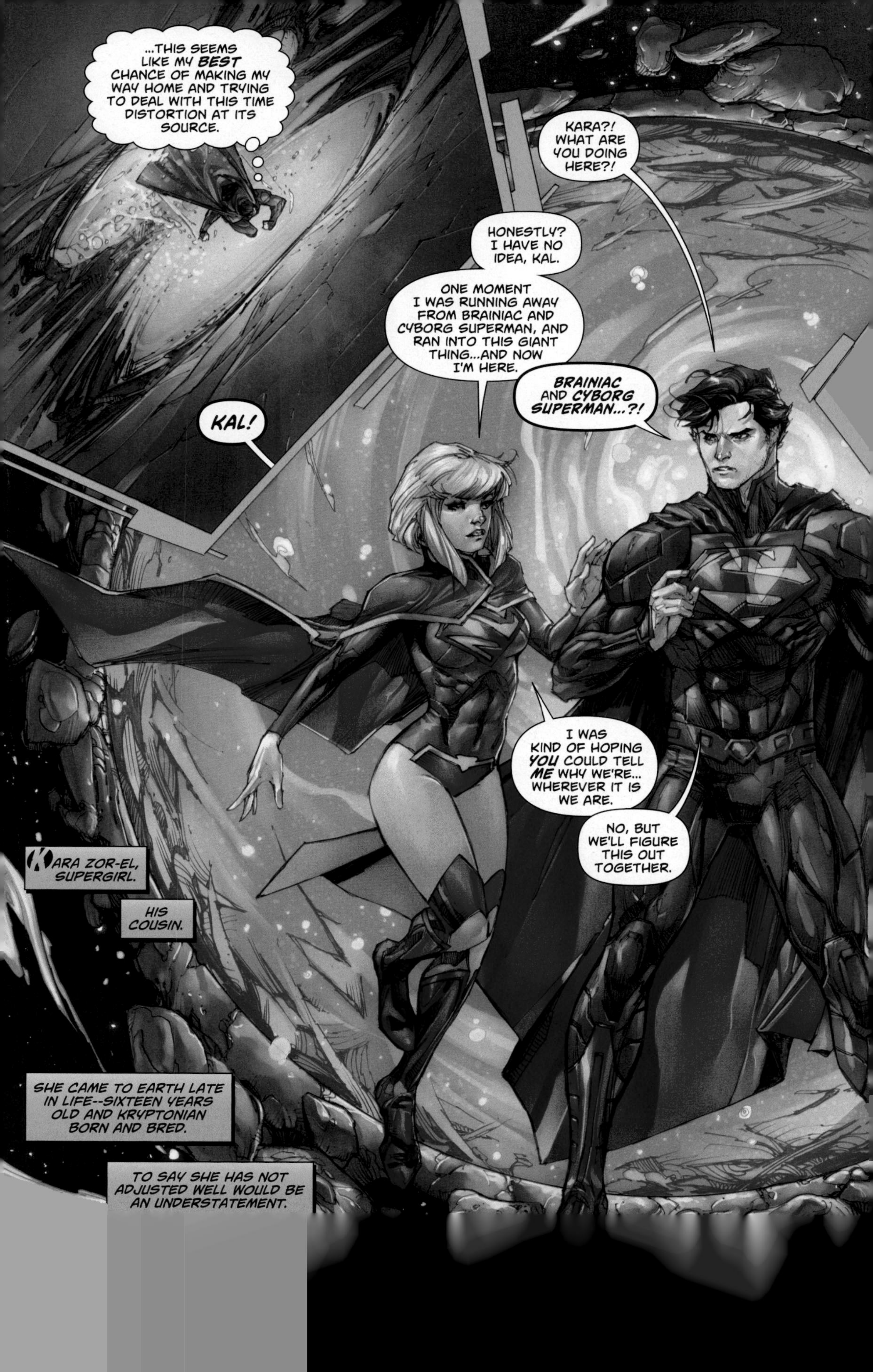
...THIS SEEMS LIKE MY BEST CHANCE OF MAKING MY WAY HOME AND TRYING TO DEAL WITH THIS TIME DISTORTION AT ITS SOURCE.
KARA?! WHAT ARE YOU DOING HERE?!
HONESTLY? I HAVE NO IDEA, KAL.
ONE MOMENT I WAS RUNNING AWAY FROM BRAINIAC AND CYBORG SUPERMAN, AND RAN INTO THIS GIANT THING...AND NOW I'M HERE.
KAL!
BRAINIAC AND CYBORG SUPERMAN...?!
I WAS KIND OF HOPING YOU COULD TELL ME WHY WE'RE... WHEREVER IT IS WE ARE.
NO, BUT WE'LL FIGURE THIS OUT TOGETHER.
KARA ZOR-EL, SUPERGIRL.
HIS COUSIN.
SHE CAME TO EARTH LATE IN LIFE--SIXTEEN YEARS OLD AND KRYPTONIAN BORN AND BRED.
TO SAY SHE HAS NOT ADJUSTED WELL WOULD BE AN UNDERSTATEMENT.

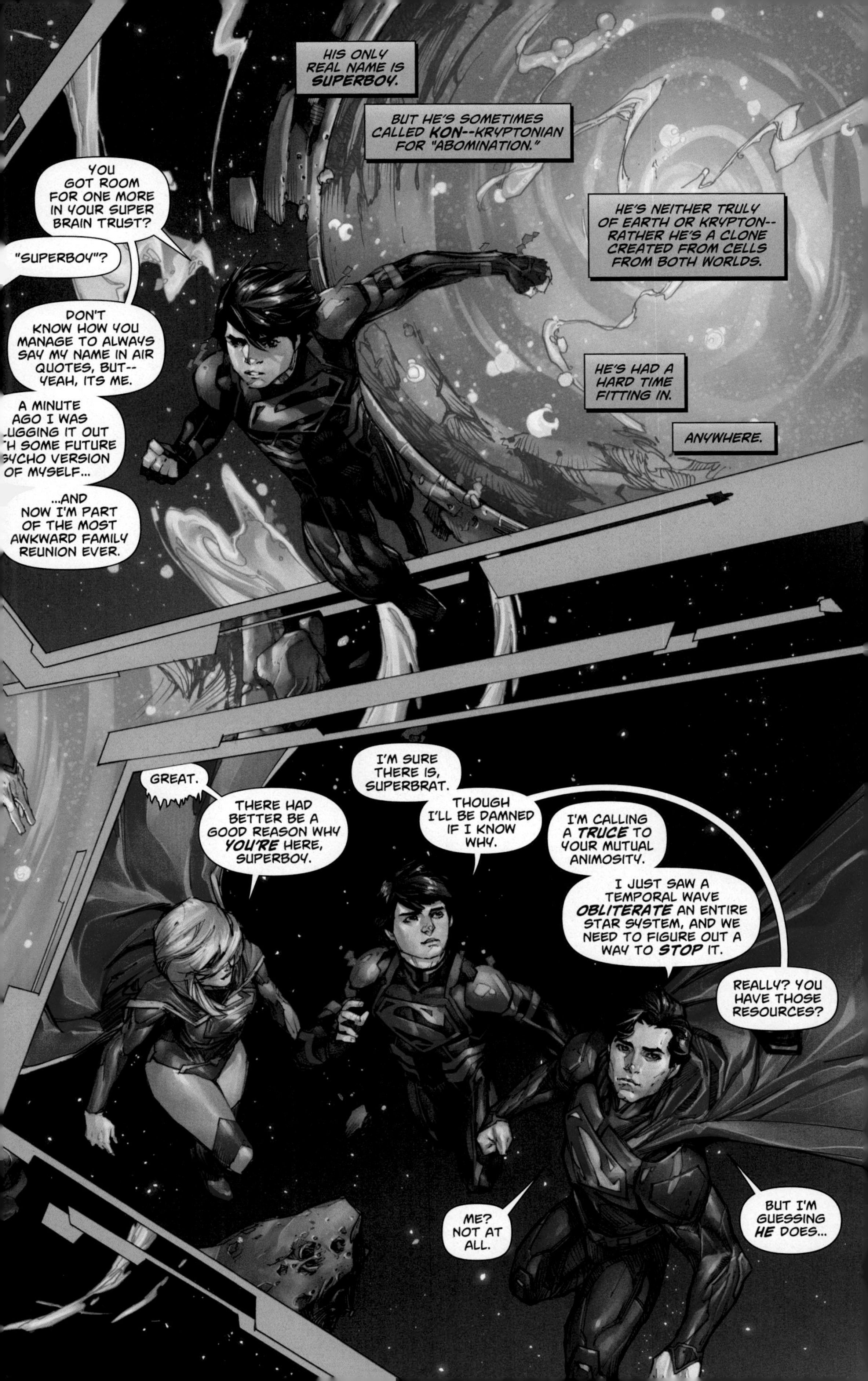

HIS ONLY REAL NAME IS SUPERBOY.
BUT HE'S SOMETIMES CALLED KON--KRYPTONIAN FOR "ABOMINATION."
YOU GOT ROOM FOR ONE MORE IN YOUR SUPER BRAIN TRUST?
"SUPERBOY"?
DON'T KNOW HOW YOU MANAGE TO ALWAYS SAY MY NAME IN AIR QUOTES, BUT-- YEAH, ITS ME.
HE'S NEITHER TRULY OF EARTH OR KRYPTON-- RATHER HE'S A CLONE CREATED FROM CELLS FROM BOTH WORLDS.
A MINUTE AGO I WAS
OF MYSELF...
...AND NOW I'M PART OF THE MOST AWKWARD FAMILY REUNION EVER.
HE'S HAD A HARD TIME FITTING IN.
ANYWHERE.
GREAT.
THERE HAD BETTER BE A GOOD REASON WHY YOU'RE HERE, SUPERBOY.
I'M SURE THERE IS, SUPERBRAT.
THOUGH I'LL BE DAMNED IF I KNOW WHY.
I'M CALLING A TRUCE TO YOUR MUTUAL ANIMOSITY.
I JUST SAW A TEMPORAL WAVE OBLITERATE AN ENTIRE STAR SYSTEM, AND WE NEED TO FIGURE OUT A WAY TO STOP IT.
REALLY? YOU HAVE THOSE RESOURCES?
ME? NOT AT ALL.
BUT I'M GUESSING HE DOES...

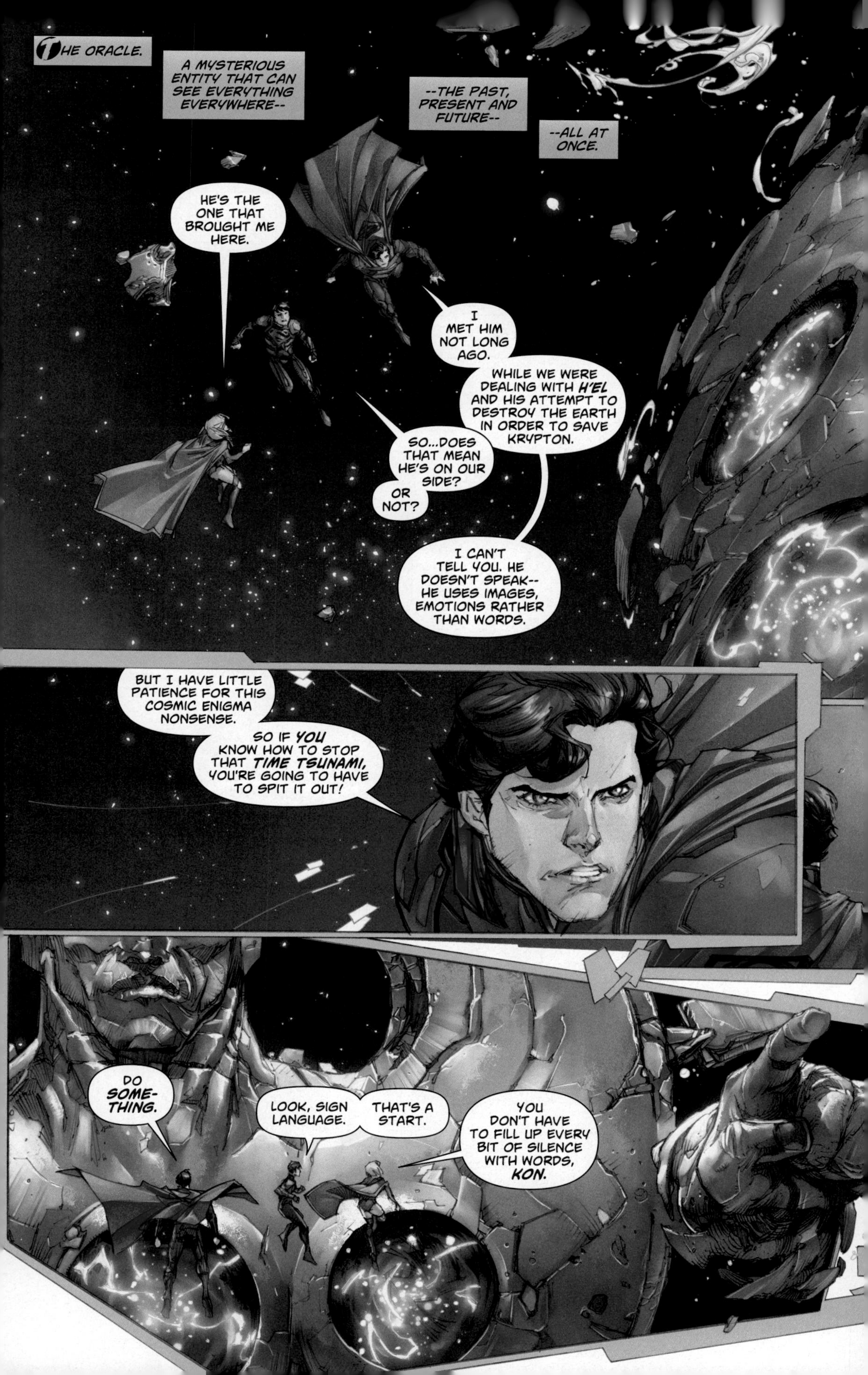
THE ORACLE.
A MYSTERIOUS ENTITY THAT CAN SEE EVERYTHING EVERYWHERE--
--THE PAST, PRESENT AND FUTURE--
--ALL AT ONCE.
HE'S THE ONE THAT BROUGHT ME HERE.
I MET HIM NOT LONG AGO.
WHILE WE WERE DEALING WITH H'EL AND HIS ATTEMPT TO DESTROY THE EARTH IN ORDER TO SAVE KRYPTON.
SO...DOES THAT MEAN HE'S ON OUR SIDE?
OR NOT?
I CAN'T TELL YOU. HE DOESN'T SPEAK-- HE USES IMAGES, EMOTIONS RATHER THAN WORDS.
BUT I HAVE LITTLE PATIENCE FOR THIS COSMIC ENIGMA NONSENSE.
SO IF YOU KNOW HOW TO STOP THAT TIME TSUNAMI, YOU'RE GOING TO HAVE TO SPIT IT OUT!
DO SOME- THING.
LOOK, SIGN LANGUAGE.
THAT'S A START.
YOU DON'T HAVE TO FILL UP EVERY BIT OF SILENCE WITH WORDS, KON.

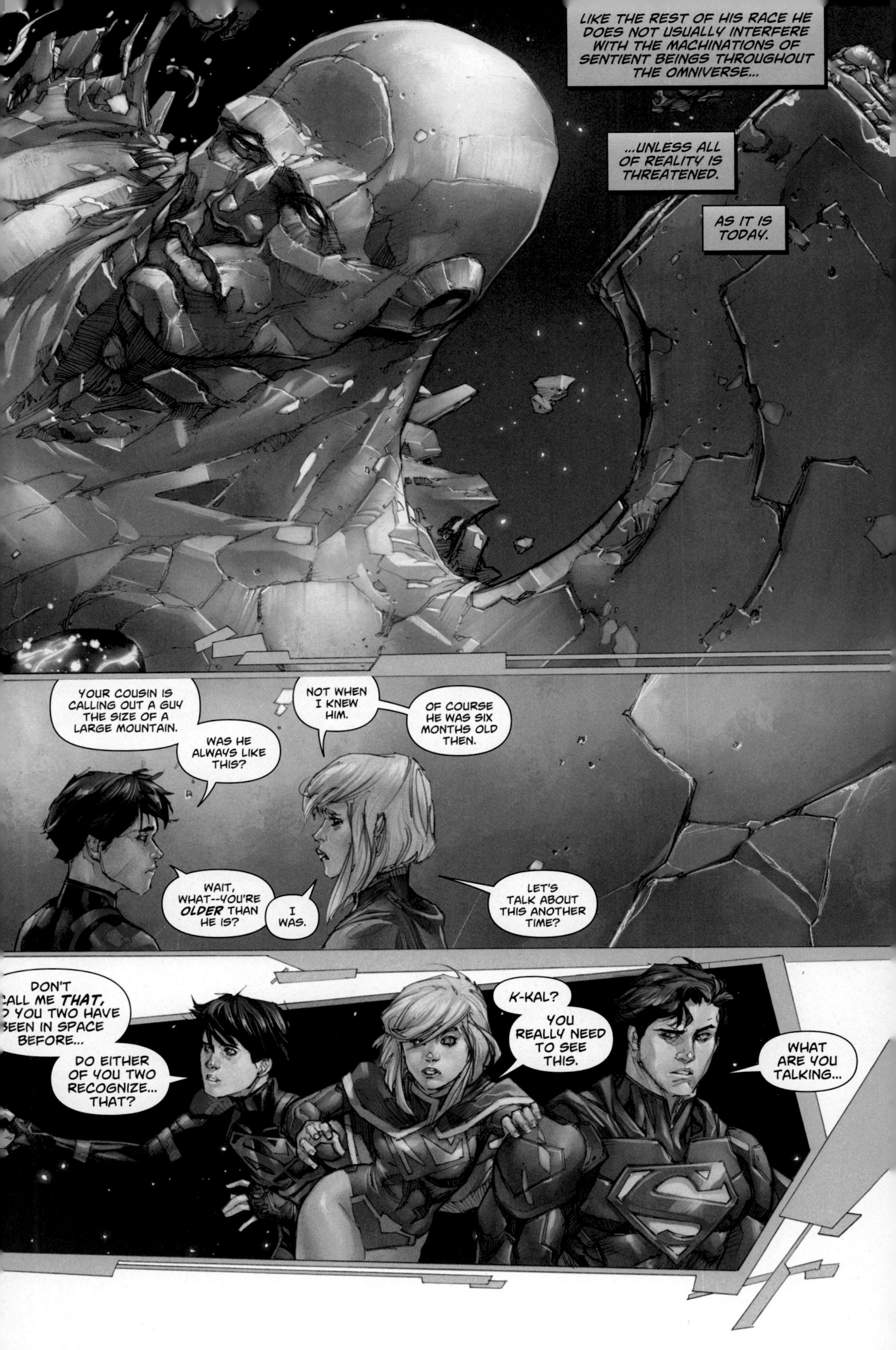
LIKE THE REST OF HIS RACE HE DOES NOT USUALLY INTERFERE WITH THE MACHINATIONS OF SENTIENT BEINGS THROUGHOUT THE OMNIVERSE...
...UNLESS ALL OF REALITY IS THREATENED.
AS IT IS TODAY.
YOUR COUSIN IS CALLING OUT A GUY THE SIZE OF A LARGE MOUNTAIN.
WAS HE ALWAYS LIKE THIS?
NOT WHEN I KNEW HIM.
OF COURSE HE WAS SIX MONTHS OLD THEN.
WAIT, WHAT--YOU'RE OLDER THAN HE IS?
I WAS.
LET'S TALK ABOUT THIS ANOTHER TIME?
DON'T CALL ME THAT, O YOU TWO HAVE BEEN IN SPACE BEFORE...
DO EITHER OF YOU TWO RECOGNIZE... THAT?
K-KAL?
YOU REALLY NEED TO SEE THIS.
WHAT ARE YOU TALKING...

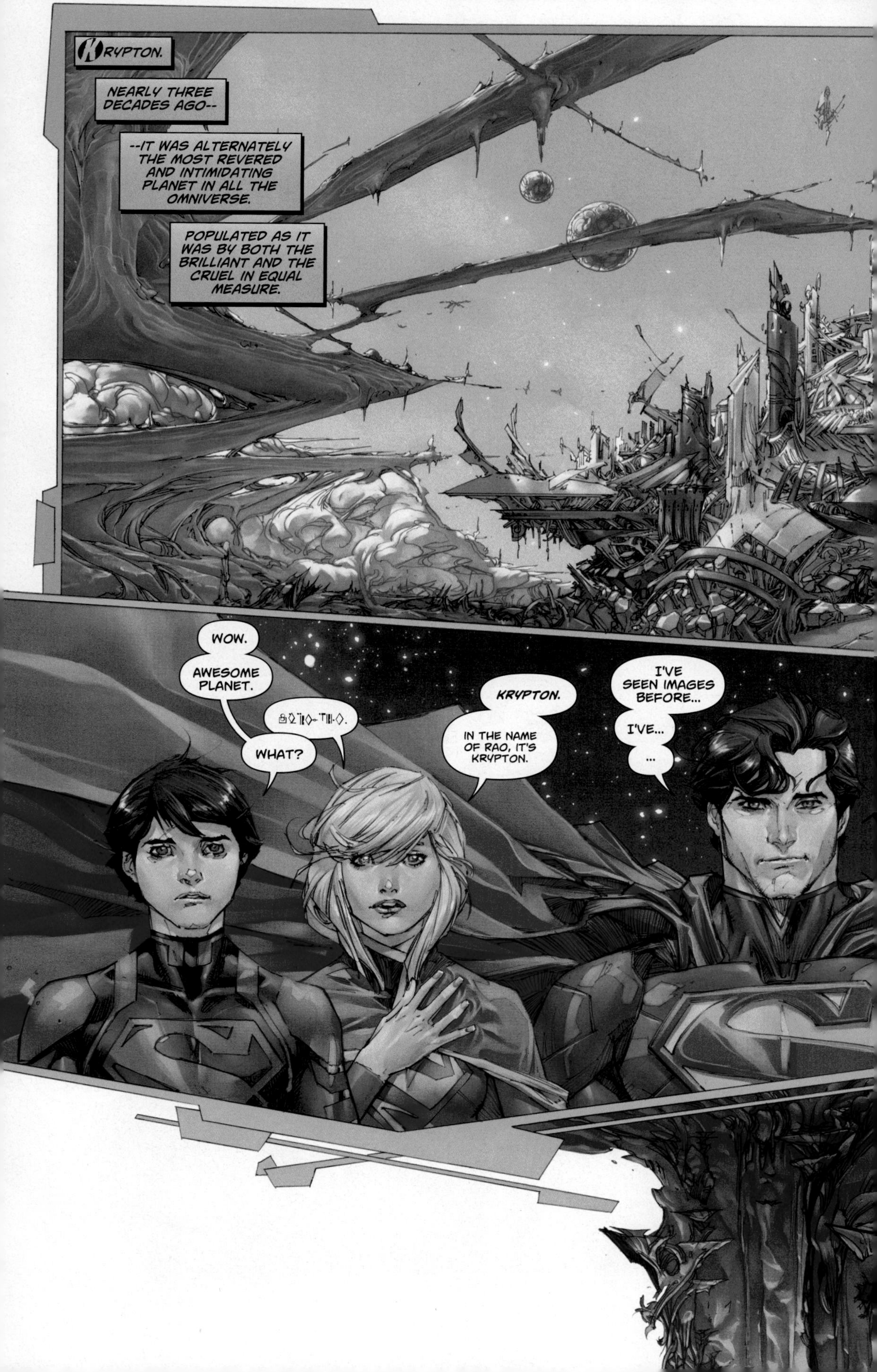
KRYPTON.
NEARLY THREE DECADES AGO--
--IT WAS ALTERNATELY THE MOST REVERED AND INTIMIDATING PLANET IN ALL THE OMNIVERSE.
POPULATED AS IT WAS BY BOTH THE BRILLIANT AND THE CRUEL IN EQUAL MEASURE.
WOW.
AWESOME PLANET.
WHAT?
KRYPTON.
IN THE NAME OF RAO, IT'S KRYPTON.
I'VE SEEN IMAGES BEFORE...
I'VE...
...

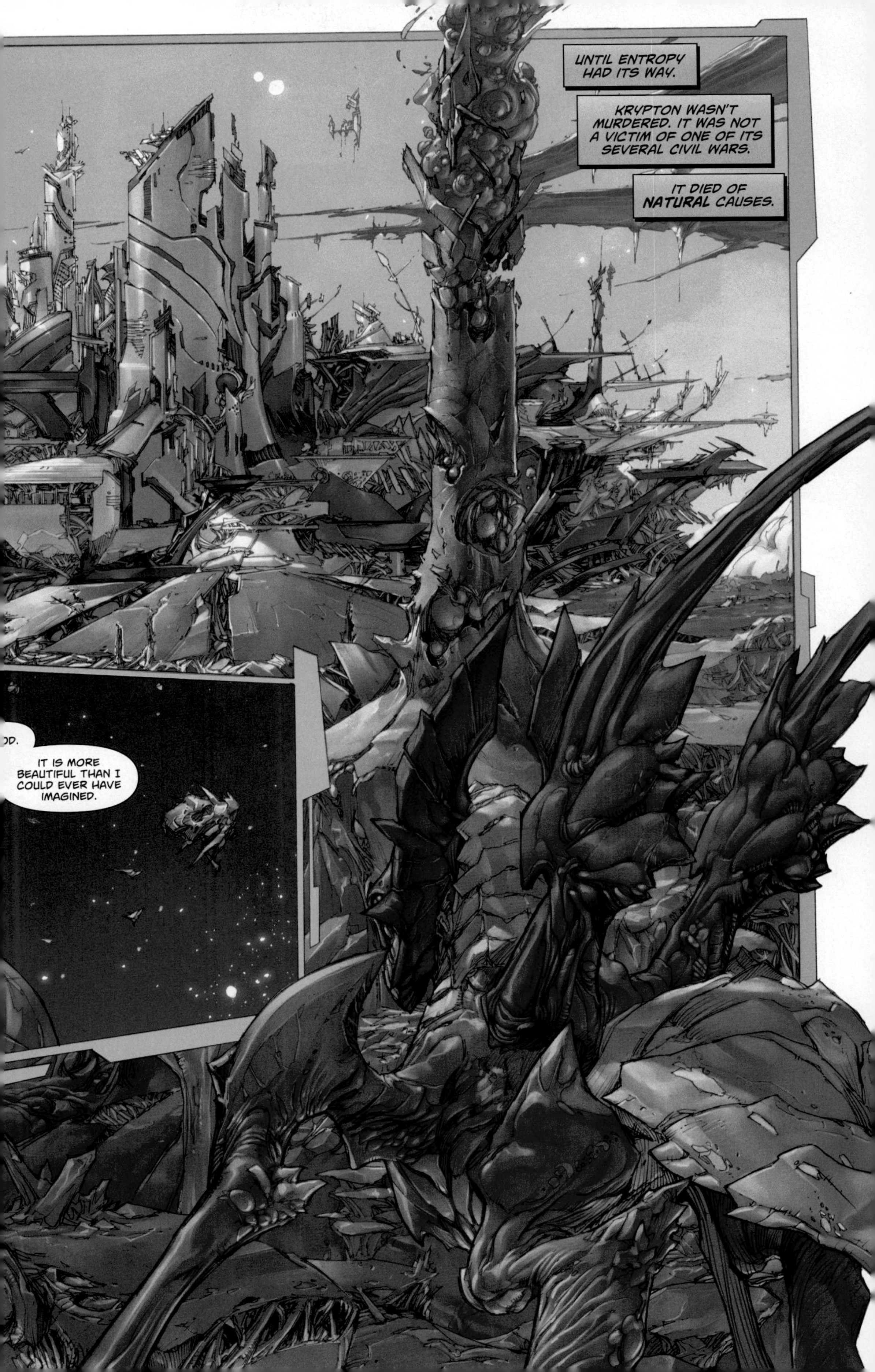
UNTIL ENTROPY HAD ITS WAY.
KRYPTON WASN'T MURDERED. IT WAS NOT A VICTIM OF ONE OF ITS SEVERAL CIVIL WARS.
IT DIED OF NATURAL CAUSES.
IT IS MORE BEAUTIFUL THAN I COULD EVER HAVE IMAGINED.

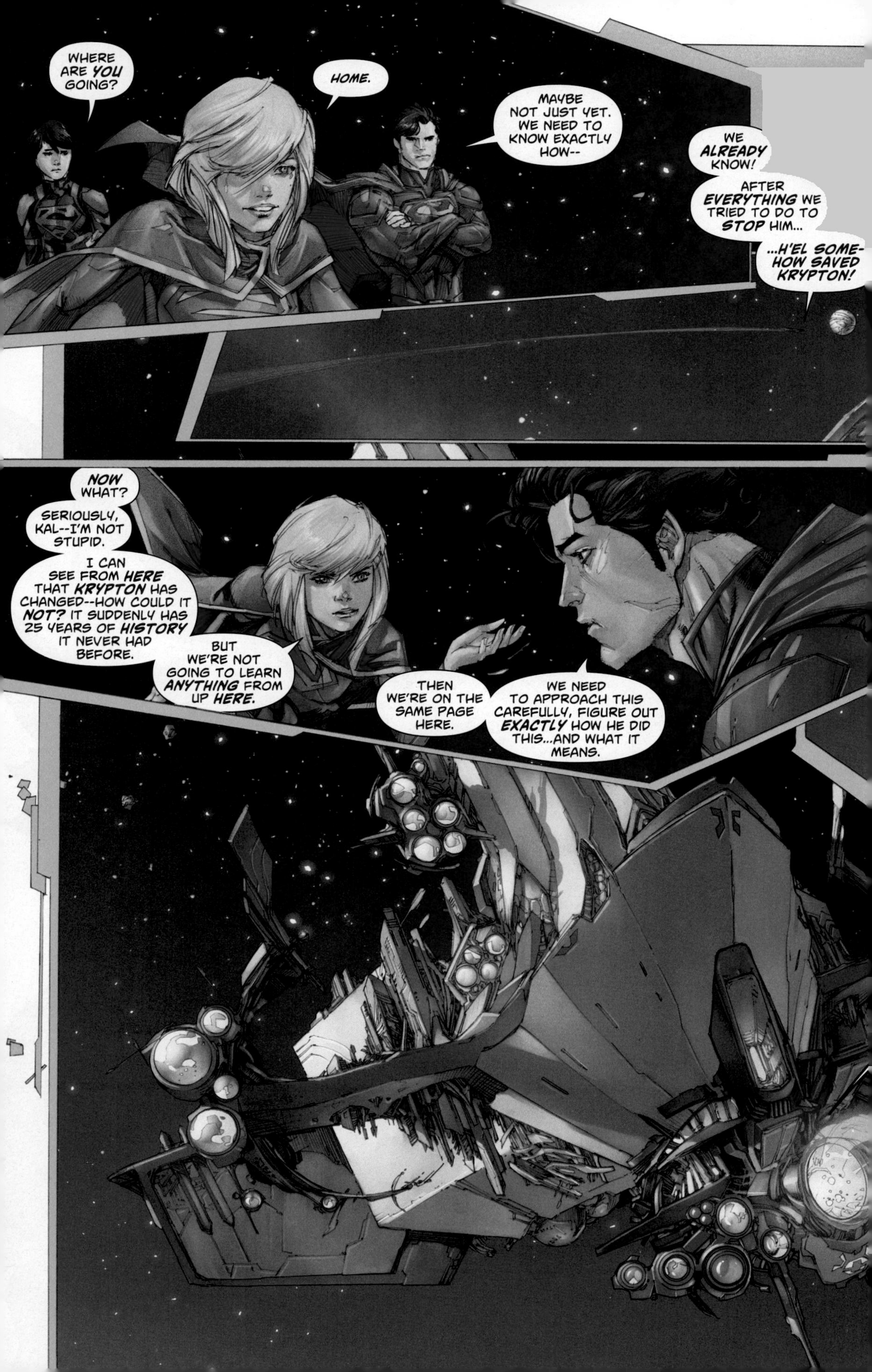
WHERE ARE YOU GOING?
HOME.
MAYBE NOT JUST YET. WE NEED TO KNOW EXACTLY HOW--
WE ALREADY KNOW!
AFTER EVERYTHING WE TRIED TO DO TO STOP HIM...
...H'EL SOMEHOW SAVED KRYPTON!
NOW WHAT?
SERIOUSLY, KAL--I'M NOT STUPID.
I CAN SEE FROM HERE THAT KRYPTON HAS CHANGED--HOW COULD IT NOT? IT SUDDENLY HAS 25 YEARS OF HISTORY IT NEVER HAD BEFORE.
BUT WE'RE NOT GOING TO LEARN ANYTHING FROM UP HERE.
THEN WE'RE ON THE SAME PAGE HERE.
WE NEED TO APPROACH THIS CAREFULLY, FIGURE OUT EXACTLY HOW HE DID THIS...AND WHAT IT MEANS.

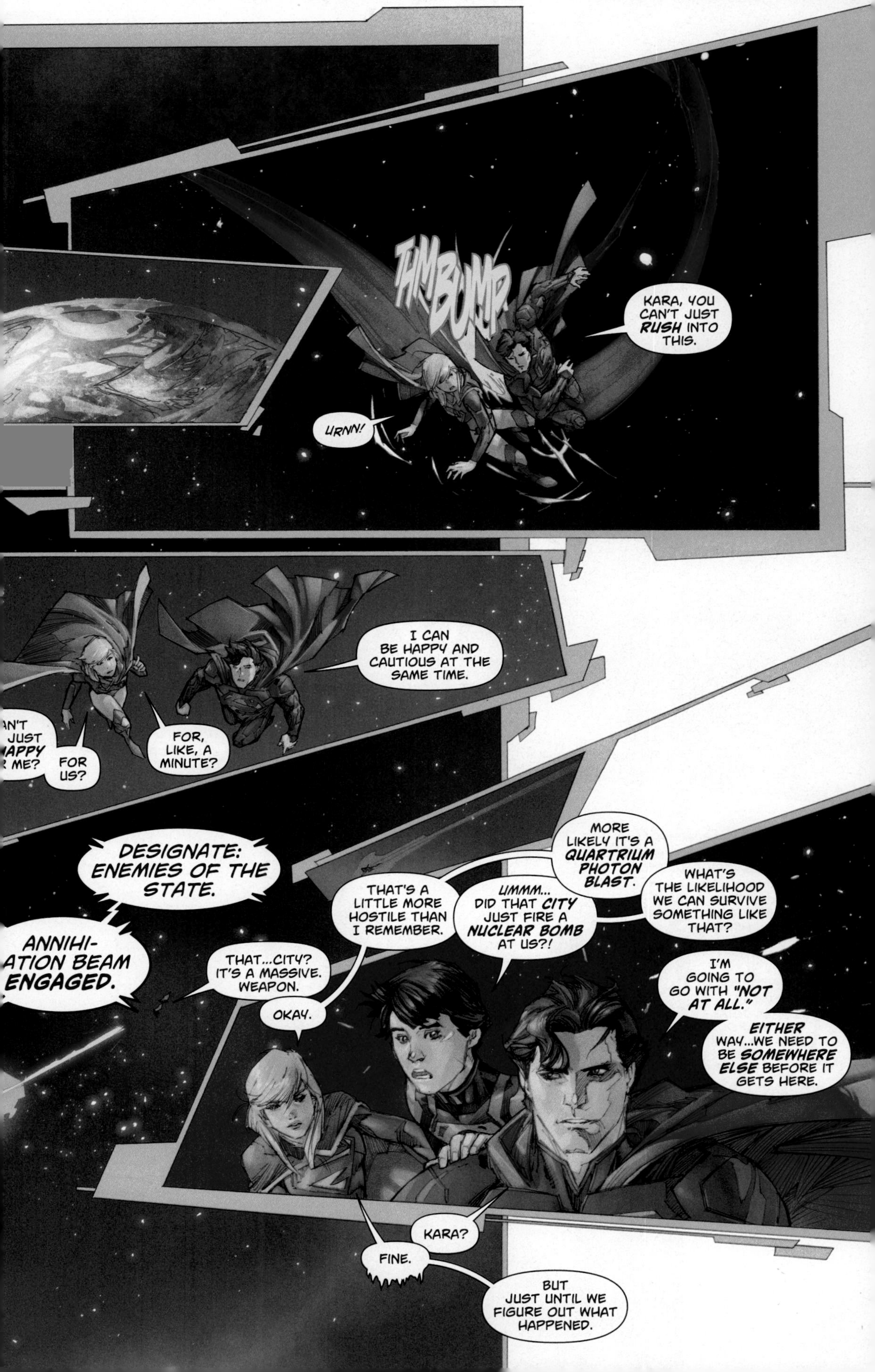
THMBUMP
KARA, YOU CAN'T JUST RUSH INTO THIS.
URNN!
I CAN BE HAPPY AND CAUTIOUS AT THE SAME TIME.
AN'T JUST HAPPY R ME?
FOR US?
FOR, LIKE, A MINUTE?
DESIGNATE: ENEMIES OF THE STATE.
ANNIHI- ATION BEAM ENGAGED.
THAT...CITY? IT'S A MASSIVE. WEAPON.
OKAY.
THAT'S A LITTLE MORE HOSTILE THAN I REMEMBER.
UMMM... DID THAT CITY JUST FIRE A NUCLEAR BOMB AT US?!
MORE LIKELY IT'S A QUARTRIUM PHOTON BLAST.
WHAT'S THE LIKELIHOOD WE CAN SURVIVE SOMETHING LIKE THAT?
I'M GOING TO GO WITH "NOT AT ALL."
EITHER WAY...WE NEED TO BE SOMEWHERE ELSE BEFORE IT GETS HERE.
KARA?
FINE.
BUT JUST UNTIL WE FIGURE OUT WHAT HAPPENED.

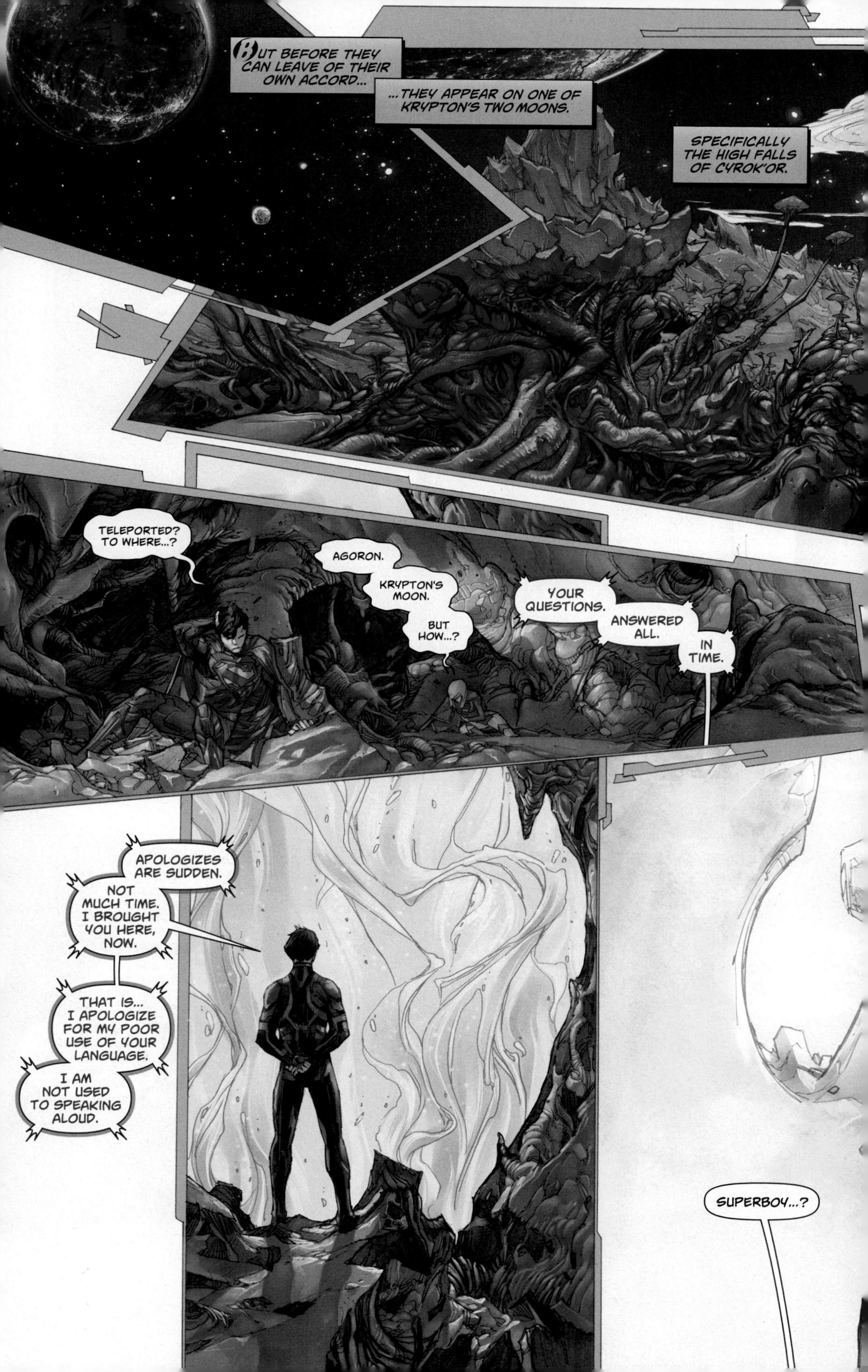
BUT BEFORE THEY CAN LEAVE OF THEIR OWN ACCORD...
...THEY APPEAR ON ONE OF KRYPTON'S TWO MOONS.
SPECIFICALLY THE HIGH FALLS OF CYROK'OR.
TELEPORTED? TO WHERE...?
AGORON.
KRYPTON'S MOON.
BUT HOW...?
YOUR QUESTIONS.
ANSWERED ALL.
IN TIME.
APOLOGIZES ARE SUDDEN.
NOT MUCH TIME. I BROUGHT YOU HERE, NOW.
THAT IS... I APOLOGIZE FOR MY POOR USE OF YOUR LANGUAGE.
I AM NOT USED TO SPEAKING ALOUD.
SUPERBOY...?

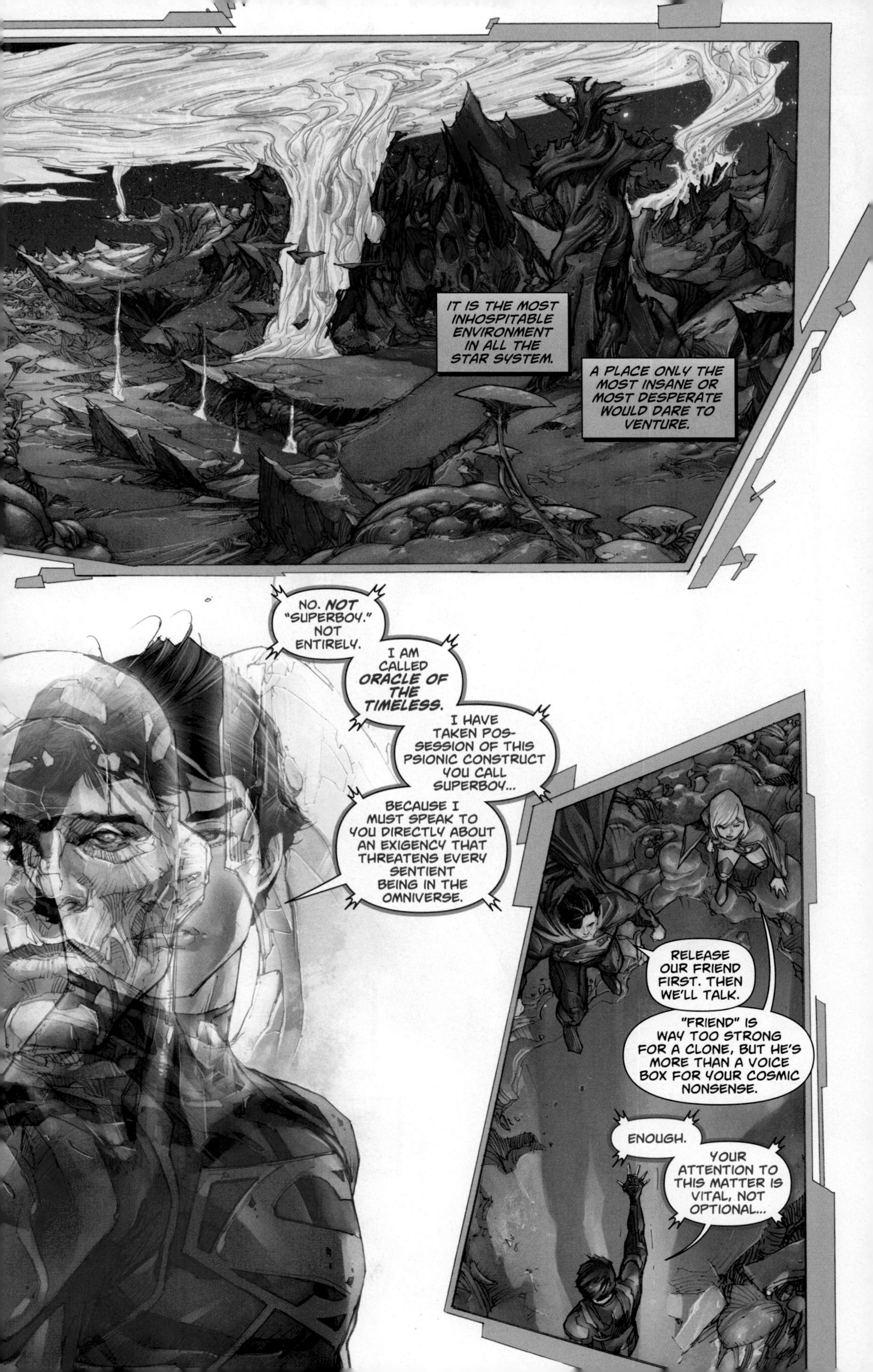
IT IS THE MOST INHOSPITABLE ENVIRONMENT IN ALL THE STAR SYSTEM.
A PLACE ONLY THE MOST INSANE OR MOST DESPERATE WOULD DARE TO VENTURE.
NO. NOT "SUPERBOY." NOT ENTIRELY.
I AM CALLED ORACLE OF THE TIMELESS.
I HAVE TAKEN POSSESSION OF THIS PSIONIC CONSTRUCT YOU CALL SUPERBOY...
BECAUSE I MUST SPEAK TO YOU DIRECTLY ABOUT AN EXIGENCY THAT THREATENS EVERY SENTIENT BEING IN THE OMNIVERSE.
RELEASE OUR FRIEND FIRST. THEN WE'LL TALK.
"FRIEND" IS WAY TOO STRONG FOR A CLONE, BUT HE'S MORE THAN A VOICE BOX FOR YOUR COSMIC NONSENSE.
ENOUGH.
YOUR ATTENTION TO THIS MATTER IS VITAL, NOT OPTIONAL...

...CONSIDERING IT WAS YOUR ACTIONS THAT CAUSED THIS COSMIC CATACLYSM.

KNOW THIS: MY PEOPLE HAVE OBSERVED ALL LIFE SINCE BEFORE THE BEGINNING OF TIME.

WE ALL EXIST IN THE PAST, PRESENT AND FUTURE SIMULTANEOUSLY.

ALMOST BEFORE THE PLANET STARTED TO COOL, IT WAS CLEAR THAT KRYPTON PRESENTED A PROBLEM.

"EVEN LONG AFTER IT WAS OBLITERATED--

KEEP TALKING LIKE *THAT* AND YOU *ARE* GOING TO HAVE A PROBLEM, "ORACLE."

"...IT WAS H'EL WHO WA[S] LEARNING THE MOST ABOUT THE WORLD AROUND HIM.

"ABOU[T] HIMSEL[F.]

"UNTIL THEN HE HAD ALWAYS BELIEVED HE WAS A NATIVE OF KRYPTON.

"THE TRUTH? HE WAS LITTLE MORE THAN CELL SAMPLES DISPATCHED BY A YOUNG JOR-EL IN AN UNMANNED SHIP.

"NOTHING MORE THAN A GENETIC ACCIDENT.

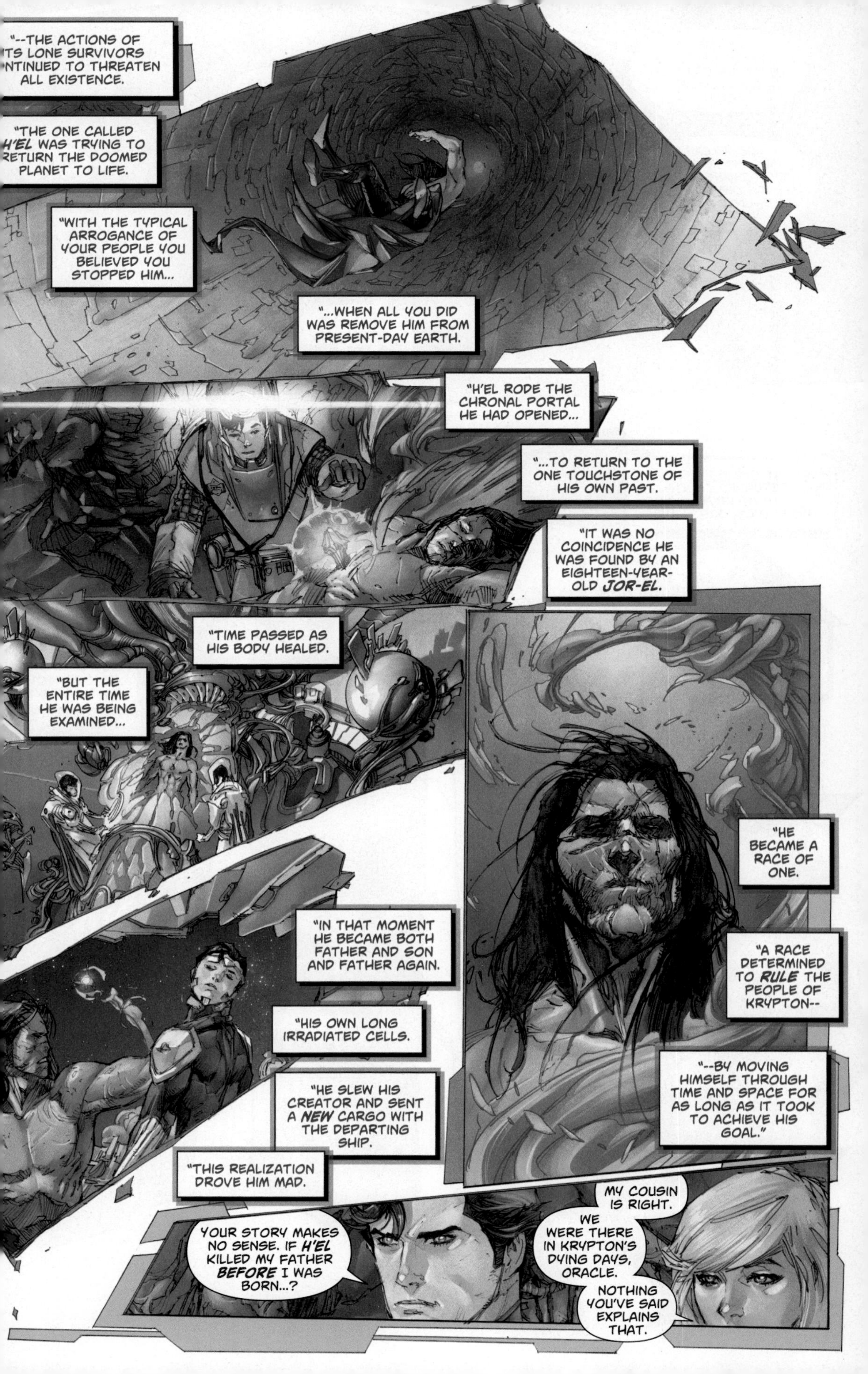

"--THE ACTIONS OF ITS LONE SURVIVORS CONTINUED TO THREATEN ALL EXISTENCE.
"THE ONE CALLED H'EL WAS TRYING TO RETURN THE DOOMED PLANET TO LIFE.
"WITH THE TYPICAL ARROGANCE OF YOUR PEOPLE YOU BELIEVED YOU STOPPED HIM...
"...WHEN ALL YOU DID WAS REMOVE HIM FROM PRESENT-DAY EARTH.
"H'EL RODE THE CHRONAL PORTAL HE HAD OPENED...
"...TO RETURN TO THE ONE TOUCHSTONE OF HIS OWN PAST.
"IT WAS NO COINCIDENCE HE WAS FOUND BY AN EIGHTEEN-YEAR-OLD JOR-EL.
"TIME PASSED AS HIS BODY HEALED.
"BUT THE ENTIRE TIME HE WAS BEING EXAMINED...
"HE BECAME A RACE OF ONE.
"A RACE DETERMINED TO RULE THE PEOPLE OF KRYPTON--
"--BY MOVING HIMSELF THROUGH TIME AND SPACE FOR AS LONG AS IT TOOK TO ACHIEVE HIS GOAL."
"IN THAT MOMENT HE BECAME BOTH FATHER AND SON AND FATHER AGAIN.
"HIS OWN LONG IRRADIATED CELLS.
"HE SLEW HIS CREATOR AND SENT A NEW CARGO WITH THE DEPARTING SHIP.
"THIS REALIZATION DROVE HIM MAD.
YOUR STORY MAKES NO SENSE. IF H'EL KILLED MY FATHER BEFORE I WAS BORN...?
MY COUSIN IS RIGHT.
WE WERE THERE IN KRYPTON'S DYING DAYS, ORACLE.
NOTHING YOU'VE SAID EXPLAINS THAT.

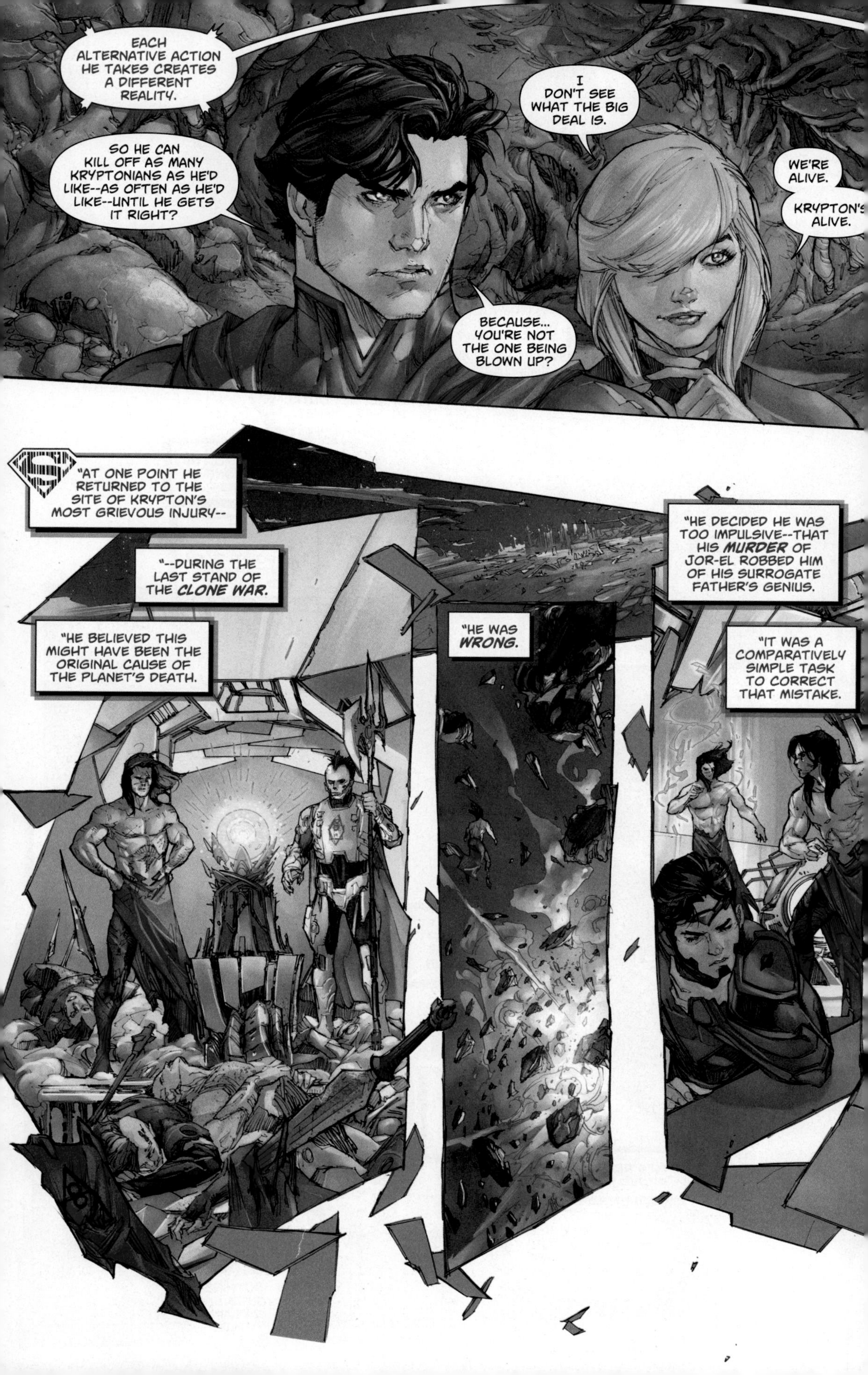
EACH ALTERNATIVE ACTION HE TAKES CREATES A DIFFERENT REALITY.
SO HE CAN KILL OFF AS MANY KRYPTONIANS AS HE'D LIKE--AS OFTEN AS HE'D LIKE--UNTIL HE GETS IT RIGHT?
I DON'T SEE WHAT THE BIG DEAL IS.
WE'RE ALIVE.
KRYPTON'S ALIVE.
BECAUSE... YOU'RE NOT THE ONE BEING BLOWN UP?
"AT ONE POINT HE RETURNED TO THE SITE OF KRYPTON'S MOST GRIEVOUS INJURY--
"--DURING THE LAST STAND OF THE CLONE WAR.
"HE BELIEVED THIS MIGHT HAVE BEEN THE ORIGINAL CAUSE OF THE PLANET'S DEATH.
"HE WAS WRONG.
"HE DECIDED HE WAS TOO IMPULSIVE--THAT HIS MURDER OF JOR-EL ROBBED HIM OF HIS SURROGATE FATHER'S GENIUS.
"IT WAS A COMPARATIVELY SIMPLE TASK TO CORRECT THAT MISTAKE.

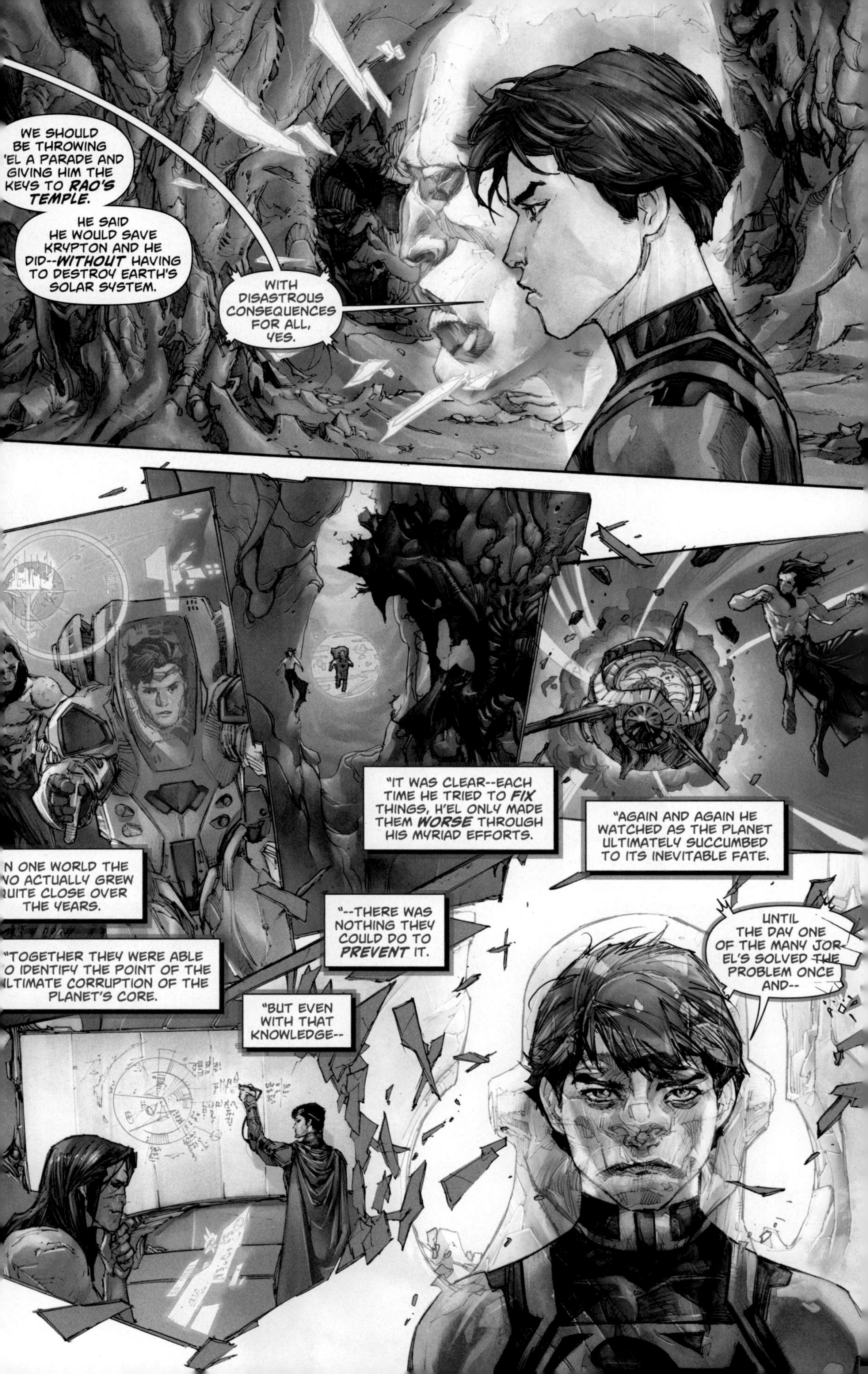
WE SHOULD BE THROWING 'EL A PARADE AND GIVING HIM THE KEYS TO RAO'S TEMPLE.
HE SAID HE WOULD SAVE KRYPTON AND HE DID--WITHOUT HAVING TO DESTROY EARTH'S SOLAR SYSTEM.
WITH DISASTROUS CONSEQUENCES FOR ALL, YES.
"IT WAS CLEAR--EACH TIME HE TRIED TO FIX THINGS, H'EL ONLY MADE THEM WORSE THROUGH HIS MYRIAD EFFORTS.
"AGAIN AND AGAIN HE WATCHED AS THE PLANET ULTIMATELY SUCCUMBED TO ITS INEVITABLE FATE.
N ONE WORLD THE VO ACTUALLY GREW UITE CLOSE OVER THE YEARS.
"TOGETHER THEY WERE ABLE O IDENTIFY THE POINT OF THE LTIMATE CORRUPTION OF THE PLANET'S CORE.
"BUT EVEN WITH THAT KNOWLEDGE--
"--THERE WAS NOTHING THEY COULD DO TO PREVENT IT.
UNTIL THE DAY ONE OF THE MANY JOR-EL'S SOLVED THE PROBLEM ONCE AND--

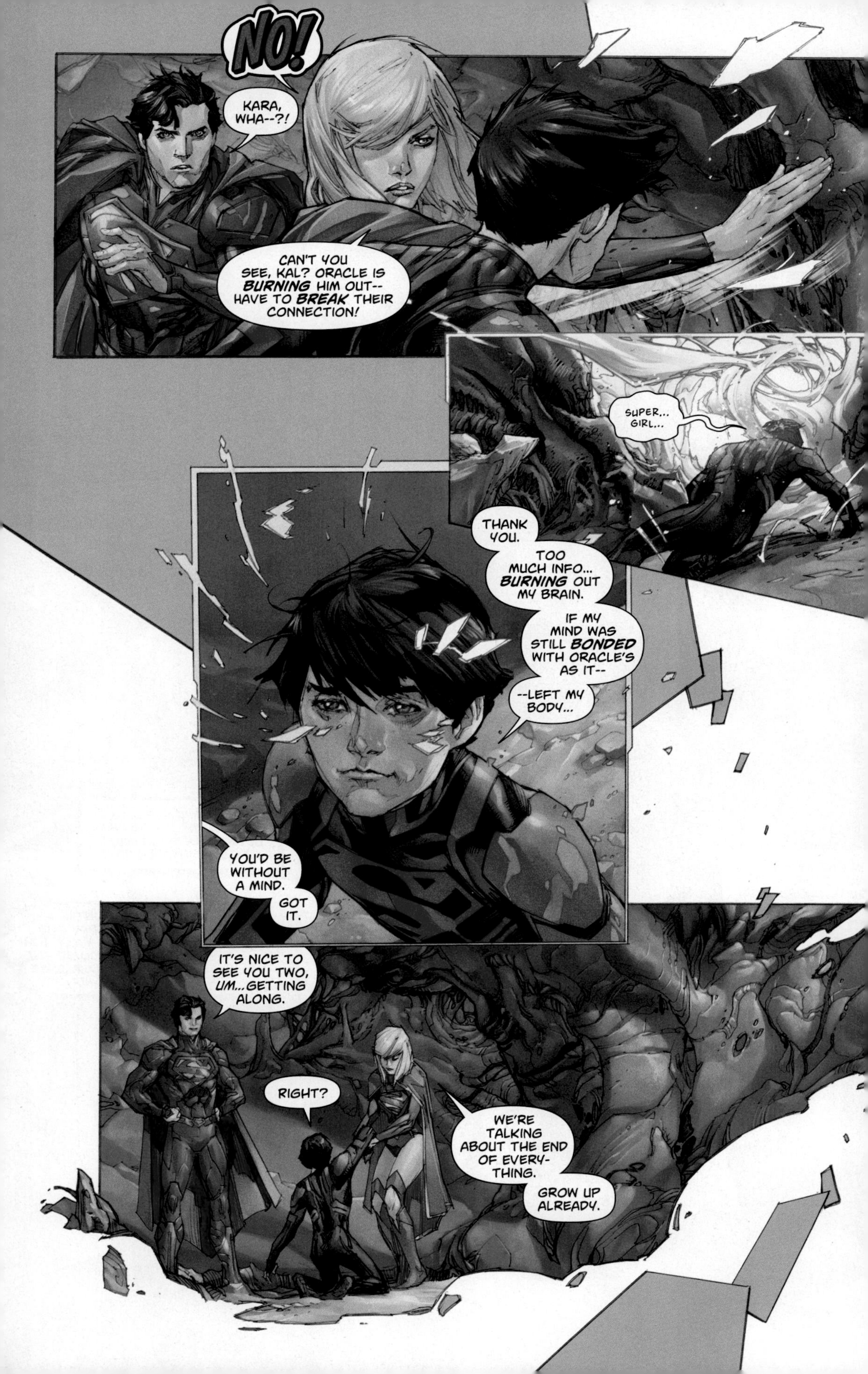
NO!
KARA, WHA--?!
CAN'T YOU SEE, KAL? ORACLE IS BURNING HIM OUT-- HAVE TO BREAK THEIR CONNECTION!
SUPER... GIRL...
THANK YOU.
TOO MUCH INFO... BURNING OUT MY BRAIN.
IF MY MIND WAS STILL BONDED WITH ORACLE'S AS IT--
--LEFT MY BODY...
YOU'D BE WITHOUT A MIND.
GOT IT.
IT'S NICE TO SEE YOU TWO, UM... GETTING ALONG.
RIGHT?
WE'RE TALKING ABOUT THE END OF EVERY-THING.
GROW UP ALREADY.

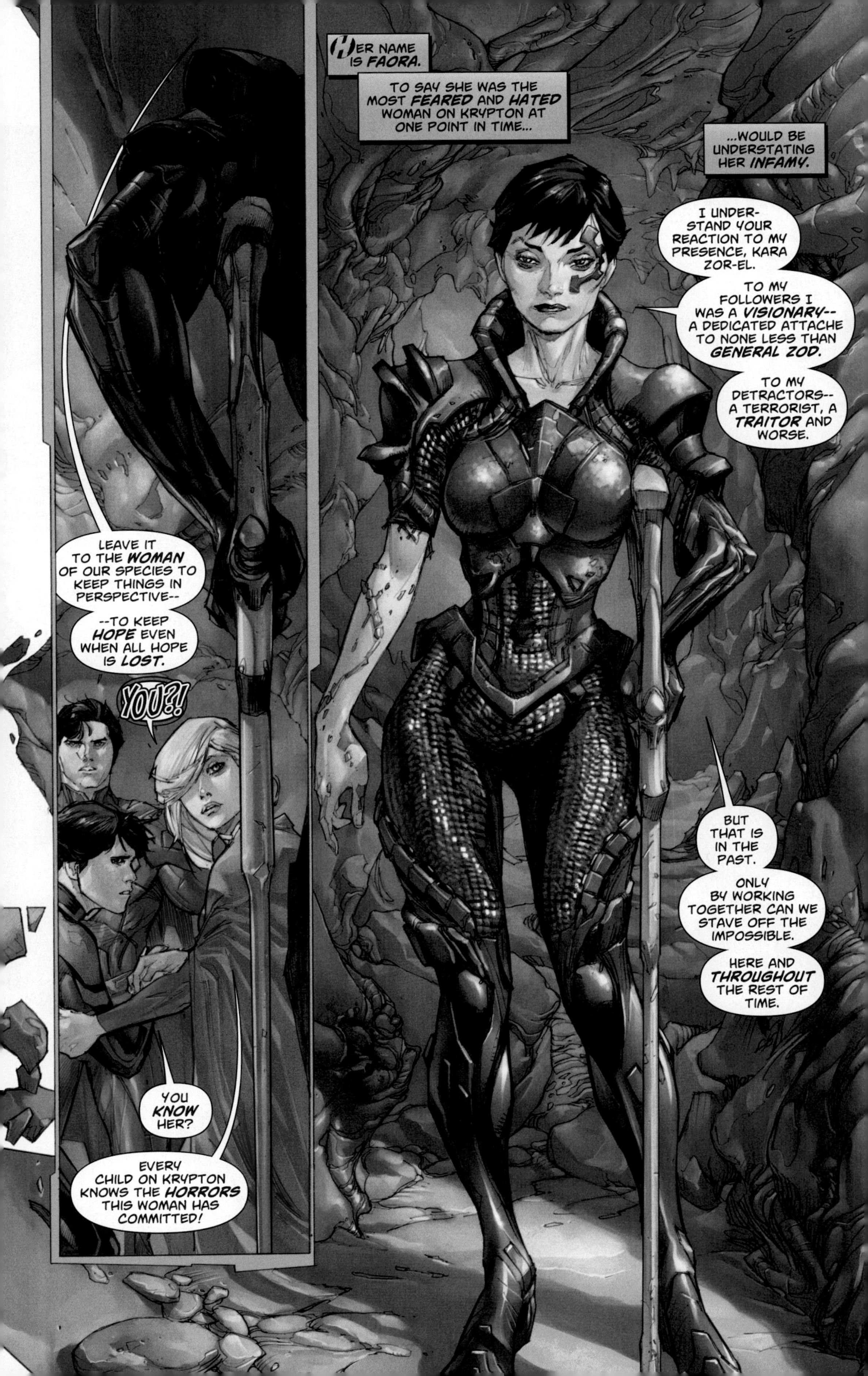
HER NAME IS FAORA.
TO SAY SHE WAS THE MOST FEARED AND HATED WOMAN ON KRYPTON AT ONE POINT IN TIME...
...WOULD BE UNDERSTATING HER INFAMY.
I UNDER-STAND YOUR REACTION TO MY PRESENCE, KARA ZOR-EL.
TO MY FOLLOWERS I WAS A VISIONARY-- A DEDICATED ATTACHE TO NONE LESS THAN GENERAL ZOD.
TO MY DETRACTORS-- A TERRORIST, A TRAITOR AND WORSE.
LEAVE IT TO THE WOMAN OF OUR SPECIES TO KEEP THINGS IN PERSPECTIVE--
--TO KEEP HOPE EVEN WHEN ALL HOPE IS LOST.
YOU?!
BUT THAT IS IN THE PAST.
ONLY BY WORKING TOGETHER CAN WE STAVE OFF THE IMPOSSIBLE.
HERE AND THROUGHOUT THE REST OF TIME.
YOU KNOW HER?
EVERY CHILD ON KRYPTON KNOWS THE HORRORS THIS WOMAN HAS COMMITTED!

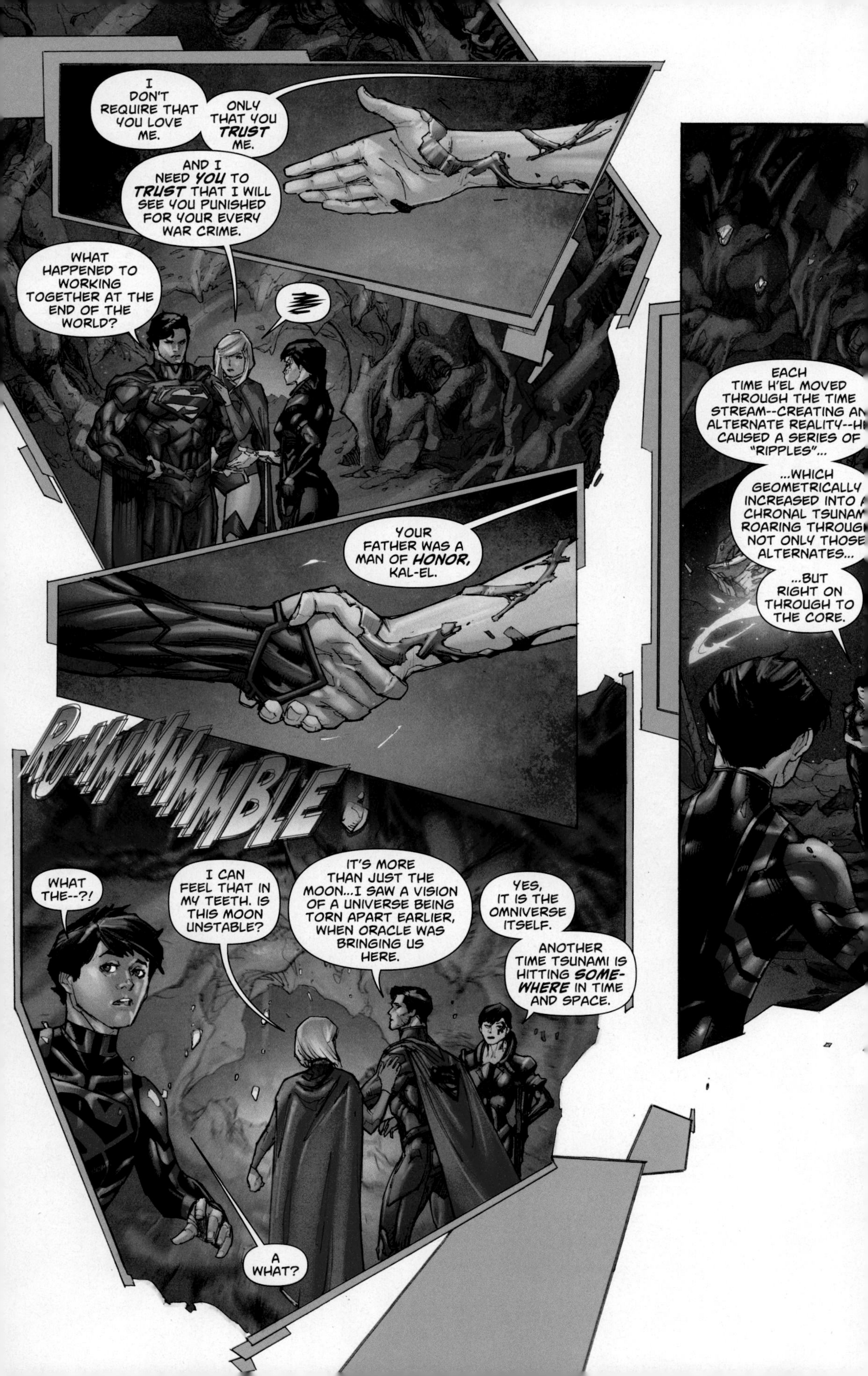
I DON'T REQUIRE THAT YOU LOVE ME.
ONLY THAT YOU TRUST ME.
AND I NEED YOU TO TRUST THAT I WILL SEE YOU PUNISHED FOR YOUR EVERY WAR CRIME.
WHAT HAPPENED TO WORKING TOGETHER AT THE END OF THE WORLD?
YOUR FATHER WAS A MAN OF HONOR, KAL-EL.
RUMMMMMBLE
WHAT THE--?!
I CAN FEEL THAT IN MY TEETH. IS THIS MOON UNSTABLE?
IT'S MORE THAN JUST THE MOON...I SAW A VISION OF A UNIVERSE BEING TORN APART EARLIER, WHEN ORACLE WAS BRINGING US HERE.
YES, IT IS THE OMNIVERSE ITSELF.
ANOTHER TIME TSUNAMI IS HITTING SOMEWHERE IN TIME AND SPACE.
A WHAT?
EACH TIME H'EL MOVED THROUGH THE TIME STREAM--CREATING AN ALTERNATE REALITY--HE CAUSED A SERIES OF "RIPPLES"...
...WHICH GEOMETRICALLY INCREASED INTO A CHRONAL TSUNAMI ROARING THROUGH NOT ONLY THOSE ALTERNATES...
...BUT RIGHT ON THROUGH TO THE CORE.

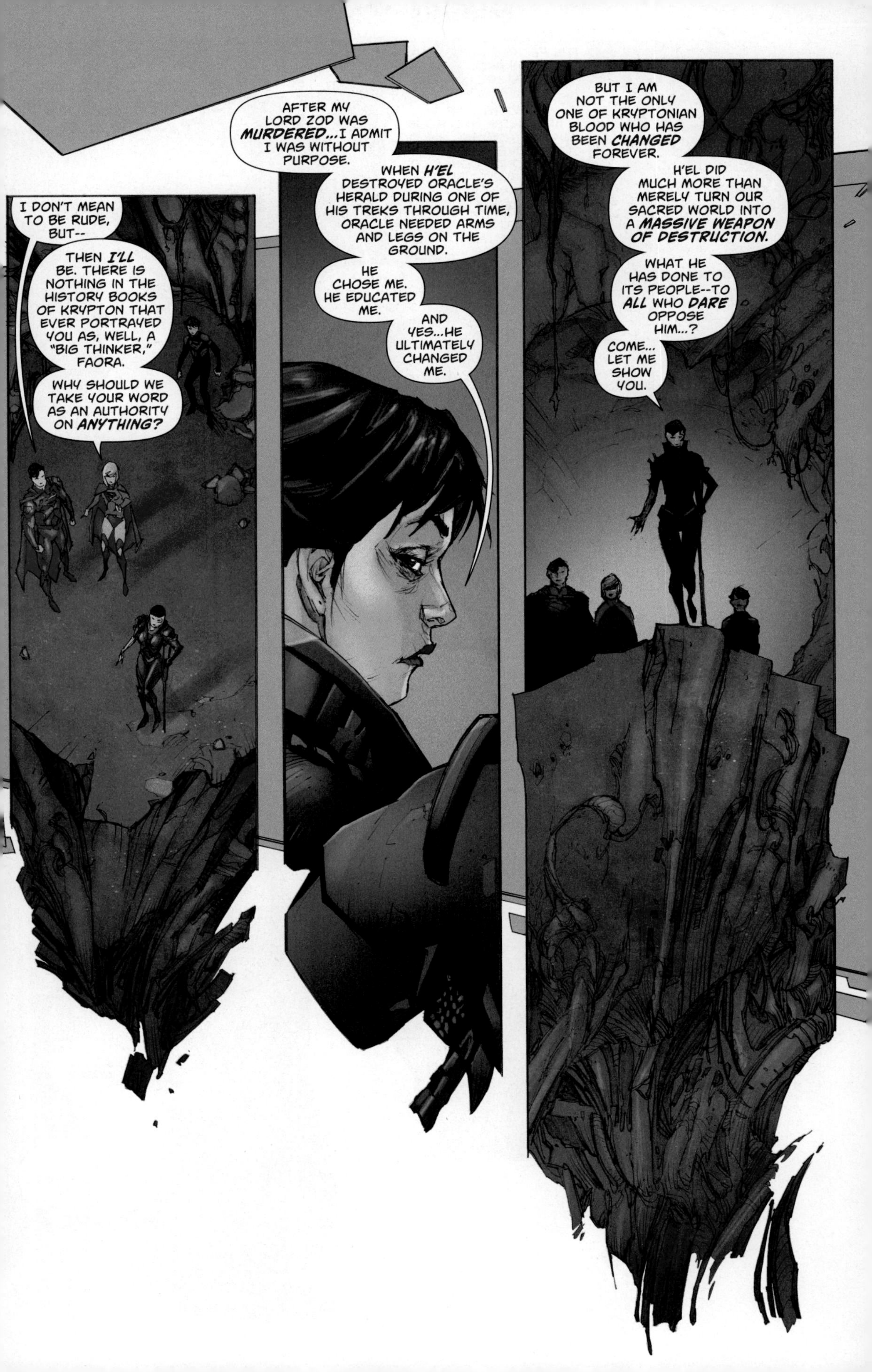
I DON'T MEAN TO BE RUDE, BUT--
THEN I'LL BE. THERE IS NOTHING IN THE HISTORY BOOKS OF KRYPTON THAT EVER PORTRAYED YOU AS, WELL, A "BIG THINKER," FAORA.
WHY SHOULD WE TAKE YOUR WORD AS AN AUTHORITY ON ANYTHING?
AFTER MY LORD ZOD WAS MURDERED... I ADMIT I WAS WITHOUT PURPOSE.
WHEN H'EL DESTROYED ORACLE'S HERALD DURING ONE OF HIS TREKS THROUGH TIME, ORACLE NEEDED ARMS AND LEGS ON THE GROUND.
HE CHOSE ME. HE EDUCATED ME.
AND YES...HE ULTIMATELY CHANGED ME.
BUT I AM NOT THE ONLY ONE OF KRYPTONIAN BLOOD WHO HAS BEEN CHANGED FOREVER.
H'EL DID MUCH MORE THAN MERELY TURN OUR SACRED WORLD INTO A MASSIVE WEAPON OF DESTRUCTION.
WHAT HE HAS DONE TO ITS PEOPLE--TO ALL WHO DARE OPPOSE HIM...?
COME... LET ME SHOW YOU.

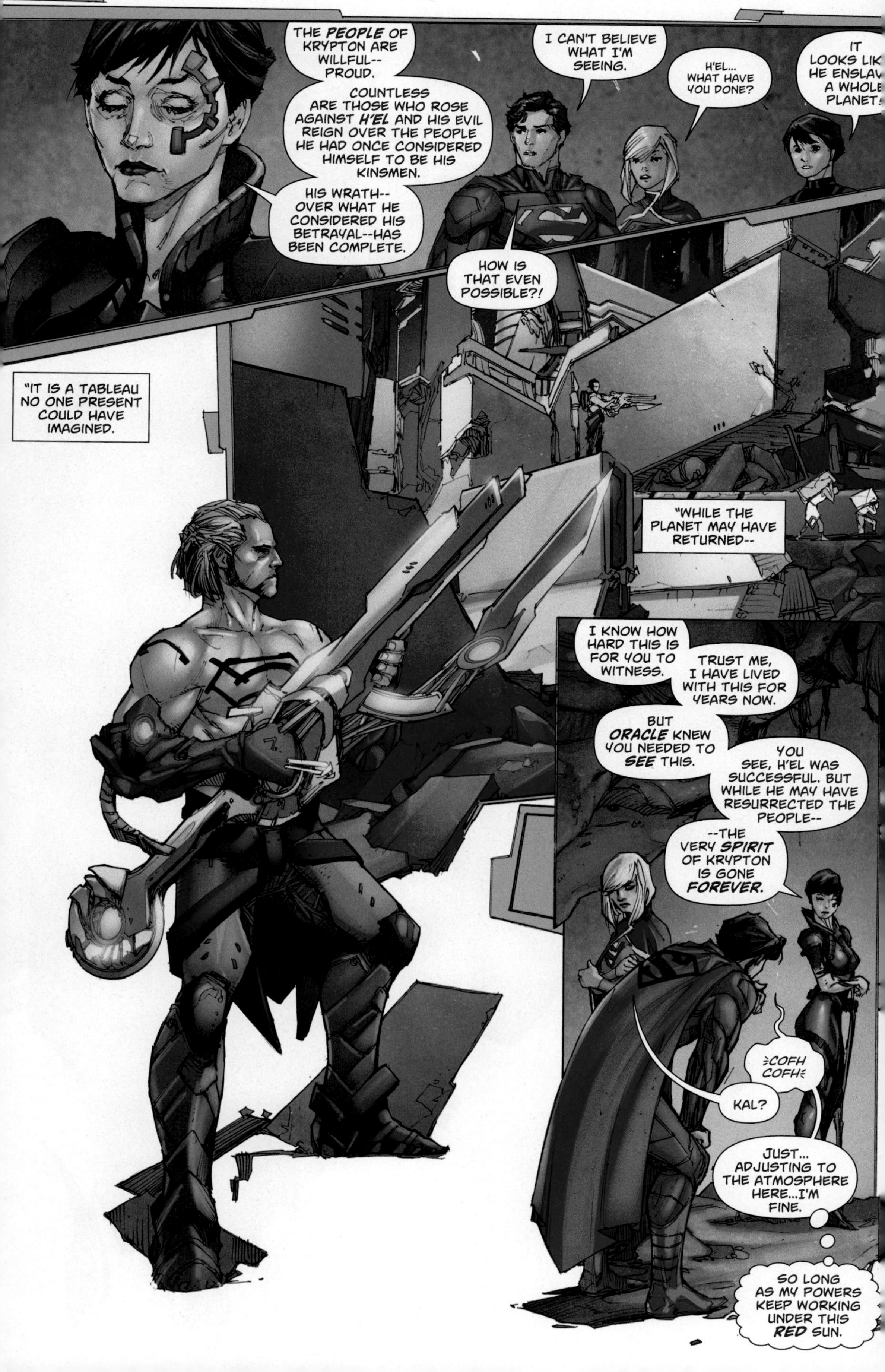

THE PEOPLE OF KRYPTON ARE WILLFUL-- PROUD.
COUNTLESS ARE THOSE WHO ROSE AGAINST H'EL AND HIS EVIL REIGN OVER THE PEOPLE HE HAD ONCE CONSIDERED HIMSELF TO BE HIS KINSMEN.
HIS WRATH-- OVER WHAT HE CONSIDERED HIS BETRAYAL--HAS BEEN COMPLETE.
I CAN'T BELIEVE WHAT I'M SEEING.
H'EL... WHAT HAVE YOU DONE?
IT LOOKS LIK HE ENSLAV A WHOLE PLANET!
HOW IS THAT EVEN POSSIBLE?!
"IT IS A TABLEAU NO ONE PRESENT COULD HAVE IMAGINED.
"WHILE THE PLANET MAY HAVE RETURNED--
I KNOW HOW HARD THIS IS FOR YOU TO WITNESS.
TRUST ME, I HAVE LIVED WITH THIS FOR YEARS NOW.
BUT ORACLE KNEW YOU NEEDED TO SEE THIS.
YOU SEE, H'EL WAS SUCCESSFUL. BUT WHILE HE MAY HAVE RESURRECTED THE PEOPLE--
--THE VERY SPIRIT OF KRYPTON IS GONE FOREVER.
COFH COFH
KAL?
JUST... ADJUSTING TO THE ATMOSPHERE HERE...I'M FINE.
SO LONG AS MY POWERS KEEP WORKING UNDER THIS RED SUN.

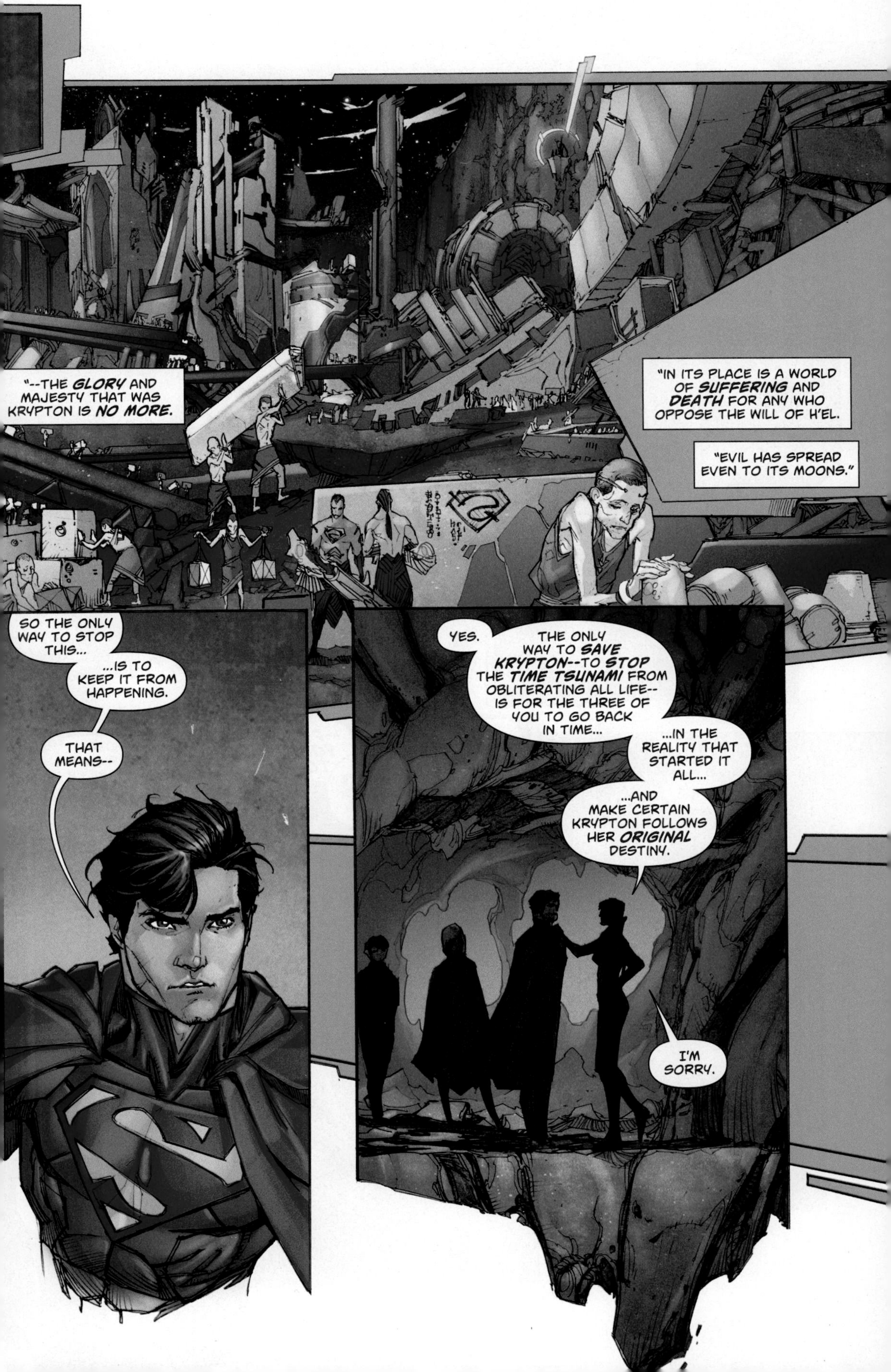
"--THE GLORY AND MAJESTY THAT WAS KRYPTON IS NO MORE.
"IN ITS PLACE IS A WORLD OF SUFFERING AND DEATH FOR ANY WHO OPPOSE THE WILL OF H'EL.
"EVIL HAS SPREAD EVEN TO ITS MOONS."
SO THE ONLY WAY TO STOP THIS...
...IS TO KEEP IT FROM HAPPENING.
THAT MEANS--
YES.
THE ONLY WAY TO SAVE KRYPTON--TO STOP THE TIME TSUNAMI FROM OBLITERATING ALL LIFE--IS FOR THE THREE OF YOU TO GO BACK IN TIME...
...IN THE REALITY THAT STARTED IT ALL...
...AND MAKE CERTAIN KRYPTON FOLLOWS HER ORIGINAL DESTINY.
I'M SORRY.

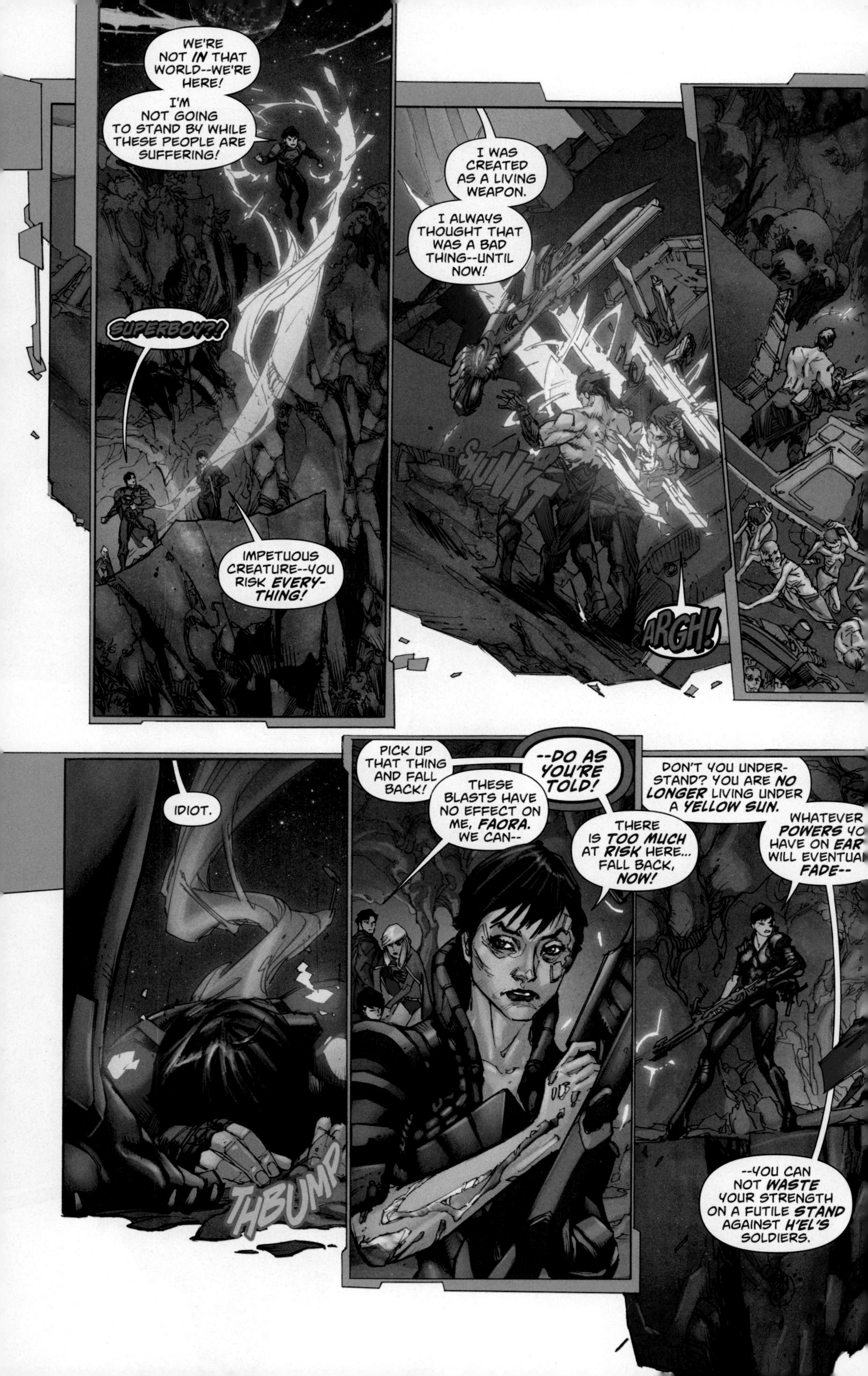
WE'RE NOT *IN* THAT WORLD--WE'RE HERE!
I'M NOT GOING TO STAND BY WHILE THESE PEOPLE ARE SUFFERING!
SUPERBOY?!
IMPETUOUS CREATURE--YOU RISK *EVERY-THING!*
I WAS CREATED AS A LIVING WEAPON.
I ALWAYS THOUGHT THAT WAS A BAD THING--UNTIL NOW!
SHUNKT
ARGH!
IDIOT.
THBUMP
PICK UP THAT THING AND FALL BACK!
--*DO AS YOU'RE TOLD!*
THESE BLASTS HAVE NO EFFECT ON ME, *FAORA.* WE CAN--
THERE IS *TOO MUCH* AT *RISK* HERE... FALL BACK, *NOW!*
DON'T YOU UNDER-STAND? YOU ARE *NO LONGER* LIVING UNDER A *YELLOW SUN.*
WHATEVER *POWERS* YO HAVE ON *EAR* WILL EVENTUA *FADE--*
--YOU CAN NOT *WASTE* YOUR STRENGTH ON A FUTILE *STAND* AGAINST *H'EL'S* SOLDIERS.

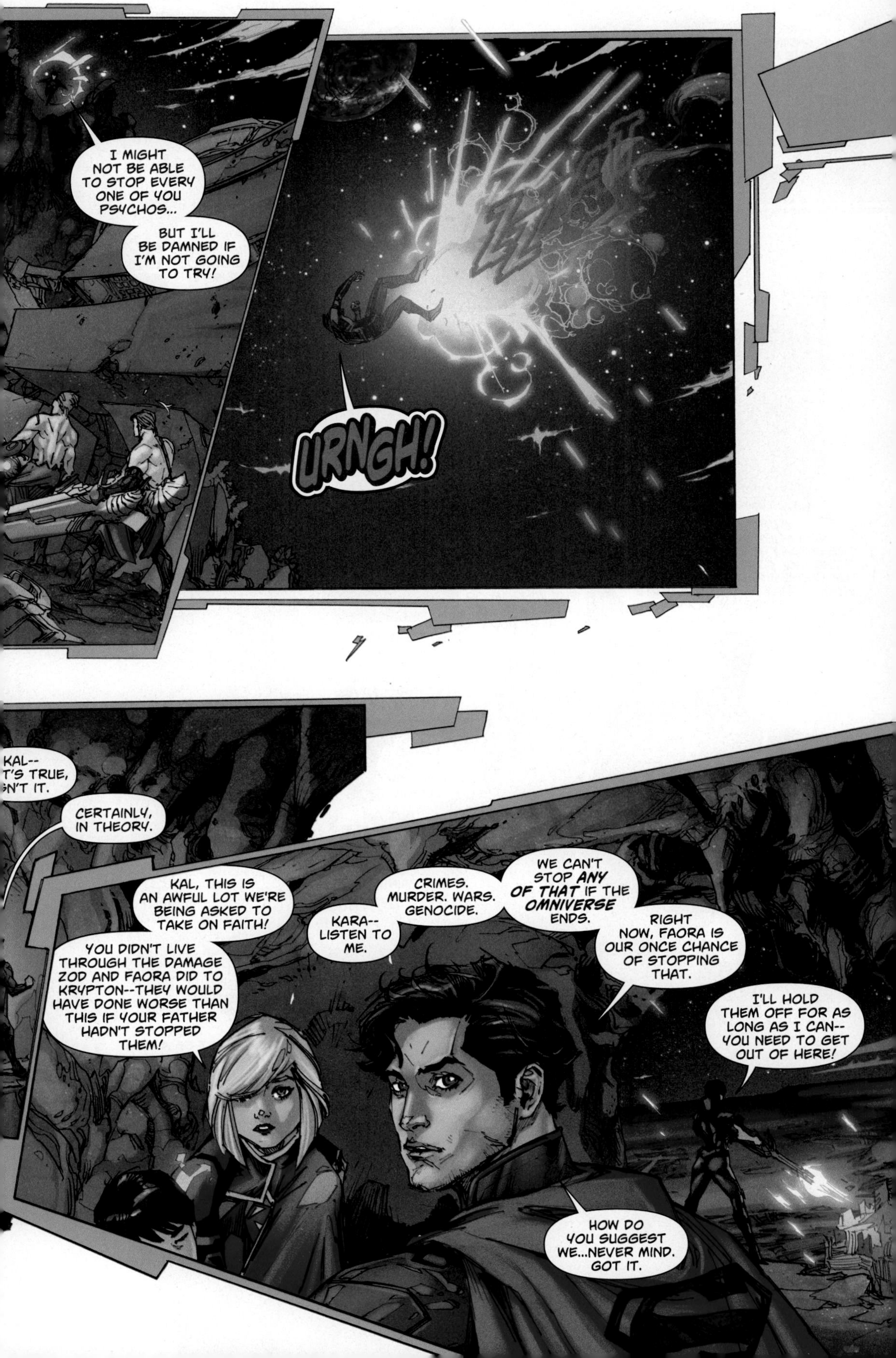
I MIGHT NOT BE ABLE TO STOP EVERY ONE OF YOU PSYCHOS...
BUT I'LL BE DAMNED IF I'M NOT GOING TO TRY!
URNGH!
KAL-- T'S TRUE, SN'T IT.
CERTAINLY, IN THEORY.
KAL, THIS IS AN AWFUL LOT WE'RE BEING ASKED TO TAKE ON FAITH!
YOU DIDN'T LIVE THROUGH THE DAMAGE ZOD AND FAORA DID TO KRYPTON--THEY WOULD HAVE DONE WORSE THAN THIS IF YOUR FATHER HADN'T STOPPED THEM!
KARA-- LISTEN TO ME.
CRIMES. MURDER. WARS. GENOCIDE.
WE CAN'T STOP ANY OF THAT IF THE OMNIVERSE ENDS.
RIGHT NOW, FAORA IS OUR ONCE CHANCE OF STOPPING THAT.
I'LL HOLD THEM OFF FOR AS LONG AS I CAN-- YOU NEED TO GET OUT OF HERE!
HOW DO YOU SUGGEST WE...NEVER MIND. GOT IT.

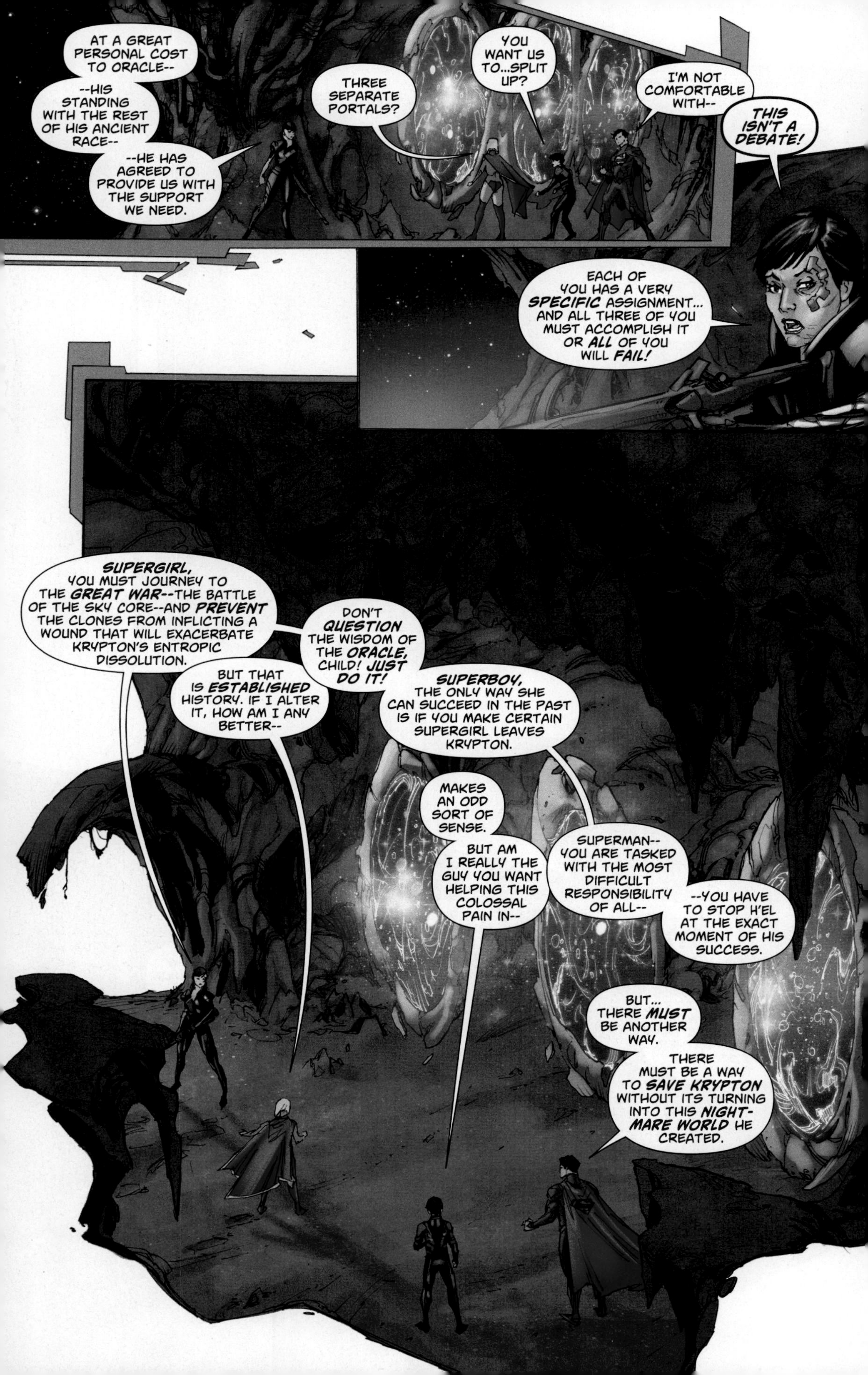
AT A GREAT PERSONAL COST TO ORACLE--
--HIS STANDING WITH THE REST OF HIS ANCIENT RACE--
--HE HAS AGREED TO PROVIDE US WITH THE SUPPORT WE NEED.
THREE SEPARATE PORTALS?
YOU WANT US TO...SPLIT UP?
I'M NOT COMFORTABLE WITH--
THIS ISN'T A DEBATE!
EACH OF YOU HAS A VERY SPECIFIC ASSIGNMENT... AND ALL THREE OF YOU MUST ACCOMPLISH IT OR ALL OF YOU WILL FAIL!
SUPERGIRL, YOU MUST JOURNEY TO THE GREAT WAR--THE BATTLE OF THE SKY CORE--AND PREVENT THE CLONES FROM INFLICTING A WOUND THAT WILL EXACERBATE KRYPTON'S ENTROPIC DISSOLUTION.
BUT THAT IS ESTABLISHED HISTORY. IF I ALTER IT, HOW AM I ANY BETTER--
DON'T QUESTION THE WISDOM OF THE ORACLE, CHILD! JUST DO IT!
SUPERBOY, THE ONLY WAY SHE CAN SUCCEED IN THE PAST IS IF YOU MAKE CERTAIN SUPERGIRL LEAVES KRYPTON.
MAKES AN ODD SORT OF SENSE.
BUT AM I REALLY THE GUY YOU WANT HELPING THIS COLOSSAL PAIN IN--
SUPERMAN-- YOU ARE TASKED WITH THE MOST DIFFICULT RESPONSIBILITY OF ALL--
--YOU HAVE TO STOP H'EL AT THE EXACT MOMENT OF HIS SUCCESS.
BUT... THERE MUST BE ANOTHER WAY.
THERE MUST BE A WAY TO SAVE KRYPTON WITHOUT ITS TURNING INTO THIS NIGHT-MARE WORLD HE CREATED.

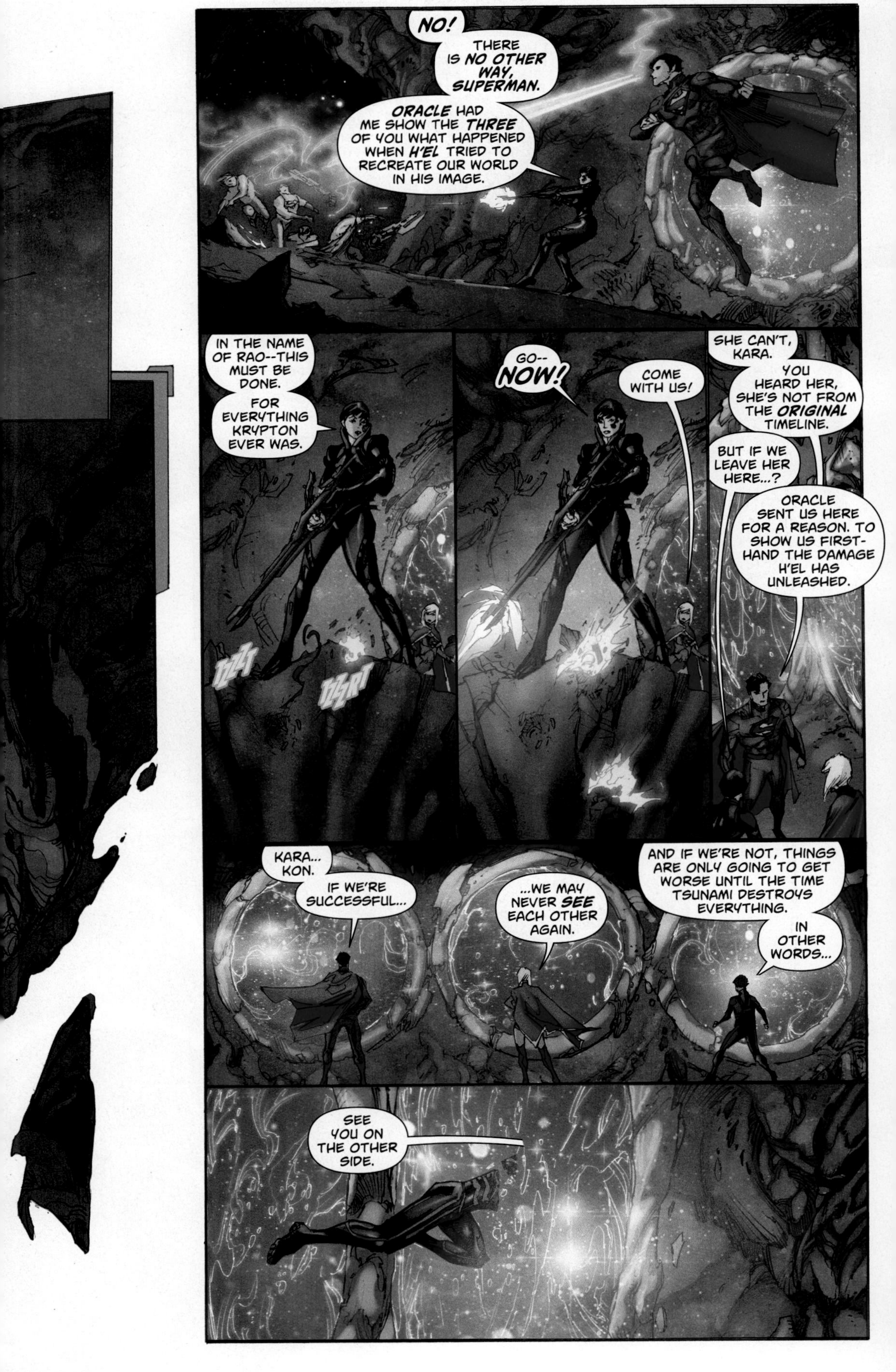
NO!
THERE IS NO OTHER WAY, SUPERMAN.
ORACLE HAD ME SHOW THE THREE OF YOU WHAT HAPPENED WHEN H'EL TRIED TO RECREATE OUR WORLD IN HIS IMAGE.
IN THE NAME OF RAO--THIS MUST BE DONE.
FOR EVERYTHING KRYPTON EVER WAS.
TZZZT
TZZZRT
GO-- NOW!
COME WITH US!
SHE CAN'T, KARA.
YOU HEARD HER, SHE'S NOT FROM THE ORIGINAL TIMELINE.
BUT IF WE LEAVE HER HERE...?
ORACLE SENT US HERE FOR A REASON. TO SHOW US FIRST-HAND THE DAMAGE H'EL HAS UNLEASHED.
KARA... KON.
IF WE'RE SUCCESSFUL...
...WE MAY NEVER SEE EACH OTHER AGAIN.
AND IF WE'RE NOT, THINGS ARE ONLY GOING TO GET WORSE UNTIL THE TIME TSUNAMI DESTROYS EVERYTHING.
IN OTHER WORDS...
SEE YOU ON THE OTHER SIDE.

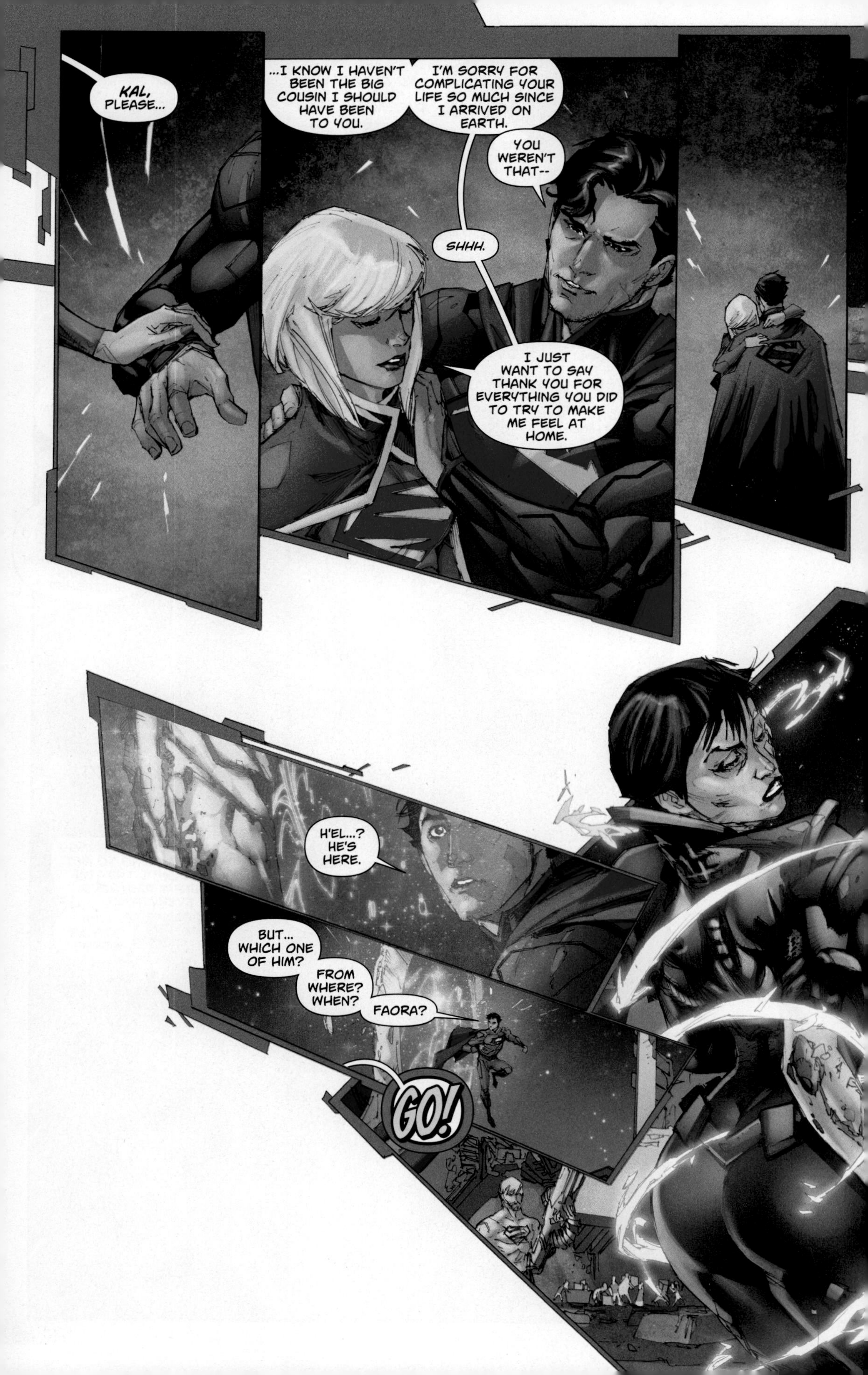
KAL, PLEASE...
...I KNOW I HAVEN'T BEEN THE BIG COUSIN I SHOULD HAVE BEEN TO YOU.
I'M SORRY FOR COMPLICATING YOUR LIFE SO MUCH SINCE I ARRIVED ON EARTH.
YOU WEREN'T THAT--
SHHH.
I JUST WANT TO SAY THANK YOU FOR EVERYTHING YOU DID TO TRY TO MAKE ME FEEL AT HOME.
H'EL...? HE'S HERE.
BUT... WHICH ONE OF HIM?
FROM WHERE? WHEN?
FAORA?
GO!

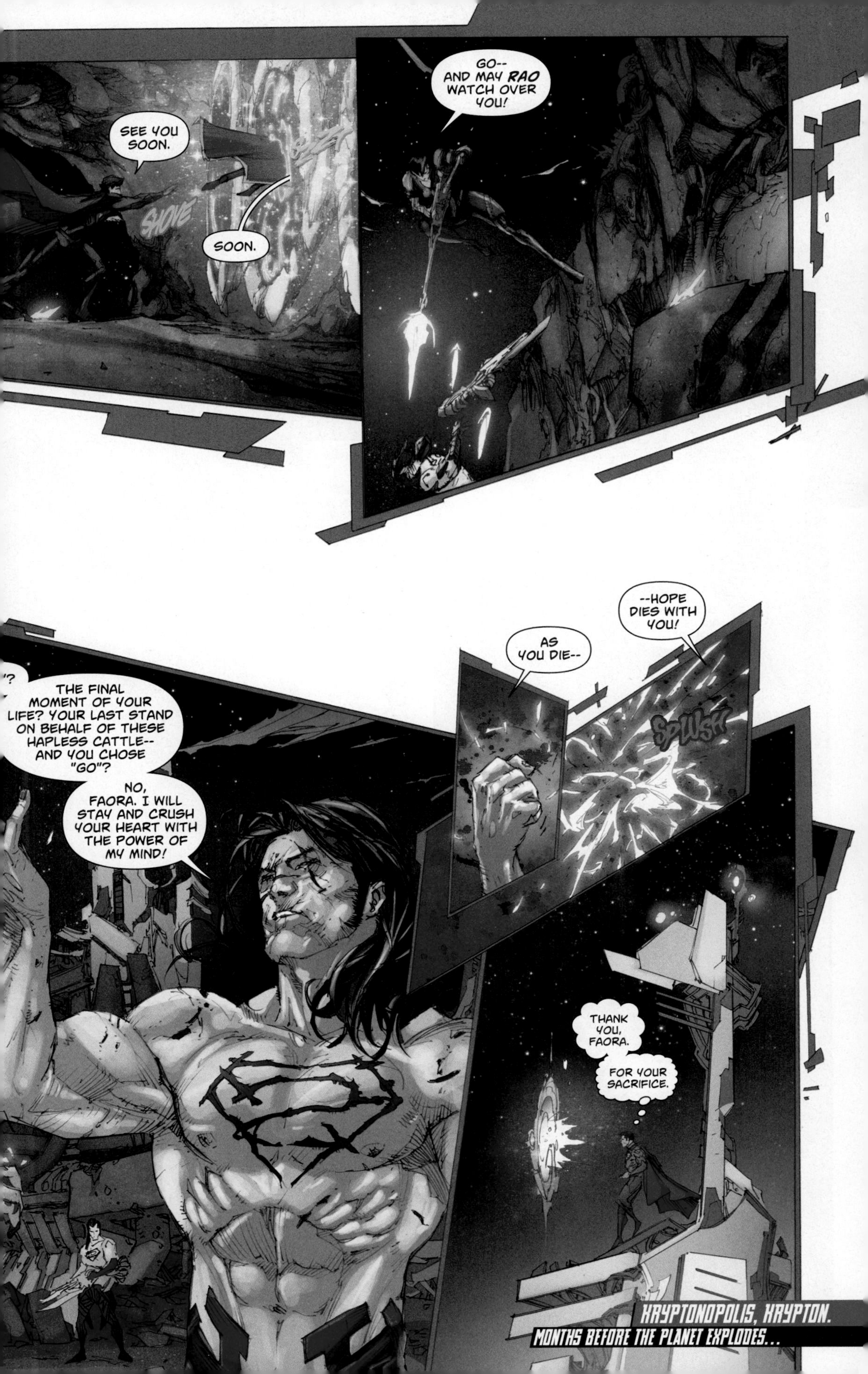
SEE YOU SOON.
SHOVE
SOON.
GO-- AND MAY RAO WATCH OVER YOU!
AS YOU DIE--
--HOPE DIES WITH YOU!
SPLUSH
THE FINAL MOMENT OF YOUR LIFE? YOUR LAST STAND ON BEHALF OF THESE HAPLESS CATTLE-- AND YOU CHOSE "GO"?
NO, FAORA. I WILL STAY AND CRUSH YOUR HEART WITH THE POWER OF MY MIND!
THANK YOU, FAORA.
FOR YOUR SACRIFICE.
KRYPTONOPOLIS, KRYPTON.
MONTHS BEFORE THE PLANET EXPLODES...

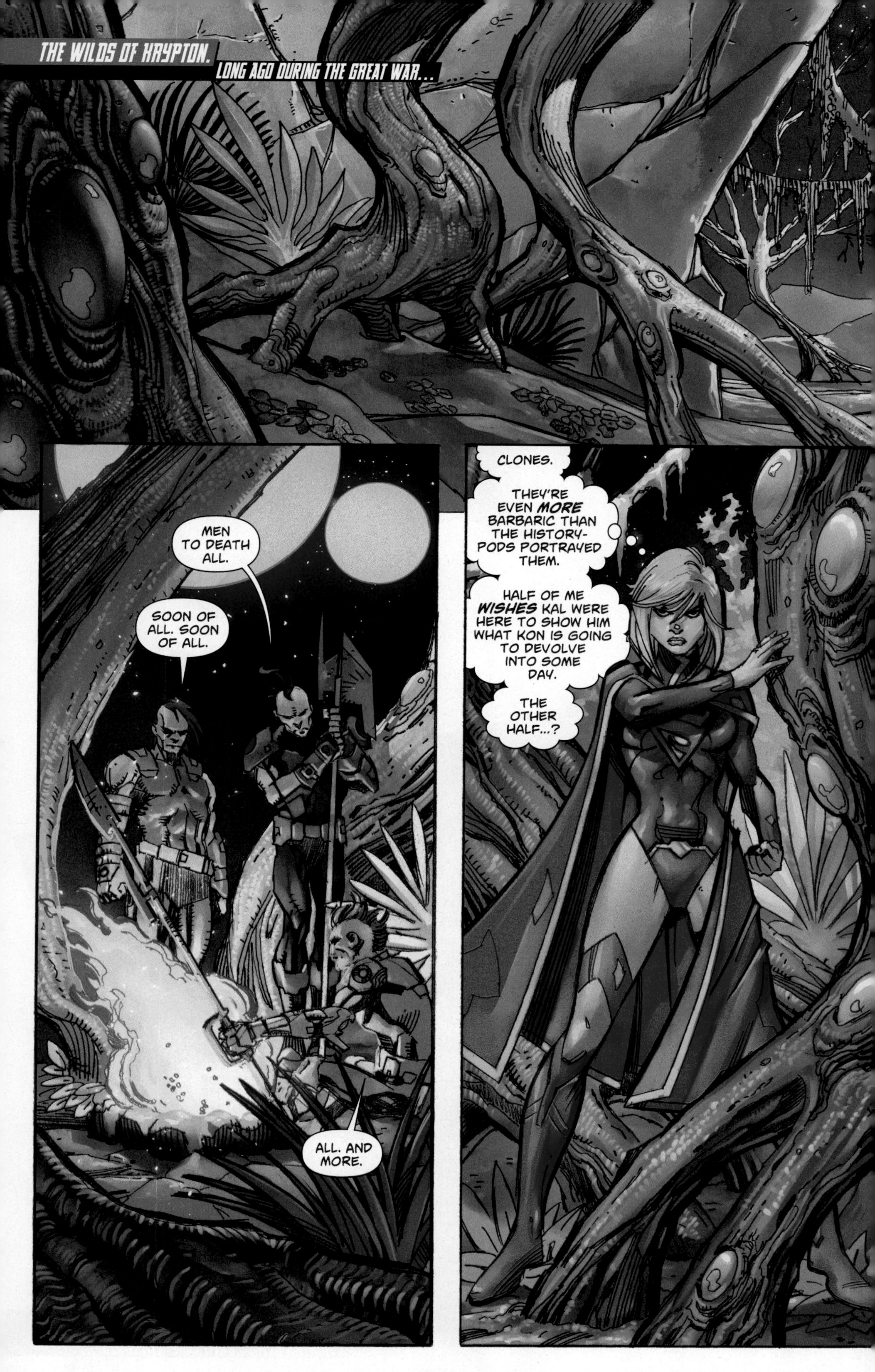
THE WILDS OF KRYPTON.
LONG AGO DURING THE GREAT WAR...
MEN TO DEATH ALL.
SOON OF ALL. SOON OF ALL.
ALL. AND MORE.
CLONES.
THEY'RE EVEN MORE BARBARIC THAN THE HISTORY-PODS PORTRAYED THEM.
HALF OF ME WISHES KAL WERE HERE TO SHOW HIM WHAT KON IS GOING TO DEVOLVE INTO SOME DAY.
THE OTHER HALF...?

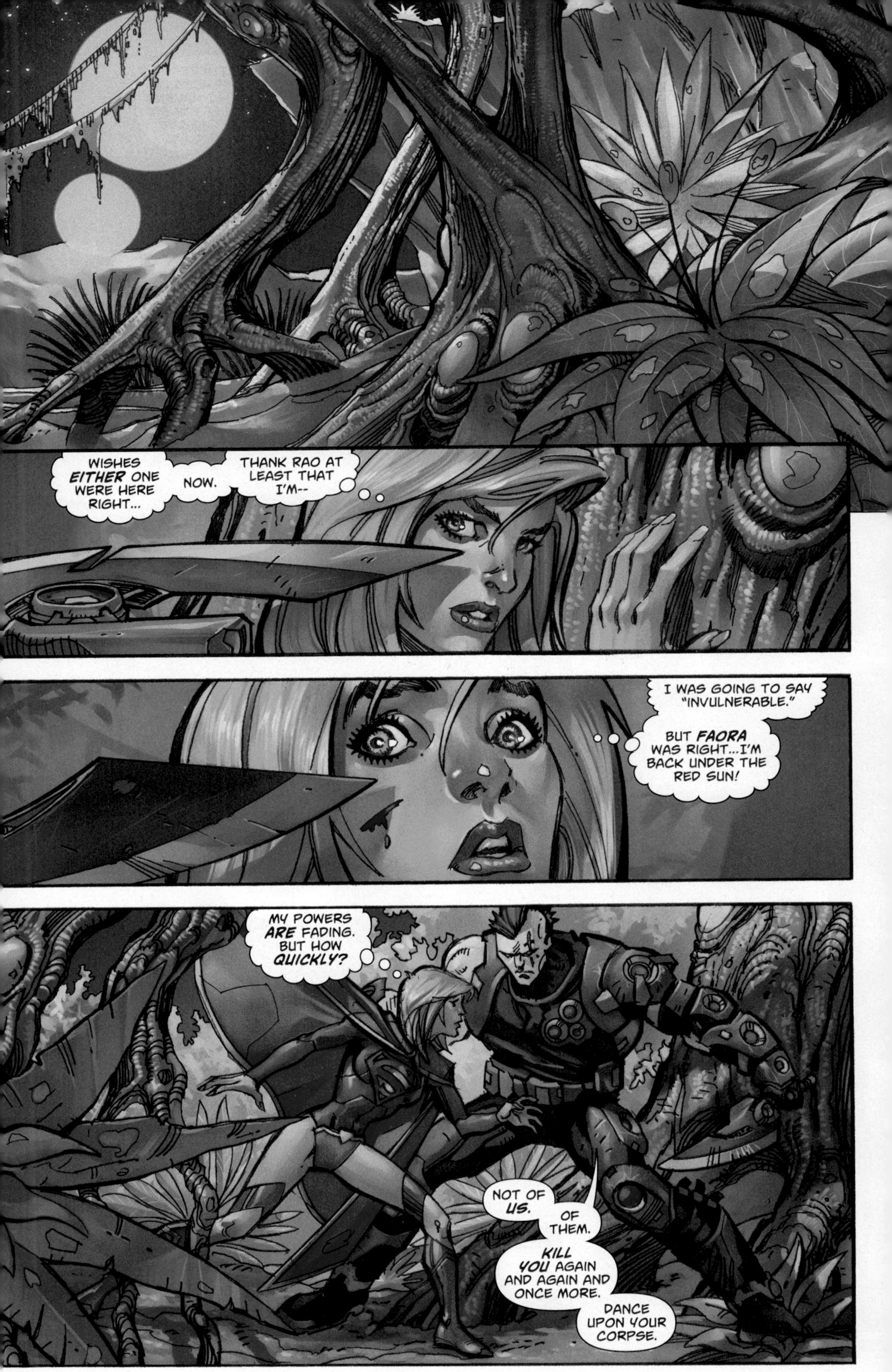
WISHES EITHER ONE WERE HERE RIGHT...
NOW.
THANK RAO AT LEAST THAT I'M--
I WAS GOING TO SAY "INVULNERABLE."
BUT FAORA WAS RIGHT...I'M BACK UNDER THE RED SUN!
MY POWERS ARE FADING. BUT HOW QUICKLY?
NOT OF US.
OF THEM.
KILL YOU AGAIN AND AGAIN AND ONCE MORE.
DANCE UPON YOUR CORPSE.

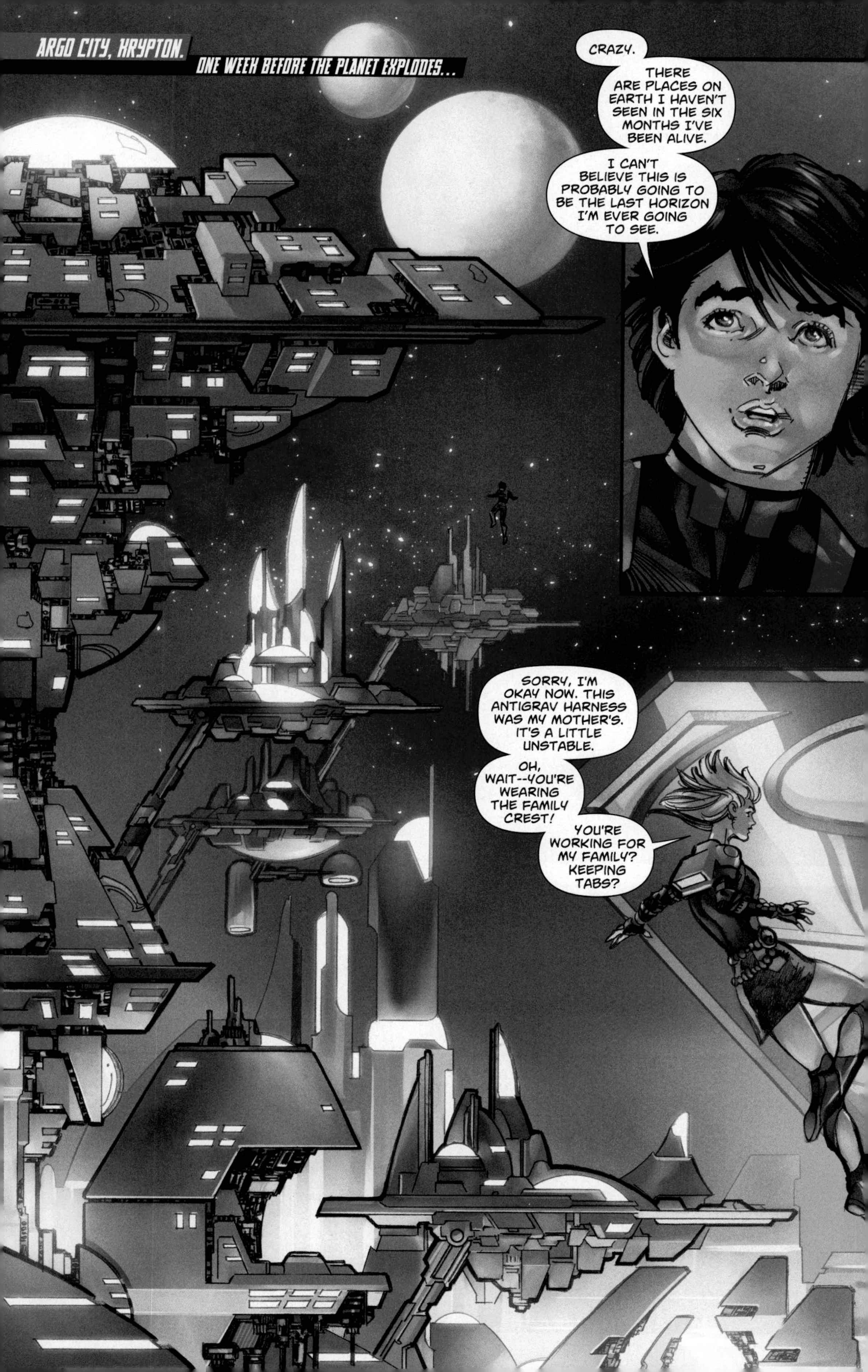
ARGO CITY, KRYPTON.
ONE WEEK BEFORE THE PLANET EXPLODES...
CRAZY.
THERE ARE PLACES ON EARTH I HAVEN'T SEEN IN THE SIX MONTHS I'VE BEEN ALIVE.
I CAN'T BELIEVE THIS IS PROBABLY GOING TO BE THE LAST HORIZON I'M EVER GOING TO SEE.
SORRY, I'M OKAY NOW. THIS ANTIGRAV HARNESS WAS MY MOTHER'S. IT'S A LITTLE UNSTABLE.
OH, WAIT--YOU'RE WEARING THE FAMILY CREST!
YOU'RE WORKING FOR MY FAMILY? KEEPING TABS?

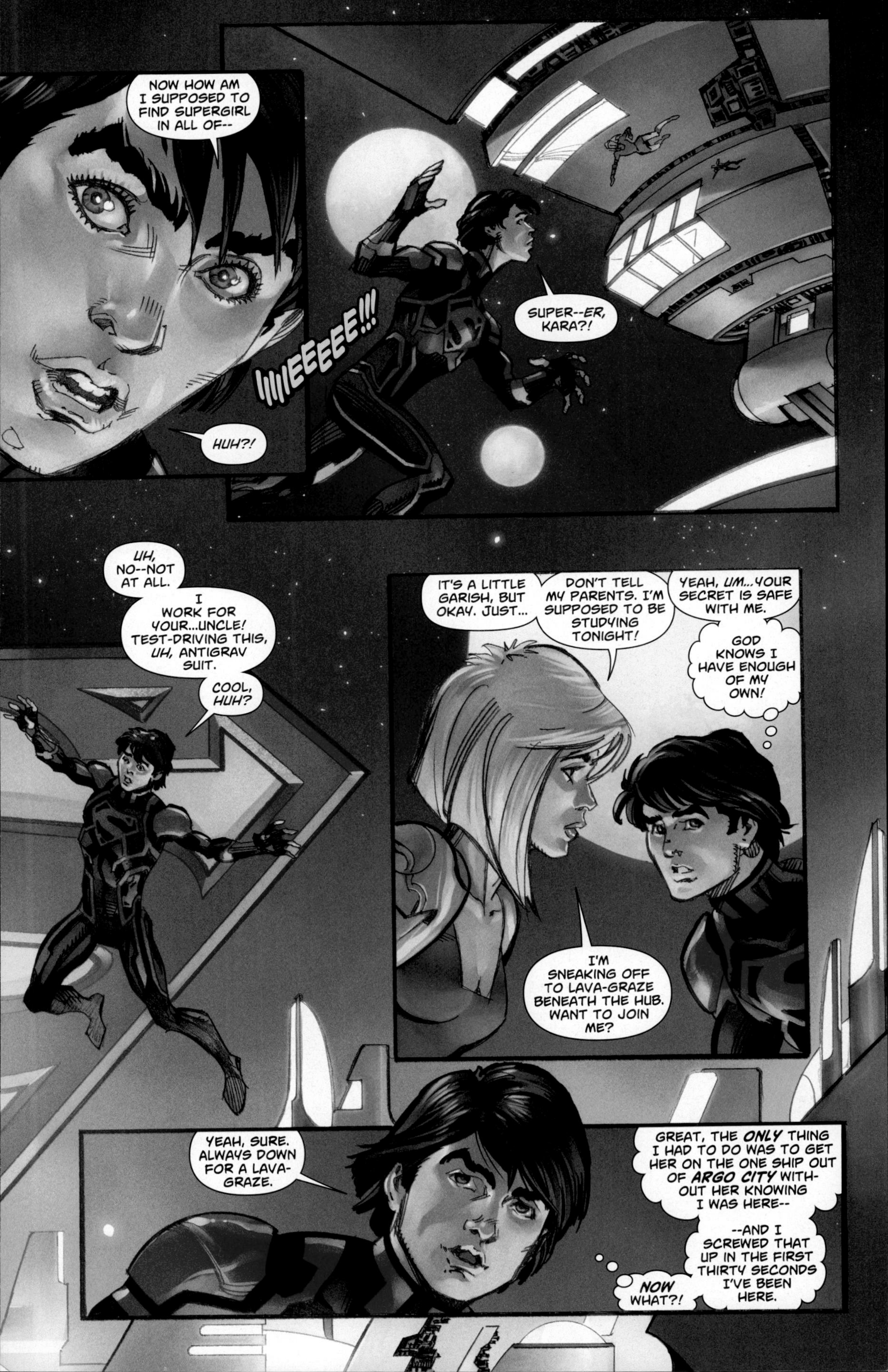
NOW HOW AM I SUPPOSED TO FIND SUPERGIRL IN ALL OF--
HUH?!
IIIIIEEEEEE!!!
SUPER--ER, KARA?!
UH, NO--NOT AT ALL.
I WORK FOR YOUR...UNCLE! TEST-DRIVING THIS, UH, ANTIGRAV SUIT.
COOL, HUH?
IT'S A LITTLE GARISH, BUT OKAY. JUST...
DON'T TELL MY PARENTS. I'M SUPPOSED TO BE STUDYING TONIGHT!
YEAH, UM...YOUR SECRET IS SAFE WITH ME.
GOD KNOWS I HAVE ENOUGH OF MY OWN!
I'M SNEAKING OFF TO LAVA-GRAZE BENEATH THE HUB. WANT TO JOIN ME?
YEAH, SURE. ALWAYS DOWN FOR A LAVA-GRAZE.
GREAT, THE ONLY THING I HAD TO DO WAS TO GET HER ON THE ONE SHIP OUT OF ARGO CITY WITH-OUT HER KNOWING I WAS HERE--
--AND I SCREWED THAT UP IN THE FIRST THIRTY SECONDS I'VE BEEN HERE.
NOW WHAT?!

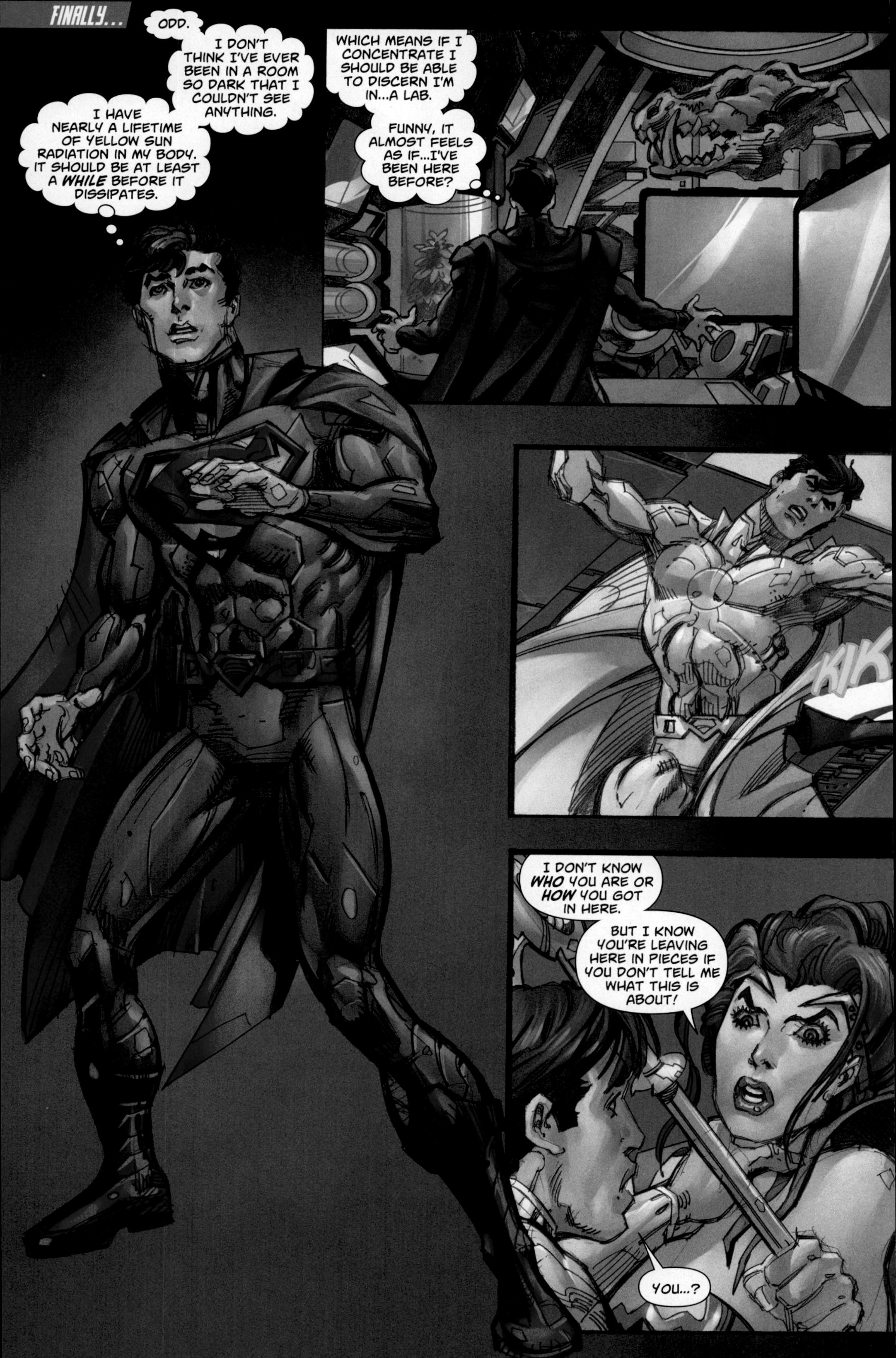
FINALLY...
ODD.
I DON'T THINK I'VE EVER BEEN IN A ROOM SO DARK THAT I COULDN'T SEE ANYTHING.
I HAVE NEARLY A LIFETIME OF YELLOW SUN RADIATION IN MY BODY. IT SHOULD BE AT LEAST A WHILE BEFORE IT DISSIPATES.
WHICH MEANS IF I CONCENTRATE I SHOULD BE ABLE TO DISCERN I'M IN...A LAB.
FUNNY, IT ALMOST FEELS AS IF...I'VE BEEN HERE BEFORE?
KIK
I DON'T KNOW WHO YOU ARE OR HOW YOU GOT IN HERE.
BUT I KNOW YOU'RE LEAVING HERE IN PIECES IF YOU DON'T TELL ME WHAT THIS IS ABOUT!
YOU...?

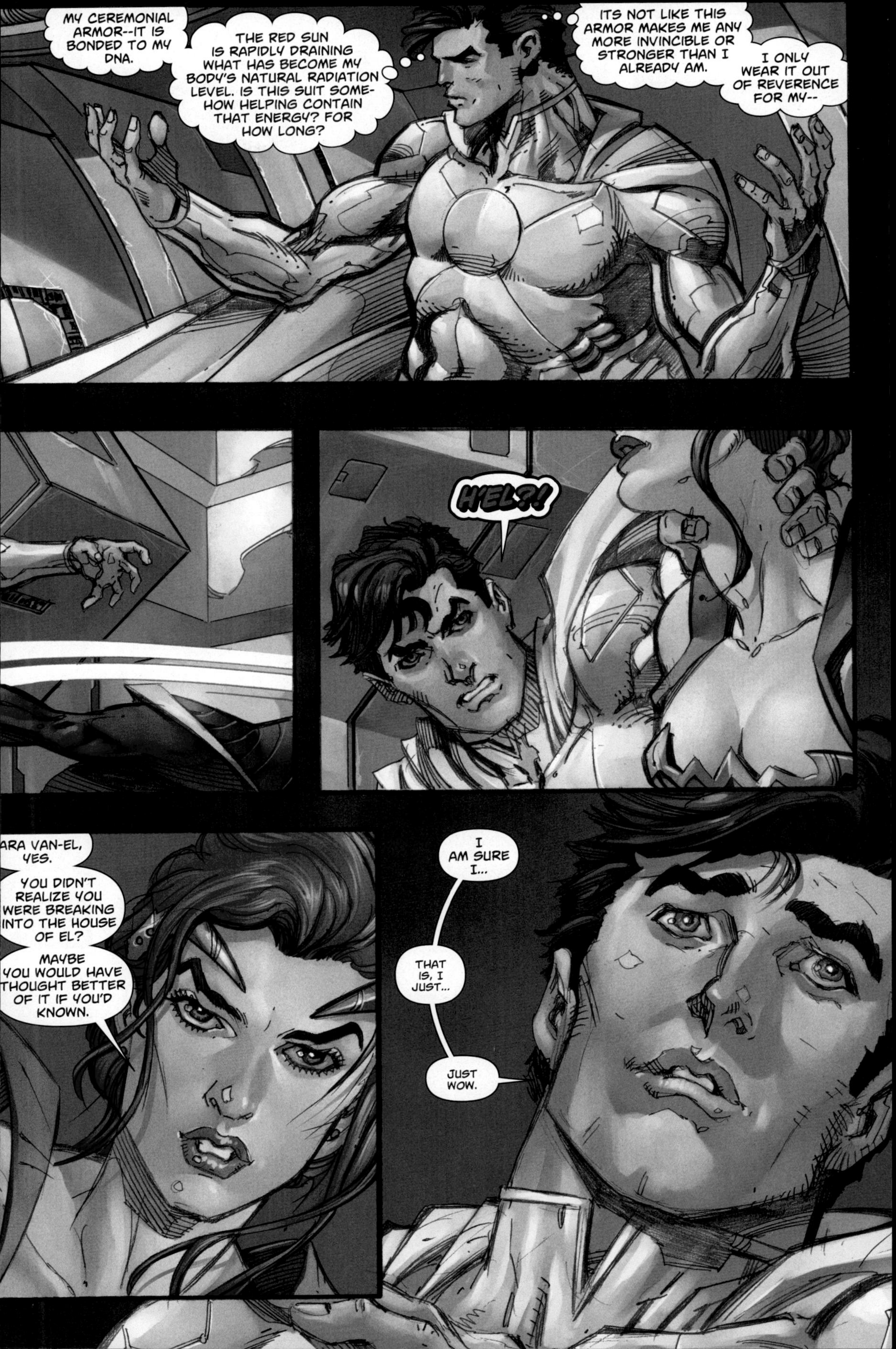

MY CEREMONIAL ARMOR--IT IS BONDED TO MY DNA.
THE RED SUN IS RAPIDLY DRAINING WHAT HAS BECOME MY BODY'S NATURAL RADIATION LEVEL. IS THIS SUIT SOME-HOW HELPING CONTAIN THAT ENERGY? FOR HOW LONG?
ITS NOT LIKE THIS ARMOR MAKES ME ANY MORE INVINCIBLE OR STRONGER THAN I ALREADY AM.
I ONLY WEAR IT OUT OF REVERENCE FOR MY--
H'EL?!
ARA VAN-EL, YES.
YOU DIDN'T REALIZE YOU WERE BREAKING INTO THE HOUSE OF EL?
MAYBE YOU WOULD HAVE THOUGHT BETTER OF IT IF YOU'D KNOWN.
I AM SURE I...
THAT IS, I JUST...
JUST WOW.

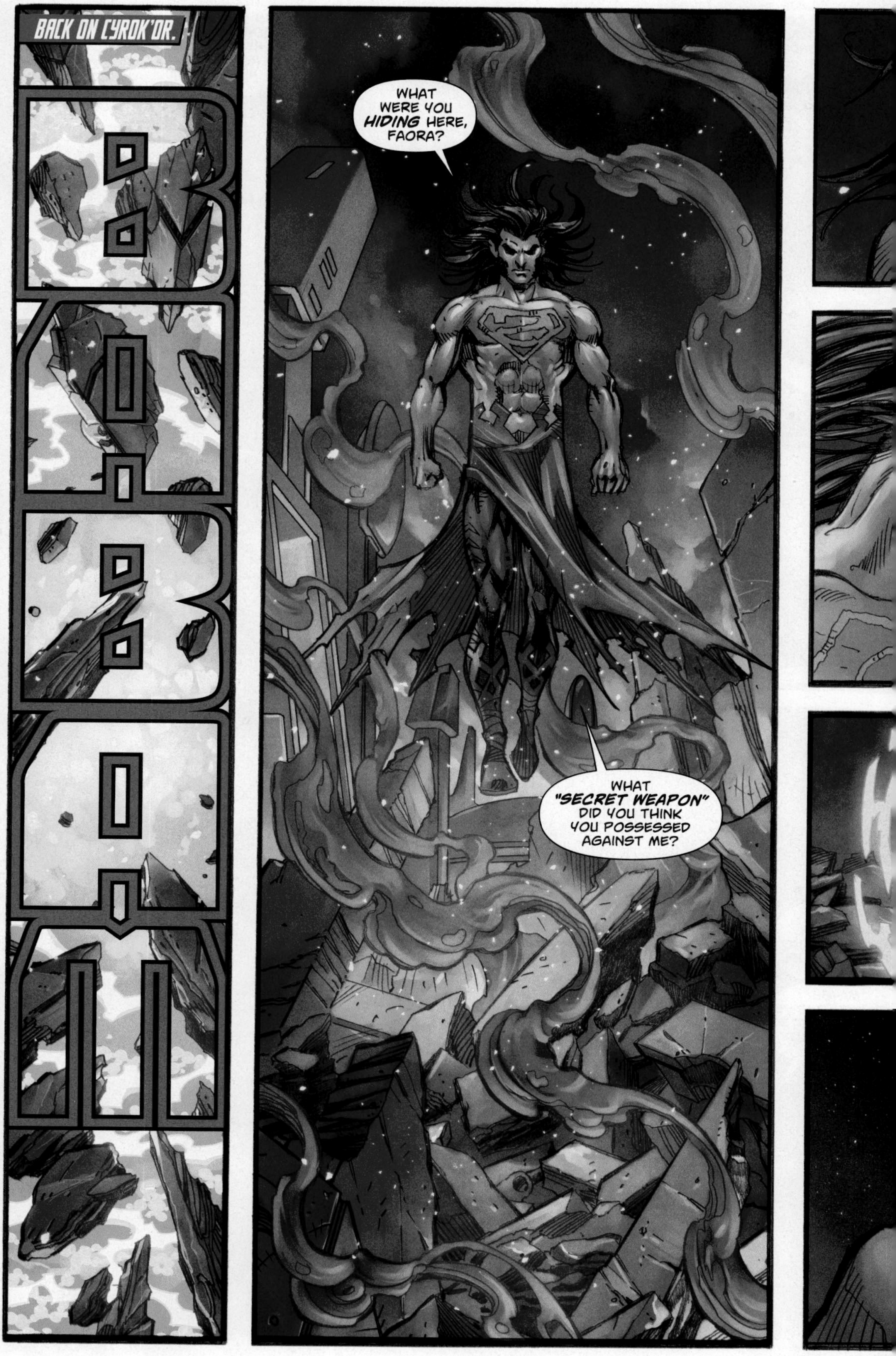
BACK ON CYROK'OR.
WHAT WERE YOU HIDING HERE, FAORA?
WHAT "SECRET WEAPON" DID YOU THINK YOU POSSESSED AGAINST ME?

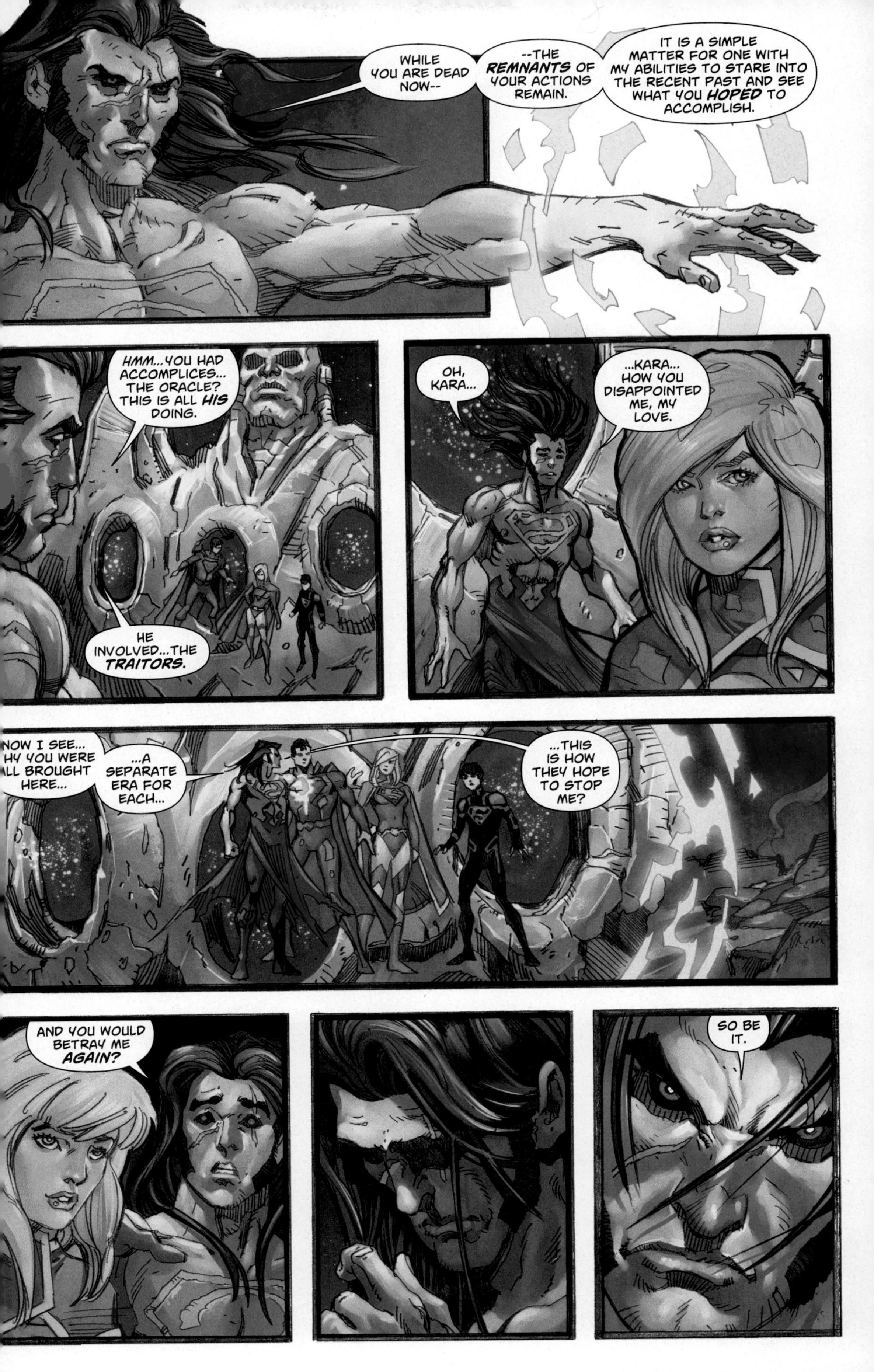
WHILE YOU ARE DEAD NOW--
--THE REMNANTS OF YOUR ACTIONS REMAIN.
IT IS A SIMPLE MATTER FOR ONE WITH MY ABILITIES TO STARE INTO THE RECENT PAST AND SEE WHAT YOU HOPED TO ACCOMPLISH.
HMM...YOU HAD ACCOMPLICES... THE ORACLE? THIS IS ALL HIS DOING.
HE INVOLVED...THE TRAITORS.
OH, KARA...
...KARA... HOW YOU DISAPPOINTED ME, MY LOVE.
NOW I SEE... HY YOU WERE LL BROUGHT HERE...
...A SEPARATE ERA FOR EACH...
...THIS IS HOW THEY HOPE TO STOP ME?
AND YOU WOULD BETRAY ME AGAIN?
SO BE IT.

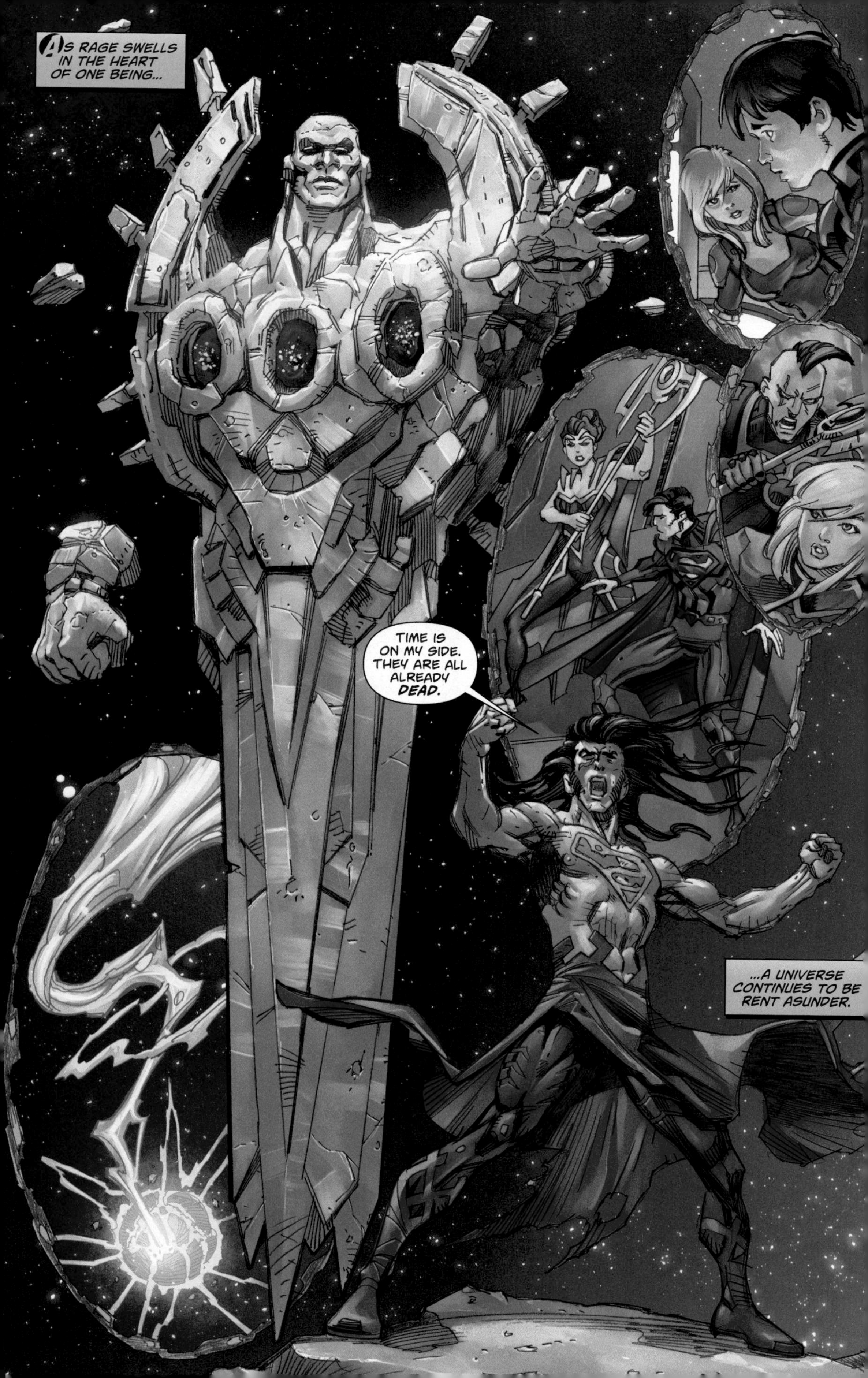
AS RAGE SWELLS IN THE HEART OF ONE BEING...
TIME IS ON MY SIDE. THEY ARE ALL ALREADY DEAD.
...A UNIVERSE CONTINUES TO BE RENT ASUNDER.

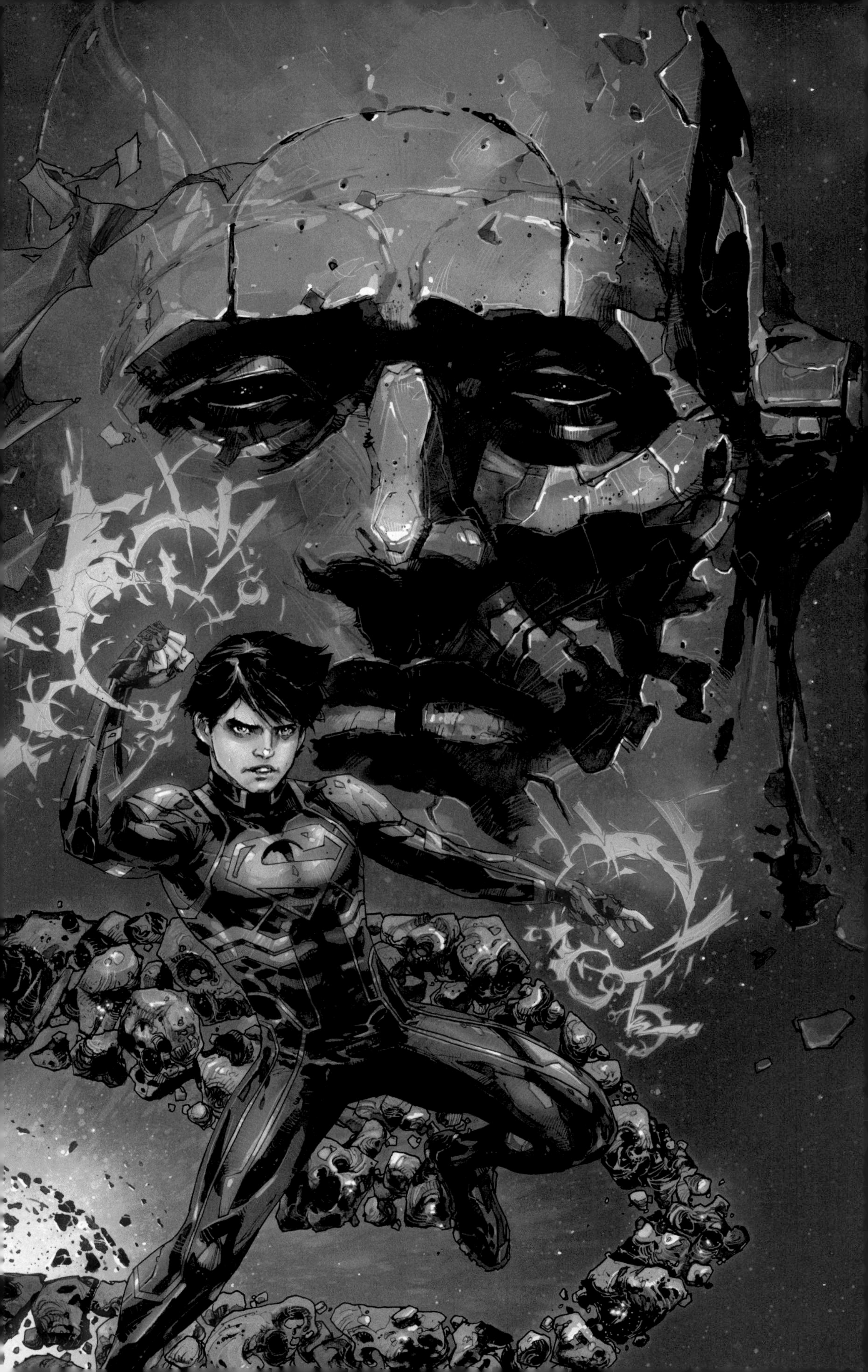

KRYPTON RETURNS PART TWO

SCOTT LOBDELL plot **SCOTT LOBDELL JUSTIN JORDAN MICHAEL ALAN NELSON** dialogue **ED BENES** artist
TANYA HORIE RICHARD HORIE colorists cover art by **KENNETH ROCAFORT**

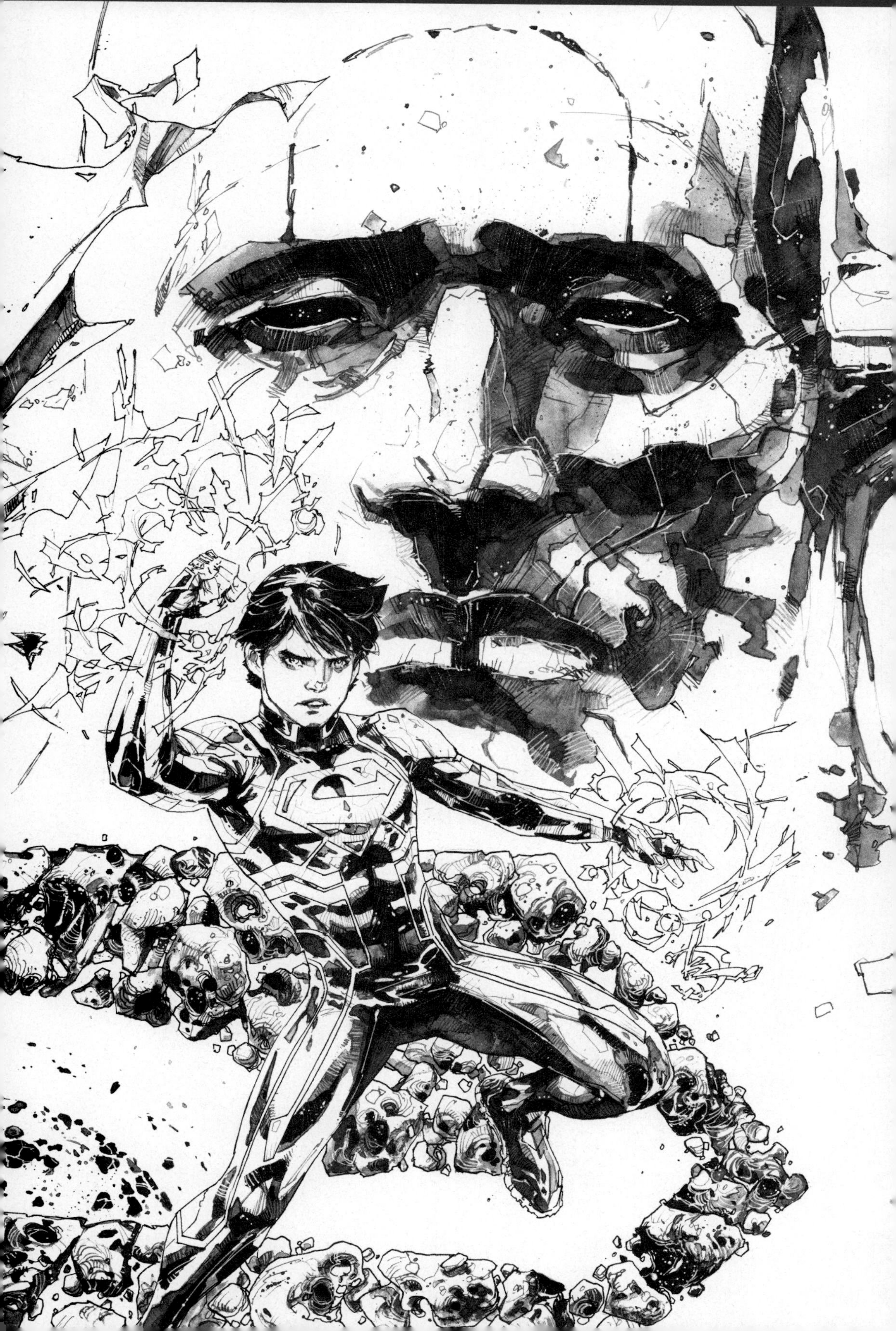

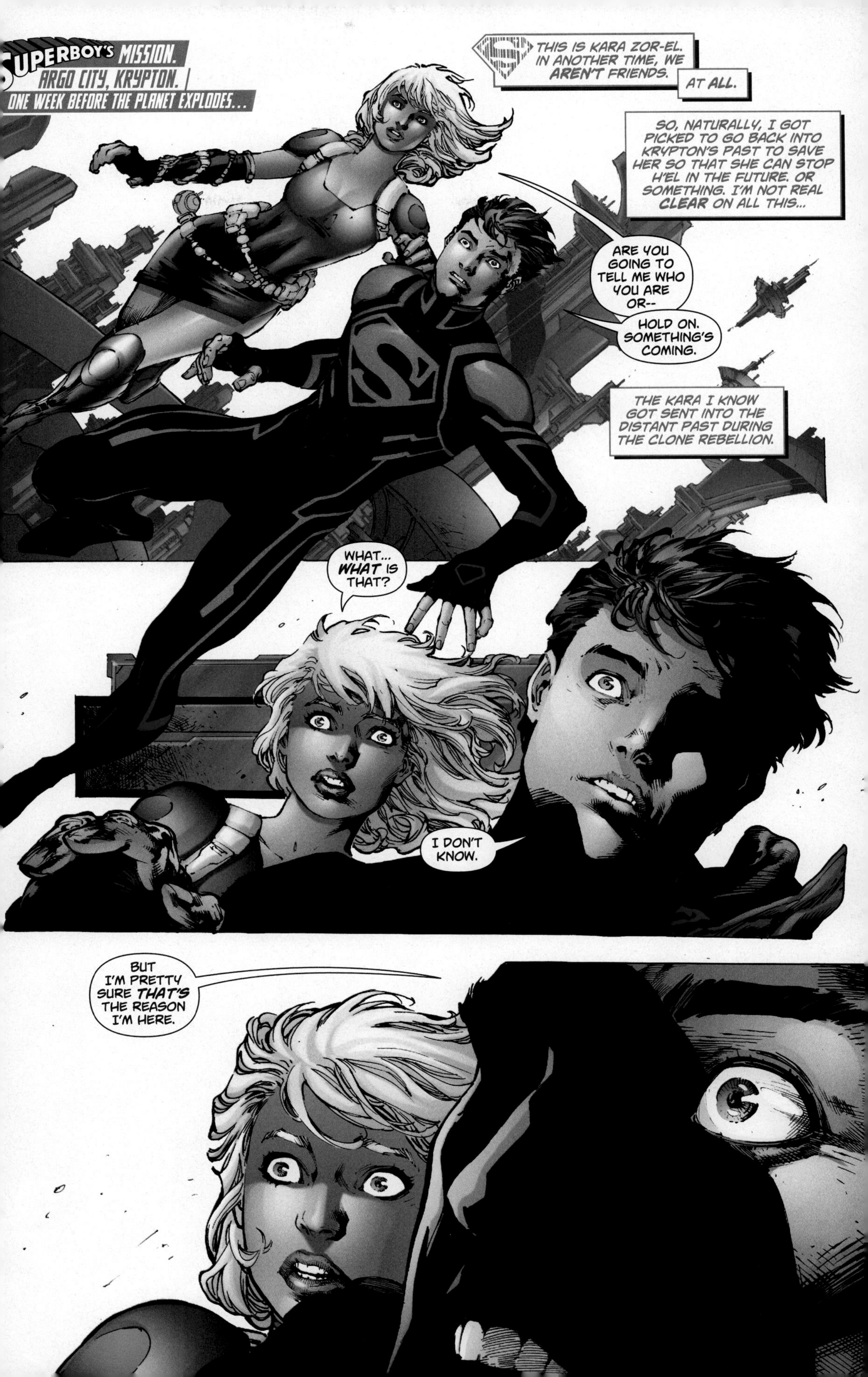
SUPERBOY'S MISSION.
ARGO CITY, KRYPTON.
ONE WEEK BEFORE THE PLANET EXPLODES...
THIS IS KARA ZOR-EL. IN ANOTHER TIME, WE AREN'T FRIENDS.
AT ALL.
SO, NATURALLY, I GOT PICKED TO GO BACK INTO KRYPTON'S PAST TO SAVE HER SO THAT SHE CAN STOP H'EL IN THE FUTURE. OR SOMETHING. I'M NOT REAL CLEAR ON ALL THIS...
ARE YOU GOING TO TELL ME WHO YOU ARE OR--
HOLD ON. SOMETHING'S COMING.
THE KARA I KNOW GOT SENT INTO THE DISTANT PAST DURING THE CLONE REBELLION.
WHAT... WHAT IS THAT?
I DON'T KNOW.
BUT I'M PRETTY SURE THAT'S THE REASON I'M HERE.

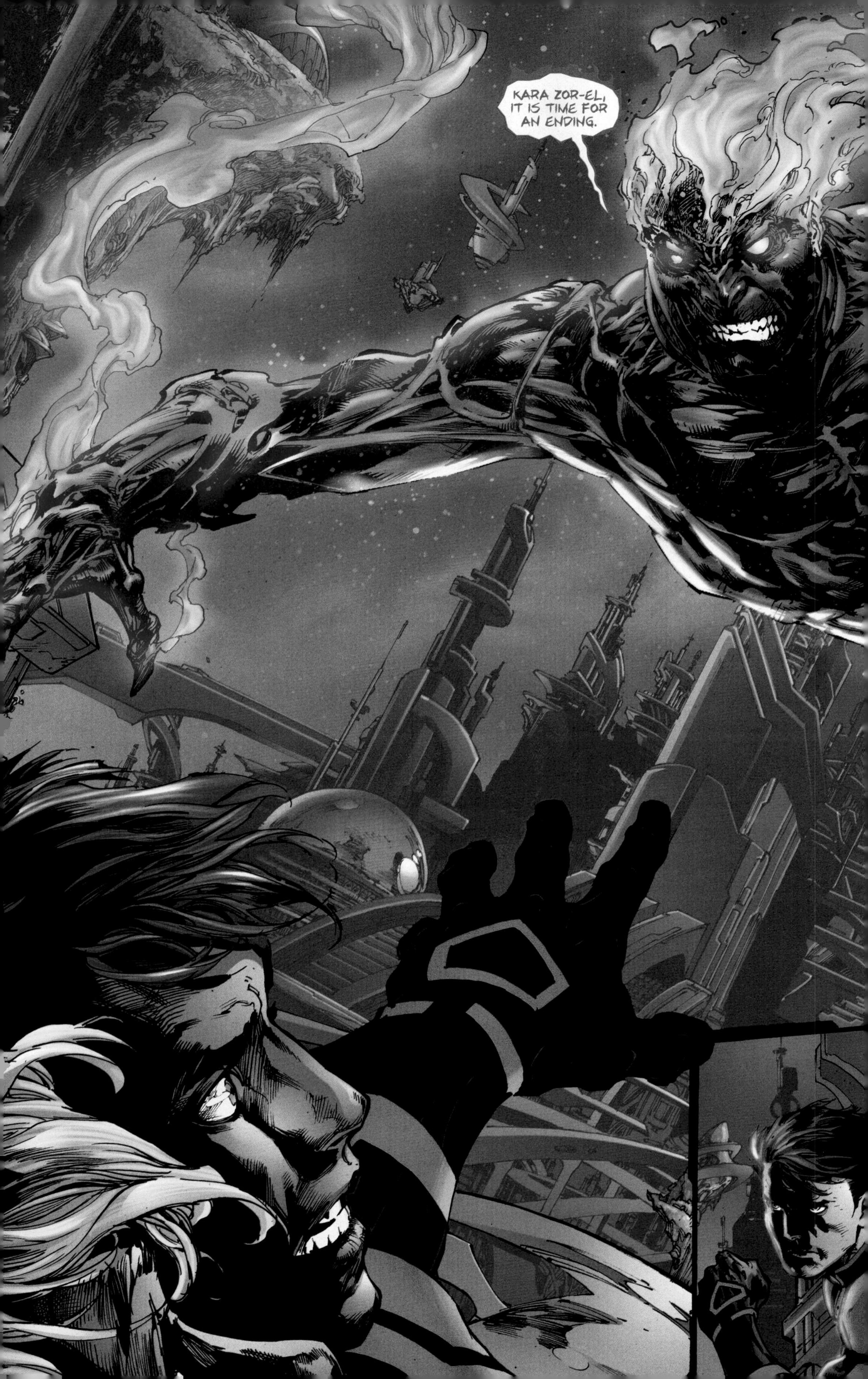
KARA ZOR-EL, IT IS TIME FOR AN ENDING.

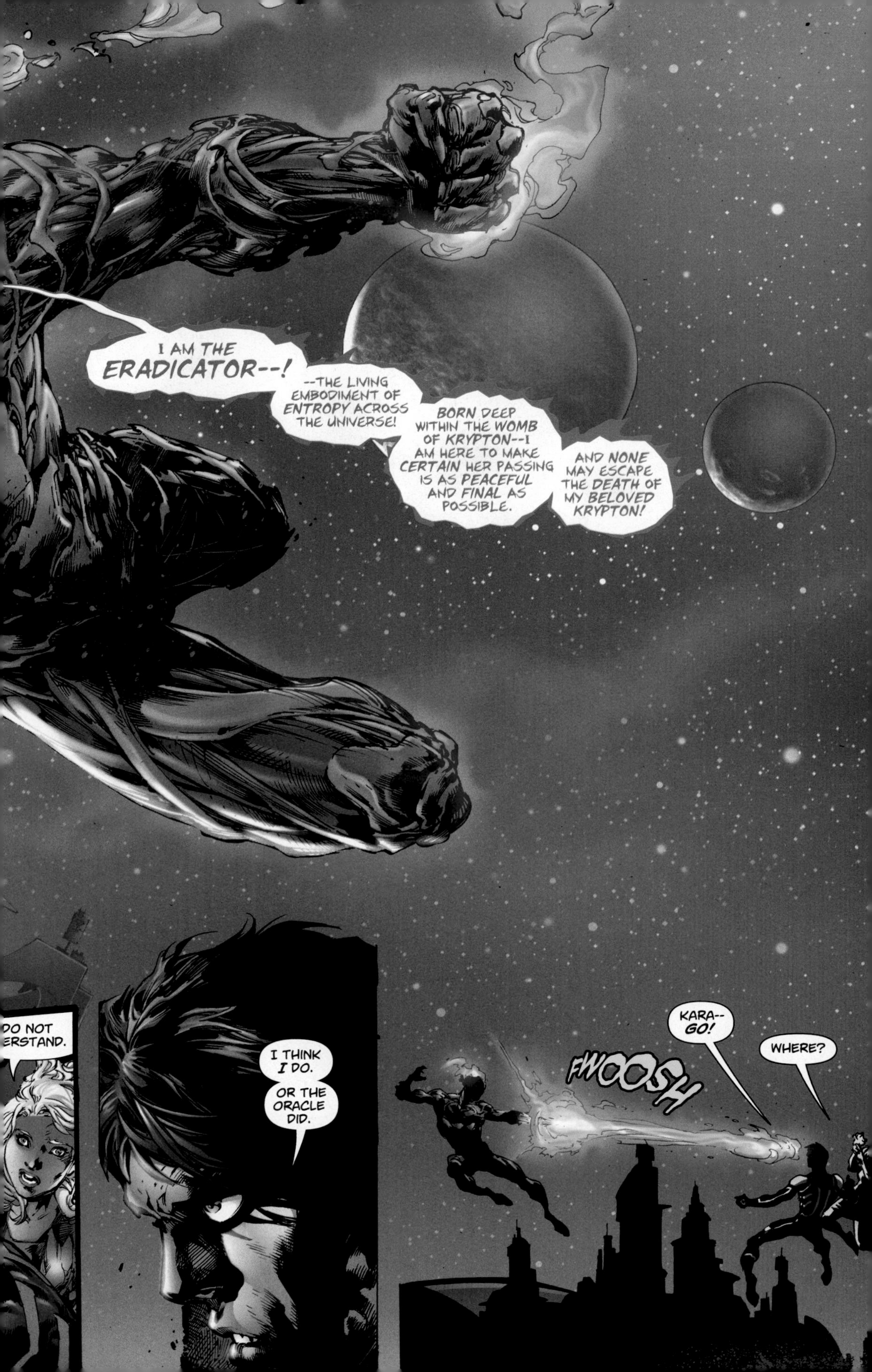
I AM THE ERADICATOR--!
--THE LIVING EMBODIMENT OF ENTROPY ACROSS THE UNIVERSE!
BORN DEEP WITHIN THE WOMB OF KRYPTON--I AM HERE TO MAKE CERTAIN HER PASSING IS AS PEACEFUL AND FINAL AS POSSIBLE.
AND NONE MAY ESCAPE THE DEATH OF MY BELOVED KRYPTON!
DO NOT ERSTAND.
I THINK I DO.
OR THE ORACLE DID.
FWOOSH
KARA-- GO!
WHERE?

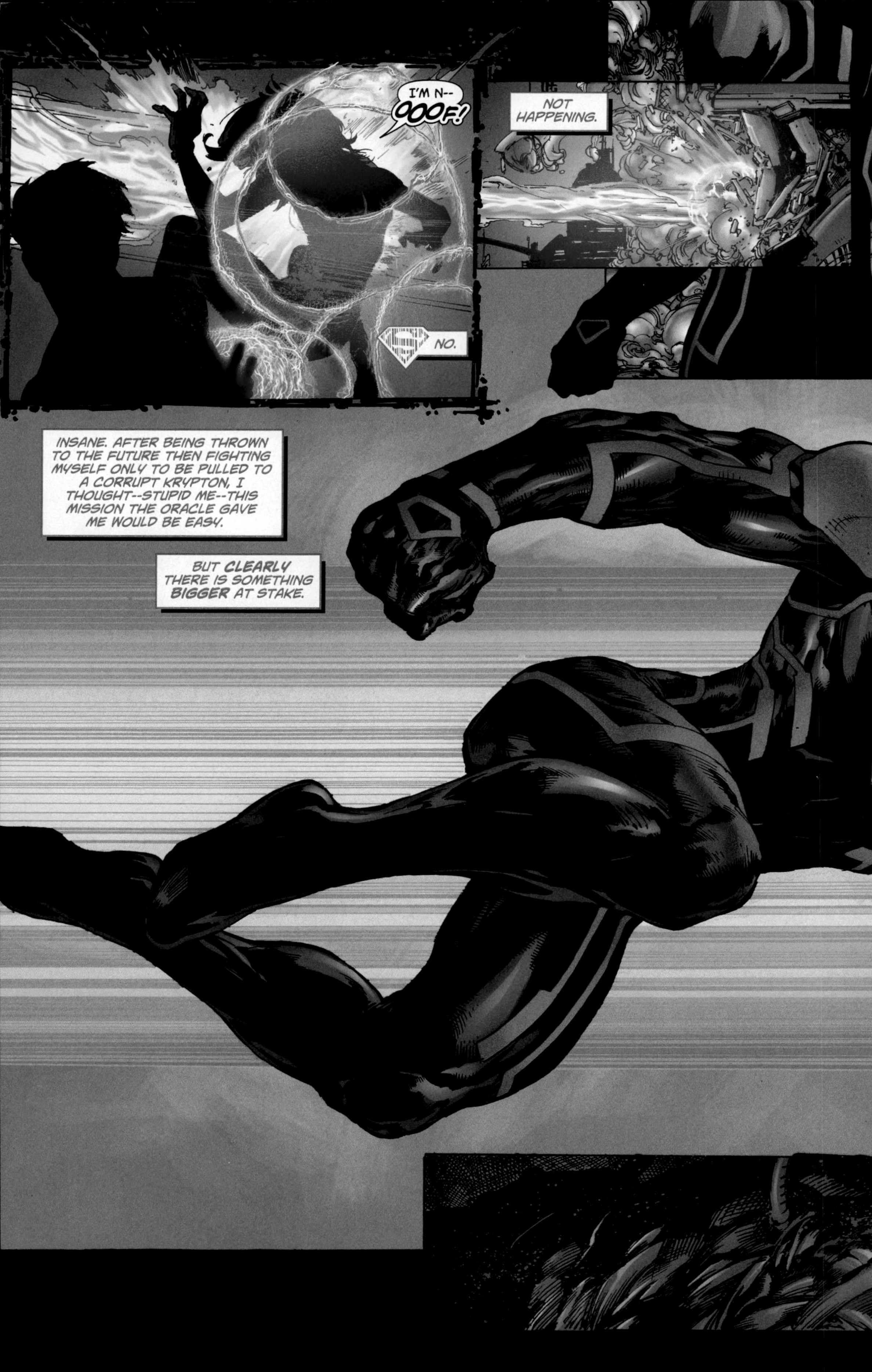
I'M N--
OOOF!
NOT HAPPENING.
NO.
INSANE. AFTER BEING THROWN TO THE FUTURE THEN FIGHTING MYSELF ONLY TO BE PULLED TO A CORRUPT KRYPTON, I THOUGHT--STUPID ME--THIS MISSION THE ORACLE GAVE ME WOULD BE EASY.
BUT CLEARLY THERE IS SOMETHING BIGGER AT STAKE.

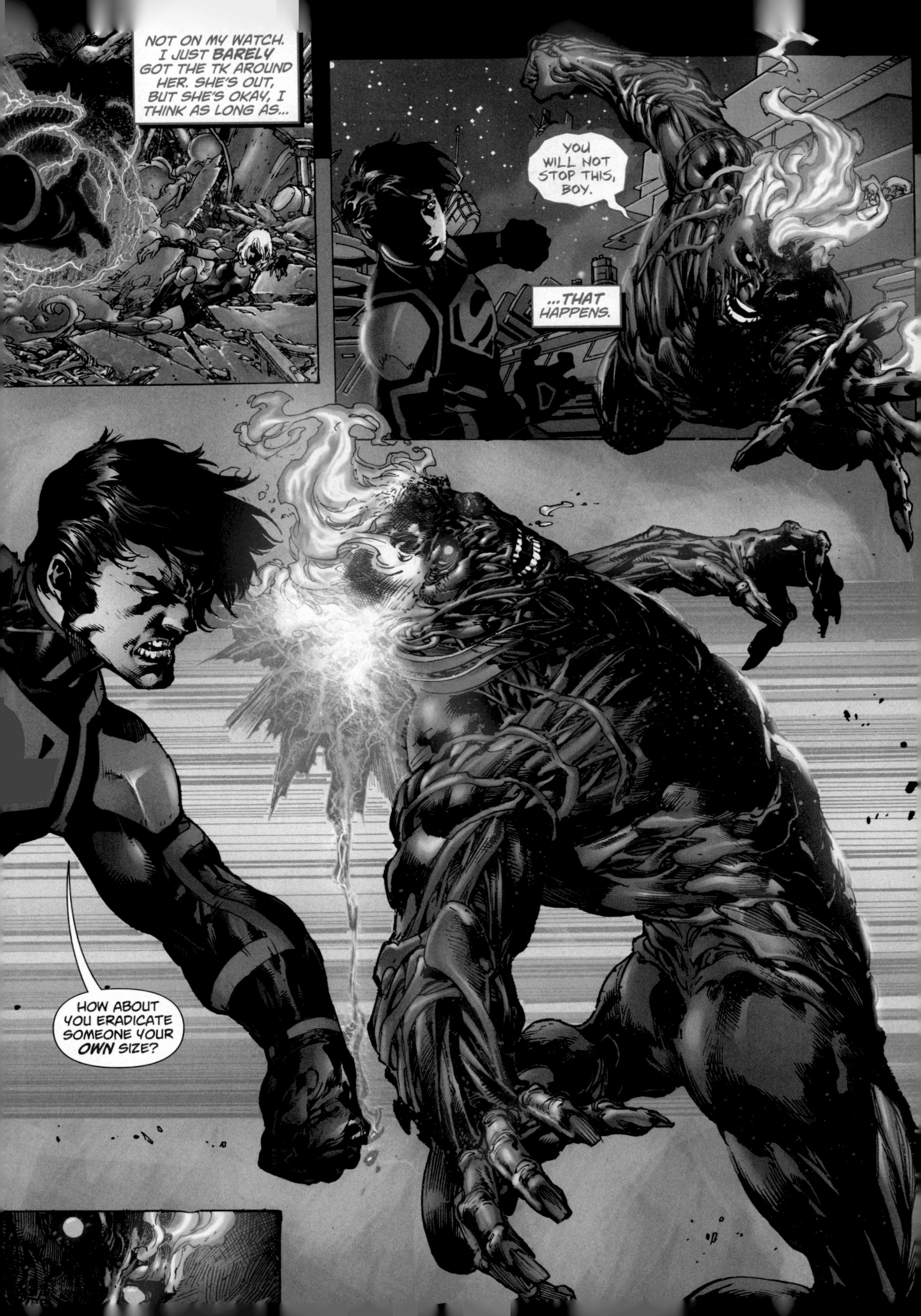
NOT ON MY WATCH. I JUST BARELY GOT THE TK AROUND HER. SHE'S OUT, BUT SHE'S OKAY, I THINK AS LONG AS...
YOU WILL NOT STOP THIS, BOY.
...THAT HAPPENS.
HOW ABOUT YOU ERADICATE SOMEONE YOUR OWN SIZE?

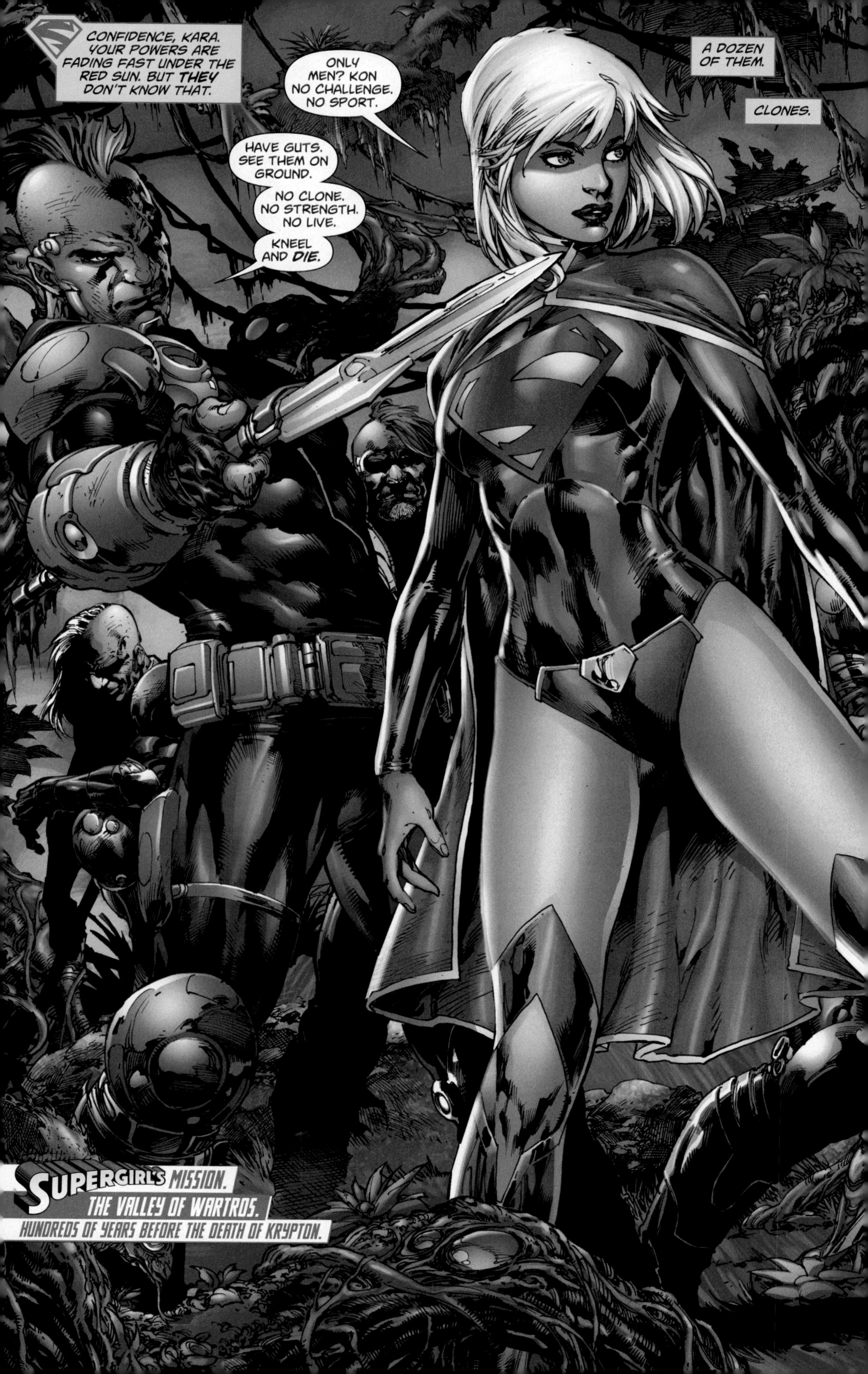

CONFIDENCE, KARA. YOUR POWERS ARE FADING FAST UNDER THE RED SUN. BUT THEY DON'T KNOW THAT.
ONLY MEN? KON NO CHALLENGE. NO SPORT.
HAVE GUTS. SEE THEM ON GROUND.
NO CLONE. NO STRENGTH. NO LIVE.
KNEEL AND DIE.
A DOZEN OF THEM.
CLONES.
SUPERGIRL'S MISSION.
THE VALLEY OF WARTROS.
HUNDREDS OF YEARS BEFORE THE DEATH OF KRYPTON.

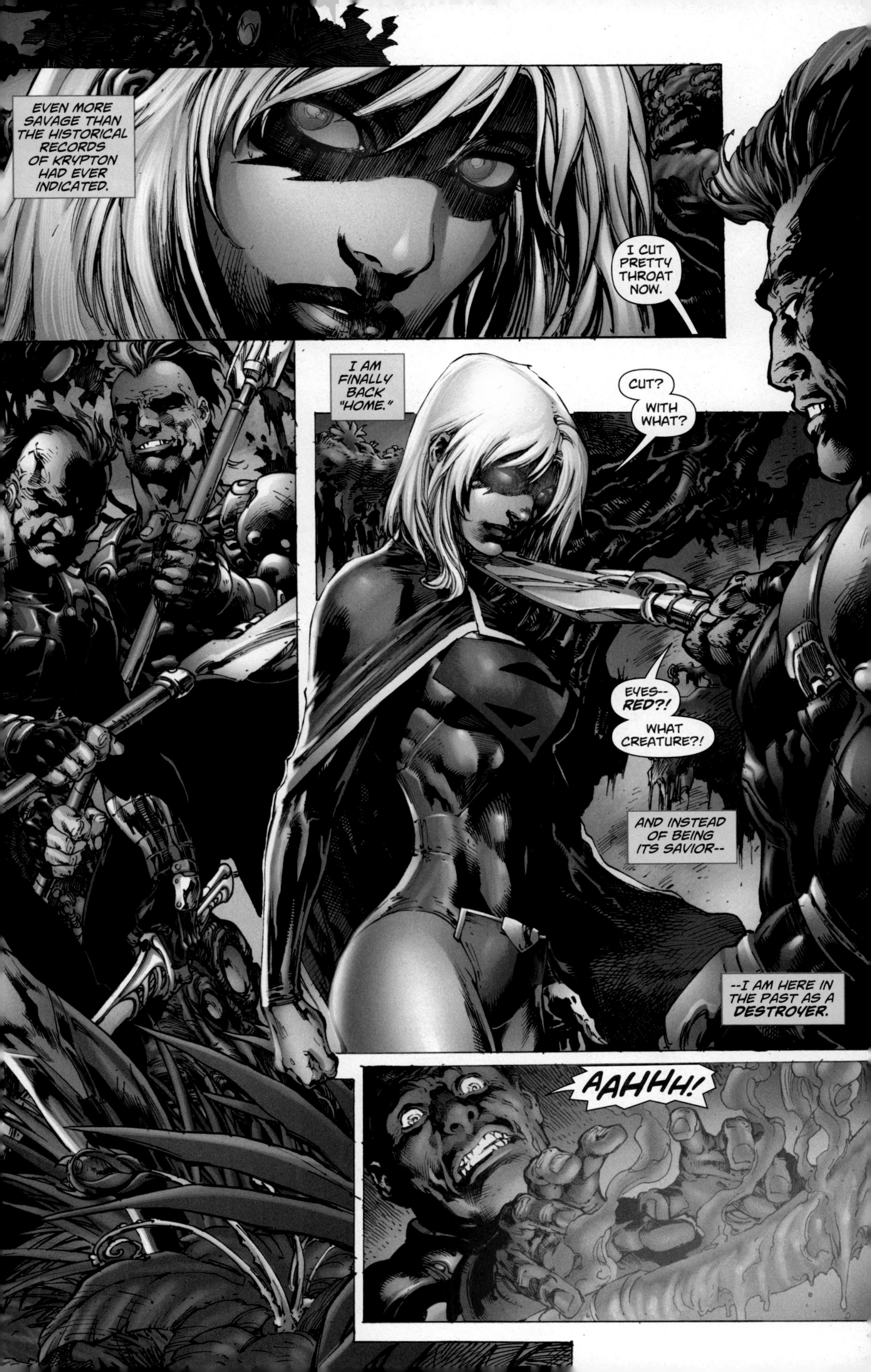
EVEN MORE SAVAGE THAN THE HISTORICAL RECORDS OF KRYPTON HAD EVER INDICATED.
I CUT PRETTY THROAT NOW.
I AM FINALLY BACK "HOME."
CUT? WITH WHAT?
EYES--RED?!
WHAT CREATURE?!
AND INSTEAD OF BEING ITS SAVIOR--
--I AM HERE IN THE PAST AS A DESTROYER.
AAHHH!

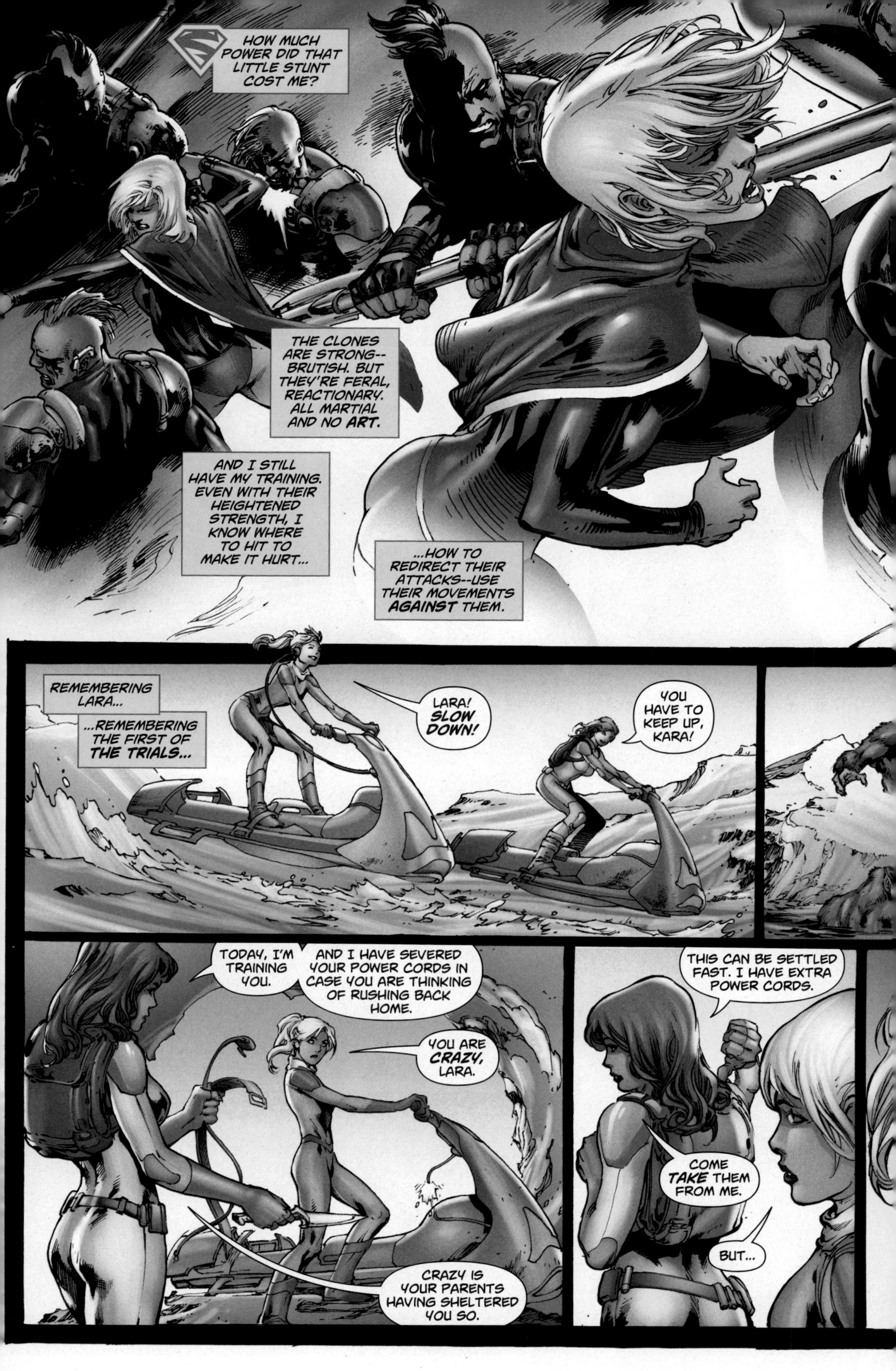
HOW MUCH POWER DID THAT LITTLE STUNT COST ME?
THE CLONES ARE STRONG-- BRUTISH. BUT THEY'RE FERAL, REACTIONARY. ALL MARTIAL AND NO ART.
AND I STILL HAVE MY TRAINING. EVEN WITH THEIR HEIGHTENED STRENGTH, I KNOW WHERE TO HIT TO MAKE IT HURT...
...HOW TO REDIRECT THEIR ATTACKS--USE THEIR MOVEMENTS AGAINST THEM.
REMEMBERING LARA...
...REMEMBERING THE FIRST OF THE TRIALS...
LARA! SLOW DOWN!
YOU HAVE TO KEEP UP, KARA!
TODAY, I'M TRAINING YOU.
AND I HAVE SEVERED YOUR POWER CORDS IN CASE YOU ARE THINKING OF RUSHING BACK HOME.
YOU ARE CRAZY, LARA.
CRAZY IS YOUR PARENTS HAVING SHELTERED YOU SO.
THIS CAN BE SETTLED FAST. I HAVE EXTRA POWER CORDS.
COME TAKE THEM FROM ME.
BUT...

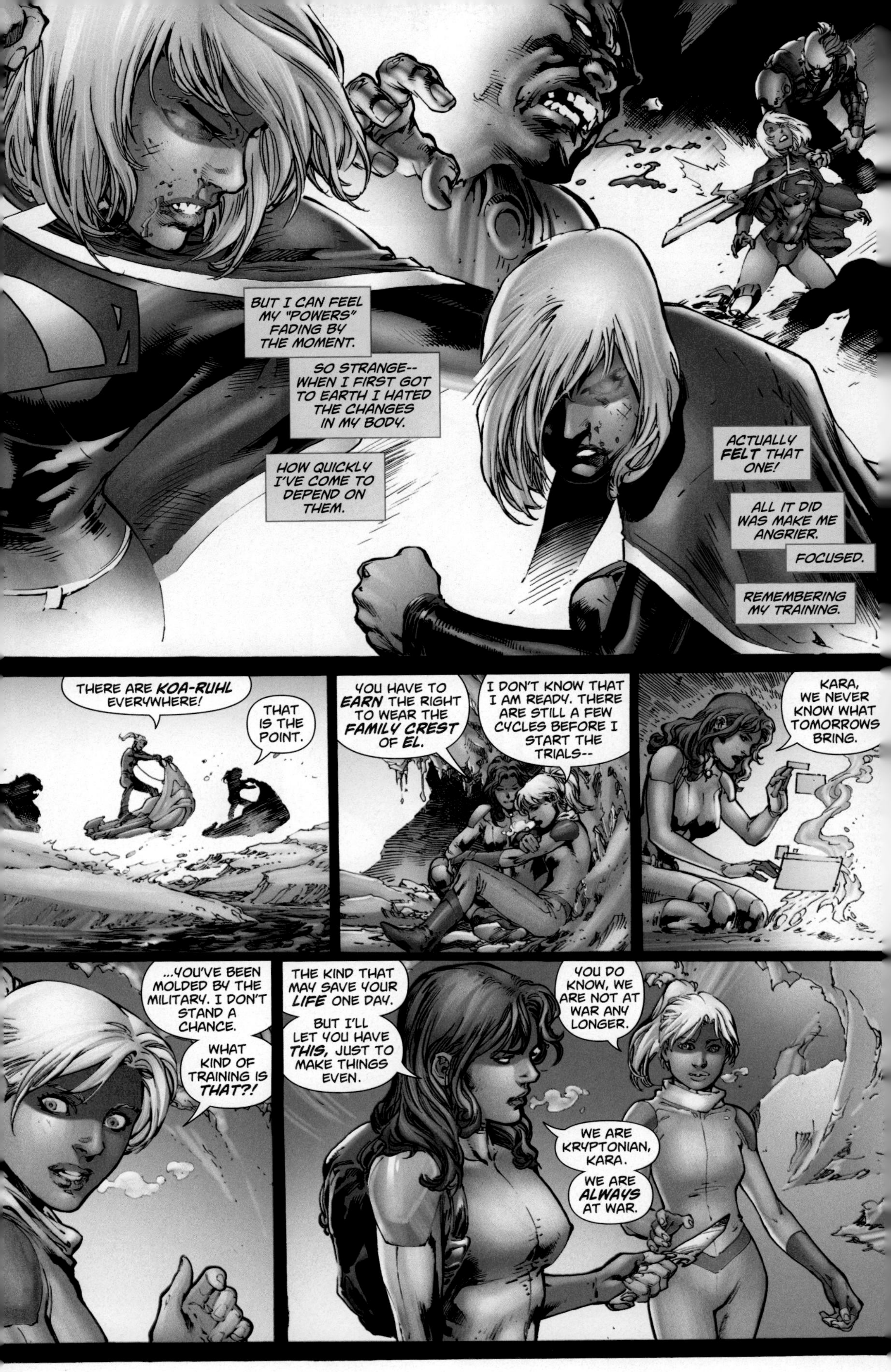
BUT I CAN FEEL MY "POWERS" FADING BY THE MOMENT.
SO STRANGE-- WHEN I FIRST GOT TO EARTH I HATED THE CHANGES IN MY BODY.
HOW QUICKLY I'VE COME TO DEPEND ON THEM.
ACTUALLY FELT THAT ONE!
ALL IT DID WAS MAKE ME ANGRIER.
FOCUSED.
REMEMBERING MY TRAINING.
THERE ARE KOA-RUHL EVERYWHERE!
THAT IS THE POINT.
YOU HAVE TO EARN THE RIGHT TO WEAR THE FAMILY CREST OF EL.
I DON'T KNOW THAT I AM READY. THERE ARE STILL A FEW CYCLES BEFORE I START THE TRIALS--
KARA, WE NEVER KNOW WHAT TOMORROWS BRING.
...YOU'VE BEEN MOLDED BY THE MILITARY. I DON'T STAND A CHANCE.
WHAT KIND OF TRAINING IS THAT?!
THE KIND THAT MAY SAVE YOUR LIFE ONE DAY.
BUT I'LL LET YOU HAVE THIS, JUST TO MAKE THINGS EVEN.
YOU DO KNOW, WE ARE NOT AT WAR ANY LONGER.
WE ARE KRYPTONIAN, KARA.
WE ARE ALWAYS AT WAR.

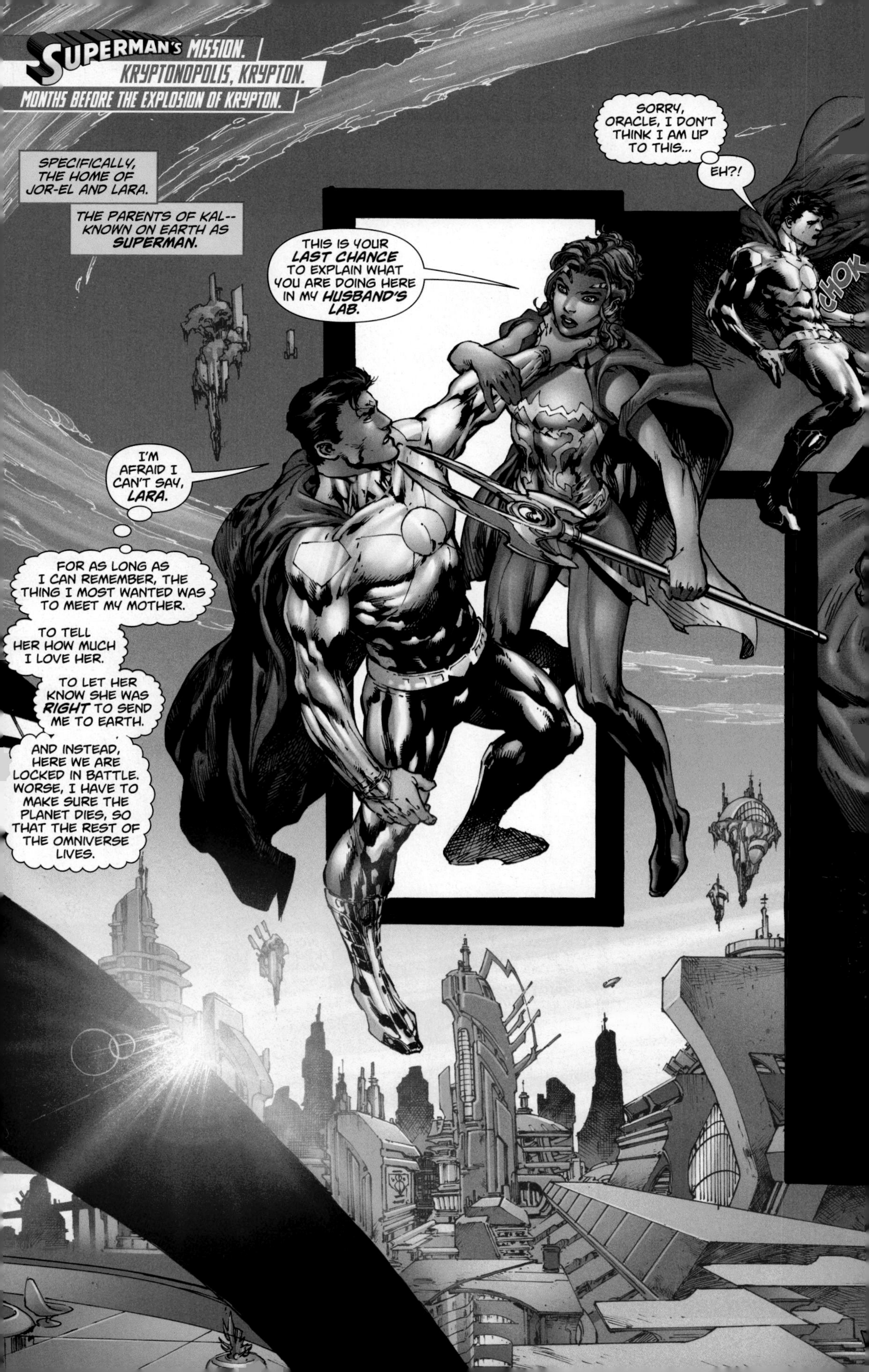
SUPERMAN's MISSION.
KRYPTONOPOLIS, KRYPTON.
MONTHS BEFORE THE EXPLOSION OF KRYPTON.
SPECIFICALLY, THE HOME OF JOR-EL AND LARA.
THE PARENTS OF KAL-- KNOWN ON EARTH AS SUPERMAN.
THIS IS YOUR LAST CHANCE TO EXPLAIN WHAT YOU ARE DOING HERE IN MY HUSBAND'S LAB.
SORRY, ORACLE, I DON'T THINK I AM UP TO THIS...
EH?!
CHOK
I'M AFRAID I CAN'T SAY, LARA.
FOR AS LONG AS I CAN REMEMBER, THE THING I MOST WANTED WAS TO MEET MY MOTHER.
TO TELL HER HOW MUCH I LOVE HER.
TO LET HER KNOW SHE WAS RIGHT TO SEND ME TO EARTH.
AND INSTEAD, HERE WE ARE LOCKED IN BATTLE. WORSE, I HAVE TO MAKE SURE THE PLANET DIES, SO THAT THE REST OF THE OMNIVERSE LIVES.

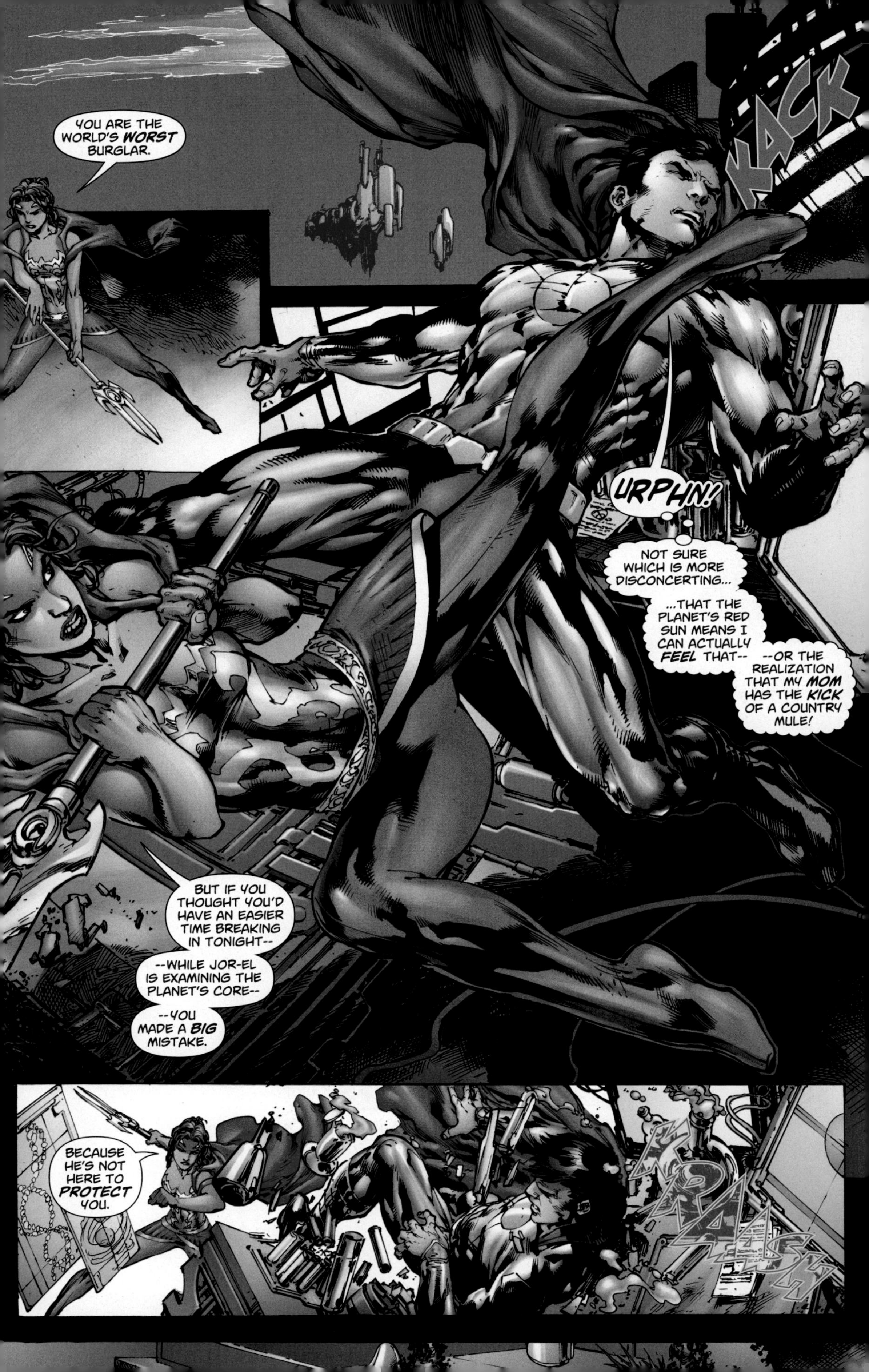
KRACK
YOU ARE THE WORLD'S WORST BURGLAR.
URPHN!
NOT SURE WHICH IS MORE DISCONCERTING...
...THAT THE PLANET'S RED SUN MEANS I CAN ACTUALLY FEEL THAT--
--OR THE REALIZATION THAT MY MOM HAS THE KICK OF A COUNTRY MULE!
BUT IF YOU THOUGHT YOU'D HAVE AN EASIER TIME BREAKING IN TONIGHT--
--WHILE JOR-EL IS EXAMINING THE PLANET'S CORE--
--YOU MADE A BIG MISTAKE.
BECAUSE HE'S NOT HERE TO PROTECT YOU.

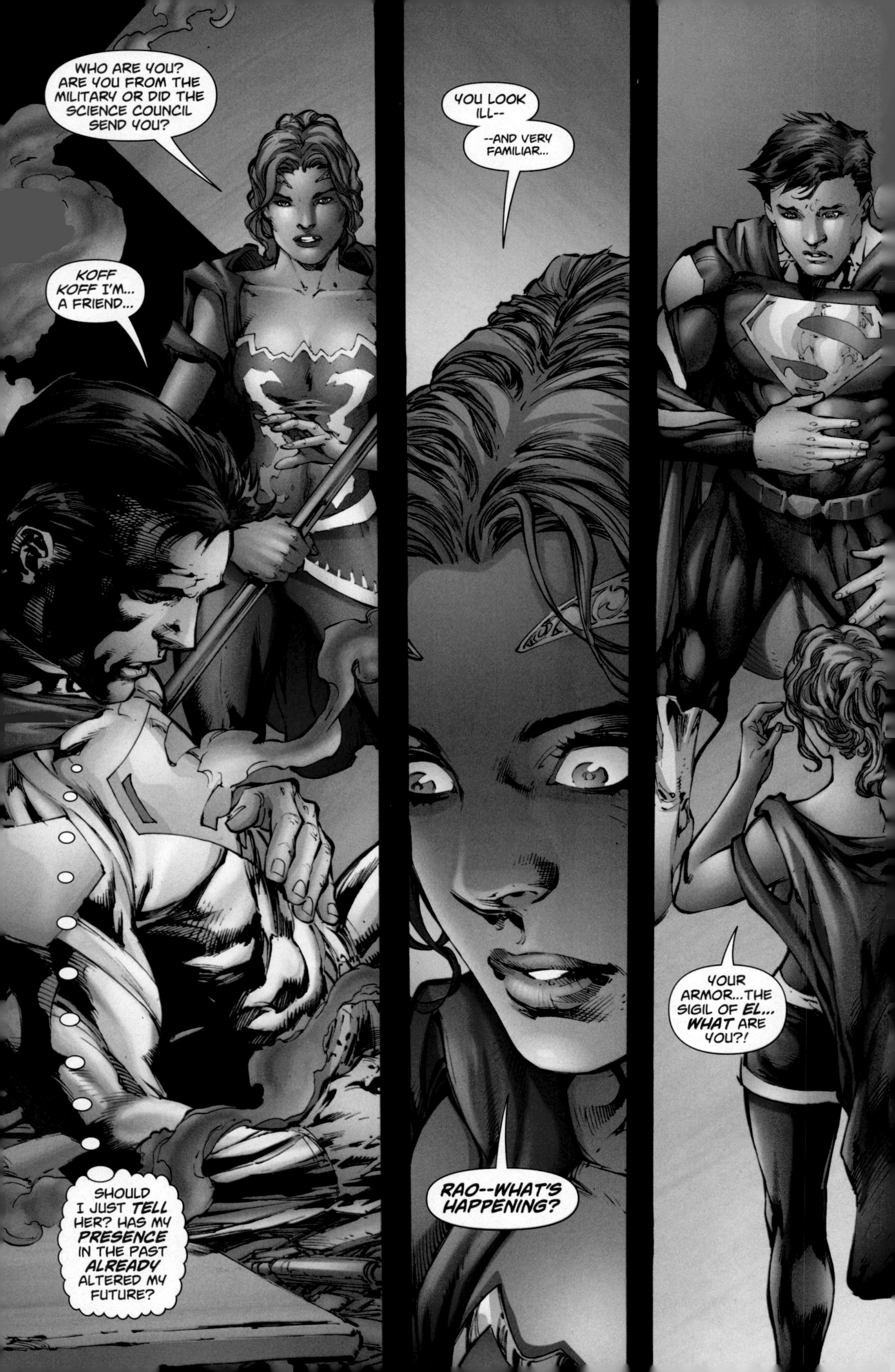

WHO ARE YOU? ARE YOU FROM THE MILITARY OR DID THE SCIENCE COUNCIL SEND YOU?
KOFF KOFF I'M... A FRIEND...
SHOULD I JUST TELL HER? HAS MY PRESENCE IN THE PAST ALREADY ALTERED MY FUTURE?
YOU LOOK ILL--
--AND VERY FAMILIAR...
RAO--WHAT'S HAPPENING?
YOUR ARMOR...THE SIGIL OF EL... WHAT ARE YOU?!

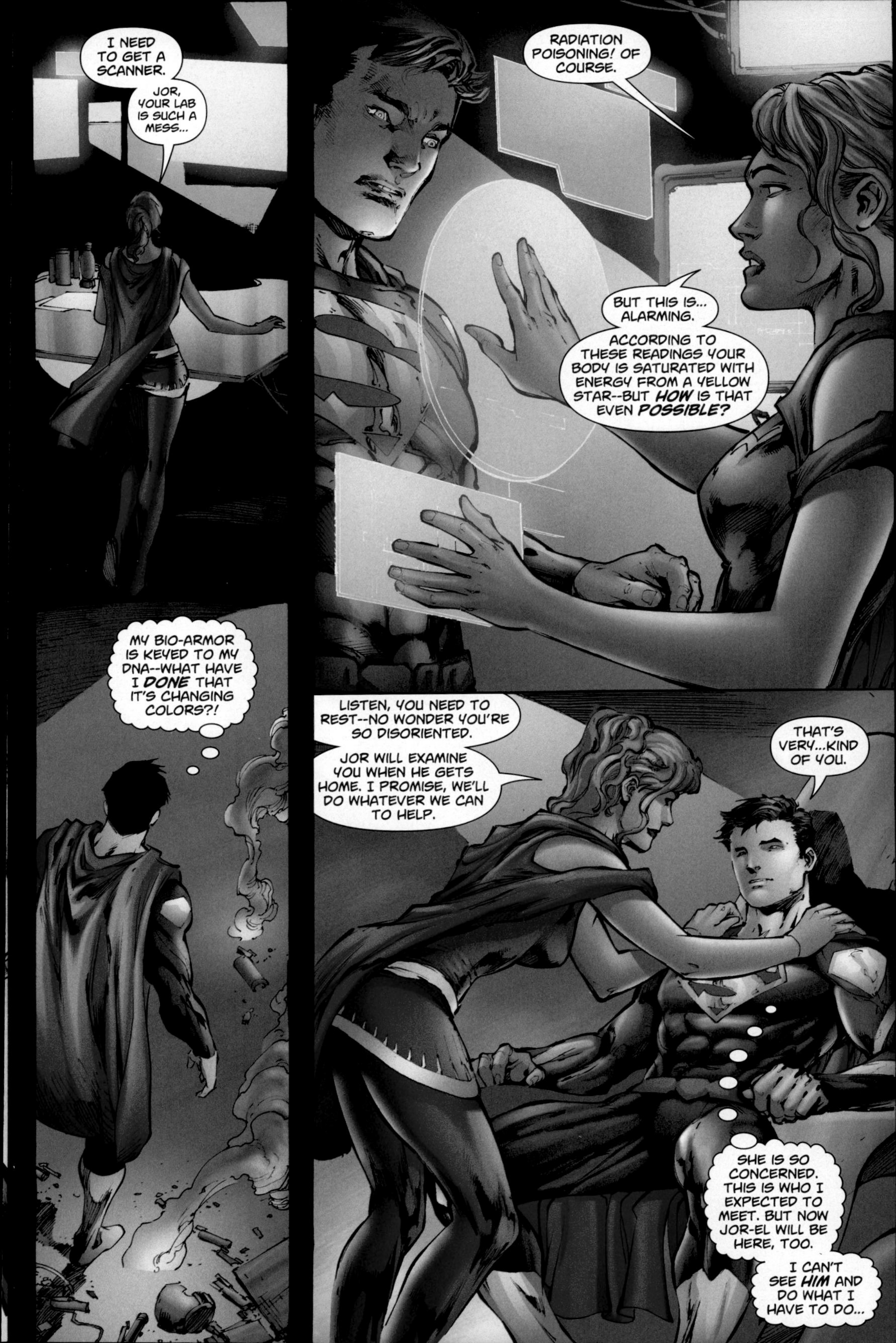
I NEED TO GET A SCANNER.
JOR, YOUR LAB IS SUCH A MESS...
RADIATION POISONING! OF COURSE.
BUT THIS IS... ALARMING.
ACCORDING TO THESE READINGS YOUR BODY IS SATURATED WITH ENERGY FROM A YELLOW STAR--BUT HOW IS THAT EVEN POSSIBLE?
MY BIO-ARMOR IS KEYED TO MY DNA--WHAT HAVE I DONE THAT IT'S CHANGING COLORS?!
LISTEN, YOU NEED TO REST--NO WONDER YOU'RE SO DISORIENTED.
JOR WILL EXAMINE YOU WHEN HE GETS HOME. I PROMISE, WE'LL DO WHATEVER WE CAN TO HELP.
THAT'S VERY...KIND OF YOU.
SHE IS SO CONCERNED. THIS IS WHO I EXPECTED TO MEET. BUT NOW JOR-EL WILL BE HERE, TOO.
I CAN'T SEE HIM AND DO WHAT I HAVE TO DO...

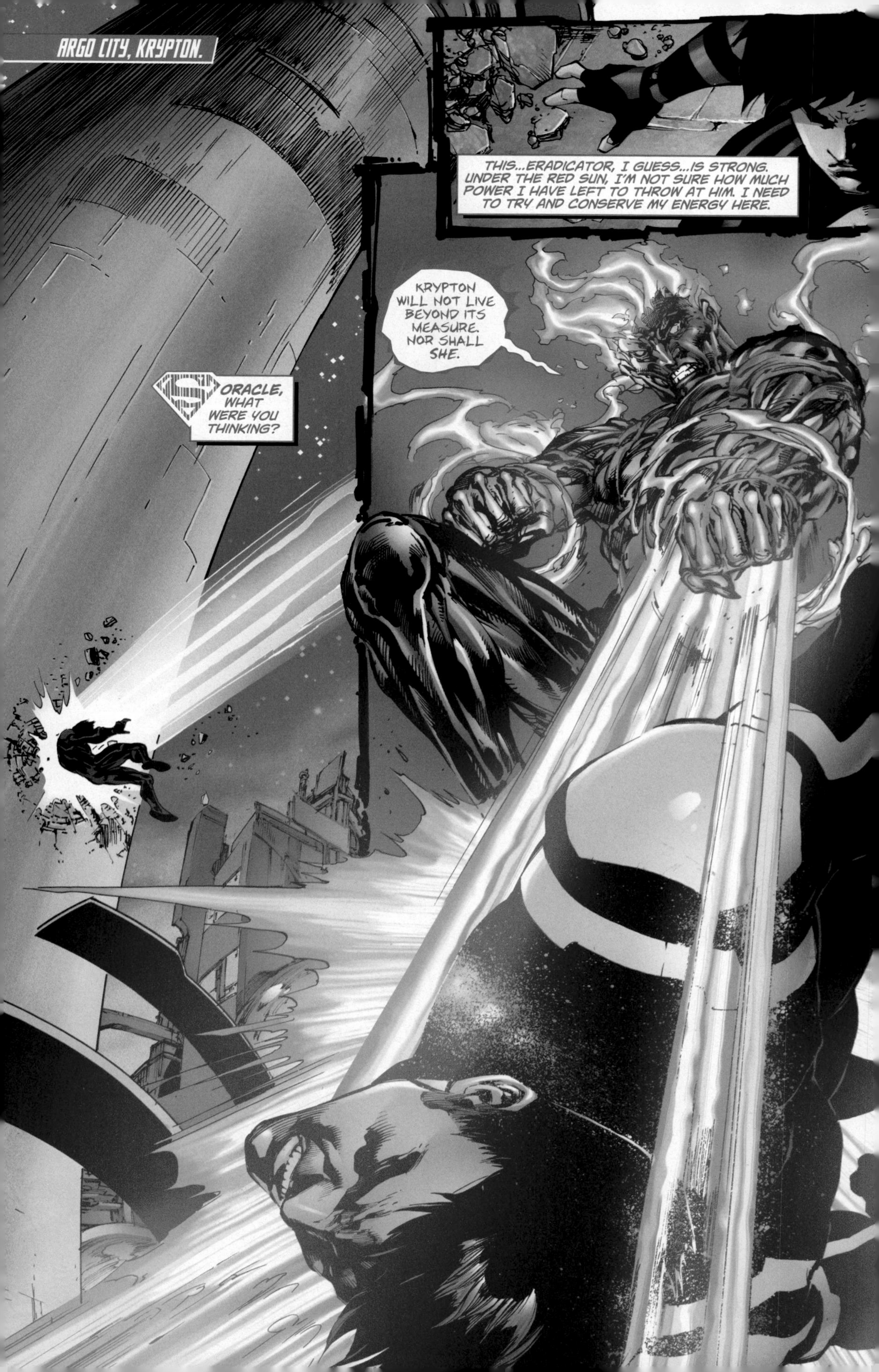
ARGO CITY, KRYPTON.
THIS...ERADICATOR, I GUESS...IS STRONG. UNDER THE RED SUN, I'M NOT SURE HOW MUCH POWER I HAVE LEFT TO THROW AT HIM. I NEED TO TRY AND CONSERVE MY ENERGY HERE.
KRYPTON WILL NOT LIVE BEYOND ITS MEASURE. NOR SHALL SHE.
ORACLE, WHAT WERE YOU THINKING?

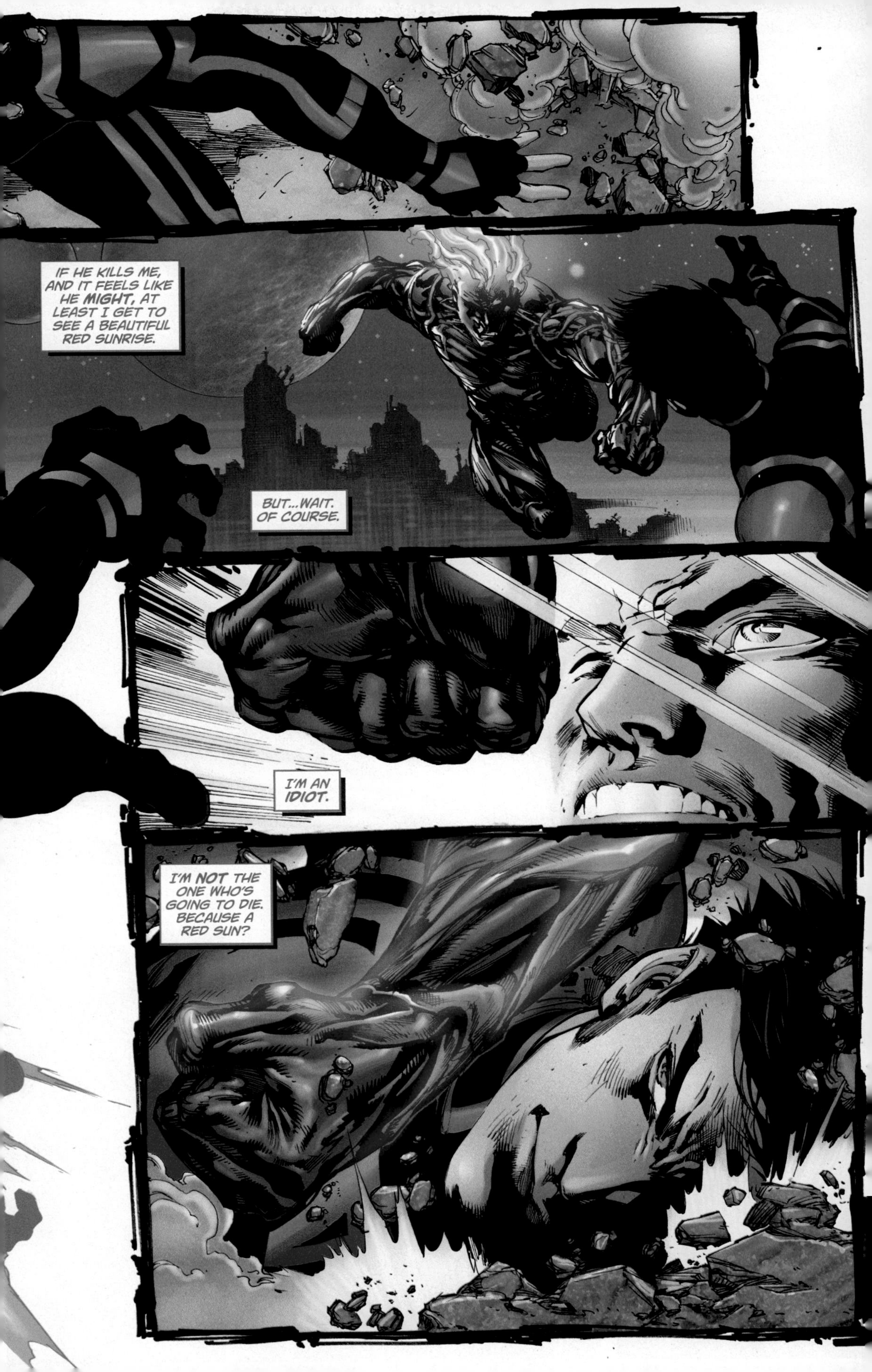
IF HE KILLS ME, AND IT FEELS LIKE HE MIGHT, AT LEAST I GET TO SEE A BEAUTIFUL RED SUNRISE.
BUT...WAIT. OF COURSE.
I'M AN IDIOT.
I'M NOT THE ONE WHO'S GOING TO DIE. BECAUSE A RED SUN?

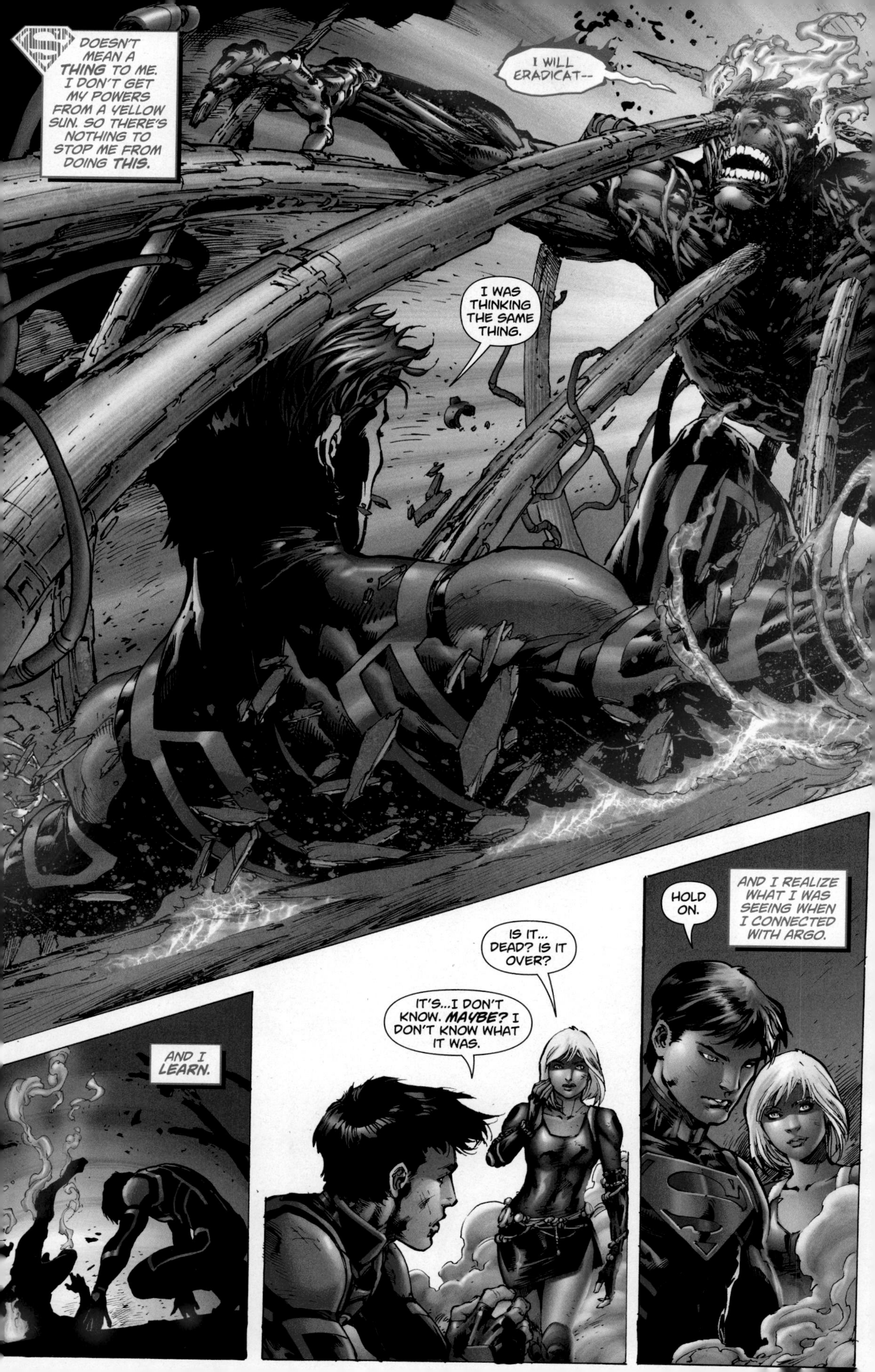
DOESN'T MEAN A THING TO ME. I DON'T GET MY POWERS FROM A YELLOW SUN. SO THERE'S NOTHING TO STOP ME FROM DOING THIS.
I WILL ERADICAT--
I WAS THINKING THE SAME THING.
AND I LEARN.
IS IT... DEAD? IS IT OVER?
IT'S...I DON'T KNOW. MAYBE? I DON'T KNOW WHAT IT WAS.
HOLD ON.
AND I REALIZE WHAT I WAS SEEING WHEN I CONNECTED WITH ARGO.

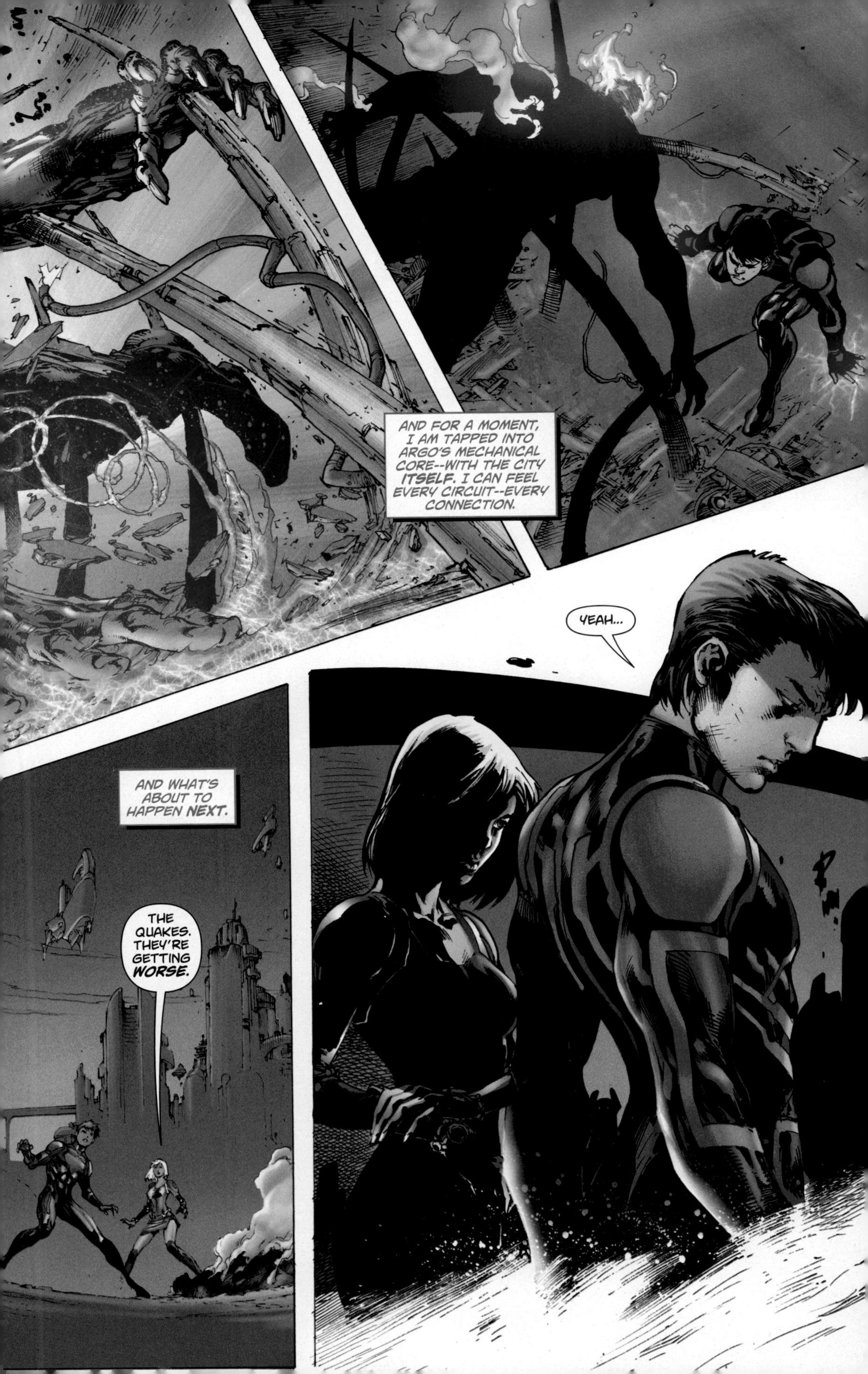
AND FOR A MOMENT, I AM TAPPED INTO ARGO'S MECHANICAL CORE--WITH THE CITY ITSELF. I CAN FEEL EVERY CIRCUIT--EVERY CONNECTION.
YEAH...
AND WHAT'S ABOUT TO HAPPEN NEXT.
THE QUAKES. THEY'RE GETTING WORSE.

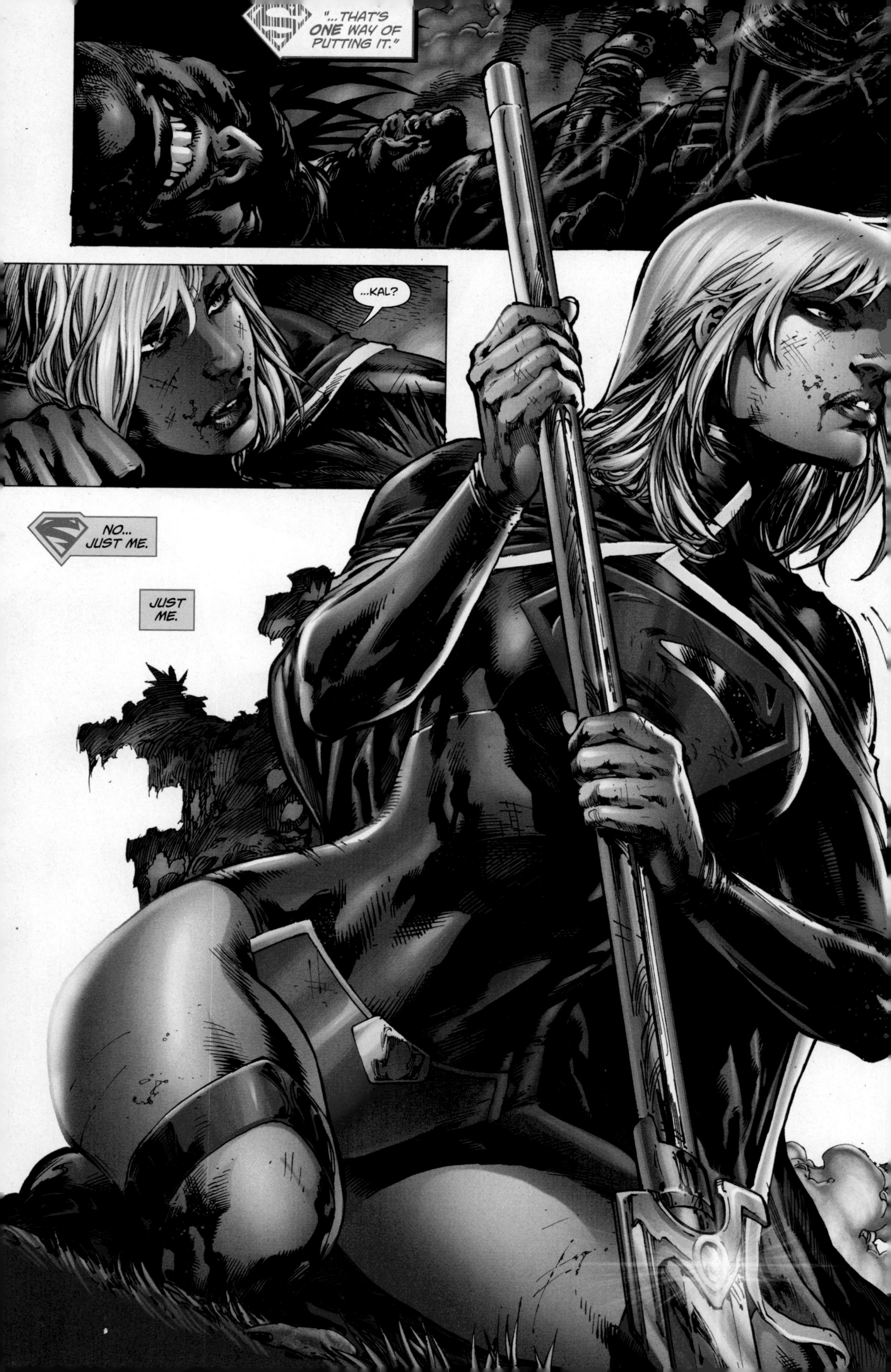
"...THAT'S ONE WAY OF PUTTING IT."
...KAL?
NO... JUST ME.
JUST ME.

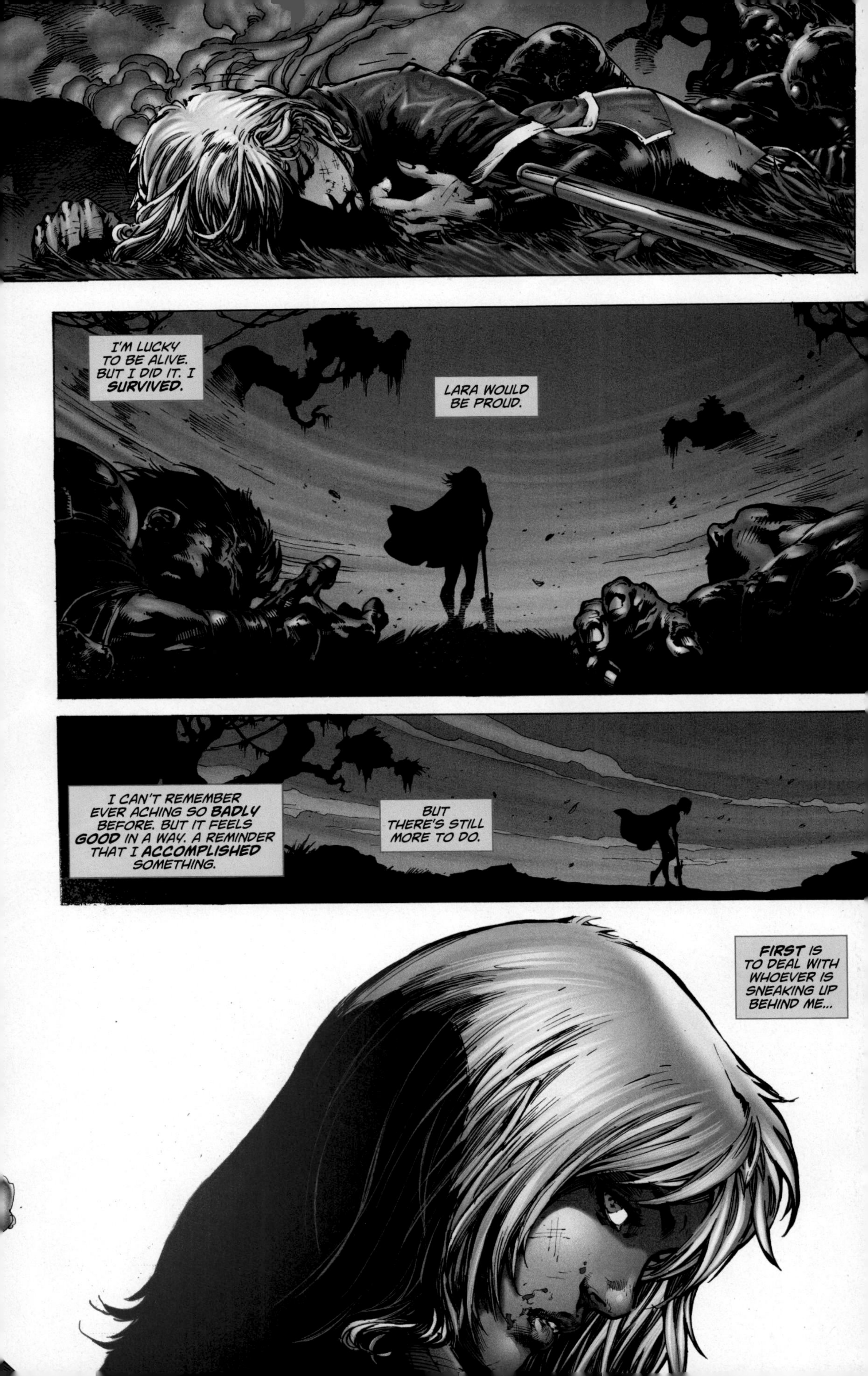
I'M LUCKY TO BE ALIVE. BUT I DID IT. I SURVIVED.
LARA WOULD BE PROUD.
I CAN'T REMEMBER EVER ACHING SO BADLY BEFORE. BUT IT FEELS GOOD IN A WAY. A REMINDER THAT I ACCOMPLISHED SOMETHING.
BUT THERE'S STILL MORE TO DO.
FIRST IS TO DEAL WITH WHOEVER IS SNEAKING UP BEHIND ME...

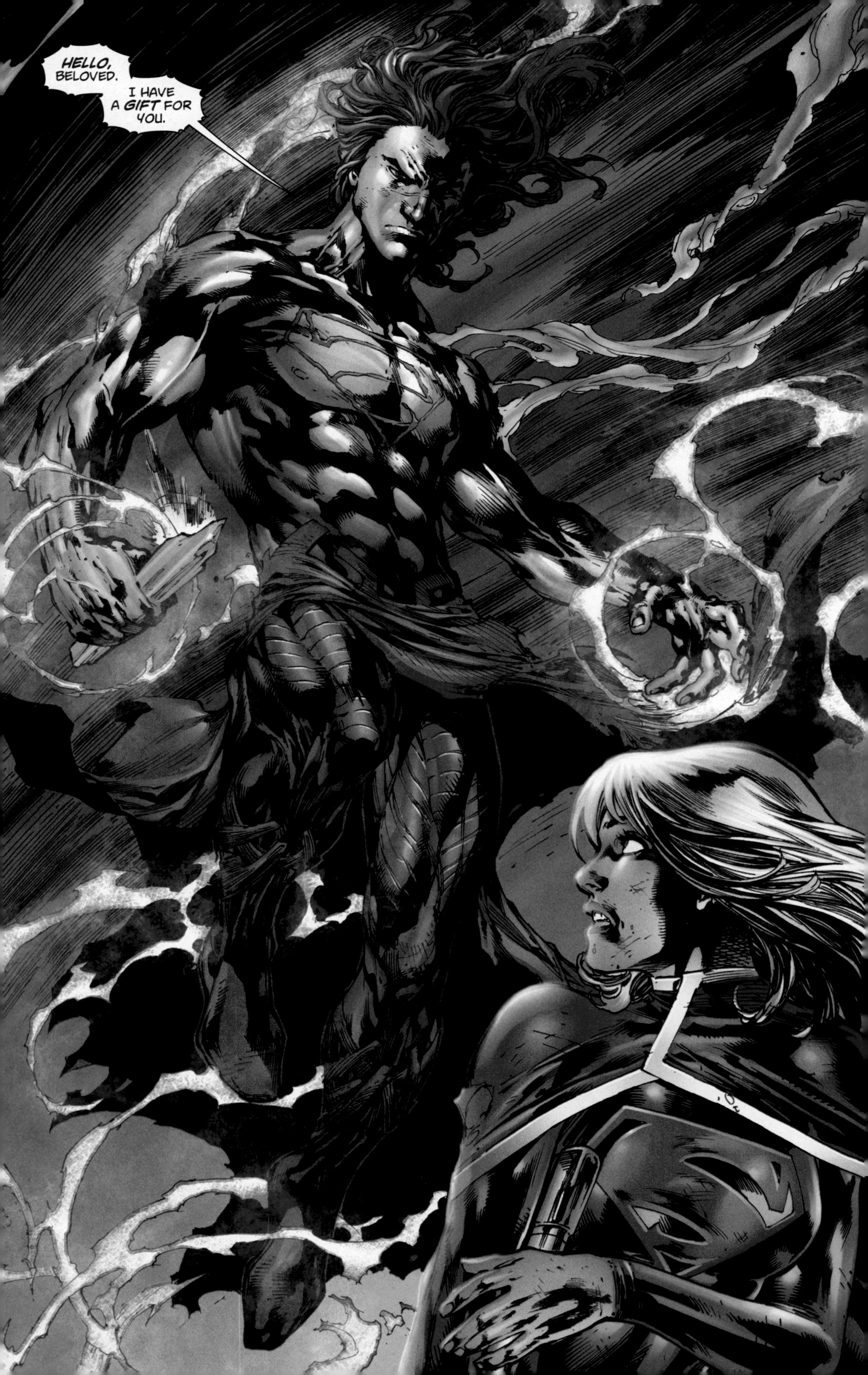
HELLO, BELOVED.
I HAVE A GIFT FOR YOU.

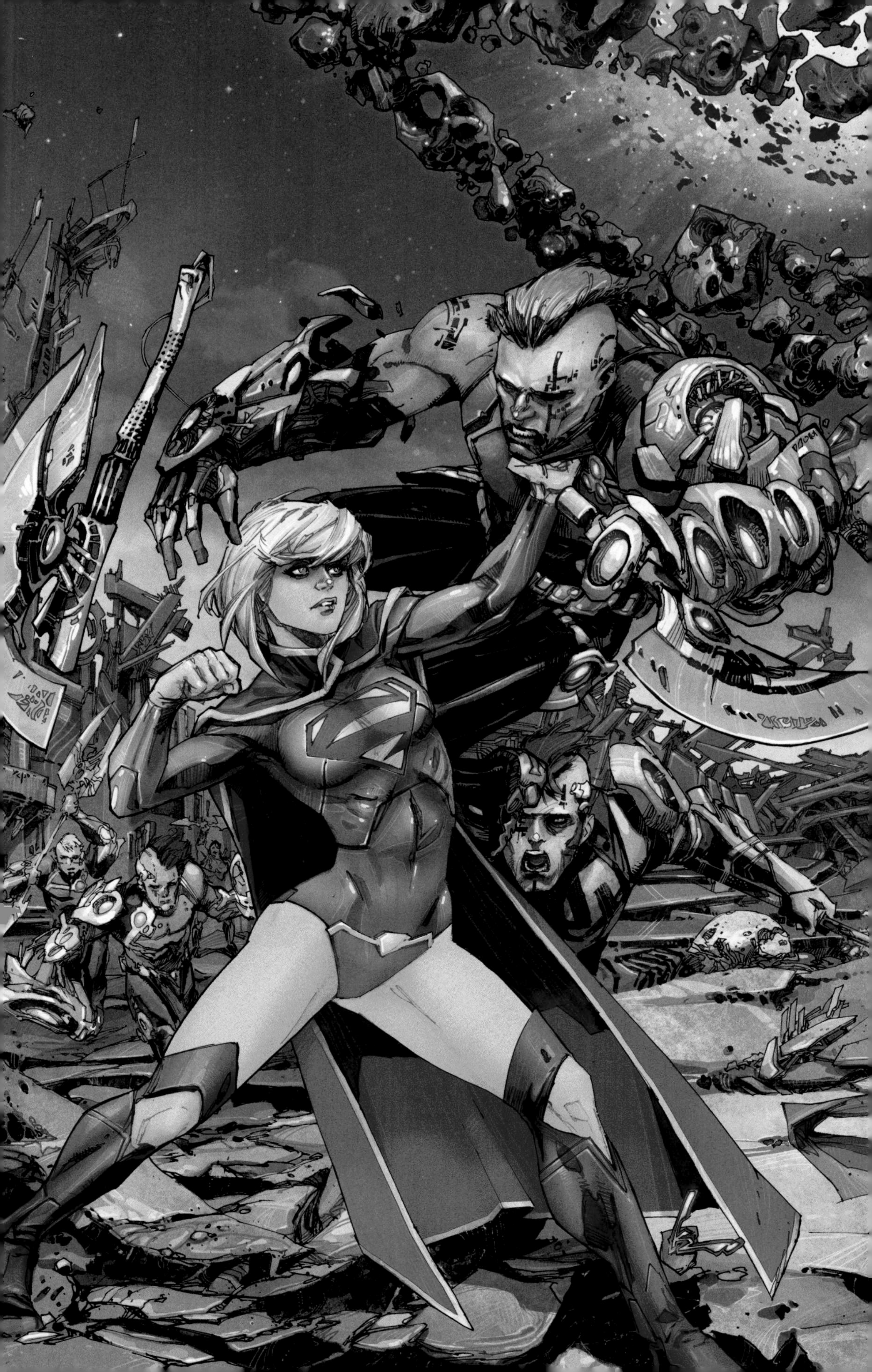

KRYPTON RETURNS PART THREE

SCOTT LOBDELL plot **SCOTT LOBDELL JUSTIN JORDAN MICHAEL ALAN NELSON** dialogue **PAULO SIQUEIRA** artist
HI-FI colorist cover art by **KENNETH ROCAFORT**

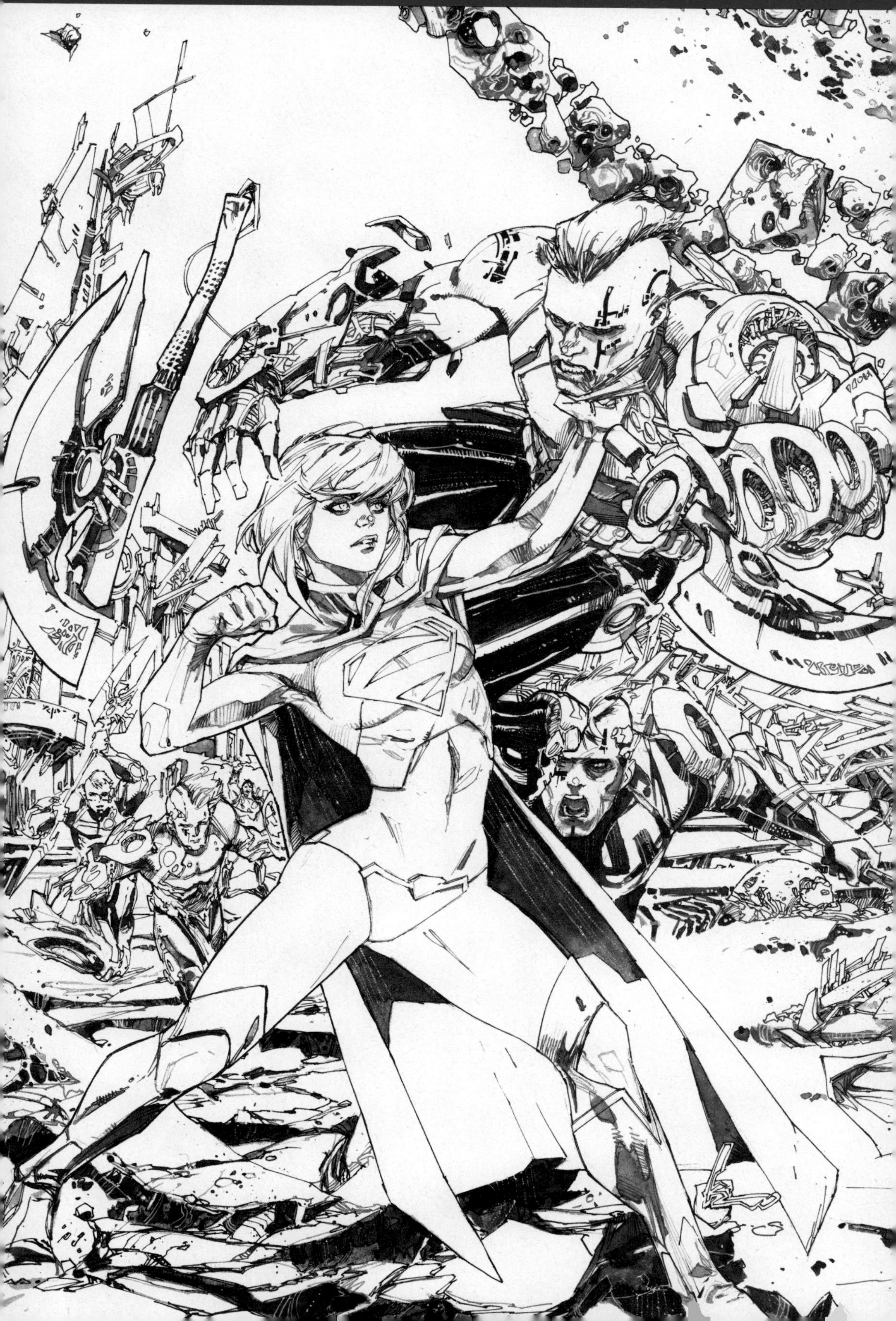

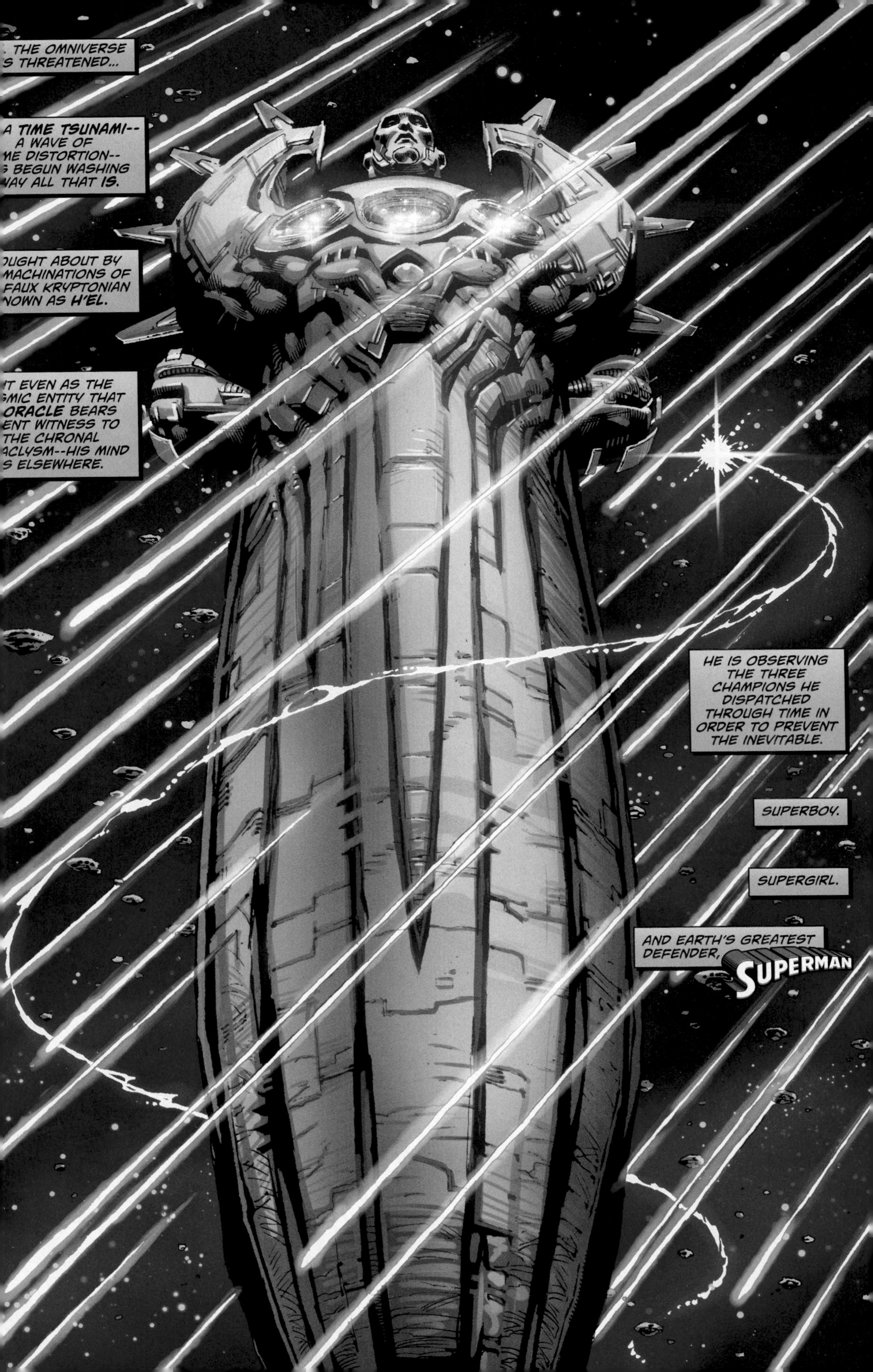

THE OMNIVERSE S THREATENED...
A TIME TSUNAMI-- A WAVE OF ME DISTORTION-- S BEGUN WASHING WAY ALL THAT IS.
OUGHT ABOUT BY MACHINATIONS OF FAUX KRYPTONIAN NOWN AS H'EL.
T EVEN AS THE SMIC ENTITY THAT ORACLE BEARS ENT WITNESS TO THE CHRONAL ACLYSM--HIS MIND S ELSEWHERE.
HE IS OBSERVING THE THREE CHAMPIONS HE DISPATCHED THROUGH TIME IN ORDER TO PREVENT THE INEVITABLE.
SUPERBOY.
SUPERGIRL.
AND EARTH'S GREATEST DEFENDER, SUPERMAN

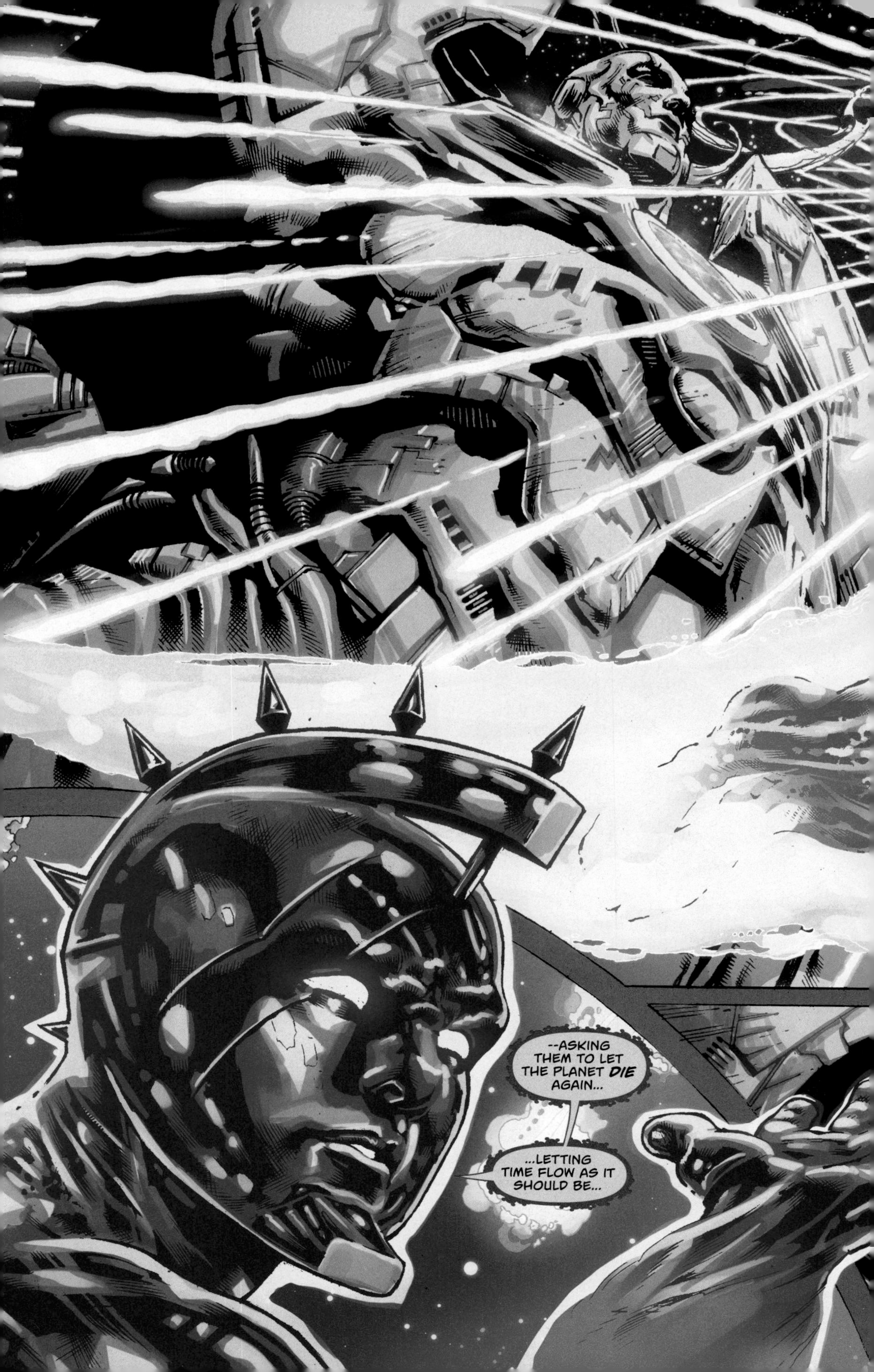
--ASKING THEM TO LET THE PLANET DIE AGAIN...
...LETTING TIME FLOW AS IT SHOULD BE...

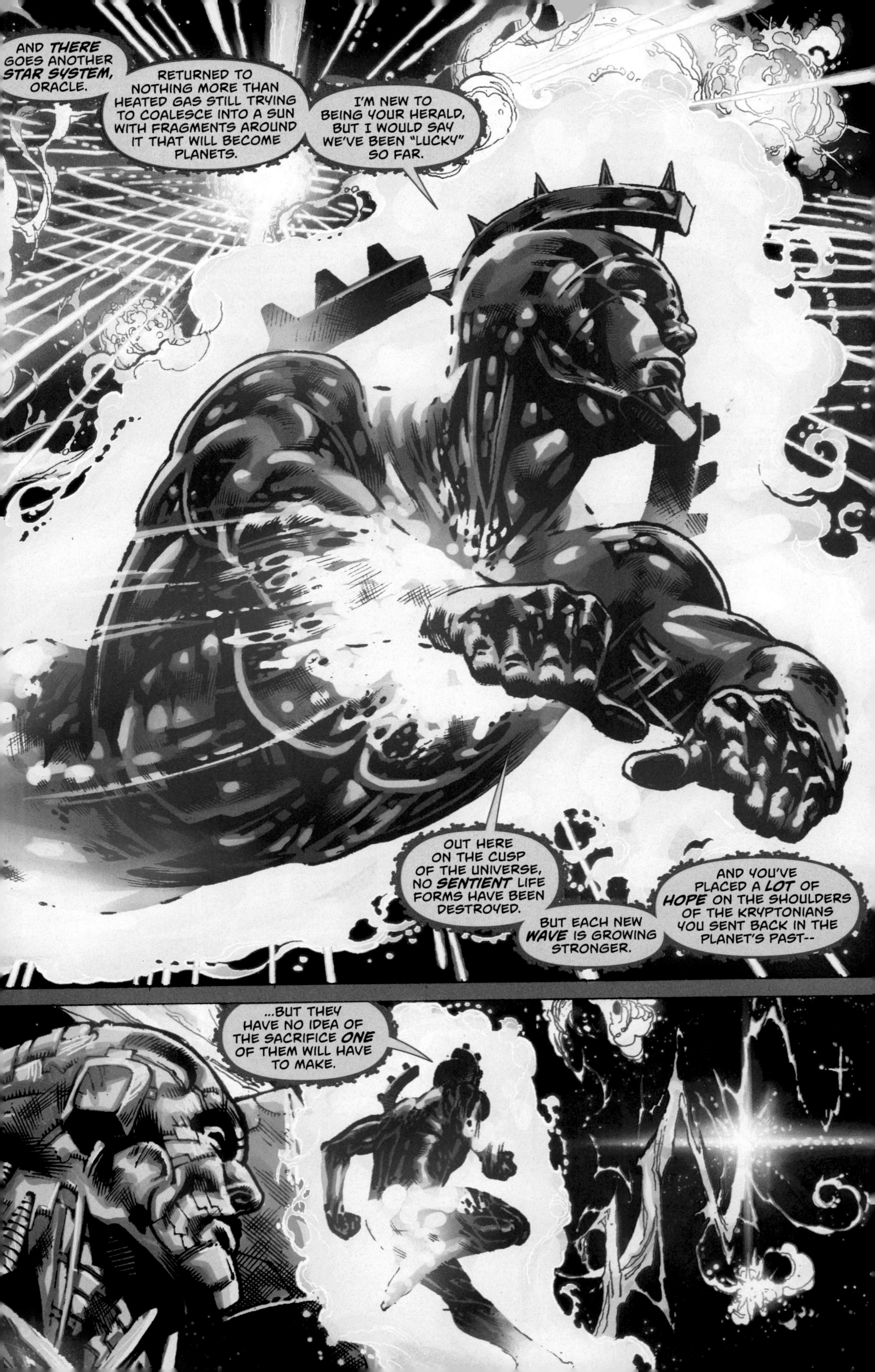
AND THERE GOES ANOTHER STAR SYSTEM, ORACLE.
RETURNED TO NOTHING MORE THAN HEATED GAS STILL TRYING TO COALESCE INTO A SUN WITH FRAGMENTS AROUND IT THAT WILL BECOME PLANETS.
I'M NEW TO BEING YOUR HERALD, BUT I WOULD SAY WE'VE BEEN "LUCKY" SO FAR.
OUT HERE ON THE CUSP OF THE UNIVERSE, NO SENTIENT LIFE FORMS HAVE BEEN DESTROYED.
BUT EACH NEW WAVE IS GROWING STRONGER.
AND YOU'VE PLACED A LOT OF HOPE ON THE SHOULDERS OF THE KRYPTONIANS YOU SENT BACK IN THE PLANET'S PAST--
...BUT THEY HAVE NO IDEA OF THE SACRIFICE ONE OF THEM WILL HAVE TO MAKE.

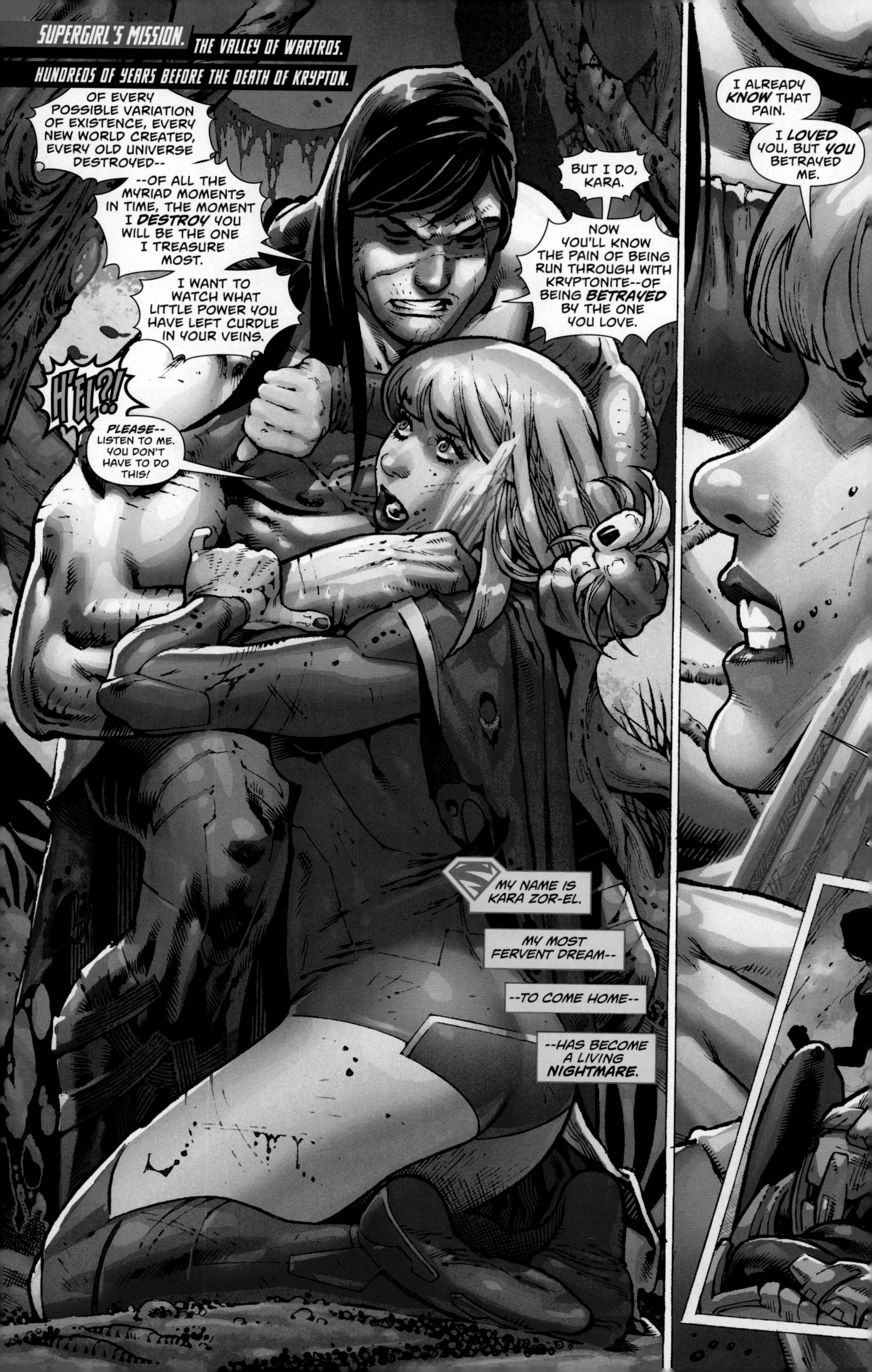
SUPERGIRL'S MISSION.
THE VALLEY OF WARTROS.
HUNDREDS OF YEARS BEFORE THE DEATH OF KRYPTON.
OF EVERY POSSIBLE VARIATION OF EXISTENCE, EVERY NEW WORLD CREATED, EVERY OLD UNIVERSE DESTROYED--
--OF ALL THE MYRIAD MOMENTS IN TIME, THE MOMENT I DESTROY YOU WILL BE THE ONE I TREASURE MOST.
I WANT TO WATCH WHAT LITTLE POWER YOU HAVE LEFT CURDLE IN YOUR VEINS.
BUT I DO, KARA.
NOW YOU'LL KNOW THE PAIN OF BEING RUN THROUGH WITH KRYPTONITE--OF BEING BETRAYED BY THE ONE YOU LOVE.
PLEASE-- LISTEN TO ME. YOU DON'T HAVE TO DO THIS!
MY NAME IS KARA ZOR-EL.
MY MOST FERVENT DREAM--
--TO COME HOME--
--HAS BECOME A LIVING NIGHTMARE.
I ALREADY KNOW THAT PAIN.
I LOVED YOU, BUT YOU BETRAYED ME.

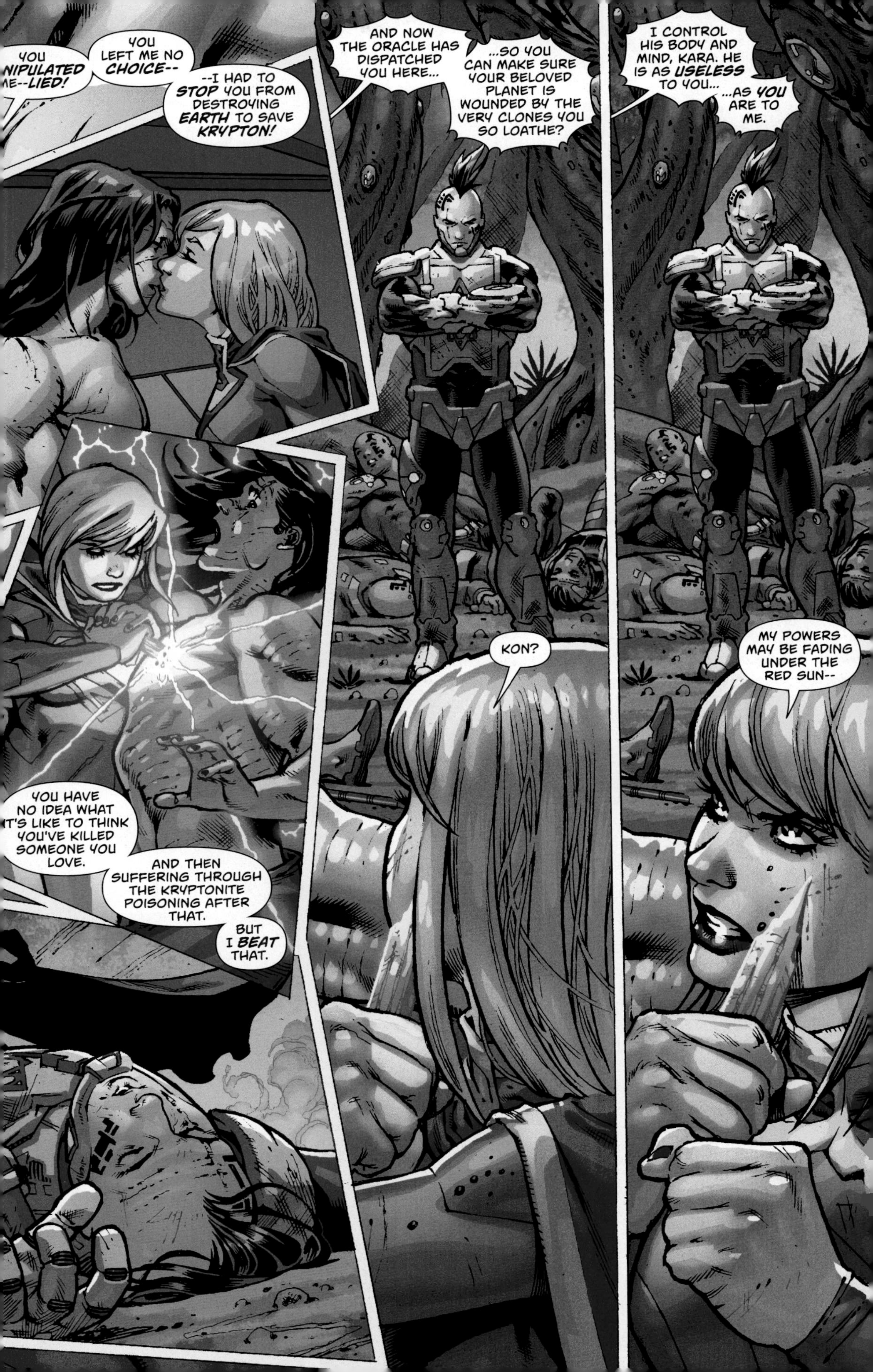
YOU NIPULATED ME--LIED!
YOU LEFT ME NO CHOICE--
--I HAD TO STOP YOU FROM DESTROYING EARTH TO SAVE KRYPTON!
YOU HAVE NO IDEA WHAT IT'S LIKE TO THINK YOU'VE KILLED SOMEONE YOU LOVE.
AND THEN SUFFERING THROUGH THE KRYPTONITE POISONING AFTER THAT.
BUT I BEAT THAT.
AND NOW THE ORACLE HAS DISPATCHED YOU HERE...
...SO YOU CAN MAKE SURE YOUR BELOVED PLANET IS WOUNDED BY THE VERY CLONES YOU SO LOATHE?
KON?
I CONTROL HIS BODY AND MIND, KARA. HE IS AS USELESS TO YOU...
...AS YOU ARE TO ME.
MY POWERS MAY BE FADING UNDER THE RED SUN--

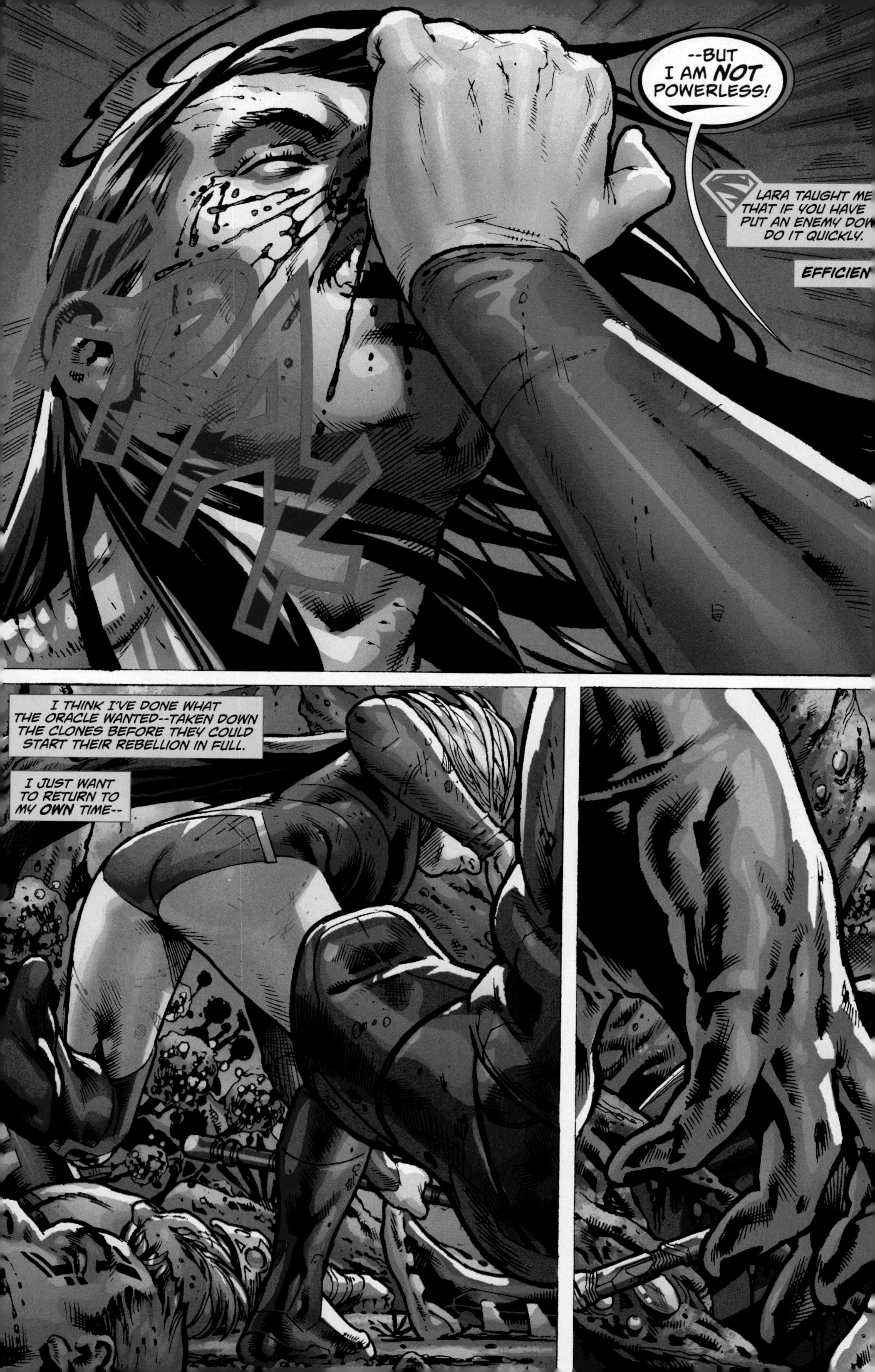
--BUT I AM **NOT** POWERLESS!
LARA TAUGHT ME THAT IF YOU HAVE PUT AN ENEMY DOW DO IT QUICKLY.
EFFICIEN
I THINK I'VE DONE WHAT THE ORACLE WANTED--TAKEN DOWN THE CLONES BEFORE THEY COULD START THEIR REBELLION IN FULL.
I JUST WANT TO RETURN TO MY **OWN** TIME--

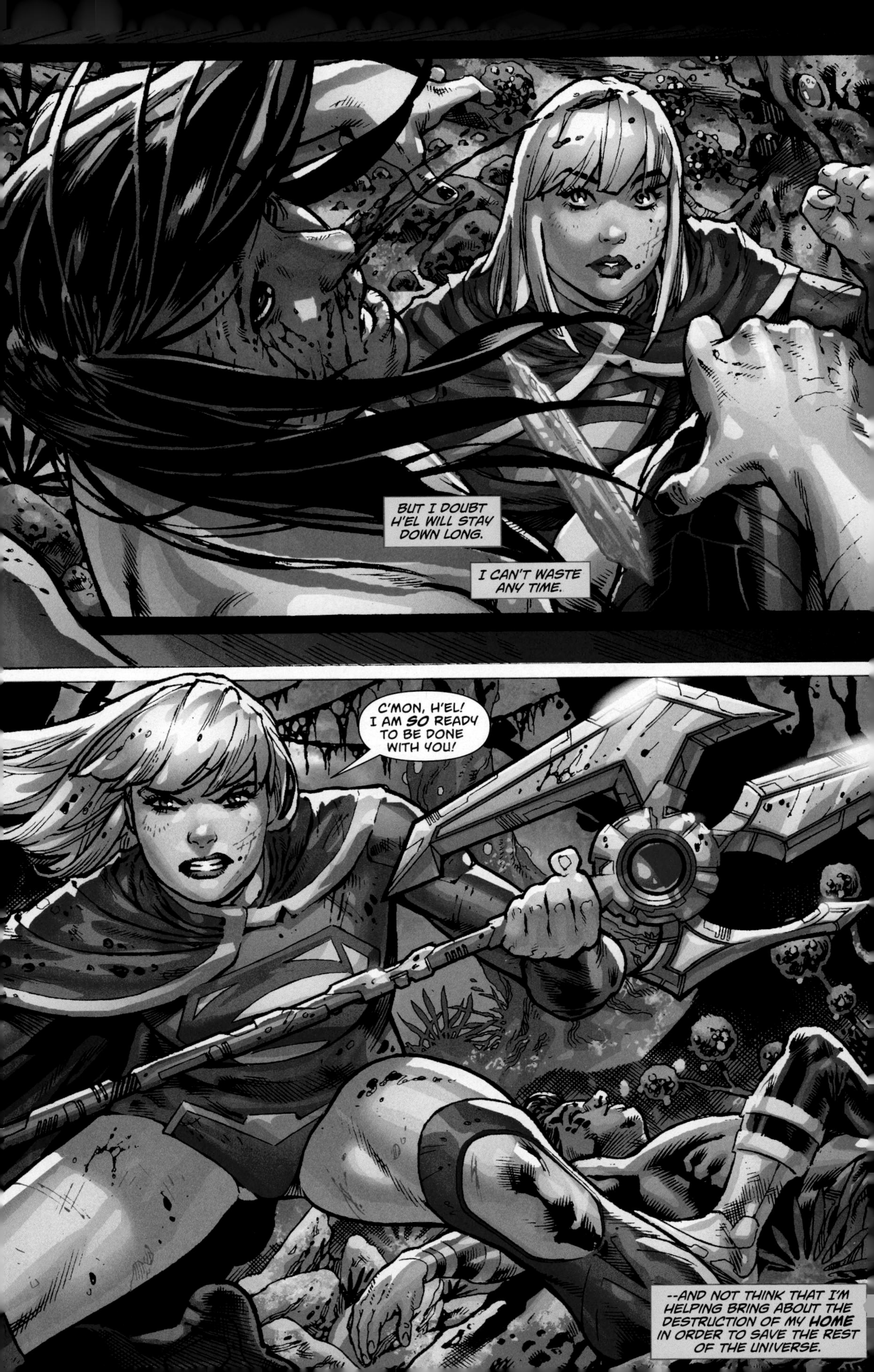
BUT I DOUBT H'EL WILL STAY DOWN LONG.
I CAN'T WASTE ANY TIME.
C'MON, H'EL! I AM SO READY TO BE DONE WITH YOU!
--AND NOT THINK THAT I'M HELPING BRING ABOUT THE DESTRUCTION OF MY HOME IN ORDER TO SAVE THE REST OF THE UNIVERSE.

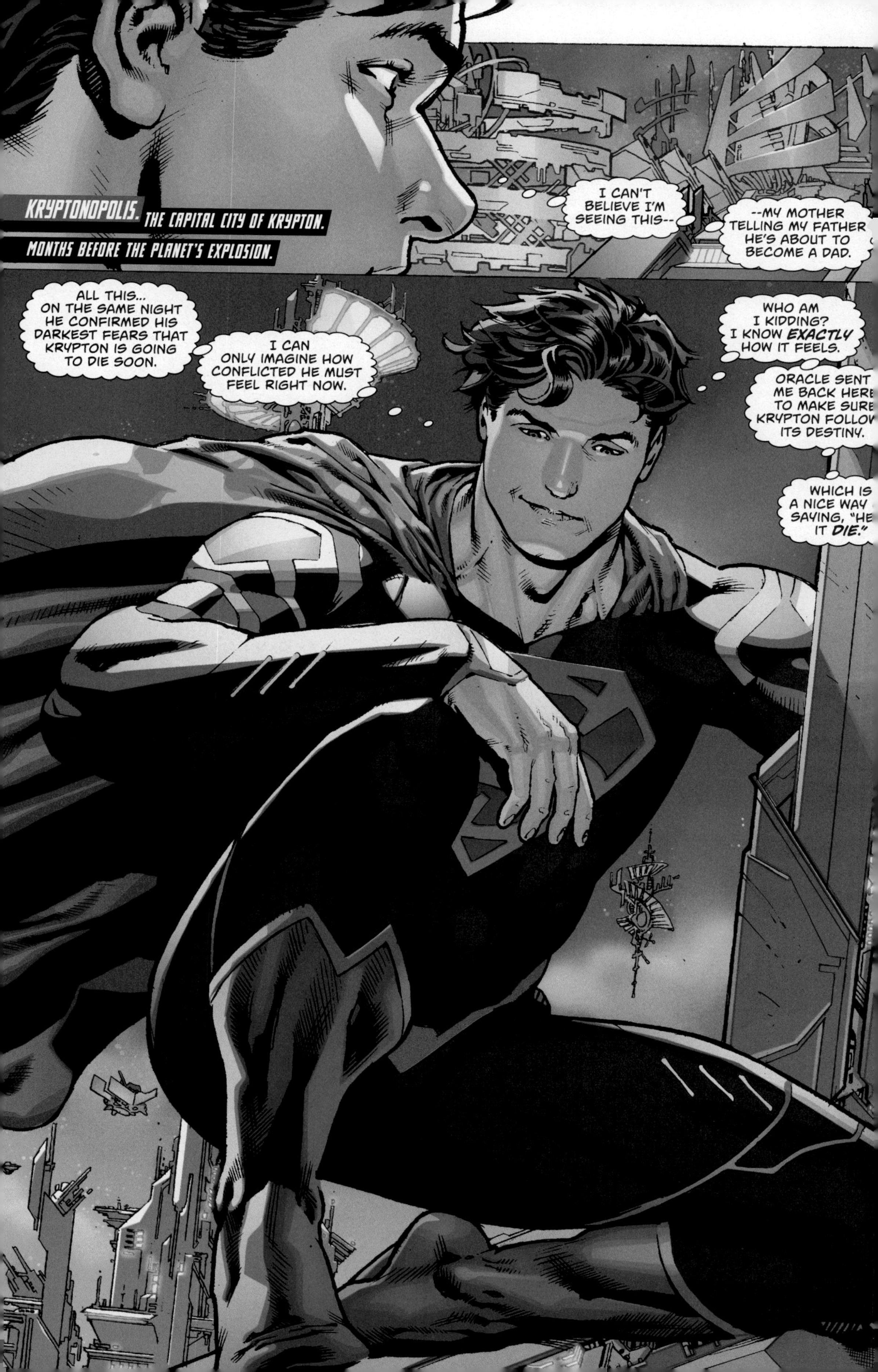

KRYPTONOPOLIS. THE CAPITAL CITY OF KRYPTON.
MONTHS BEFORE THE PLANET'S EXPLOSION.
I CAN'T BELIEVE I'M SEEING THIS--
--MY MOTHER TELLING MY FATHER HE'S ABOUT TO BECOME A DAD.
ALL THIS... ON THE SAME NIGHT HE CONFIRMED HIS DARKEST FEARS THAT KRYPTON IS GOING TO DIE SOON.
I CAN ONLY IMAGINE HOW CONFLICTED HE MUST FEEL RIGHT NOW.
WHO AM I KIDDING? I KNOW EXACTLY HOW IT FEELS.
ORACLE SENT ME BACK HERE TO MAKE SURE KRYPTON FOLLOW ITS DESTINY.
WHICH IS A NICE WAY SAYING, "HE IT DIE."

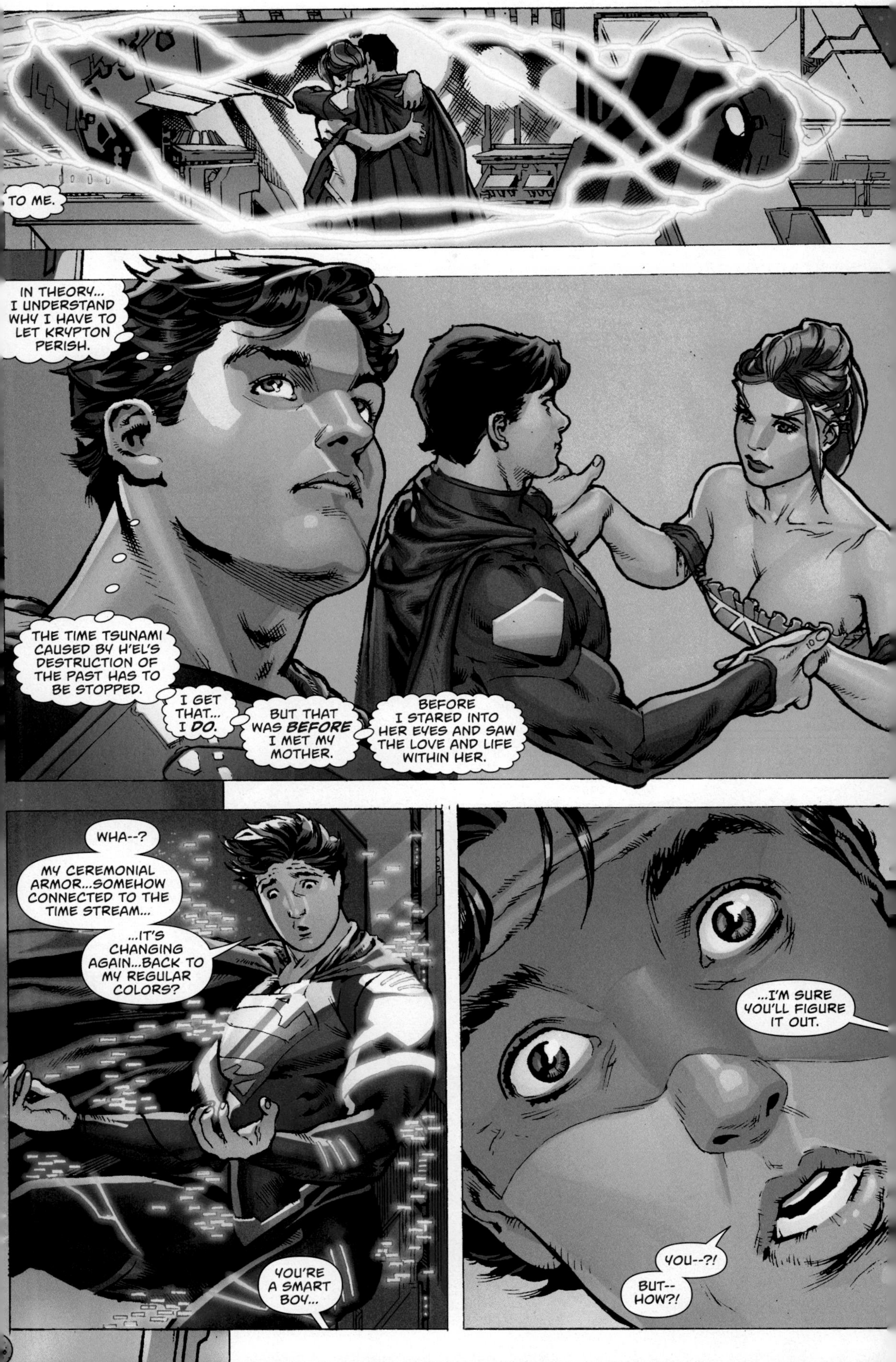
TO ME.
IN THEORY... I UNDERSTAND WHY I HAVE TO LET KRYPTON PERISH.
THE TIME TSUNAMI CAUSED BY H'EL'S DESTRUCTION OF THE PAST HAS TO BE STOPPED.
I GET THAT... I *DO*.
BUT THAT WAS *BEFORE* I MET MY MOTHER.
BEFORE I STARED INTO HER EYES AND SAW THE LOVE AND LIFE WITHIN HER.
WHA--?
MY CEREMONIAL ARMOR...SOMEHOW CONNECTED TO THE TIME STREAM...
...IT'S CHANGING AGAIN...BACK TO MY REGULAR COLORS?
YOU'RE A SMART BOY...
...I'M SURE YOU'LL FIGURE IT OUT.
YOU--?!
BUT-- HOW?!

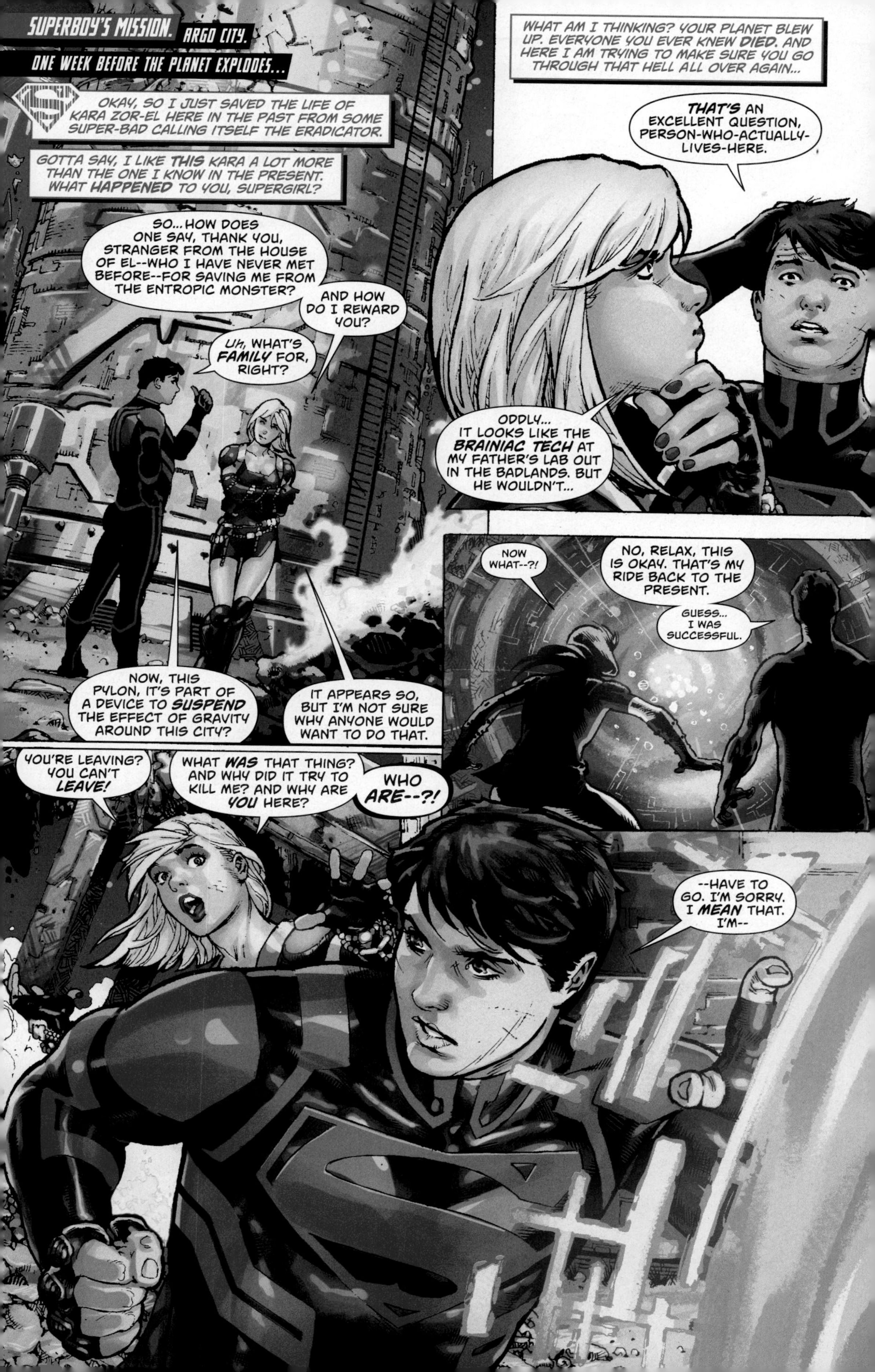

SUPERBOY'S MISSION. ARGO CITY.
ONE WEEK BEFORE THE PLANET EXPLODES...
OKAY, SO I JUST SAVED THE LIFE OF KARA ZOR-EL HERE IN THE PAST FROM SOME SUPER-BAD CALLING ITSELF THE ERADICATOR.
GOTTA SAY, I LIKE THIS KARA A LOT MORE THAN THE ONE I KNOW IN THE PRESENT. WHAT HAPPENED TO YOU, SUPERGIRL?
SO...HOW DOES ONE SAY, THANK YOU, STRANGER FROM THE HOUSE OF EL--WHO I HAVE NEVER MET BEFORE--FOR SAVING ME FROM THE ENTROPIC MONSTER?
AND HOW DO I REWARD YOU?
UH, WHAT'S FAMILY FOR, RIGHT?
NOW, THIS PYLON, IT'S PART OF A DEVICE TO SUSPEND THE EFFECT OF GRAVITY AROUND THIS CITY?
IT APPEARS SO, BUT I'M NOT SURE WHY ANYONE WOULD WANT TO DO THAT.
WHAT AM I THINKING? YOUR PLANET BLEW UP. EVERYONE YOU EVER KNEW DIED. AND HERE I AM TRYING TO MAKE SURE YOU GO THROUGH THAT HELL ALL OVER AGAIN...
THAT'S AN EXCELLENT QUESTION, PERSON-WHO-ACTUALLY-LIVES-HERE.
ODDLY... IT LOOKS LIKE THE BRAINIAC TECH AT MY FATHER'S LAB OUT IN THE BADLANDS. BUT HE WOULDN'T...
NOW WHAT--?!
NO, RELAX, THIS IS OKAY. THAT'S MY RIDE BACK TO THE PRESENT.
GUESS... I WAS SUCCESSFUL.
YOU'RE LEAVING? YOU CAN'T LEAVE!
WHAT WAS THAT THING? AND WHY DID IT TRY TO KILL ME? AND WHY ARE YOU HERE?
WHO ARE--?!
--HAVE TO GO. I'M SORRY. I MEAN THAT. I'M--

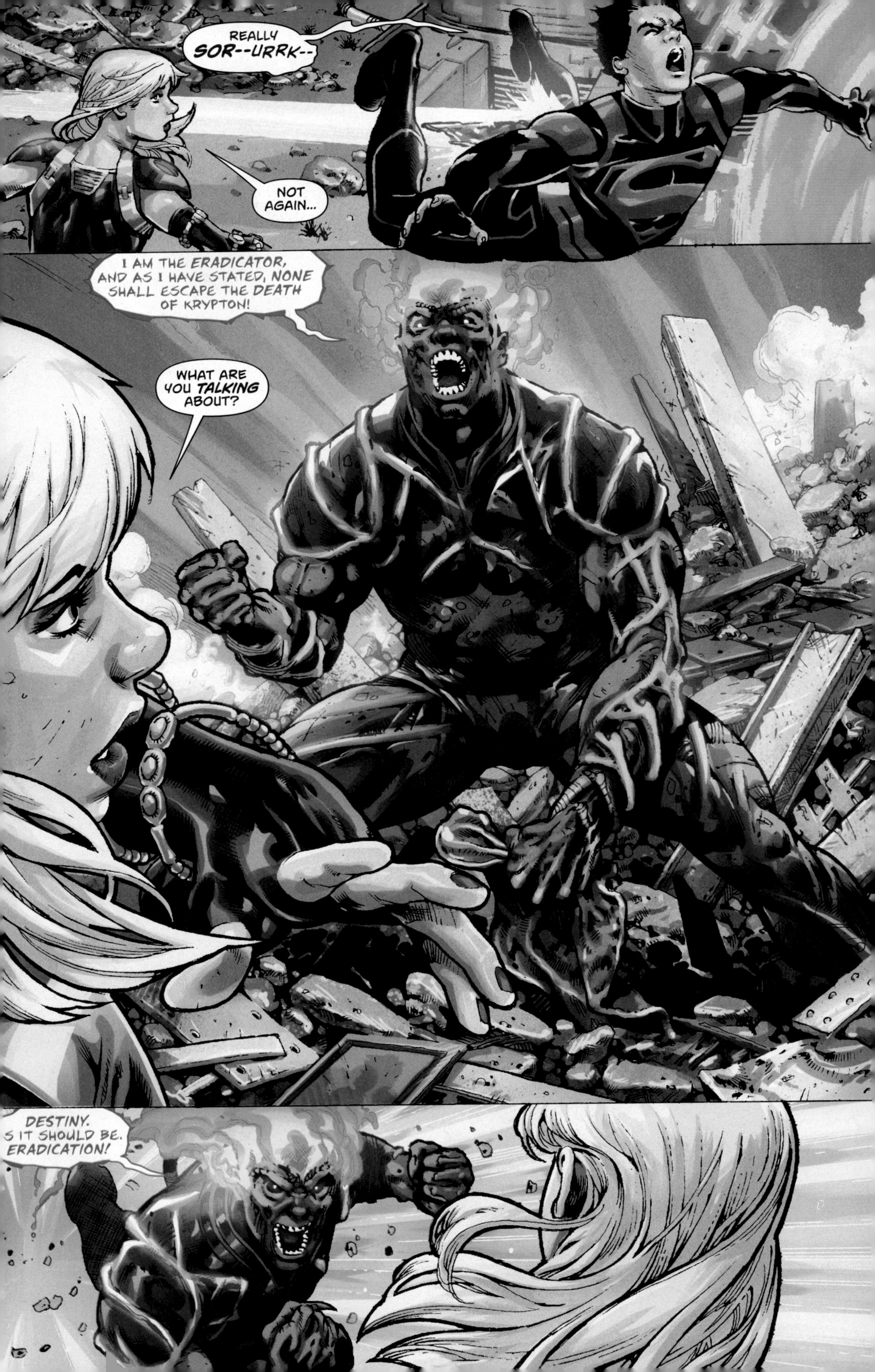
REALLY SOR--URRK--
NOT AGAIN...
I AM THE ERADICATOR, AND AS I HAVE STATED, NONE SHALL ESCAPE THE DEATH OF KRYPTON!
WHAT ARE YOU TALKING ABOUT?
DESTINY. S IT SHOULD BE. ERADICATION!

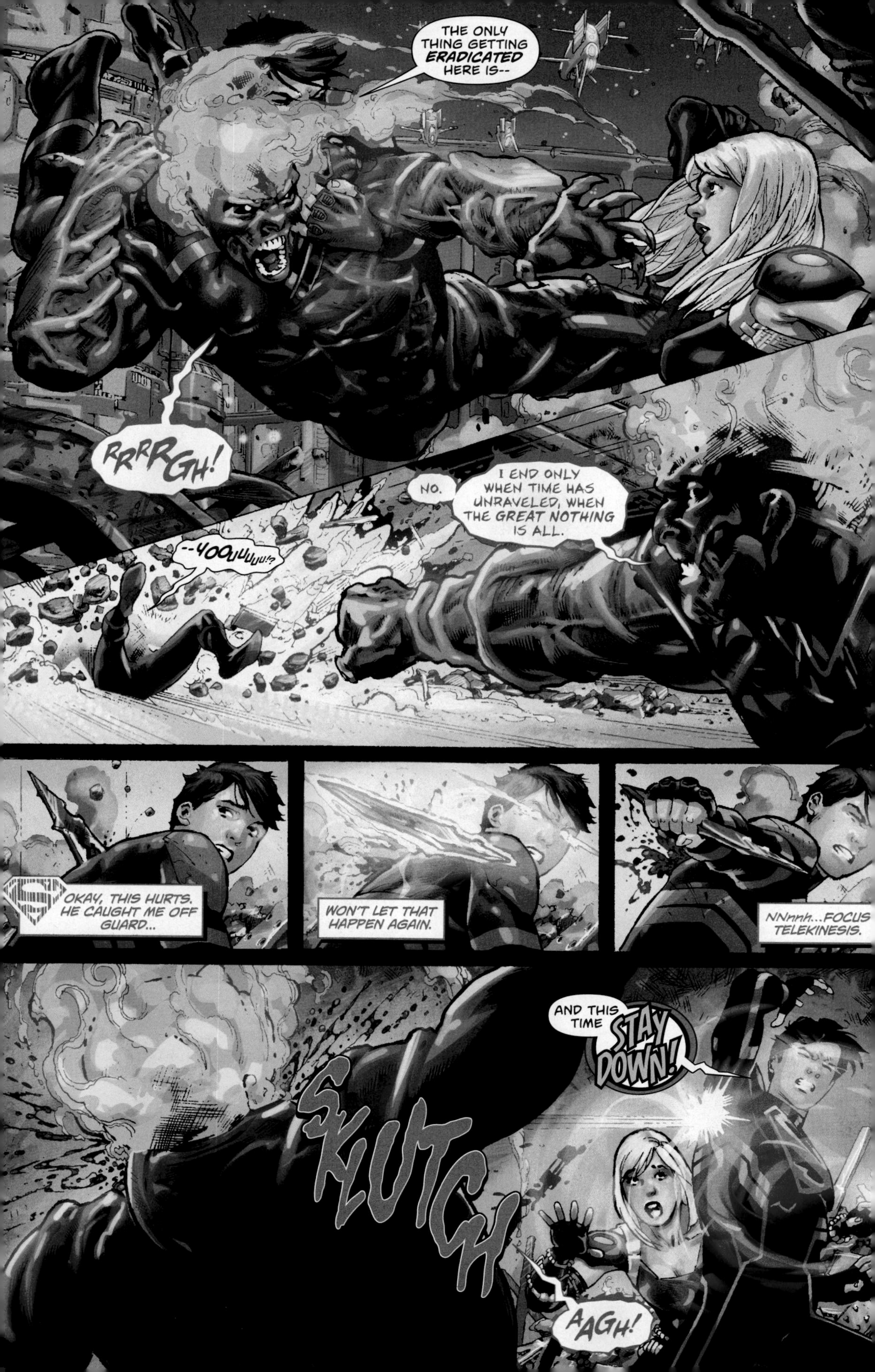
THE ONLY THING GETTING ERADICATED HERE IS--
RRRRGH!
NO.
I END ONLY WHEN TIME HAS UNRAVELED, WHEN THE GREAT NOTHING IS ALL.
--YOOUUUUU!?
OKAY, THIS HURTS. HE CAUGHT ME OFF GUARD...
WON'T LET THAT HAPPEN AGAIN.
NNnnh...FOCUS TELEKINESIS.
AND THIS TIME
STAY DOWN!
SKLUTCH
AAGH!

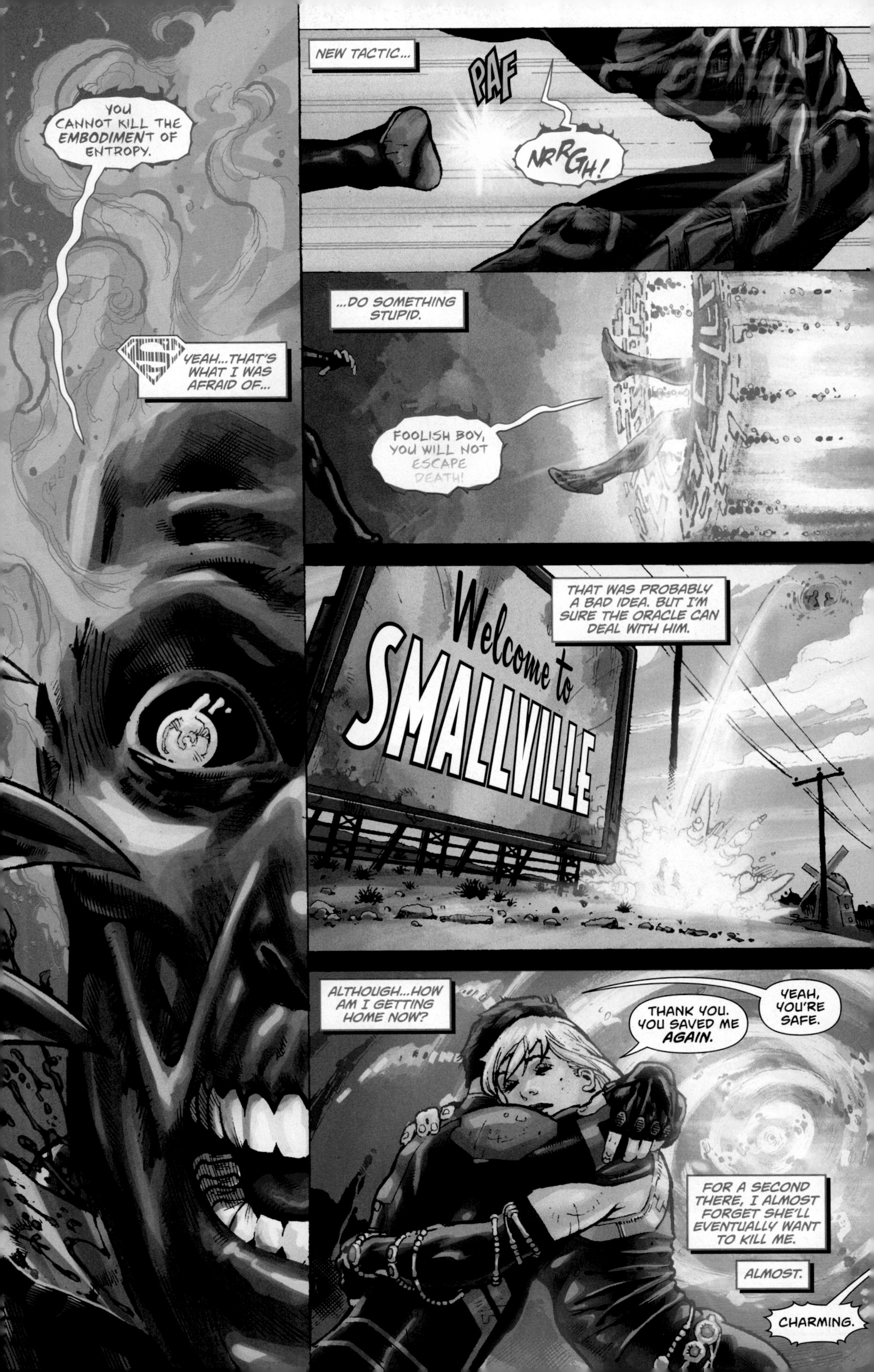

YOU CANNOT KILL THE EMBODIMENT OF ENTROPY.
YEAH...THAT'S WHAT I WAS AFRAID OF...
NEW TACTIC...
PAF
NRRGH!
...DO SOMETHING STUPID.
FOOLISH BOY, YOU WILL NOT ESCAPE DEATH!
Welcome to SMALLVILLE
THAT WAS PROBABLY A BAD IDEA. BUT I'M SURE THE ORACLE CAN DEAL WITH HIM.
ALTHOUGH...HOW AM I GETTING HOME NOW?
THANK YOU. YOU SAVED ME AGAIN.
YEAH, YOU'RE SAFE.
FOR A SECOND THERE, I ALMOST FORGET SHE'LL EVENTUALLY WANT TO KILL ME.
ALMOST.
CHARMING.

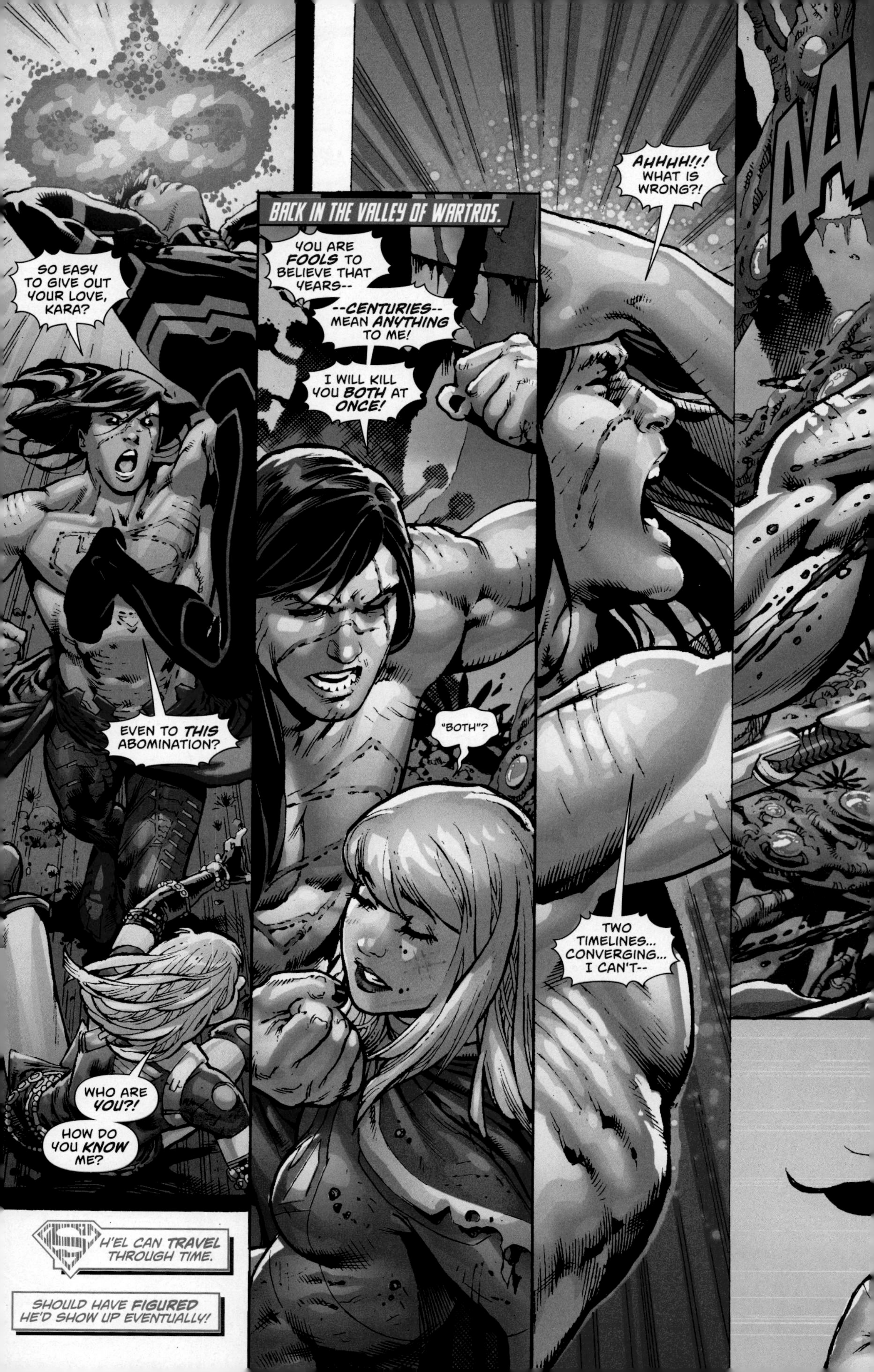
SO EASY TO GIVE OUT YOUR LOVE, KARA?
EVEN TO THIS ABOMINATION?
WHO ARE YOU?!
HOW DO YOU KNOW ME?
H'EL CAN TRAVEL THROUGH TIME.
SHOULD HAVE FIGURED HE'D SHOW UP EVENTUALLY!
BACK IN THE VALLEY OF WARTROS.
YOU ARE FOOLS TO BELIEVE THAT YEARS--
--CENTURIES-- MEAN ANYTHING TO ME!
I WILL KILL YOU BOTH AT ONCE!
"BOTH"?
AHHHH!!! WHAT IS WRONG?!
TWO TIMELINES... CONVERGING... I CAN'T--

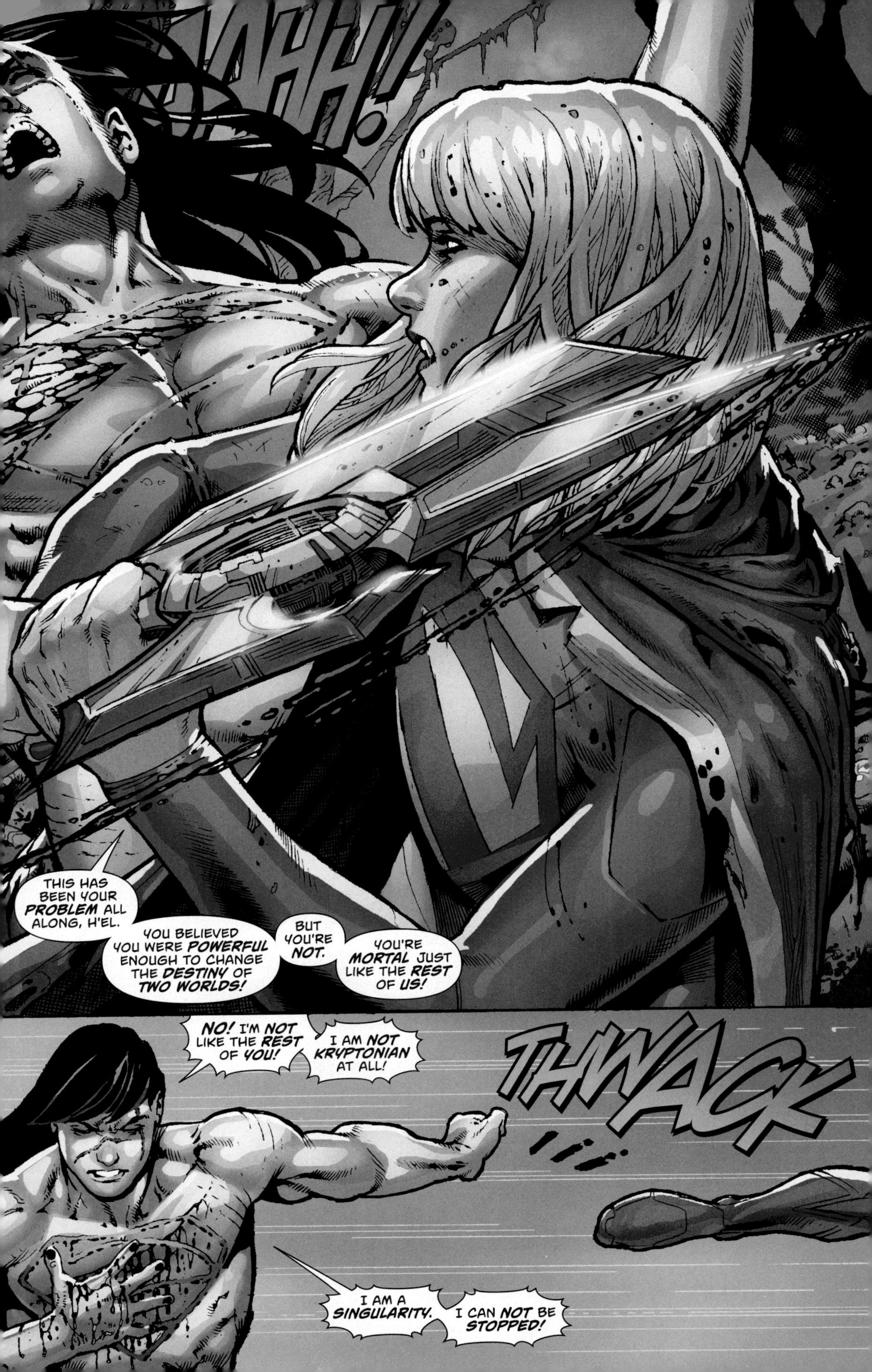
AHH!
THIS HAS BEEN YOUR PROBLEM ALL ALONG, H'EL.
YOU BELIEVED YOU WERE POWERFUL ENOUGH TO CHANGE THE DESTINY OF TWO WORLDS!
BUT YOU'RE NOT.
YOU'RE MORTAL JUST LIKE THE REST OF US!
NO! I'M NOT LIKE THE REST OF YOU!
I AM NOT KRYPTONIAN AT ALL!
THWACK
I AM A SINGULARITY.
I CAN NOT BE STOPPED!

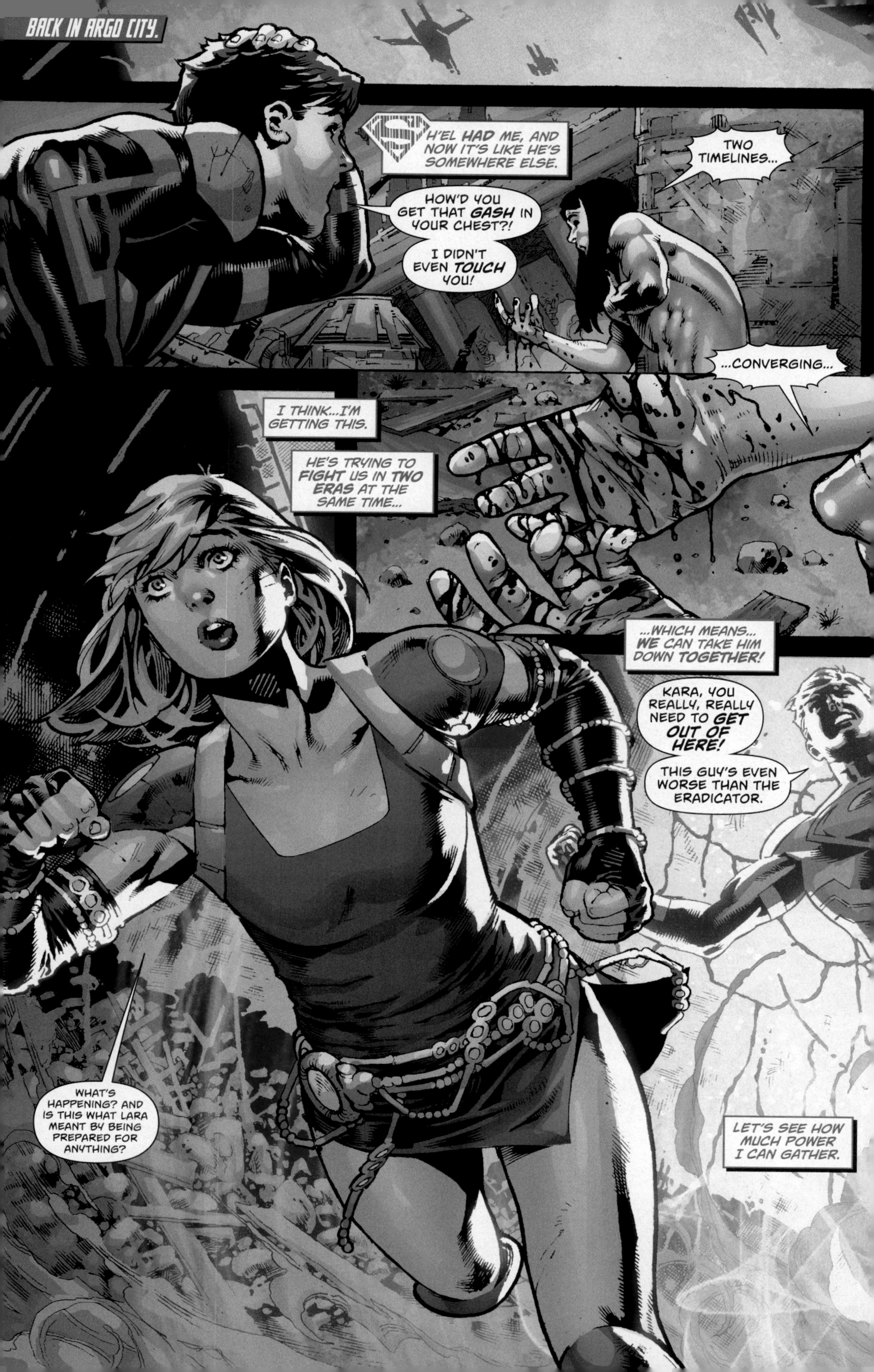
BACK IN ARGO CITY.
H'EL HAD ME, AND NOW IT'S LIKE HE'S SOMEWHERE ELSE.
HOW'D YOU GET THAT GASH IN YOUR CHEST?!
I DIDN'T EVEN TOUCH YOU!
TWO TIMELINES...
...CONVERGING...
I THINK...I'M GETTING THIS.
HE'S TRYING TO FIGHT US IN TWO ERAS AT THE SAME TIME...
...WHICH MEANS... WE CAN TAKE HIM DOWN TOGETHER!
KARA, YOU REALLY, REALLY NEED TO GET OUT OF HERE!
THIS GUY'S EVEN WORSE THAN THE ERADICATOR.
WHAT'S HAPPENING? AND IS THIS WHAT LARA MEANT BY BEING PREPARED FOR ANYTHING?
LET'S SEE HOW MUCH POWER I CAN GATHER.

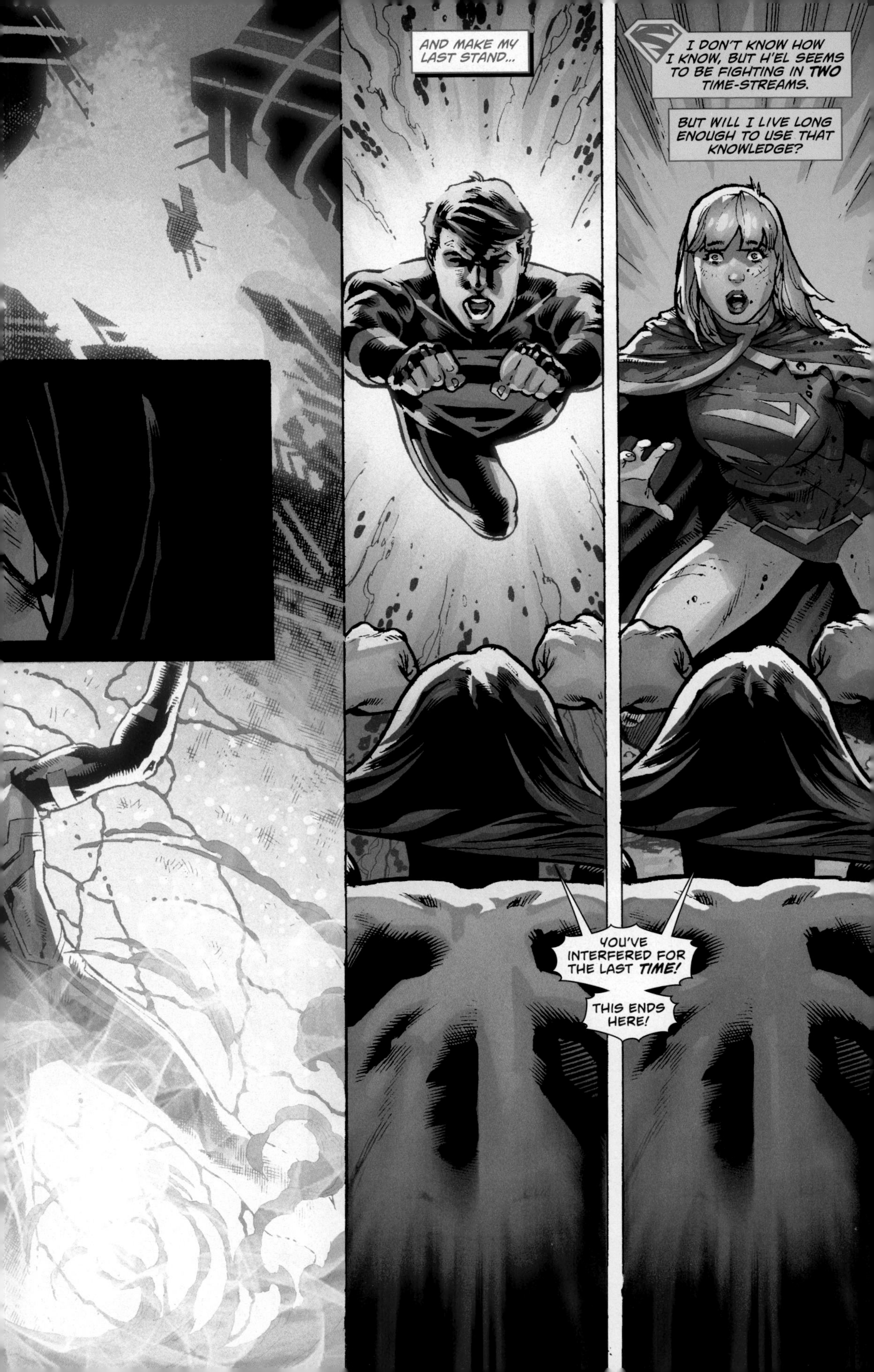
AND MAKE MY LAST STAND...
I DON'T KNOW HOW I KNOW, BUT H'EL SEEMS TO BE FIGHTING IN **TWO** TIME-STREAMS.
BUT WILL I LIVE LONG ENOUGH TO USE THAT KNOWLEDGE?
YOU'VE INTERFERED FOR THE LAST *TIME!*
THIS ENDS HERE!

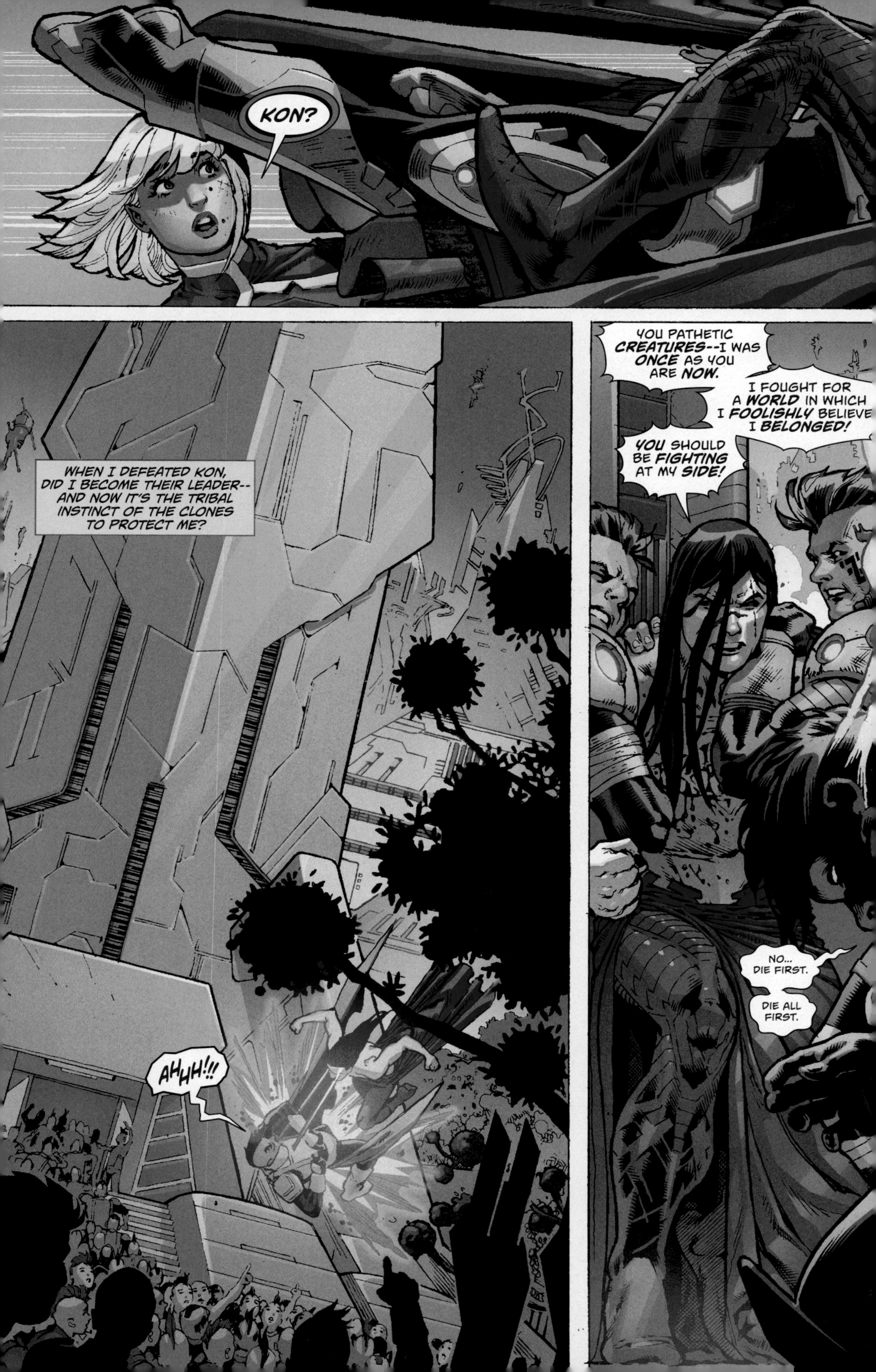
KON?
WHEN I DEFEATED KON, DID I BECOME THEIR LEADER-- AND NOW IT'S THE TRIBAL INSTINCT OF THE CLONES TO PROTECT ME?
AHHH!!!
YOU PATHETIC CREATURES--I WAS ONCE AS YOU ARE NOW.
I FOUGHT FOR A WORLD IN WHICH I FOOLISHLY BELIEVE I BELONGED!
YOU SHOULD BE FIGHTING AT MY SIDE!
NO... DIE FIRST.
DIE ALL FIRST.

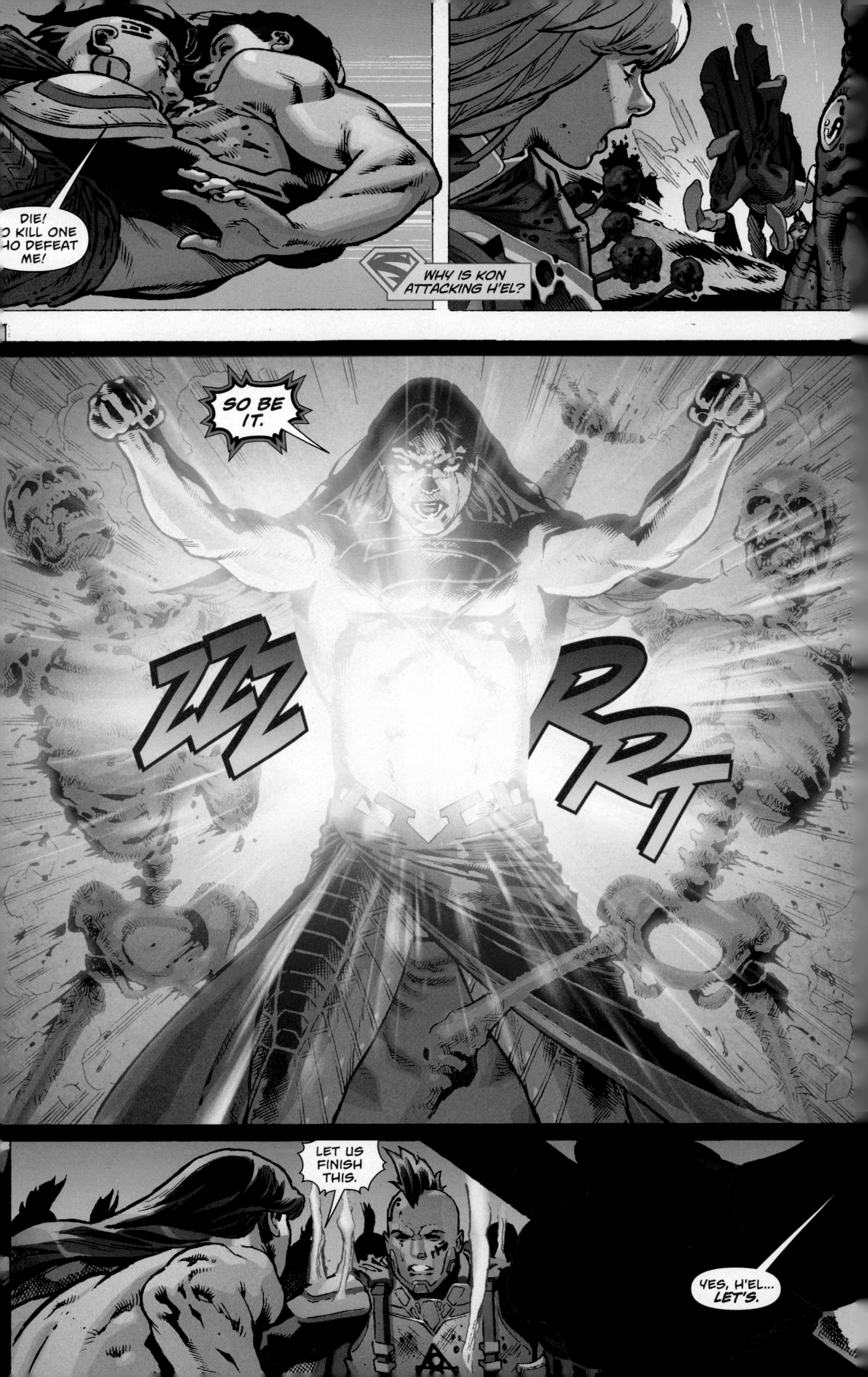
DIE! O KILL ONE HO DEFEAT ME!
WHY IS KON ATTACKING H'EL?
SO BE IT.
ZZZRRRT
LET US FINISH THIS.
YES, H'EL... LET'S.

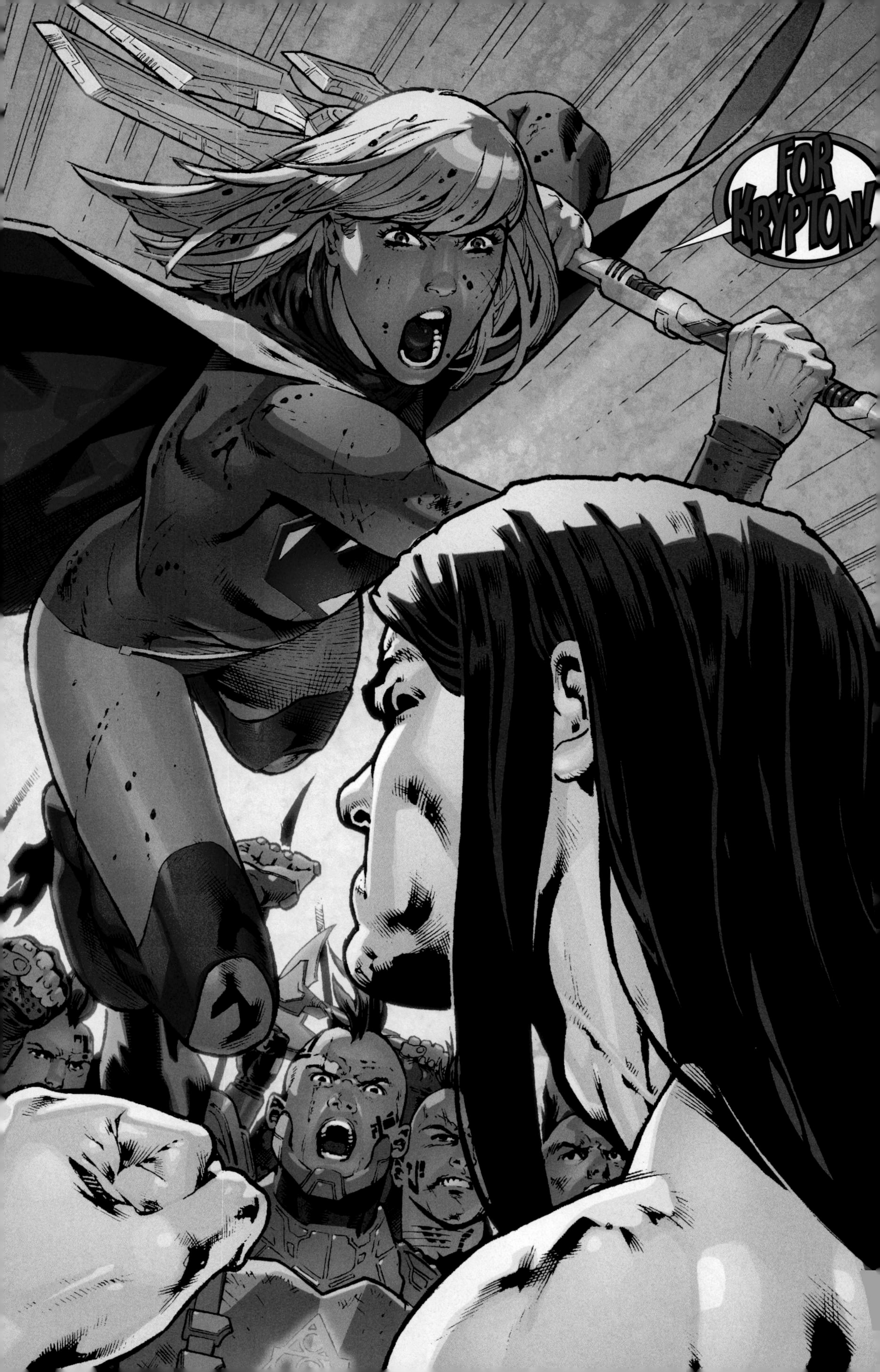
FOR KRYPTON!

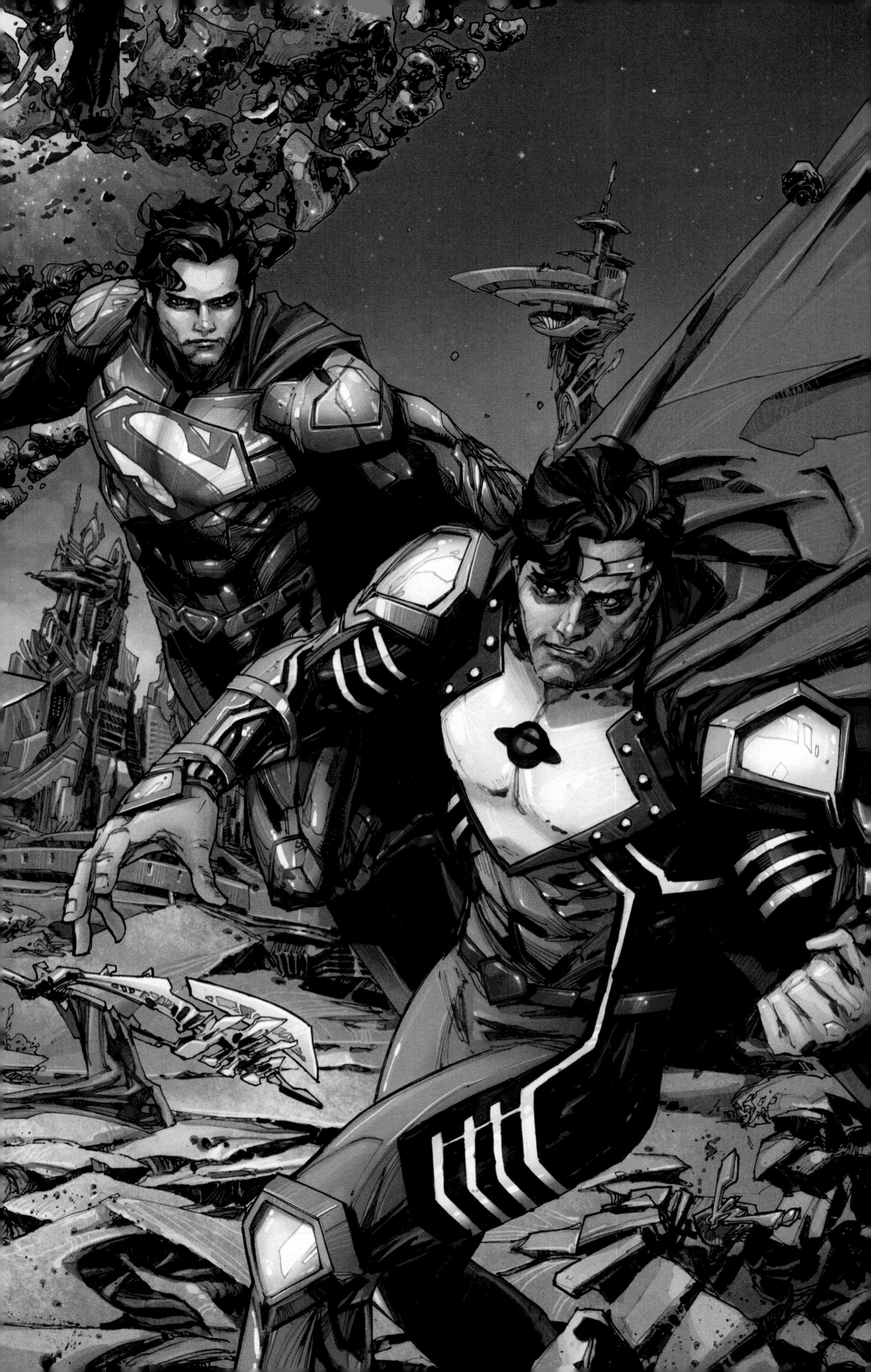

KRYPTON RETURNS PART FOUR

SCOTT LOBDELL writer **KENNETH ROCAFORT** artist **BLOND** colorist

cover art by **KENNETH ROCAFORT**

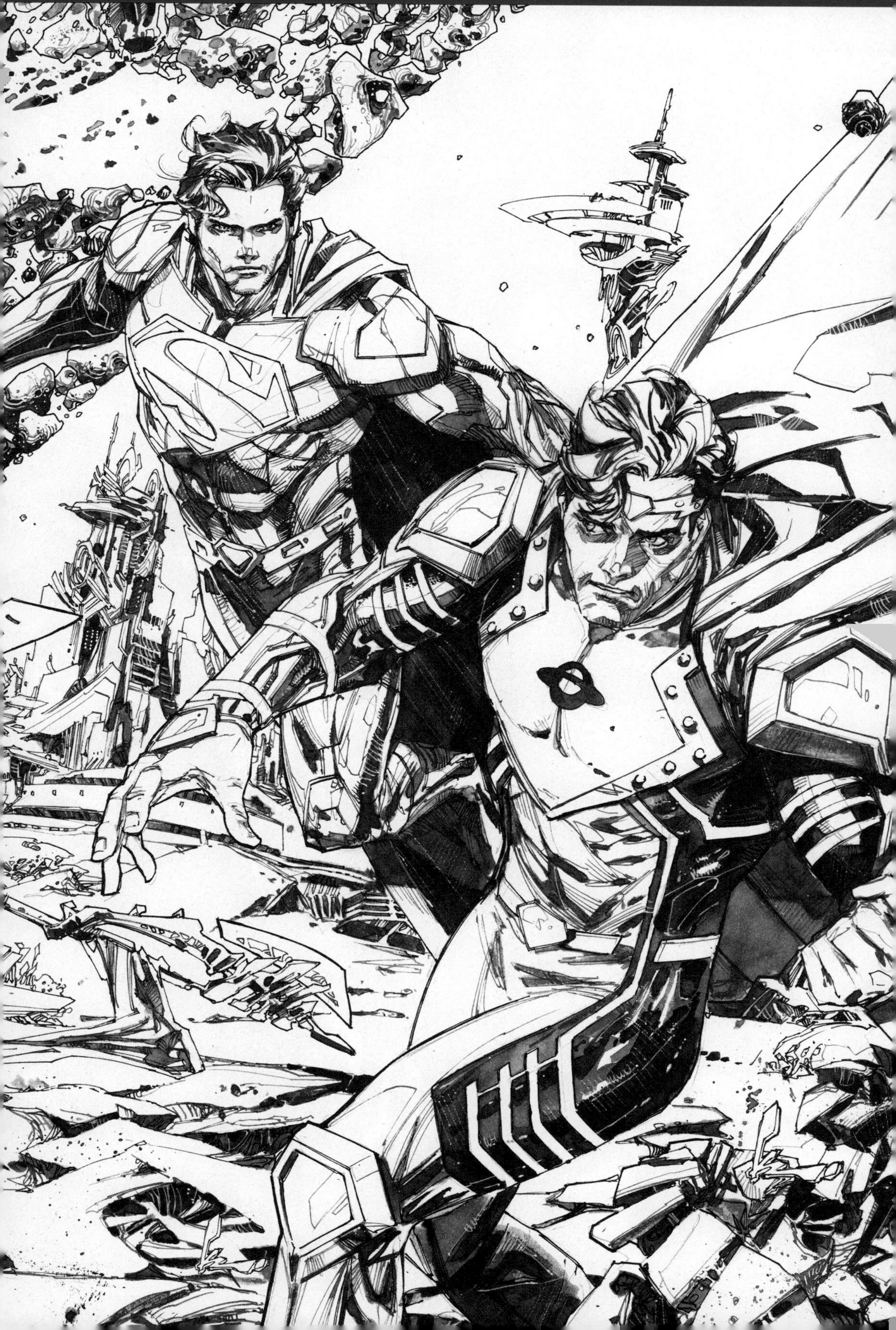

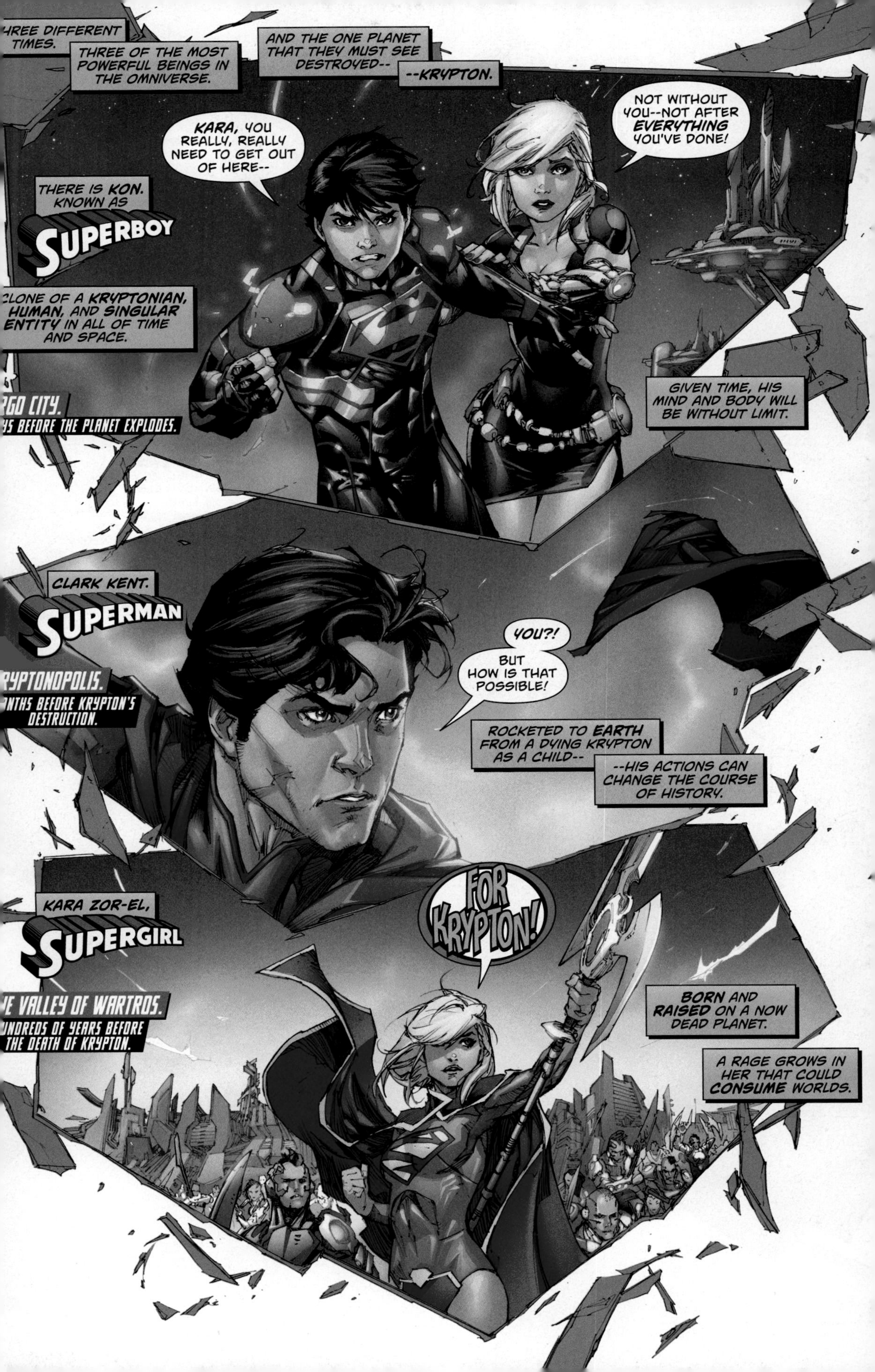
THREE DIFFERENT TIMES.
THREE OF THE MOST POWERFUL BEINGS IN THE OMNIVERSE.
AND THE ONE PLANET THAT THEY MUST SEE DESTROYED--
--KRYPTON.
KARA, YOU REALLY, REALLY NEED TO GET OUT OF HERE--
NOT WITHOUT YOU--NOT AFTER EVERYTHING YOU'VE DONE!
THERE IS KON. KNOWN AS
SUPERBOY
CLONE OF A KRYPTONIAN, HUMAN, AND SINGULAR ENTITY IN ALL OF TIME AND SPACE.
GIVEN TIME, HIS MIND AND BODY WILL BE WITHOUT LIMIT.
RGO CITY.
YS BEFORE THE PLANET EXPLODES.
CLARK KENT.
SUPERMAN
RYPTONOPOLIS.
NTHS BEFORE KRYPTON'S DESTRUCTION.
YOU?! BUT HOW IS THAT POSSIBLE!
ROCKETED TO EARTH FROM A DYING KRYPTON AS A CHILD--
--HIS ACTIONS CAN CHANGE THE COURSE OF HISTORY.
KARA ZOR-EL,
SUPERGIRL
E VALLEY OF WARTROS.
UNDREDS OF YEARS BEFORE THE DEATH OF KRYPTON.
FOR KRYPTON!
BORN AND RAISED ON A NOW DEAD PLANET.
A RAGE GROWS IN HER THAT COULD CONSUME WORLDS.

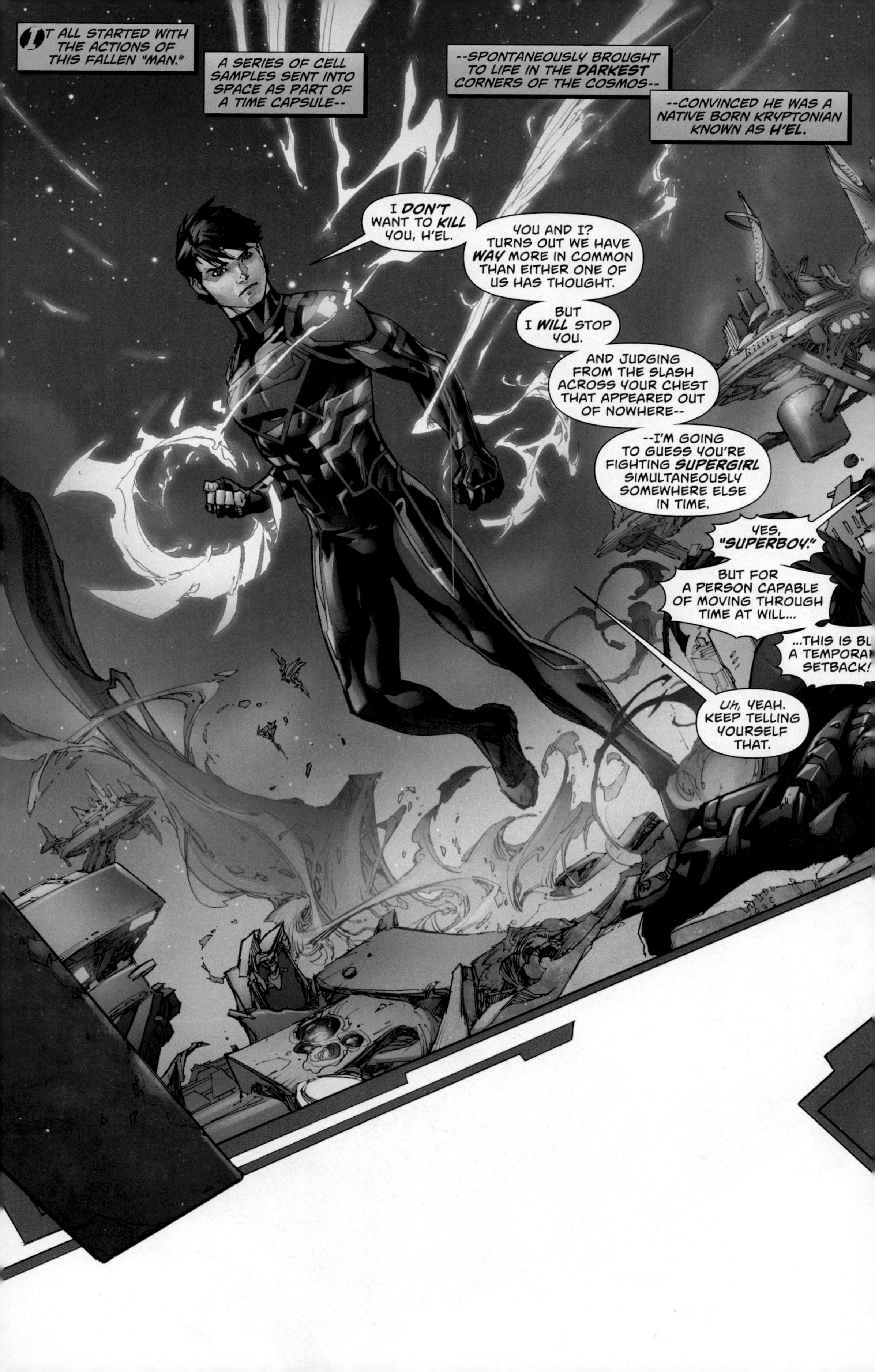
IT ALL STARTED WITH THE ACTIONS OF THIS FALLEN "MAN."
A SERIES OF CELL SAMPLES SENT INTO SPACE AS PART OF A TIME CAPSULE--
--SPONTANEOUSLY BROUGHT TO LIFE IN THE DARKEST CORNERS OF THE COSMOS--
--CONVINCED HE WAS A NATIVE BORN KRYPTONIAN KNOWN AS H'EL.
I DON'T WANT TO KILL YOU, H'EL.
YOU AND I? TURNS OUT WE HAVE WAY MORE IN COMMON THAN EITHER ONE OF US HAS THOUGHT.
BUT I WILL STOP YOU.
AND JUDGING FROM THE SLASH ACROSS YOUR CHEST THAT APPEARED OUT OF NOWHERE--
--I'M GOING TO GUESS YOU'RE FIGHTING SUPERGIRL SIMULTANEOUSLY SOMEWHERE ELSE IN TIME.
YES, "SUPERBOY."
BUT FOR A PERSON CAPABLE OF MOVING THROUGH TIME AT WILL...
UH, YEAH. KEEP TELLING YOURSELF THAT.

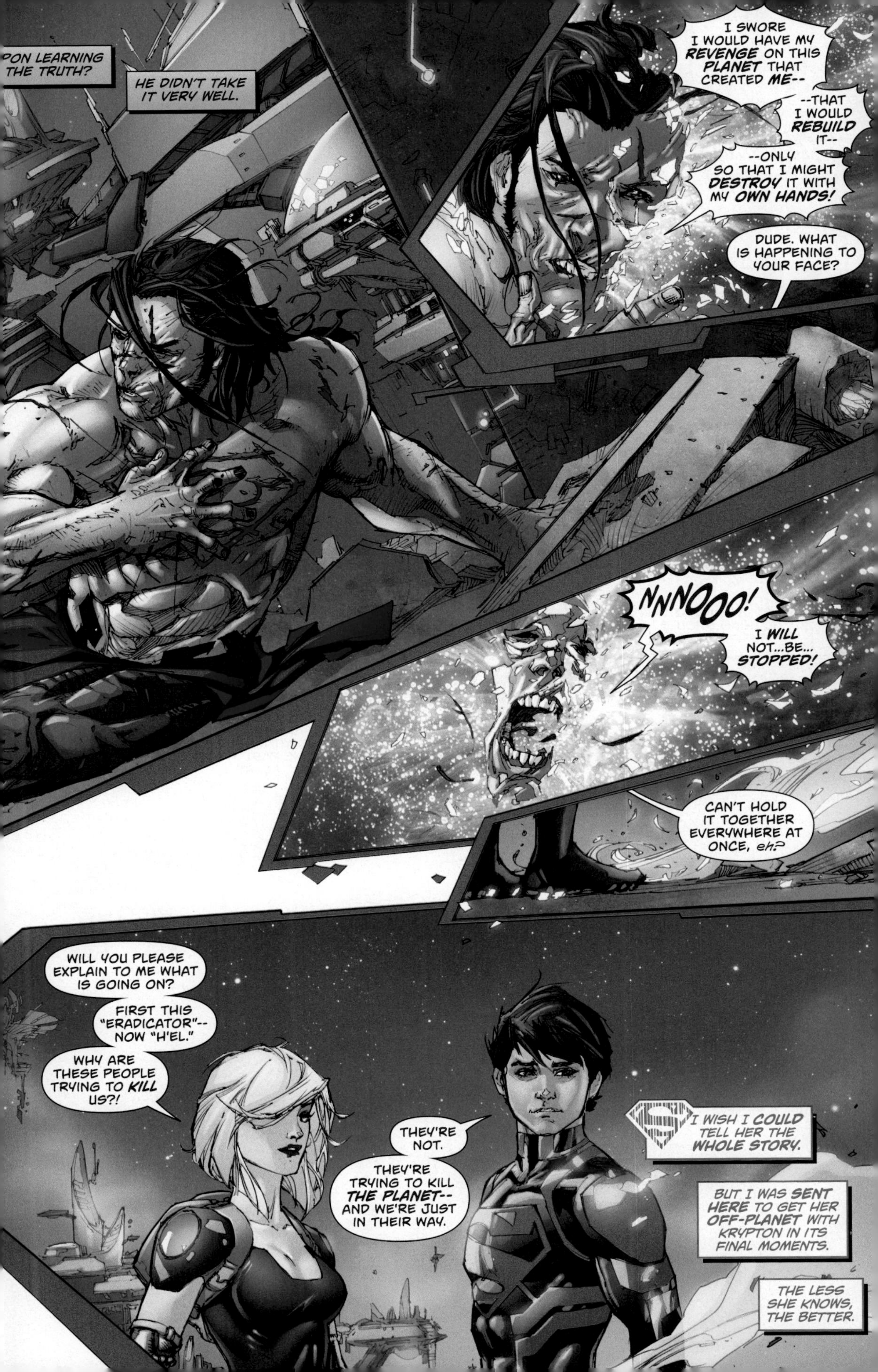
PON LEARNING THE TRUTH?
HE DIDN'T TAKE IT VERY WELL.
I SWORE I WOULD HAVE MY REVENGE ON THIS PLANET THAT CREATED ME--
--THAT I WOULD REBUILD IT--
--ONLY SO THAT I MIGHT DESTROY IT WITH MY OWN HANDS!
DUDE. WHAT IS HAPPENING TO YOUR FACE?
NNNOOO!
I WILL NOT...BE... STOPPED!
CAN'T HOLD IT TOGETHER EVERYWHERE AT ONCE, eh?
WILL YOU PLEASE EXPLAIN TO ME WHAT IS GOING ON?
FIRST THIS "ERADICATOR"-- NOW "H'EL."
WHY ARE THESE PEOPLE TRYING TO KILL US?!
THEY'RE NOT.
THEY'RE TRYING TO KILL THE PLANET-- AND WE'RE JUST IN THEIR WAY.
I WISH I COULD TELL HER THE WHOLE STORY.
BUT I WAS SENT HERE TO GET HER OFF-PLANET WITH KRYPTON IN ITS FINAL MOMENTS.
THE LESS SHE KNOWS, THE BETTER.

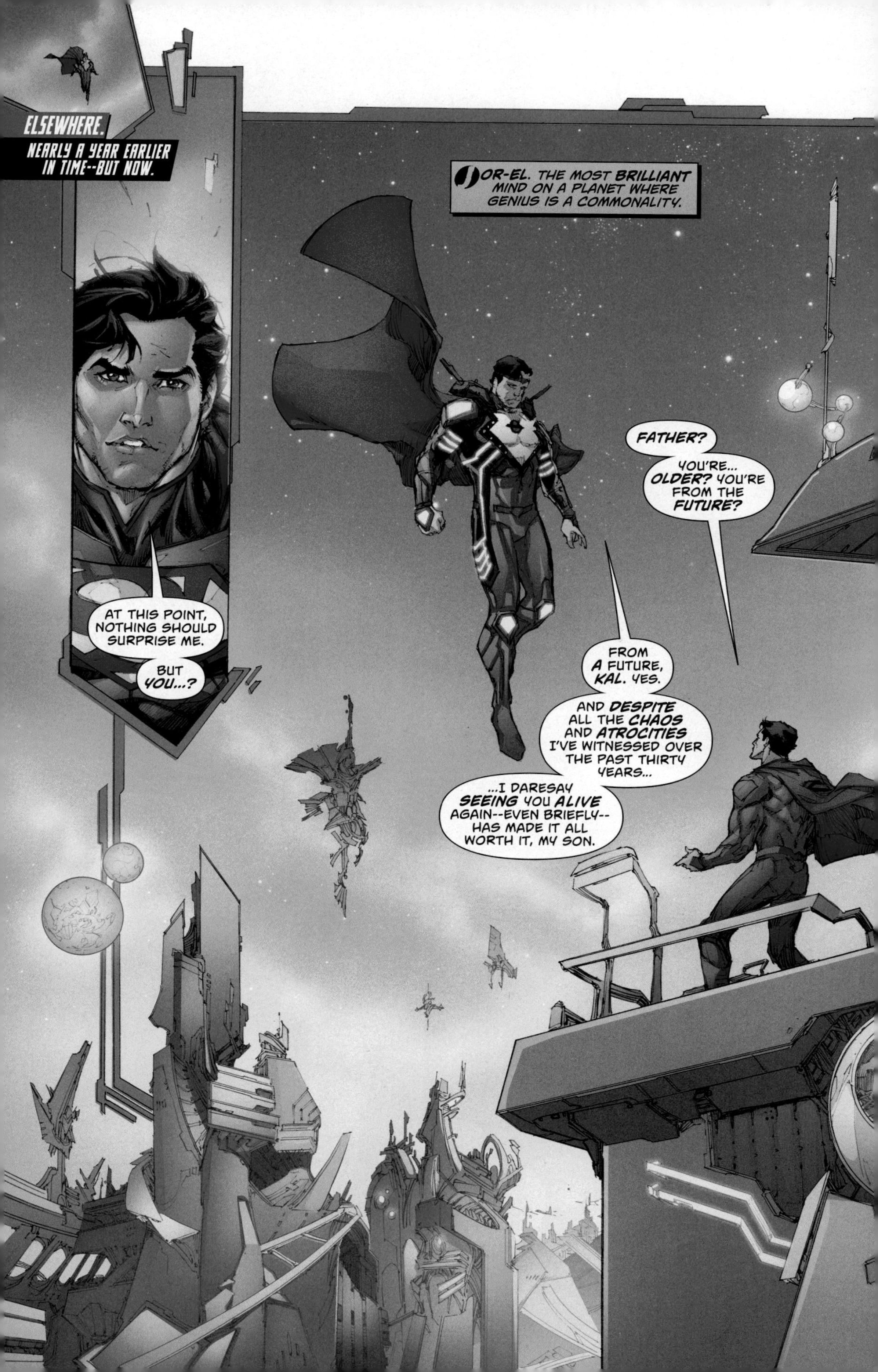
ELSEWHERE.
NEARLY A YEAR EARLIER IN TIME--BUT NOW.
AT THIS POINT, NOTHING SHOULD SURPRISE ME.
BUT YOU...?
JOR-EL. THE MOST BRILLIANT MIND ON A PLANET WHERE GENIUS IS A COMMONALITY.
FATHER?
YOU'RE... OLDER? YOU'RE FROM THE FUTURE?
FROM A FUTURE, KAL. YES.
AND DESPITE ALL THE CHAOS AND ATROCITIES I'VE WITNESSED OVER THE PAST THIRTY YEARS...
...I DARESAY SEEING YOU ALIVE AGAIN--EVEN BRIEFLY--HAS MADE IT ALL WORTH IT, MY SON.

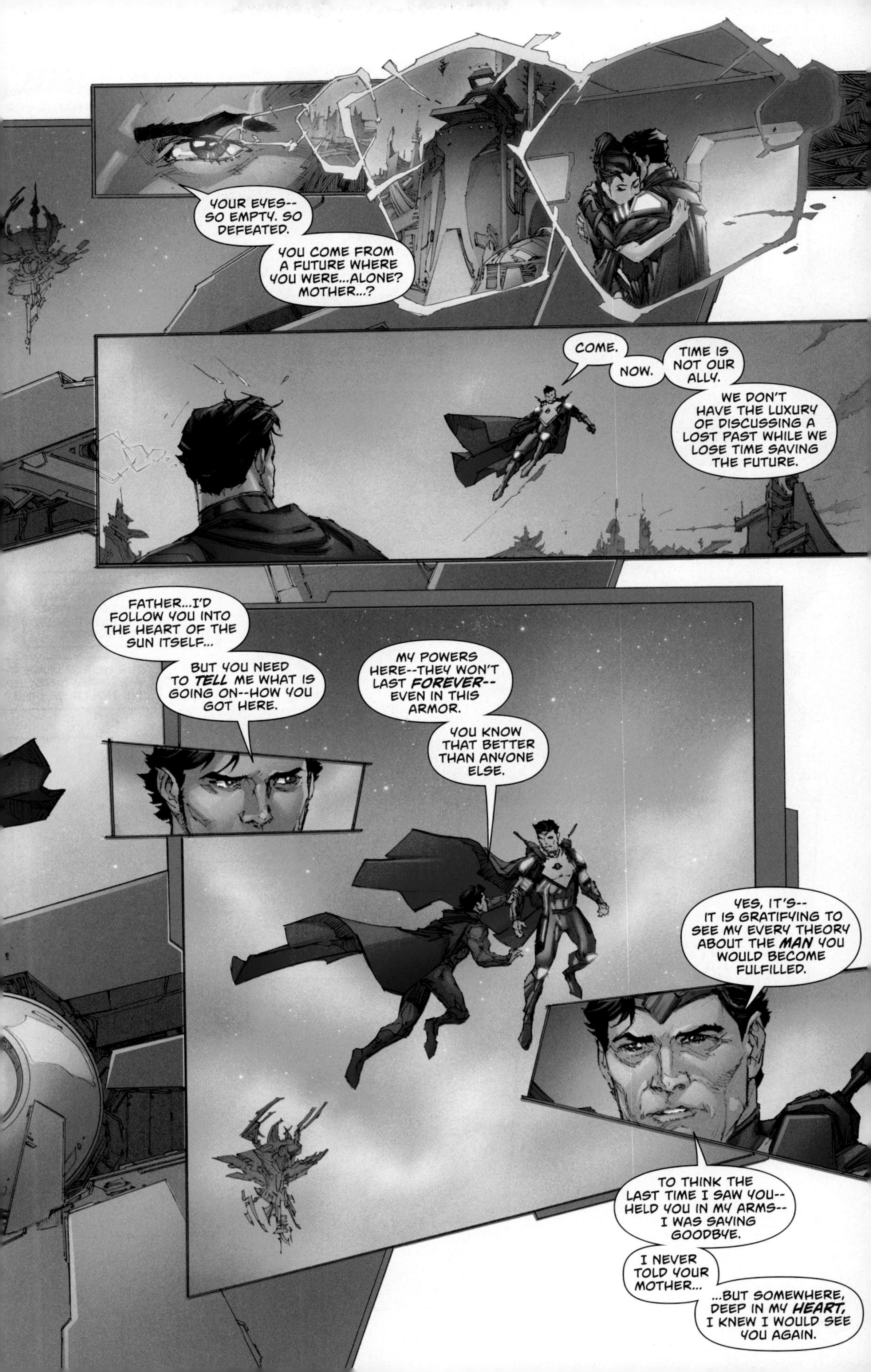
YOUR EYES-- SO EMPTY. SO DEFEATED.
YOU COME FROM A FUTURE WHERE YOU WERE...ALONE? MOTHER...?
COME.
NOW.
TIME IS NOT OUR ALLY.
WE DON'T HAVE THE LUXURY OF DISCUSSING A LOST PAST WHILE WE LOSE TIME SAVING THE FUTURE.
FATHER...I'D FOLLOW YOU INTO THE HEART OF THE SUN ITSELF...
BUT YOU NEED TO TELL ME WHAT IS GOING ON--HOW YOU GOT HERE.
MY POWERS HERE--THEY WON'T LAST FOREVER-- EVEN IN THIS ARMOR.
YOU KNOW THAT BETTER THAN ANYONE ELSE.
YES, IT'S-- IT IS GRATIFYING TO SEE MY EVERY THEORY ABOUT THE MAN YOU WOULD BECOME FULFILLED.
TO THINK THE LAST TIME I SAW YOU-- HELD YOU IN MY ARMS-- I WAS SAYING GOODBYE.
I NEVER TOLD YOUR MOTHER...
...BUT SOMEWHERE, DEEP IN MY HEART, I KNEW I WOULD SEE YOU AGAIN.

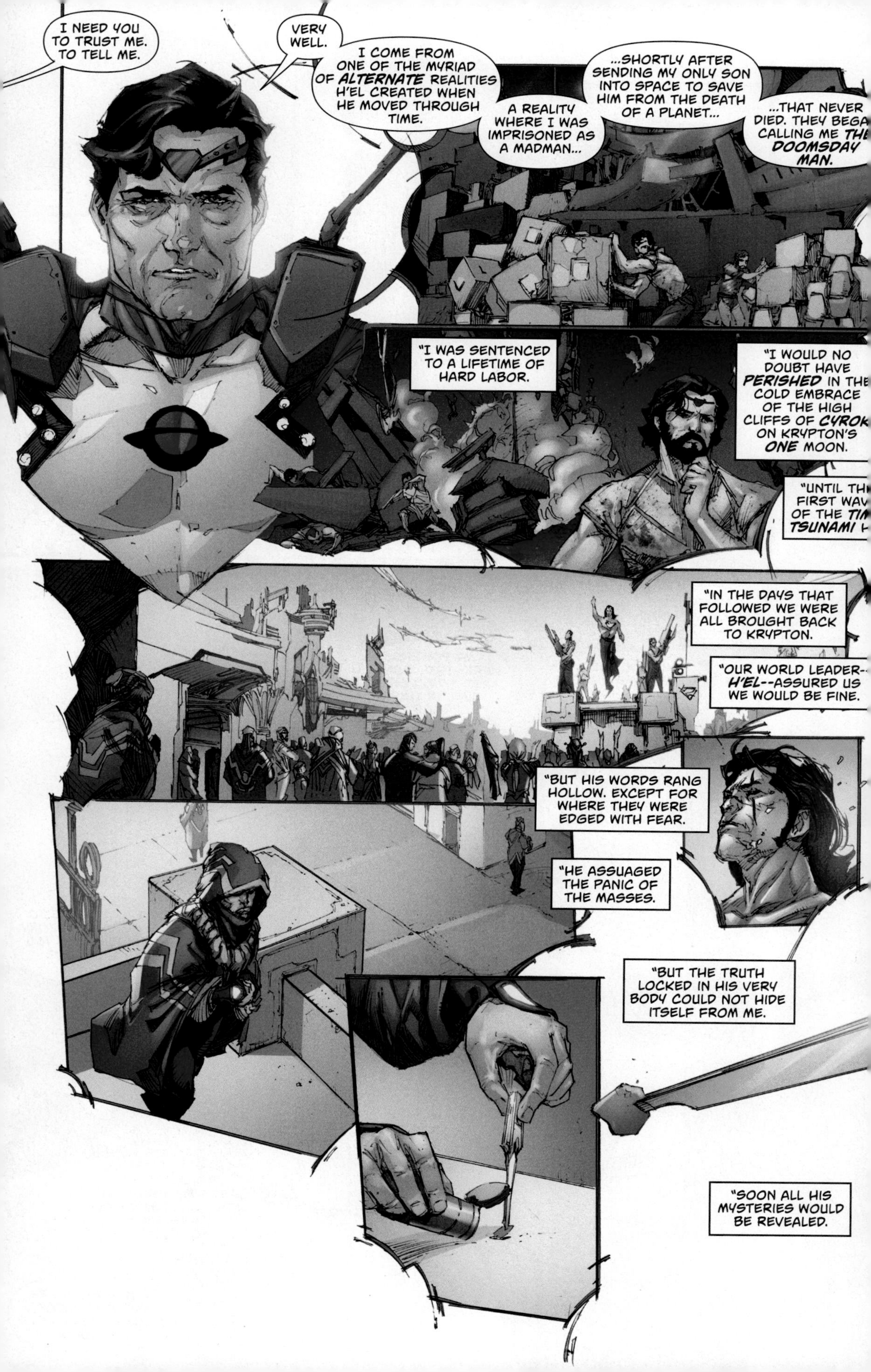

I NEED YOU TO TRUST ME. TO TELL ME.
VERY WELL.
I COME FROM ONE OF THE MYRIAD OF ALTERNATE REALITIES H'EL CREATED WHEN HE MOVED THROUGH TIME.
A REALITY WHERE I WAS IMPRISONED AS A MADMAN...
...SHORTLY AFTER SENDING MY ONLY SON INTO SPACE TO SAVE HIM FROM THE DEATH OF A PLANET...
...THAT NEVER DIED. THEY BEGA CALLING ME THE DOOMSDAY MAN.
"I WAS SENTENCED TO A LIFETIME OF HARD LABOR.
"I WOULD NO DOUBT HAVE PERISHED IN THE COLD EMBRACE OF THE HIGH CLIFFS OF CYROK ON KRYPTON'S ONE MOON.
"UNTIL TH FIRST WAV OF THE TIM TSUNAMI H
"IN THE DAYS THAT FOLLOWED WE WERE ALL BROUGHT BACK TO KRYPTON.
"OUR WORLD LEADER--H'EL--ASSURED US WE WOULD BE FINE.
"BUT HIS WORDS RANG HOLLOW. EXCEPT FOR WHERE THEY WERE EDGED WITH FEAR.
"HE ASSUAGED THE PANIC OF THE MASSES.
"BUT THE TRUTH LOCKED IN HIS VERY BODY COULD NOT HIDE ITSELF FROM ME.
"SOON ALL HIS MYSTERIES WOULD BE REVEALED.

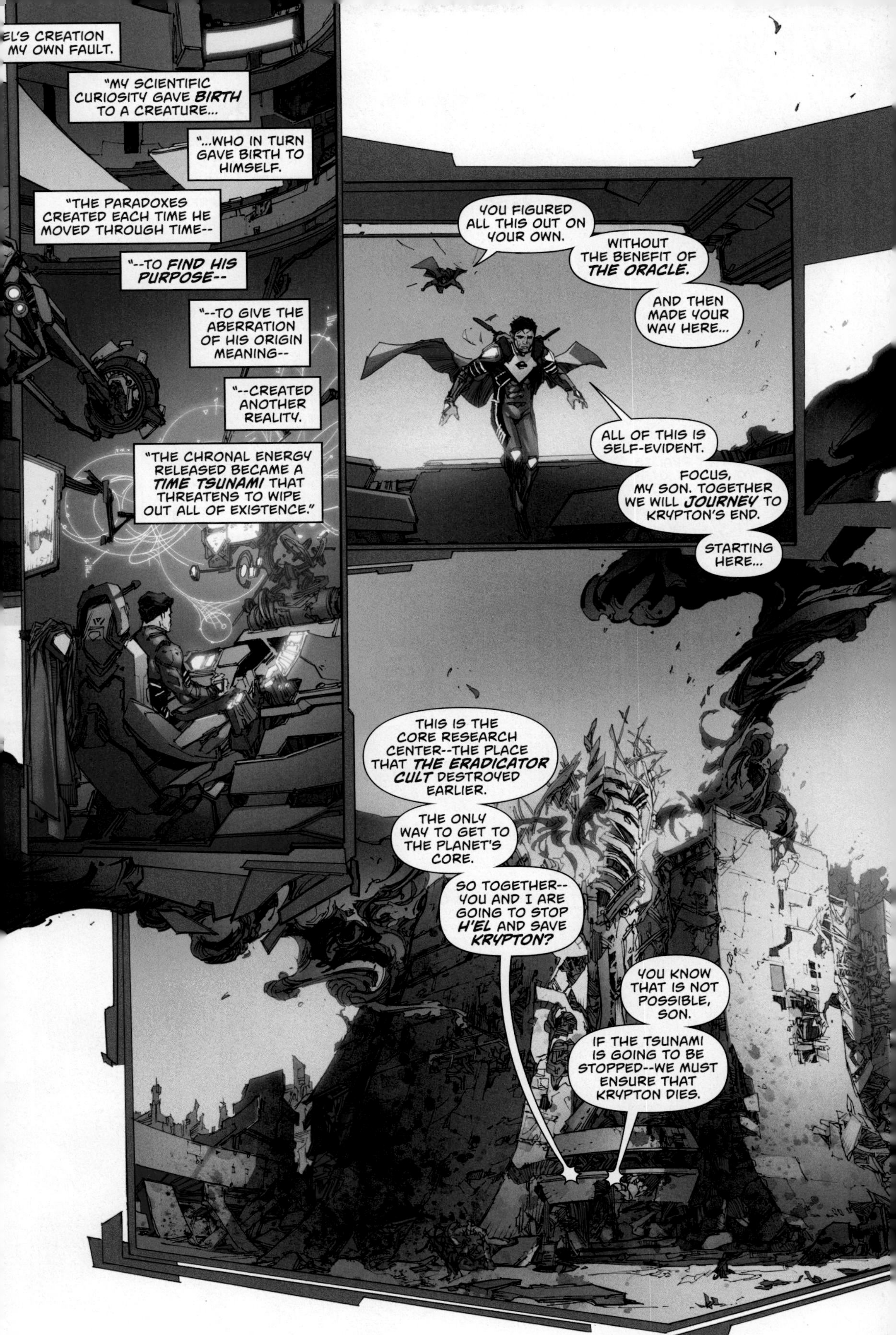

EL'S CREATION MY OWN FAULT.
"MY SCIENTIFIC CURIOSITY GAVE BIRTH TO A CREATURE...
"...WHO IN TURN GAVE BIRTH TO HIMSELF.
"THE PARADOXES CREATED EACH TIME HE MOVED THROUGH TIME--
"--TO FIND HIS PURPOSE--
"--TO GIVE THE ABERRATION OF HIS ORIGIN MEANING--
"--CREATED ANOTHER REALITY.
"THE CHRONAL ENERGY RELEASED BECAME A TIME TSUNAMI THAT THREATENS TO WIPE OUT ALL OF EXISTENCE."
YOU FIGURED ALL THIS OUT ON YOUR OWN.
WITHOUT THE BENEFIT OF THE ORACLE.
AND THEN MADE YOUR WAY HERE...
ALL OF THIS IS SELF-EVIDENT.
FOCUS, MY SON. TOGETHER WE WILL JOURNEY TO KRYPTON'S END.
STARTING HERE...
THIS IS THE CORE RESEARCH CENTER--THE PLACE THAT THE ERADICATOR CULT DESTROYED EARLIER.
THE ONLY WAY TO GET TO THE PLANET'S CORE.
SO TOGETHER--YOU AND I ARE GOING TO STOP H'EL AND SAVE KRYPTON?
YOU KNOW THAT IS NOT POSSIBLE, SON.
IF THE TSUNAMI IS GOING TO BE STOPPED--WE MUST ENSURE THAT KRYPTON DIES.

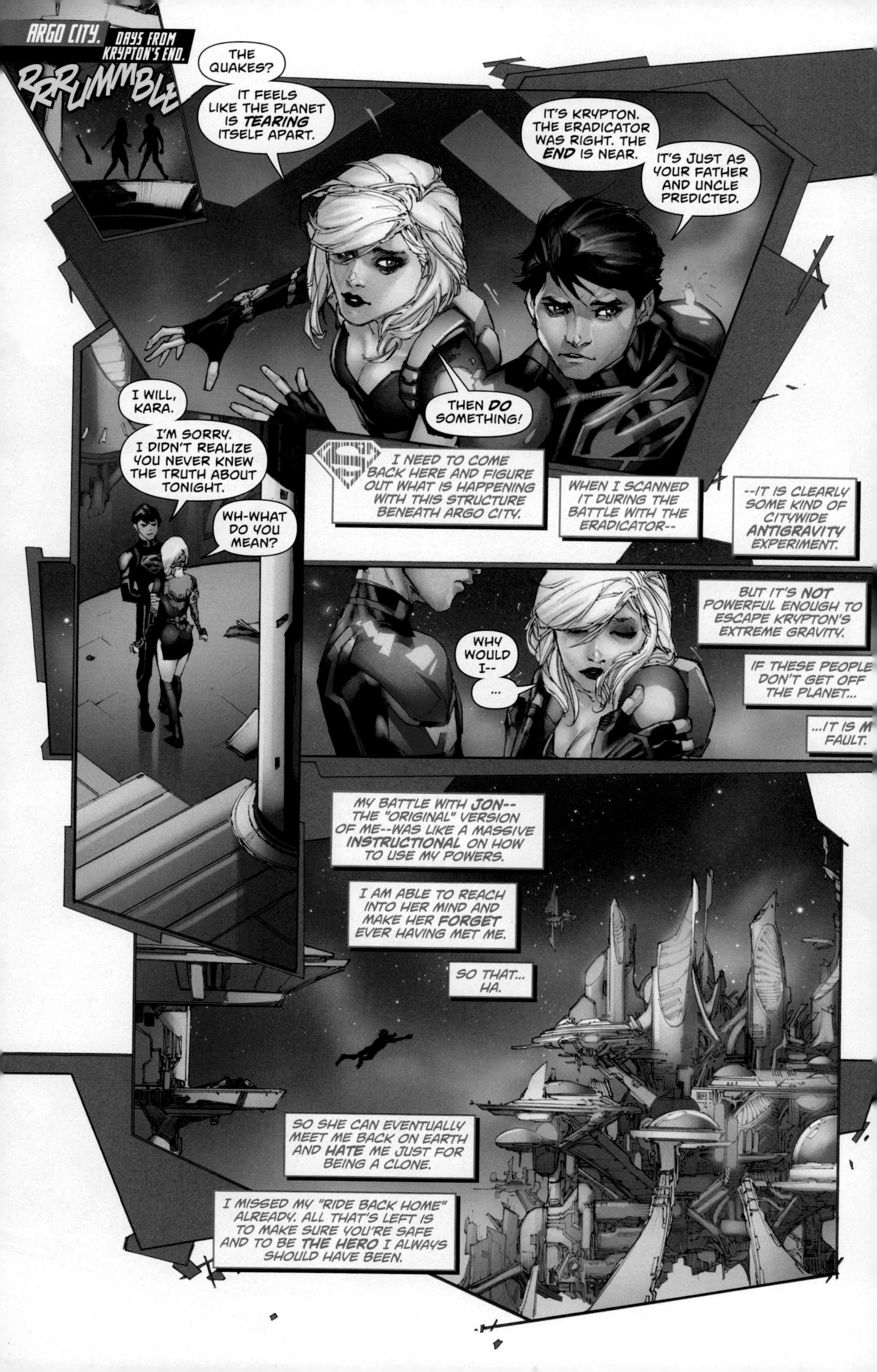
ARGO CITY.
DAYS FROM KRYPTON'S END.
RRRUMMBLE
THE QUAKES?
IT FEELS LIKE THE PLANET IS TEARING ITSELF APART.
IT'S KRYPTON. THE ERADICATOR WAS RIGHT. THE END IS NEAR.
IT'S JUST AS YOUR FATHER AND UNCLE PREDICTED.
THEN DO SOMETHING!
I WILL, KARA.
I'M SORRY. I DIDN'T REALIZE YOU NEVER KNEW THE TRUTH ABOUT TONIGHT.
WH-WHAT DO YOU MEAN?
I NEED TO COME BACK HERE AND FIGURE OUT WHAT IS HAPPENING WITH THIS STRUCTURE BENEATH ARGO CITY.
WHEN I SCANNED IT DURING THE BATTLE WITH THE ERADICATOR--
--IT IS CLEARLY SOME KIND OF CITYWIDE ANTIGRAVITY EXPERIMENT.
WHY WOULD I-- ...
BUT IT'S NOT POWERFUL ENOUGH TO ESCAPE KRYPTON'S EXTREME GRAVITY.
IF THESE PEOPLE DON'T GET OFF THE PLANET...
...IT IS M FAULT.
MY BATTLE WITH JON-- THE "ORIGINAL" VERSION OF ME--WAS LIKE A MASSIVE INSTRUCTIONAL ON HOW TO USE MY POWERS.
I AM ABLE TO REACH INTO HER MIND AND MAKE HER FORGET EVER HAVING MET ME.
SO THAT... HA.
SO SHE CAN EVENTUALLY MEET ME BACK ON EARTH AND HATE ME JUST FOR BEING A CLONE.
I MISSED MY "RIDE BACK HOME" ALREADY. ALL THAT'S LEFT IS TO MAKE SURE YOU'RE SAFE AND TO BE THE HERO I ALWAYS SHOULD HAVE BEEN.

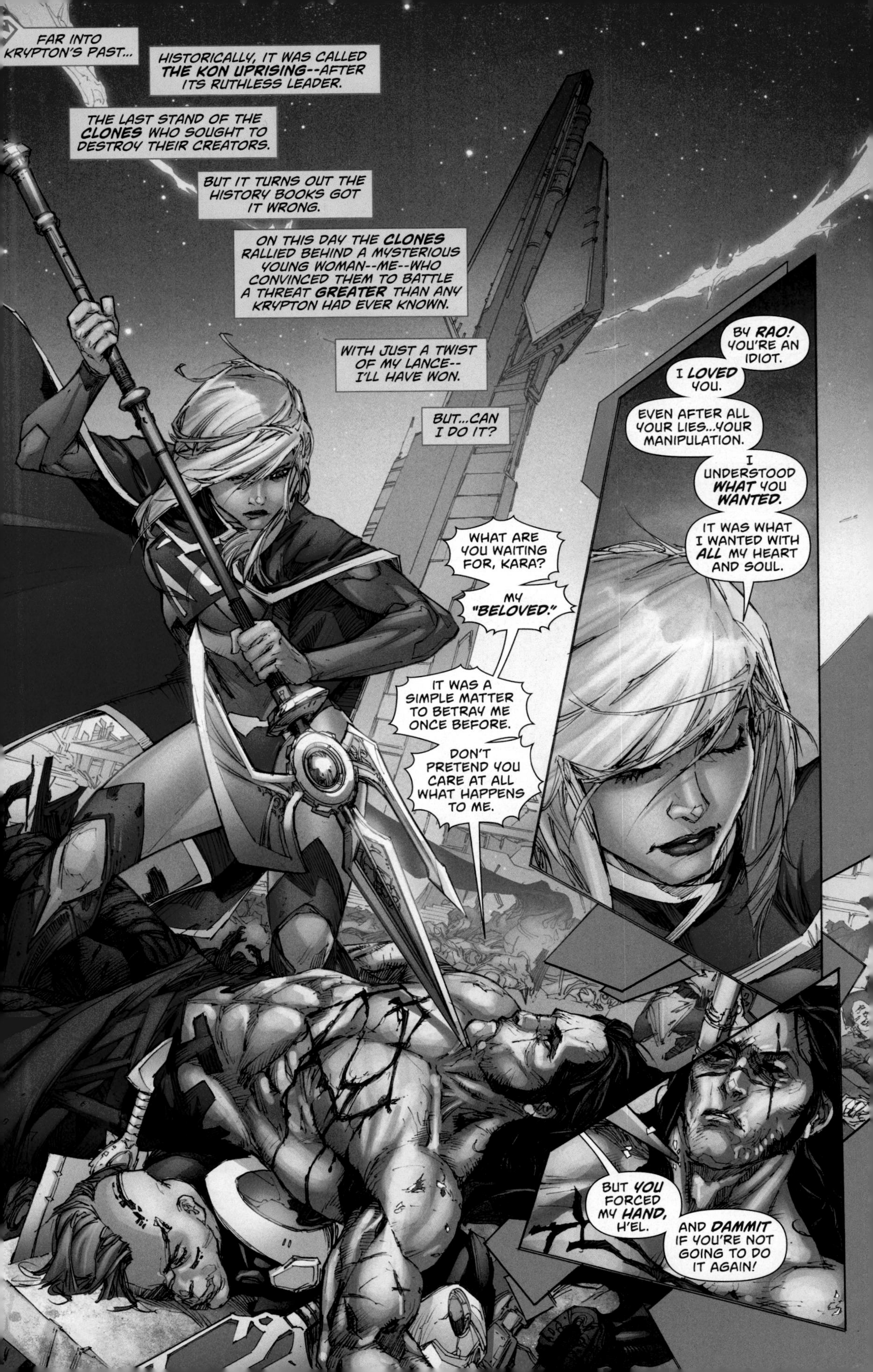
FAR INTO KRYPTON'S PAST...
HISTORICALLY, IT WAS CALLED THE KON UPRISING--AFTER ITS RUTHLESS LEADER.
THE LAST STAND OF THE CLONES WHO SOUGHT TO DESTROY THEIR CREATORS.
BUT IT TURNS OUT THE HISTORY BOOKS GOT IT WRONG.
ON THIS DAY THE CLONES RALLIED BEHIND A MYSTERIOUS YOUNG WOMAN--ME--WHO CONVINCED THEM TO BATTLE A THREAT GREATER THAN ANY KRYPTON HAD EVER KNOWN.
WITH JUST A TWIST OF MY LANCE-- I'LL HAVE WON.
BUT...CAN I DO IT?
WHAT ARE YOU WAITING FOR, KARA?
MY "BELOVED."
IT WAS A SIMPLE MATTER TO BETRAY ME ONCE BEFORE.
DON'T PRETEND YOU CARE AT ALL WHAT HAPPENS TO ME.
BY RAO! YOU'RE AN IDIOT.
I LOVED YOU.
EVEN AFTER ALL YOUR LIES...YOUR MANIPULATION.
I UNDERSTOOD WHAT YOU WANTED.
IT WAS WHAT I WANTED WITH ALL MY HEART AND SOUL.
BUT YOU FORCED MY HAND, H'EL.
AND DAMMIT IF YOU'RE NOT GOING TO DO IT AGAIN!

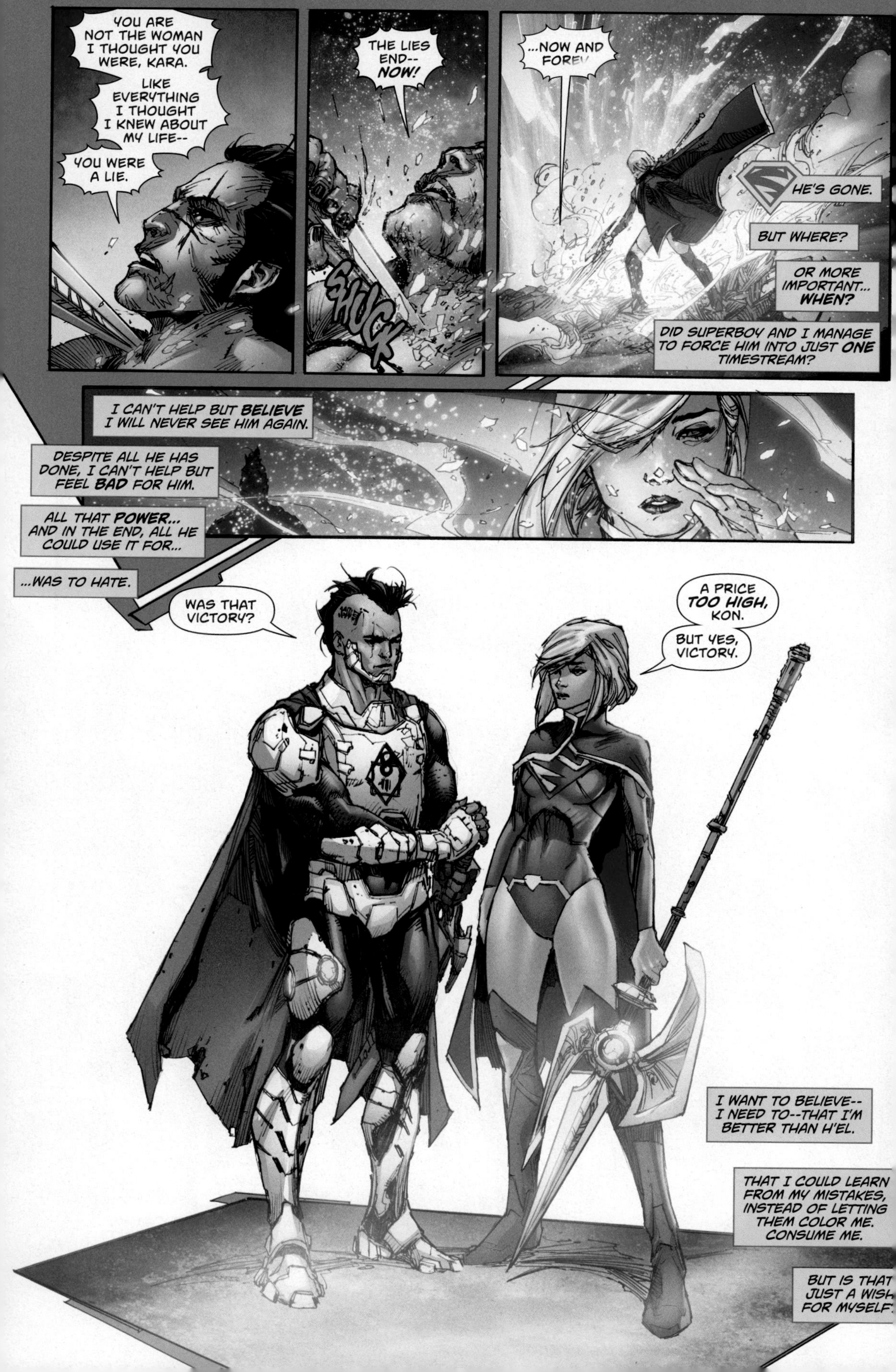

YOU ARE NOT THE WOMAN I THOUGHT YOU WERE, KARA.
LIKE EVERYTHING I THOUGHT I KNEW ABOUT MY LIFE--
YOU WERE A LIE.
THE LIES END-- NOW!
SHUCK
...NOW AND FOREV
HE'S GONE.
BUT WHERE?
OR MORE IMPORTANT... WHEN?
DID SUPERBOY AND I MANAGE TO FORCE HIM INTO JUST ONE TIMESTREAM?
I CAN'T HELP BUT BELIEVE I WILL NEVER SEE HIM AGAIN.
DESPITE ALL HE HAS DONE, I CAN'T HELP BUT FEEL BAD FOR HIM.
ALL THAT POWER... AND IN THE END, ALL HE COULD USE IT FOR...
...WAS TO HATE.
WAS THAT VICTORY?
A PRICE TOO HIGH, KON.
BUT YES, VICTORY.
I WANT TO BELIEVE-- I NEED TO--THAT I'M BETTER THAN H'EL.
THAT I COULD LEARN FROM MY MISTAKES, INSTEAD OF LETTING THEM COLOR ME. CONSUME ME.
BUT IS THAT JUST A WISH FOR MYSELF?

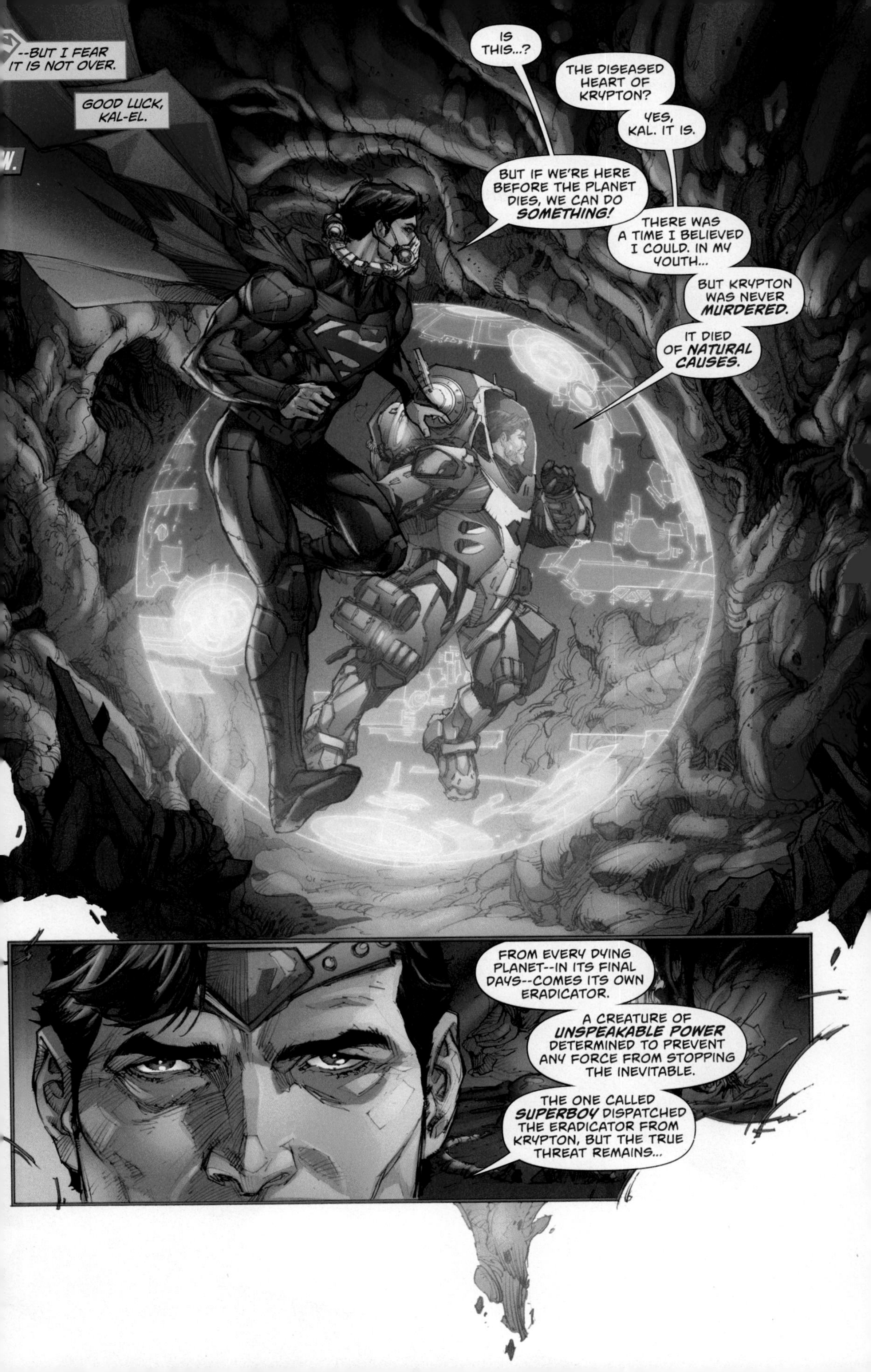

--BUT I FEAR IT IS NOT OVER.
GOOD LUCK, KAL-EL.
IS THIS...?
THE DISEASED HEART OF KRYPTON?
YES, KAL. IT IS.
BUT IF WE'RE HERE BEFORE THE PLANET DIES, WE CAN DO SOMETHING!
THERE WAS A TIME I BELIEVED I COULD. IN MY YOUTH...
BUT KRYPTON WAS NEVER MURDERED.
IT DIED OF NATURAL CAUSES.
FROM EVERY DYING PLANET--IN ITS FINAL DAYS--COMES ITS OWN ERADICATOR.
A CREATURE OF UNSPEAKABLE POWER DETERMINED TO PREVENT ANY FORCE FROM STOPPING THE INEVITABLE.
THE ONE CALLED SUPERBOY DISPATCHED THE ERADICATOR FROM KRYPTON, BUT THE TRUE THREAT REMAINS...

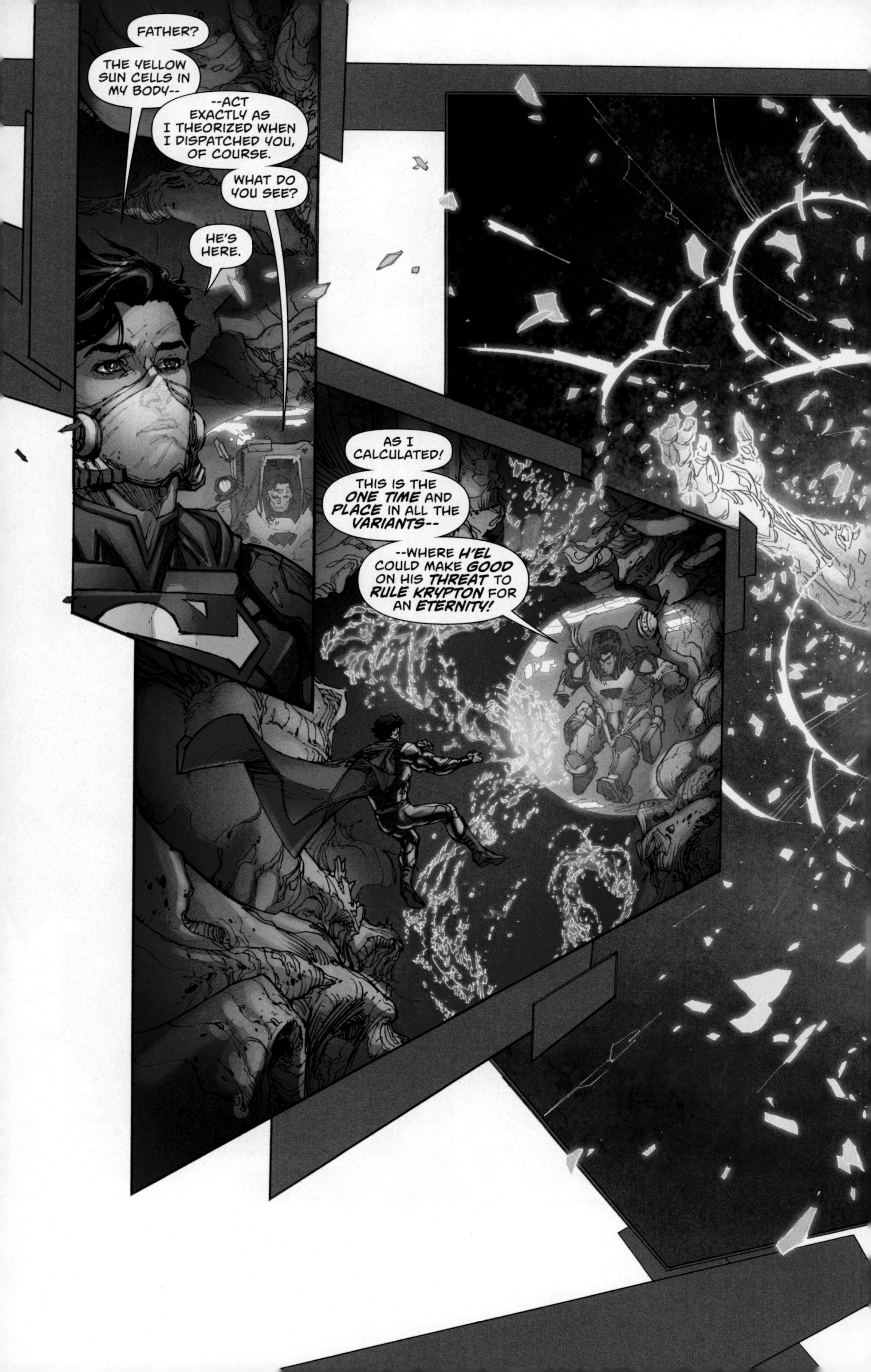
FATHER?
THE YELLOW SUN CELLS IN MY BODY--
--ACT EXACTLY AS I THEORIZED WHEN I DISPATCHED YOU, OF COURSE.
WHAT DO YOU SEE?
HE'S HERE.
AS I CALCULATED!
THIS IS THE ONE TIME AND PLACE IN ALL THE VARIANTS--
--WHERE H'EL COULD MAKE GOOD ON HIS THREAT TO RULE KRYPTON FOR AN ETERNITY!

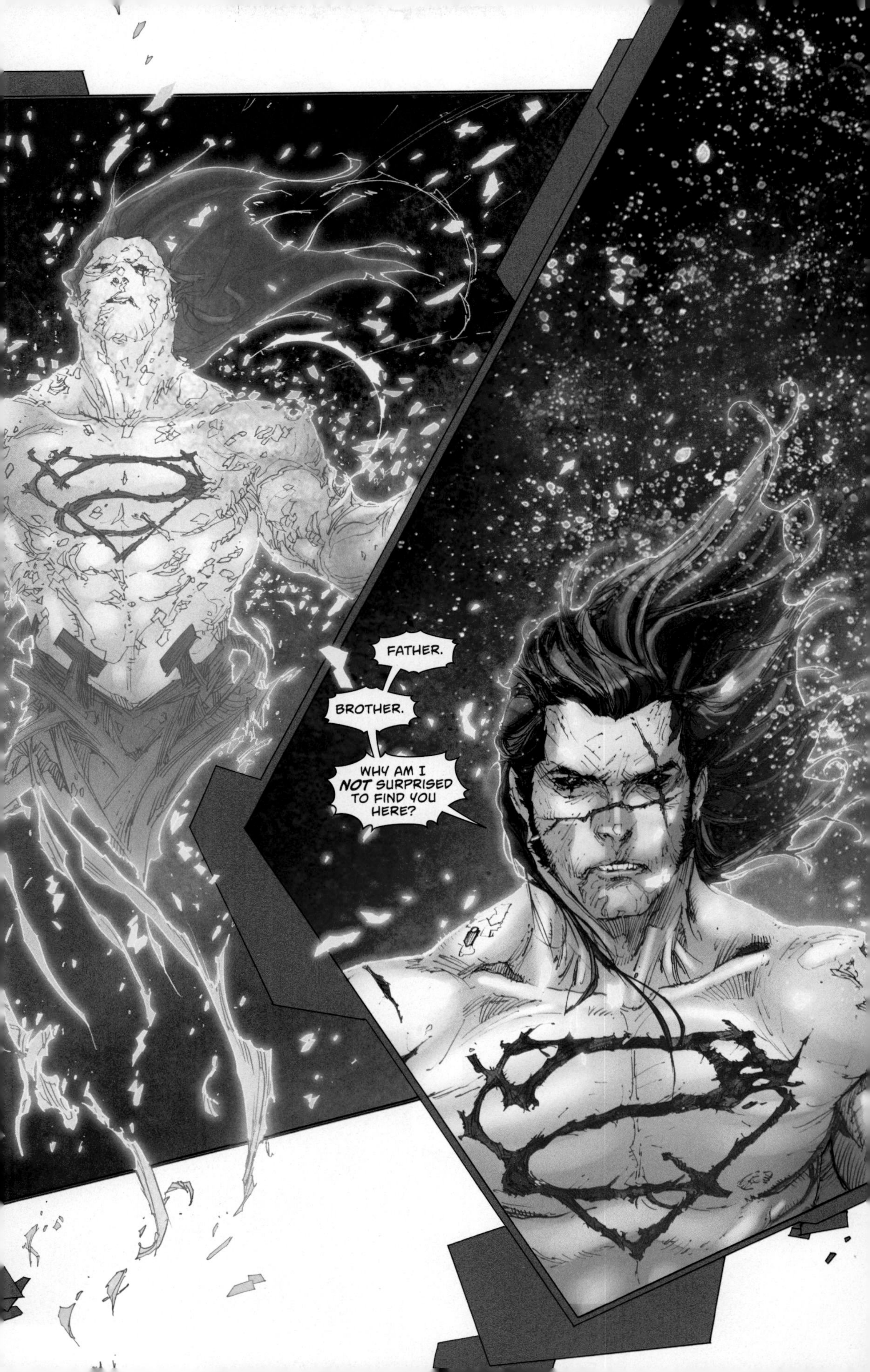
FATHER.
BROTHER.
WHY AM I NOT SURPRISED TO FIND YOU HERE?

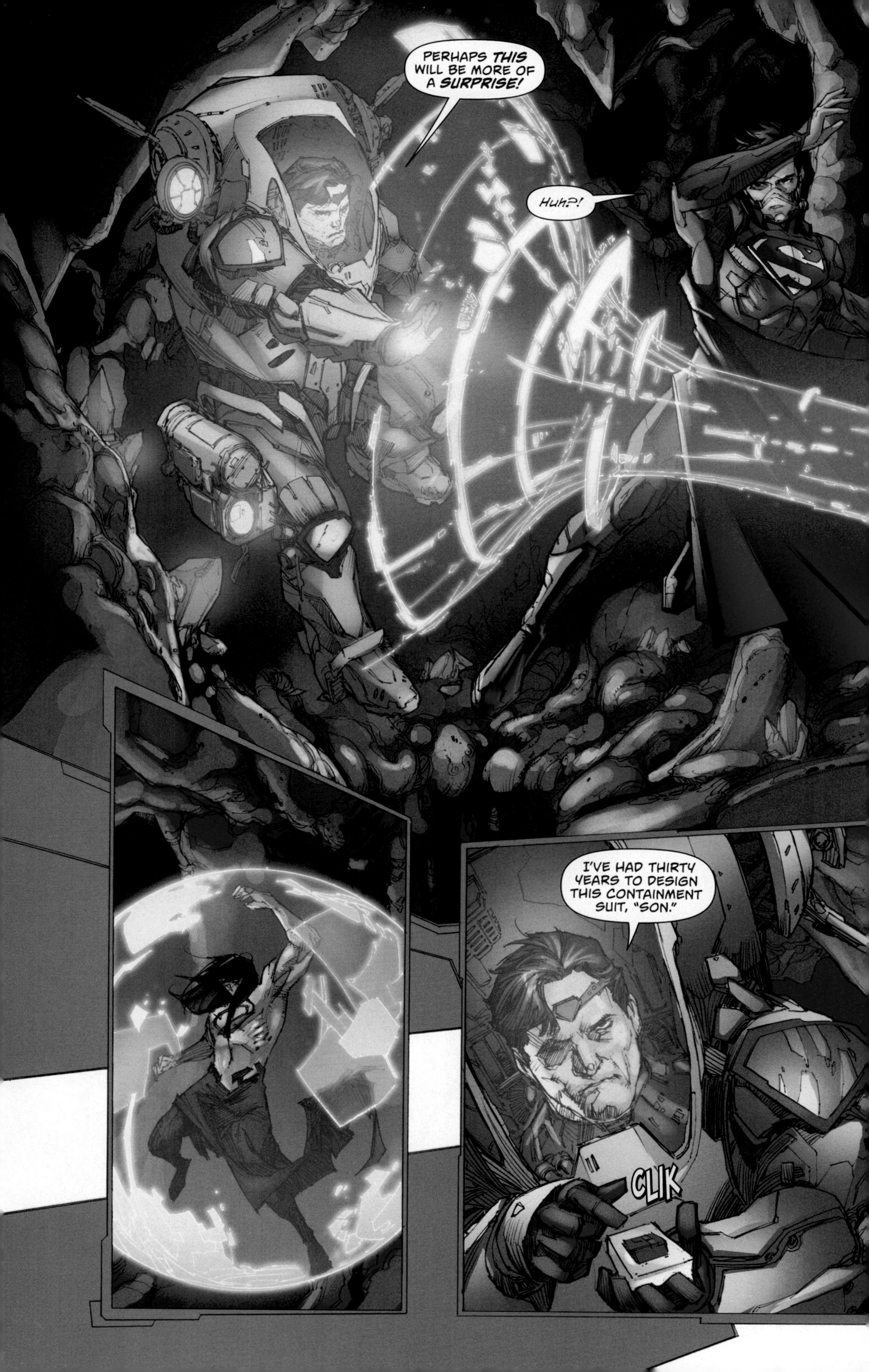
PERHAPS THIS WILL BE MORE OF A SURPRISE!
Huh?!
I'VE HAD THIRTY YEARS TO DESIGN THIS CONTAINMENT SUIT, "SON."
CLIK

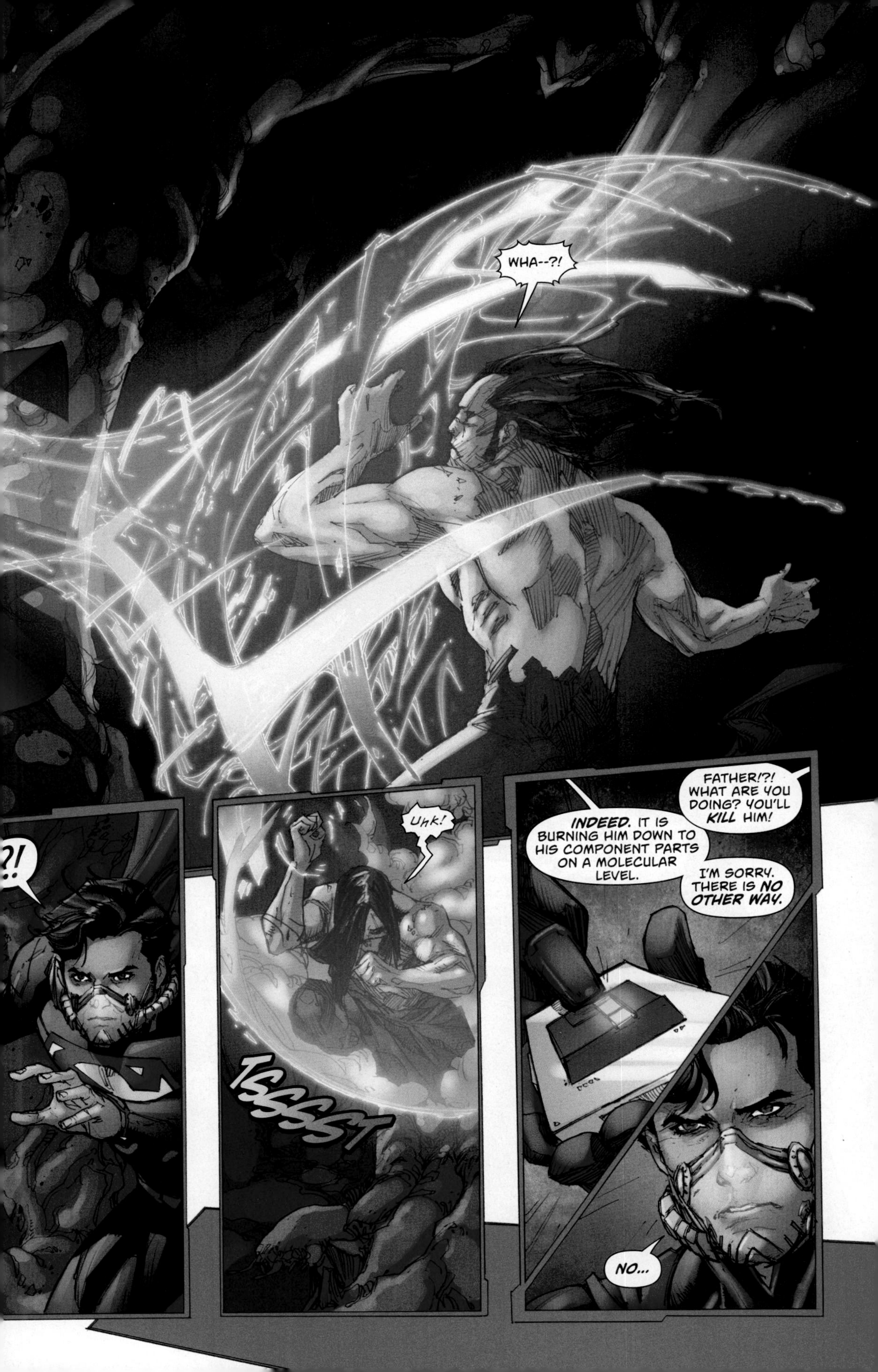
WHA--?!
?!
Unk!
TSSSST
FATHER!?! WHAT ARE YOU DOING? YOU'LL KILL HIM!
INDEED. IT IS BURNING HIM DOWN TO HIS COMPONENT PARTS ON A MOLECULAR LEVEL.
I'M SORRY. THERE IS NO OTHER WAY.
NO...

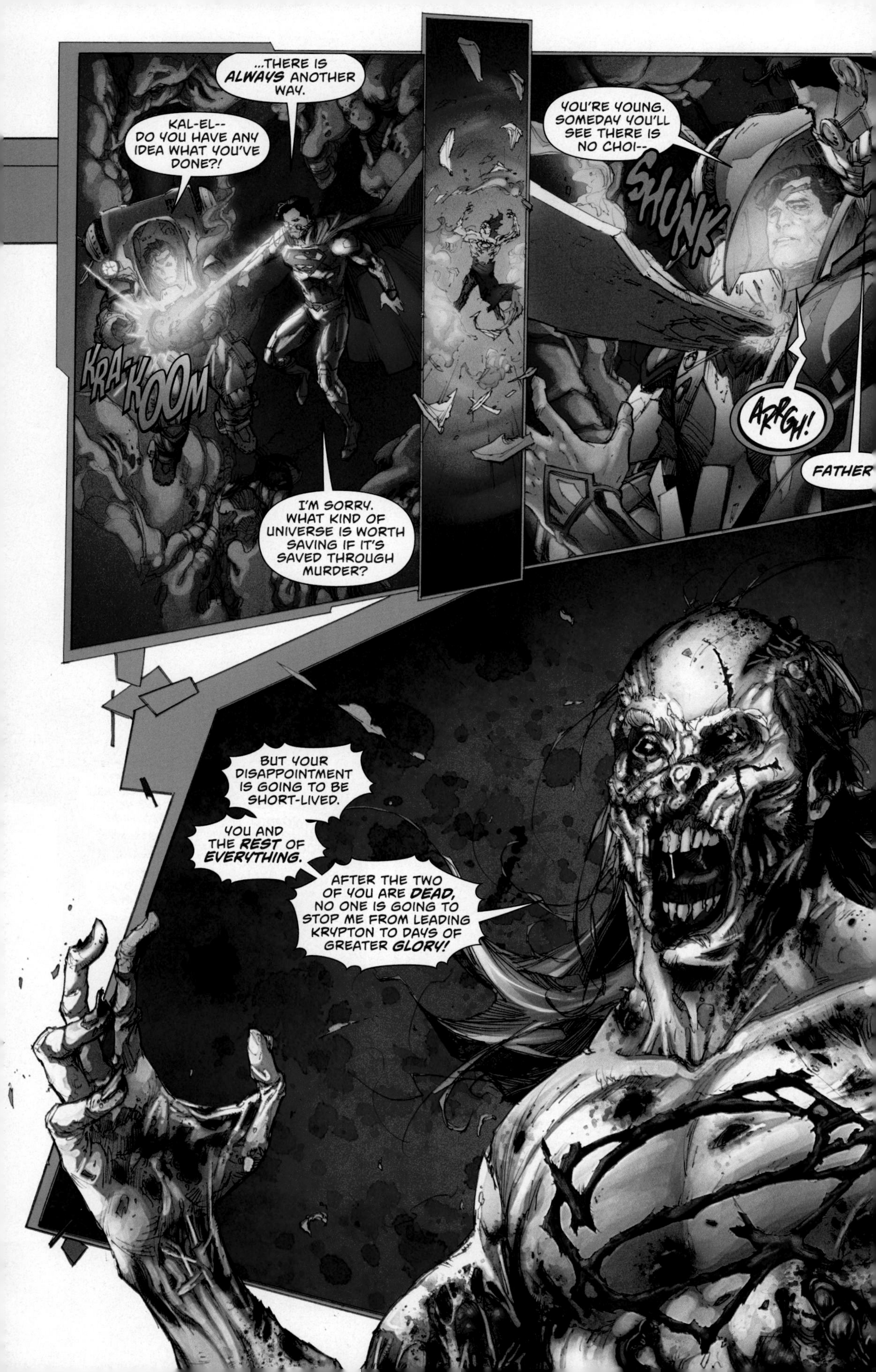
...THERE IS ALWAYS ANOTHER WAY.
KAL-EL-- DO YOU HAVE ANY IDEA WHAT YOU'VE DONE?!
KRA-KOOM
I'M SORRY. WHAT KIND OF UNIVERSE IS WORTH SAVING IF IT'S SAVED THROUGH MURDER?
YOU'RE YOUNG. SOMEDAY YOU'LL SEE THERE IS NO CHOI--
SHUNK
ARRGH!
FATHER
BUT YOUR DISAPPOINTMENT IS GOING TO BE SHORT-LIVED.
YOU AND THE REST OF EVERYTHING.
AFTER THE TWO OF YOU ARE DEAD, NO ONE IS GOING TO STOP ME FROM LEADING KRYPTON TO DAYS OF GREATER GLORY!

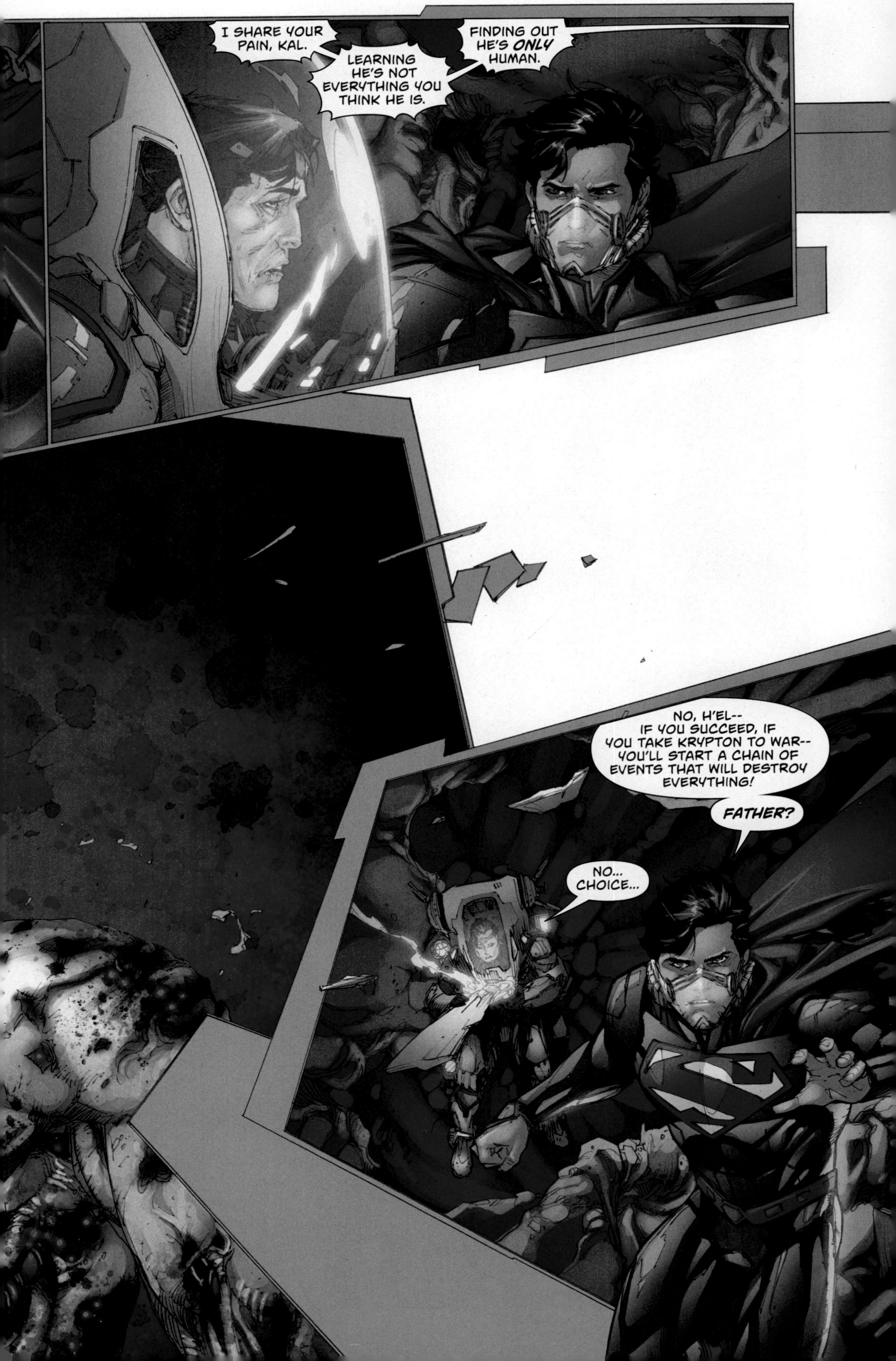
I SHARE YOUR PAIN, KAL.
LEARNING HE'S NOT EVERYTHING YOU THINK HE IS.
FINDING OUT HE'S ONLY HUMAN.
NO, H'EL-- IF YOU SUCCEED, IF YOU TAKE KRYPTON TO WAR-- YOU'LL START A CHAIN OF EVENTS THAT WILL DESTROY EVERYTHING!
FATHER?
NO... CHOICE...

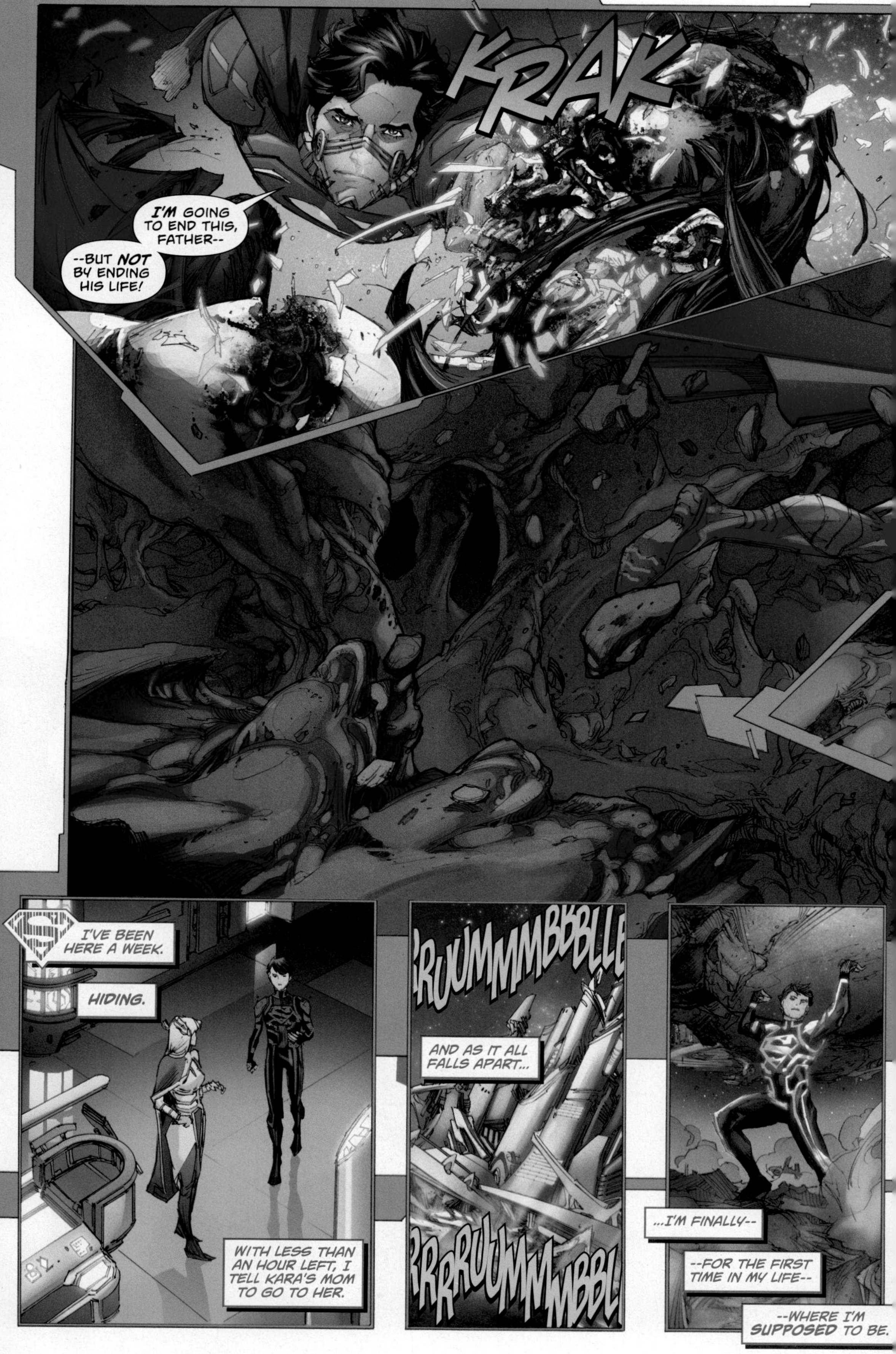
KRAK
I'M GOING TO END THIS, FATHER--
--BUT NOT BY ENDING HIS LIFE!
I'VE BEEN HERE A WEEK.
HIDING.
WITH LESS THAN AN HOUR LEFT, I TELL KARA'S MOM TO GO TO HER.
RRUUMMMBBBLLE
AND AS IT ALL FALLS APART...
RRRRUUMMMBBL
...I'M FINALLY--
--FOR THE FIRST TIME IN MY LIFE--
--WHERE I'M SUPPOSED TO BE.

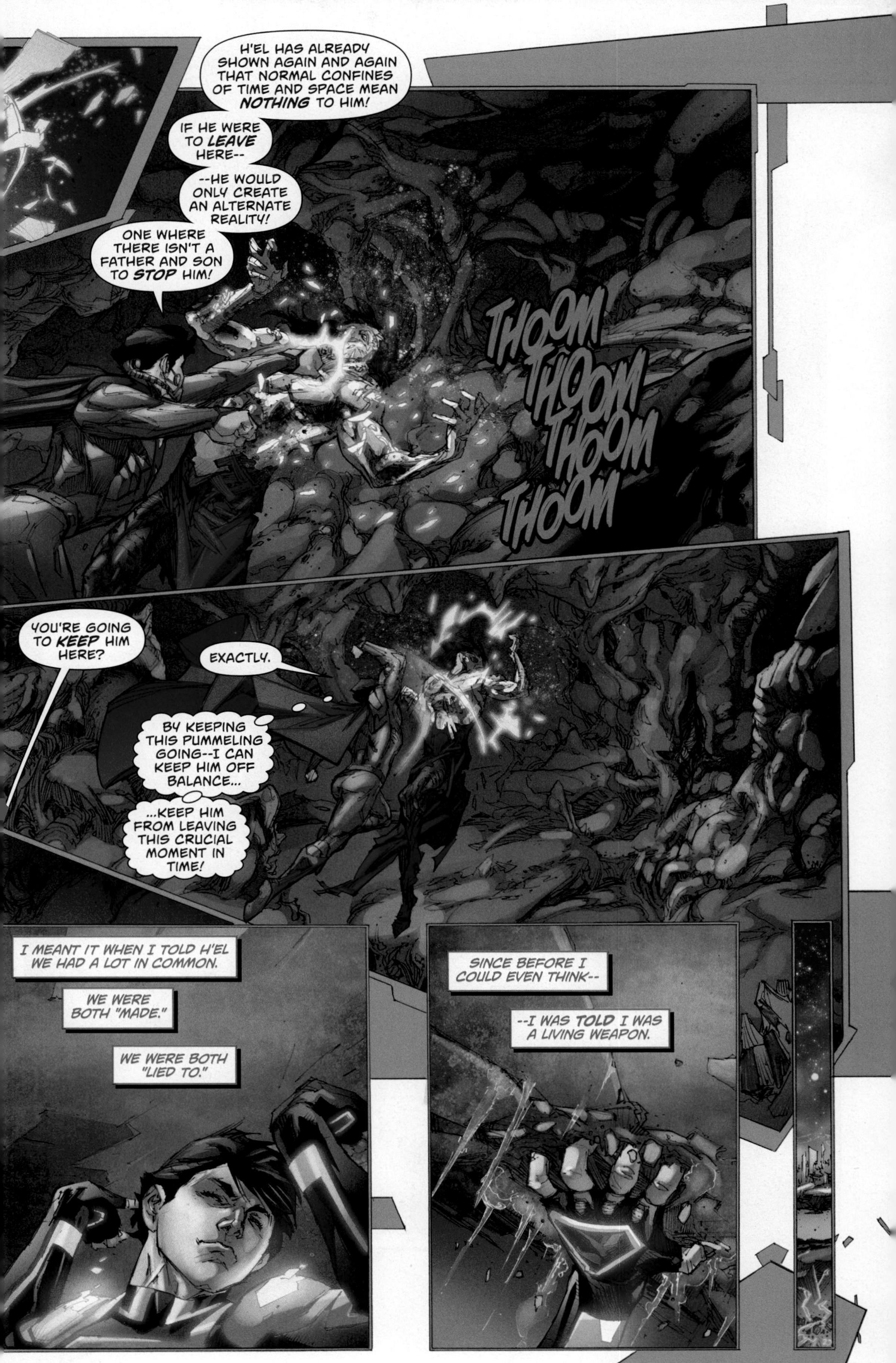
H'EL HAS ALREADY SHOWN AGAIN AND AGAIN THAT NORMAL CONFINES OF TIME AND SPACE MEAN **NOTHING** TO HIM!
IF HE WERE TO **LEAVE** HERE--
--HE WOULD ONLY CREATE AN ALTERNATE REALITY!
ONE WHERE THERE ISN'T A FATHER AND SON TO **STOP** HIM!
THOOM THOOM THOOM THOOM
YOU'RE GOING TO **KEEP** HIM HERE?
EXACTLY.
BY KEEPING THIS PUMMELING GOING--I CAN KEEP HIM OFF BALANCE...
...KEEP HIM FROM LEAVING THIS CRUCIAL MOMENT IN TIME!
I MEANT IT WHEN I TOLD H'EL WE HAD A LOT IN COMMON.
WE WERE BOTH "MADE."
WE WERE BOTH "LIED TO."
SINCE BEFORE I COULD EVEN THINK--
--I WAS **TOLD** I WAS A LIVING WEAPON.

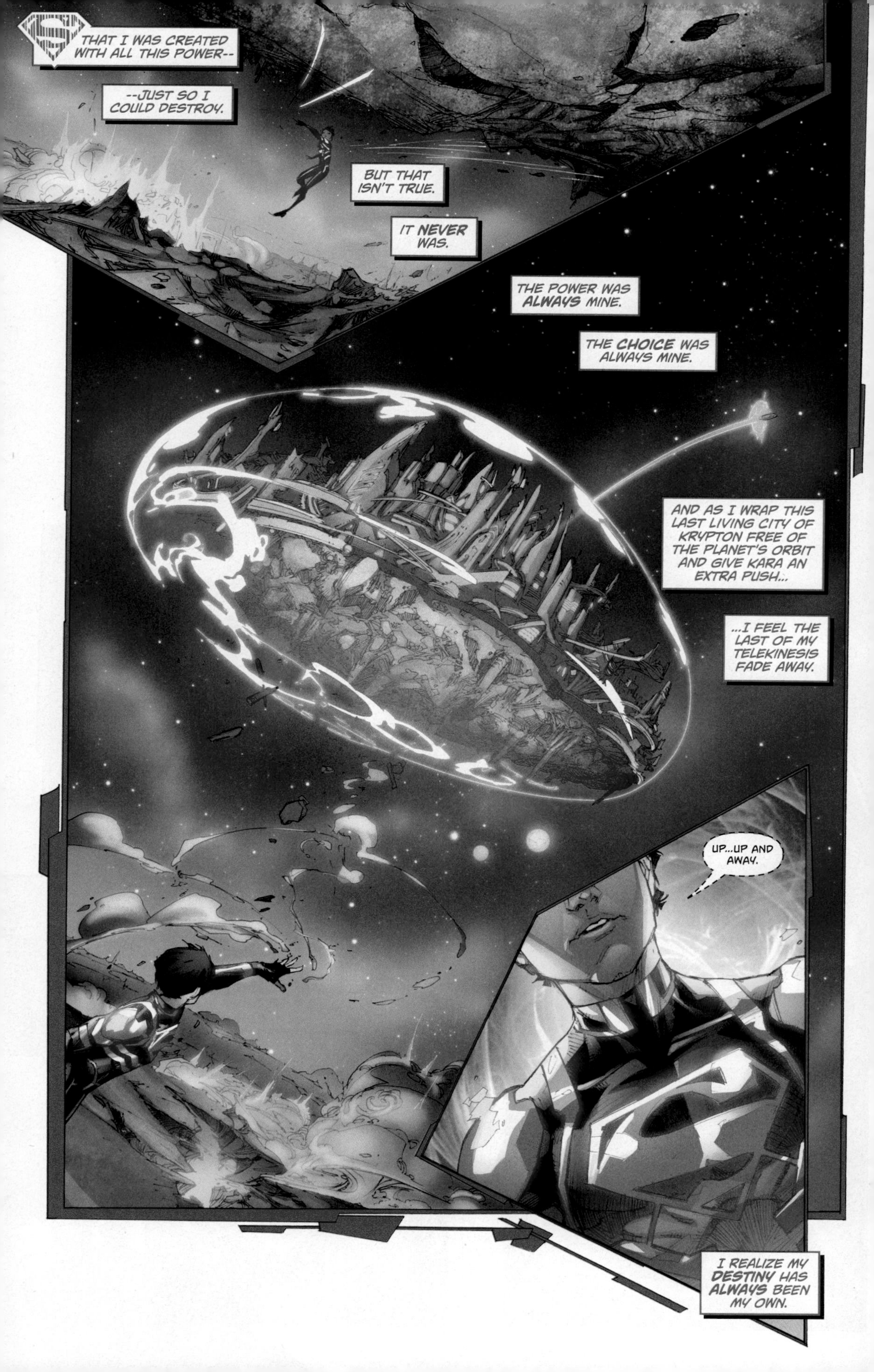
THAT I WAS CREATED WITH ALL THIS POWER--
--JUST SO I COULD DESTROY.
BUT THAT ISN'T TRUE.
IT NEVER WAS.
THE POWER WAS ALWAYS MINE.
THE CHOICE WAS ALWAYS MINE.
AND AS I WRAP THIS LAST LIVING CITY OF KRYPTON FREE OF THE PLANET'S ORBIT AND GIVE KARA AN EXTRA PUSH...
...I FEEL THE LAST OF MY TELEKINESIS FADE AWAY.
UP...UP AND AWAY.
I REALIZE MY DESTINY HAS ALWAYS BEEN MY OWN.

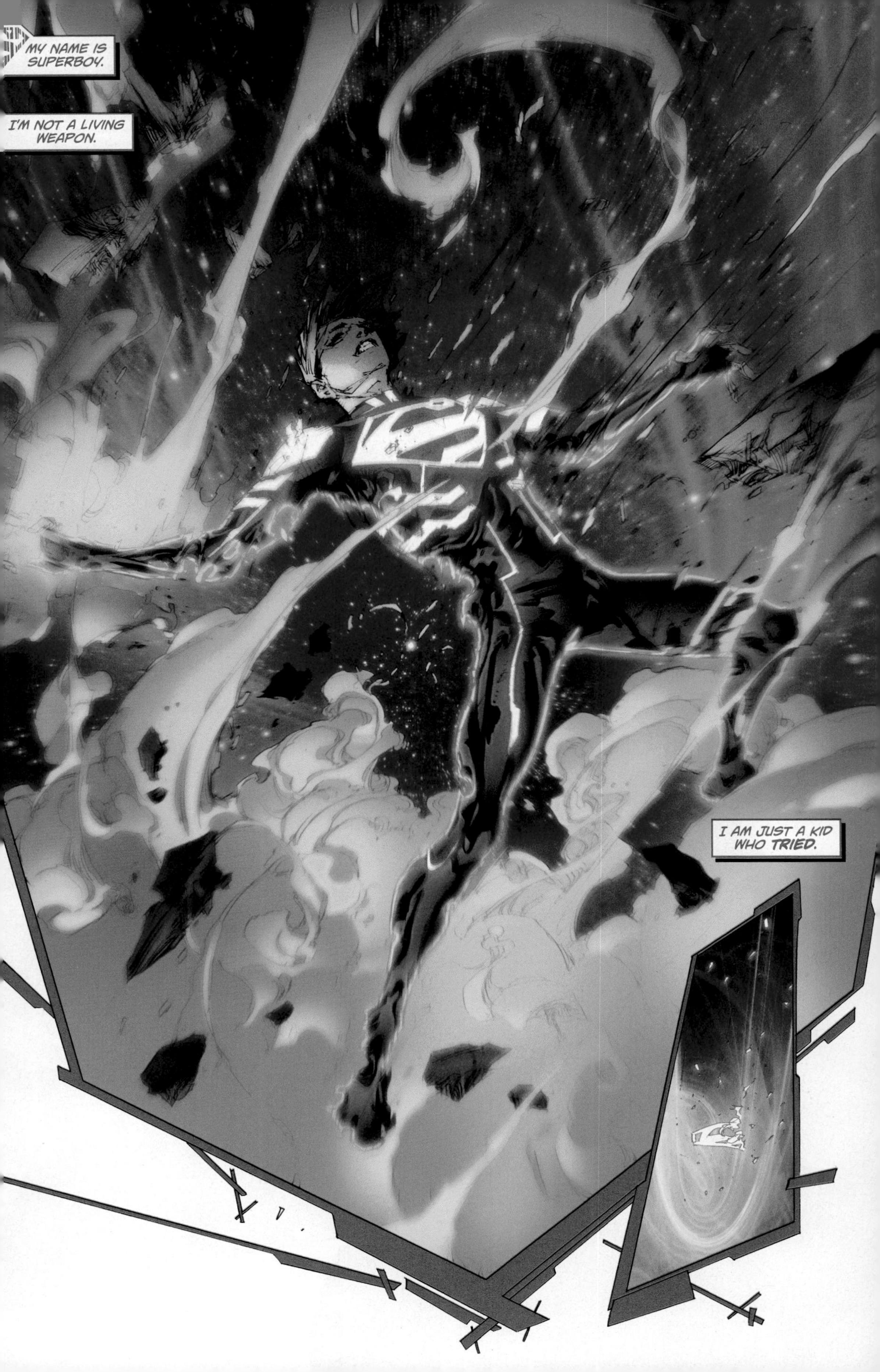
MY NAME IS SUPERBOY.
I'M NOT A LIVING WEAPON.
I AM JUST A KID WHO TRIED.

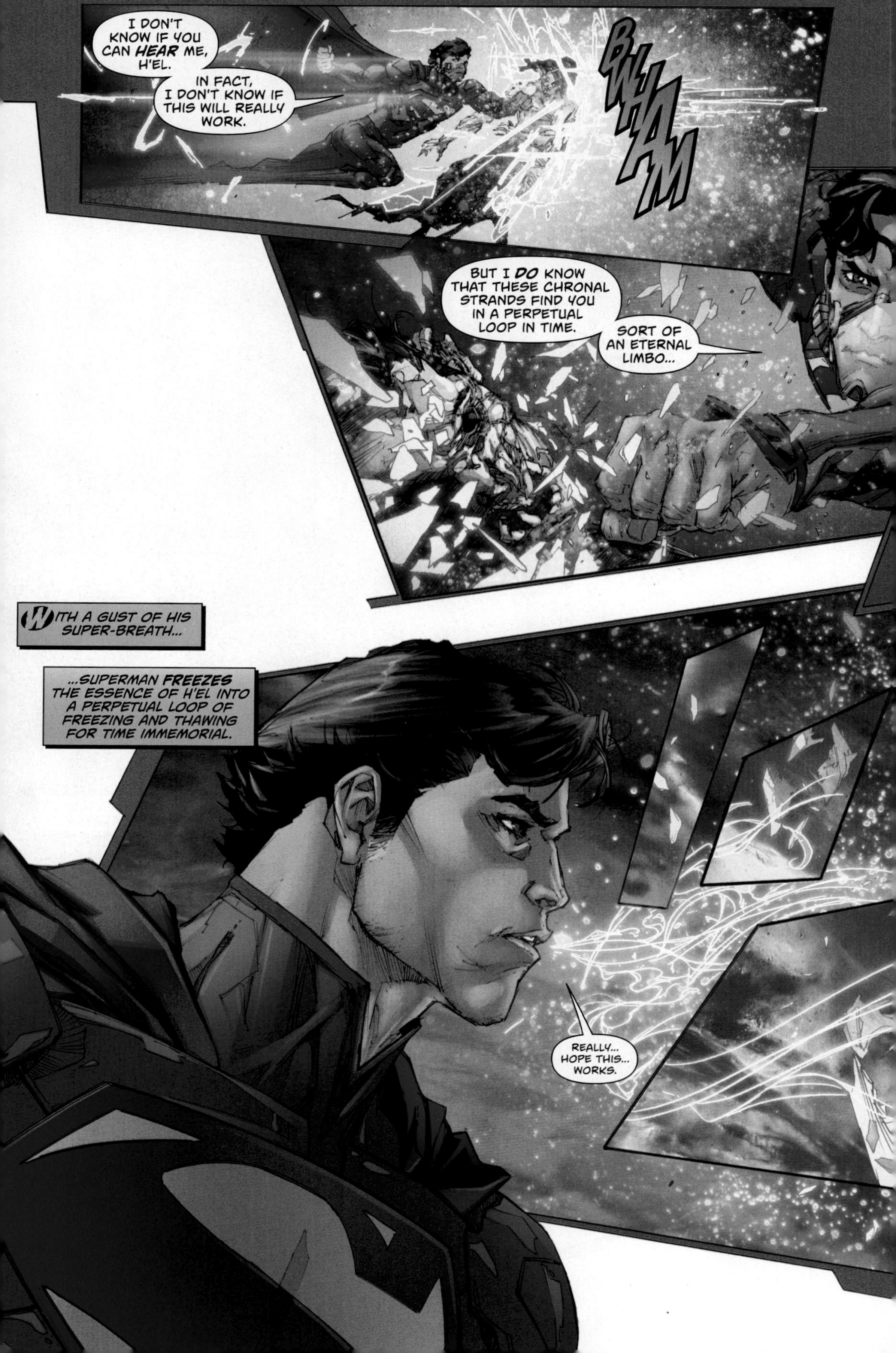
I DON'T KNOW IF YOU CAN HEAR ME, H'EL.
IN FACT, I DON'T KNOW IF THIS WILL REALLY WORK.
BWHAM
BUT I DO KNOW THAT THESE CHRONAL STRANDS FIND YOU IN A PERPETUAL LOOP IN TIME.
SORT OF AN ETERNAL LIMBO...
WITH A GUST OF HIS SUPER-BREATH...
...SUPERMAN FREEZES THE ESSENCE OF H'EL INTO A PERPETUAL LOOP OF FREEZING AND THAWING FOR TIME IMMEMORIAL.
REALLY... HOPE THIS... WORKS.

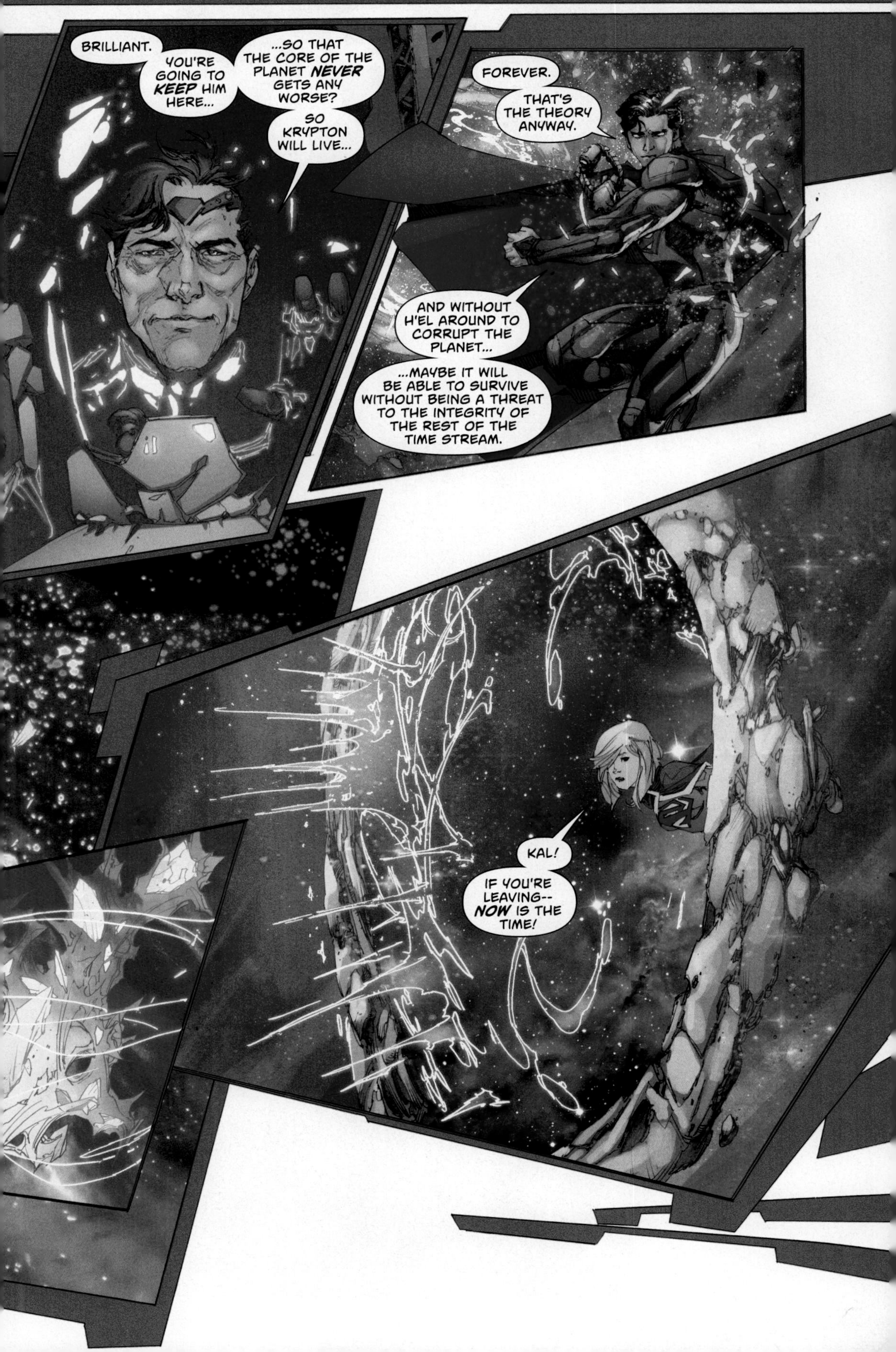

BRILLIANT.
YOU'RE GOING TO KEEP HIM HERE...
...SO THAT THE CORE OF THE PLANET NEVER GETS ANY WORSE?
SO KRYPTON WILL LIVE...
FOREVER.
THAT'S THE THEORY ANYWAY.
AND WITHOUT H'EL AROUND TO CORRUPT THE PLANET...
...MAYBE IT WILL BE ABLE TO SURVIVE WITHOUT BEING A THREAT TO THE INTEGRITY OF THE REST OF THE TIME STREAM.
KAL!
IF YOU'RE LEAVING-- NOW IS THE TIME!

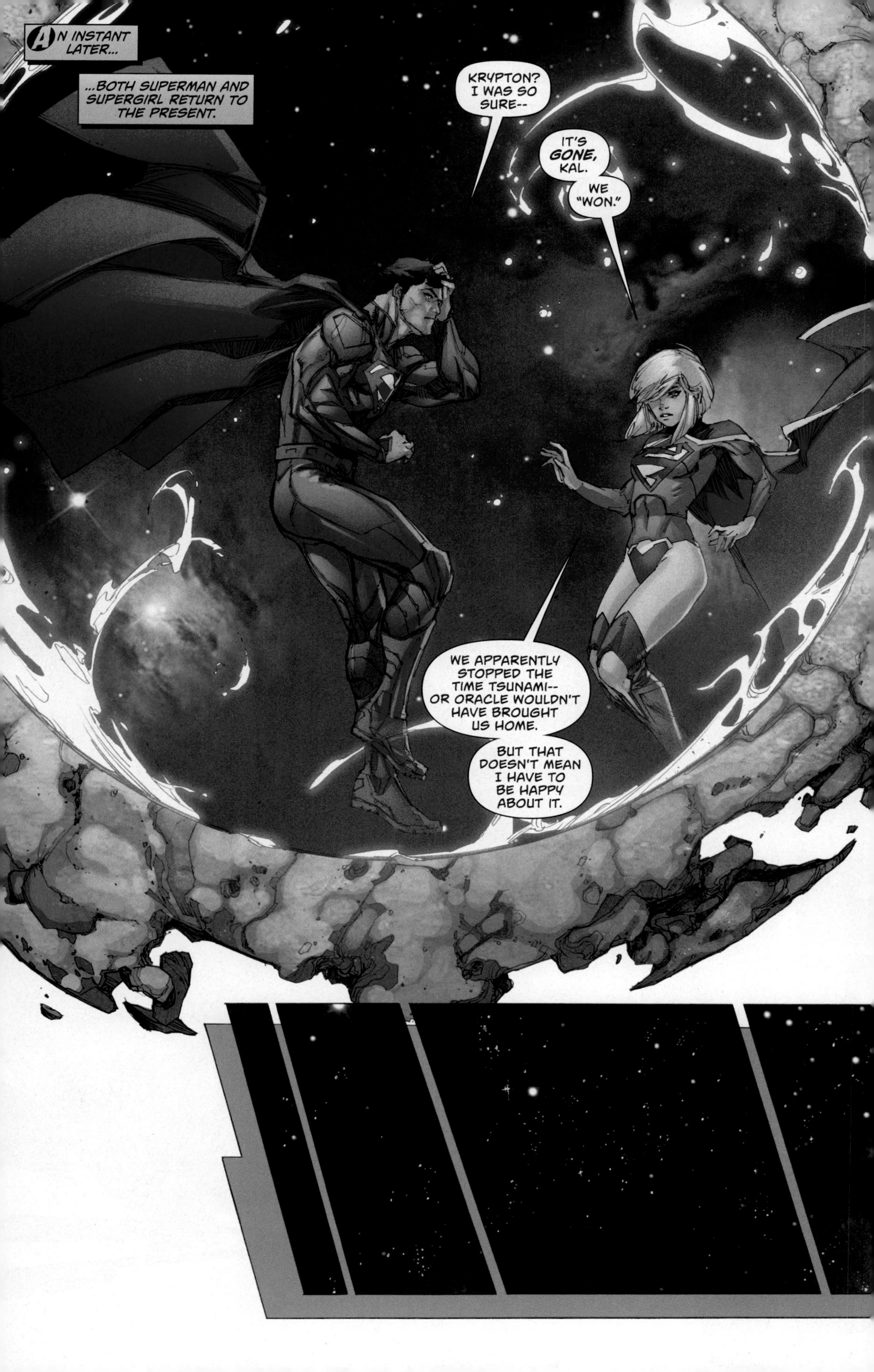
AN INSTANT LATER...
...BOTH SUPERMAN AND SUPERGIRL RETURN TO THE PRESENT.
KRYPTON? I WAS SO SURE--
IT'S GONE, KAL.
WE "WON."
WE APPARENTLY STOPPED THE TIME TSUNAMI-- OR ORACLE WOULDN'T HAVE BROUGHT US HOME.
BUT THAT DOESN'T MEAN I HAVE TO BE HAPPY ABOUT IT.

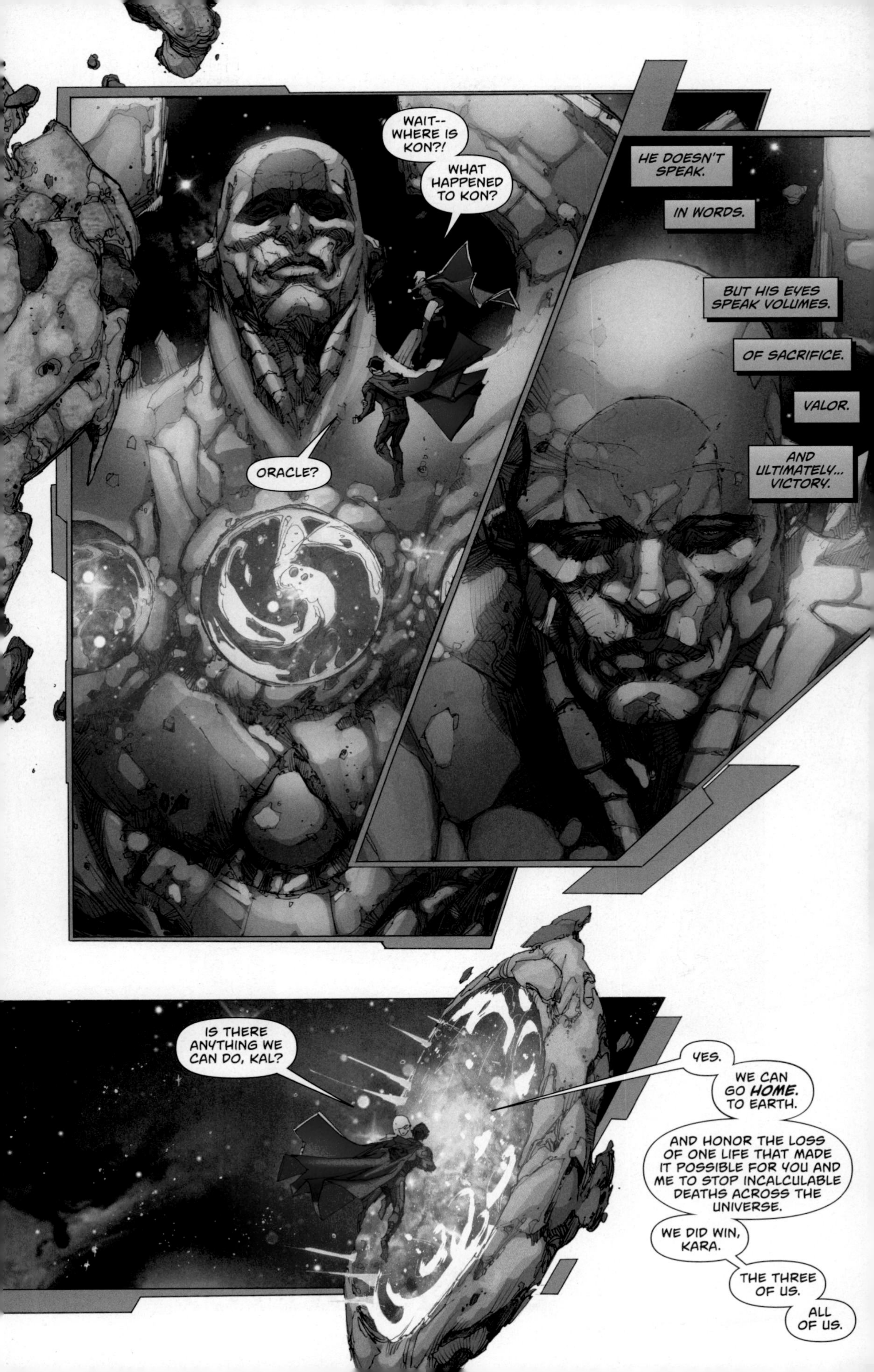
WAIT-- WHERE IS KON?!
WHAT HAPPENED TO KON?
ORACLE?
HE DOESN'T SPEAK.
IN WORDS.
BUT HIS EYES SPEAK VOLUMES.
OF SACRIFICE.
VALOR.
AND ULTIMATELY... VICTORY.
IS THERE ANYTHING WE CAN DO, KAL?
YES.
WE CAN GO HOME. TO EARTH.
AND HONOR THE LOSS OF ONE LIFE THAT MADE IT POSSIBLE FOR YOU AND ME TO STOP INCALCULABLE DEATHS ACROSS THE UNIVERSE.
WE DID WIN, KARA.
THE THREE OF US.
ALL OF US.

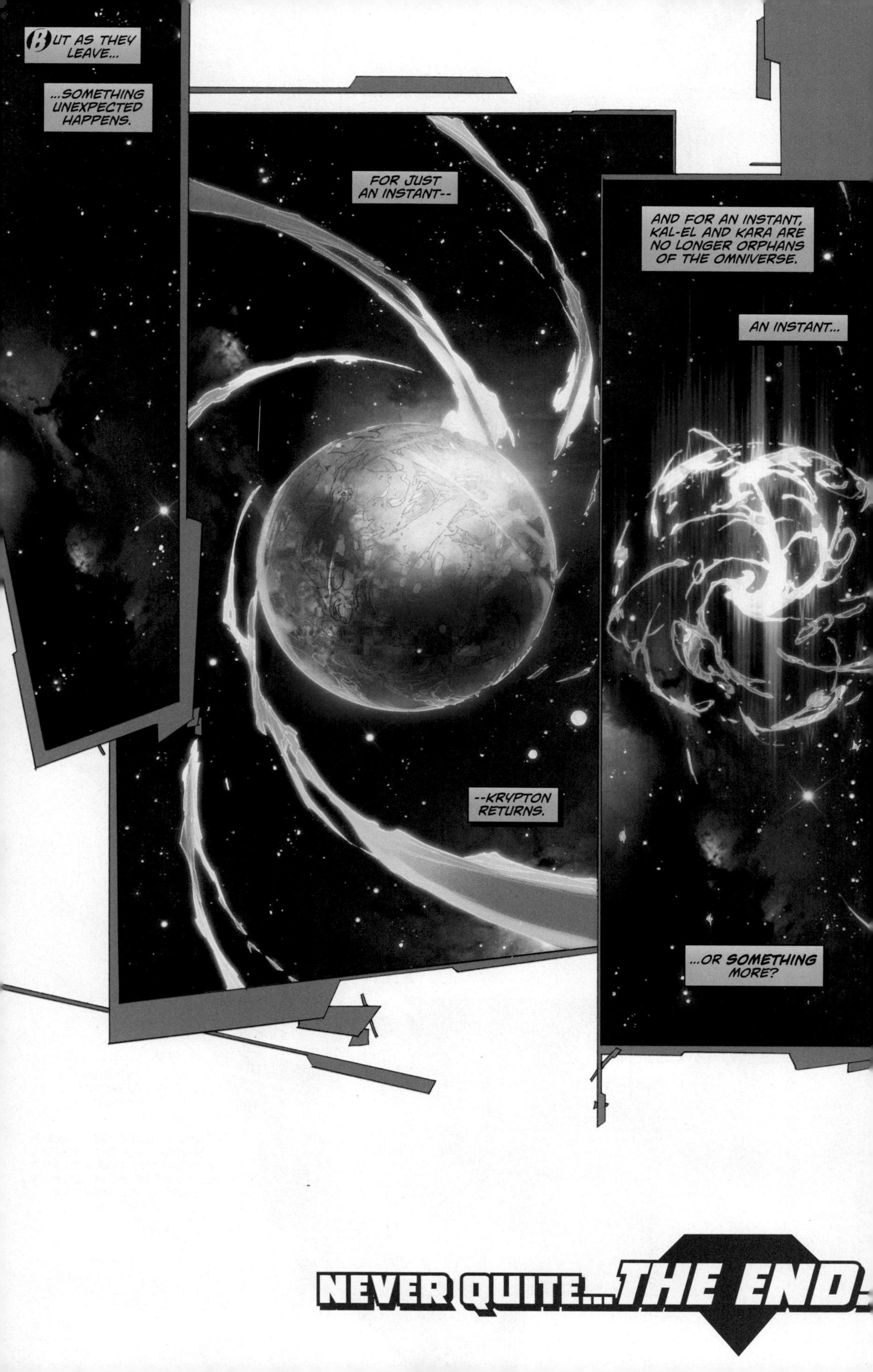
BUT AS THEY LEAVE...
...SOMETHING UNEXPECTED HAPPENS.
FOR JUST AN INSTANT--
--KRYPTON RETURNS.
AND FOR AN INSTANT, KAL-EL AND KARA ARE NO LONGER ORPHANS OF THE OMNIVERSE.
AN INSTANT...
...OR SOMETHING MORE?
NEVER QUITE...THE END.